RELUCTANT SKEPTIC

SPEKTRUM: Publications of the German Studies Association
Series Editor: David M. Luebke, University of Oregon

Published under the auspices of the German Studies Association, *Spektrum* offers current perspectives on culture, society, and political life in the German-speaking lands of central Europe—Austria, Switzerland, and the Federal Republic—from the late Middle Ages to the present day. Its titles and themes reflect the composition of the GSA and the work of its members within and across the disciplines to which they belong—literary criticism, history, cultural studies, political science, and anthropology.

Volume 1
The Holy Roman Empire, Reconsidered
Edited by Jason Philip Coy, Benjamin Marschke, and David Warren Sabean

Volume 2
Weimar Publics/Weimar Subjects: Rethinking the Political Culture of Germany in the 1920s
Edited by Kathleen Canning, Kerstin Barndt, and Kristin McGuire

Volume 3
Conversion and the Politics of Religion in Early Modern Germany
Edited by David M. Luebke, Jared Poley, Daniel C. Ryan, and David Warren Sabean

Volume 4
Walls, Borders, Boundaries:
Spatial and Cultural Practices in Europe
Edited by Marc Silberman, Karen E. Till, and Janet Ward

Volume 5
After The History of Sexuality: German Genealogies with and Beyond Foucault
Edited by Scott Spector, Helmut Puff, and Dagmar Herzog

Volume 6
Becoming East German: Socialist Structures and Sensibilities after Hitler
Edited by Mary Fulbrook and Andrew I. Port

Volume 7
Beyond Alterity:
German Encounters with Modern East Asia
Edited by Qinna Shen and Martin Rosenstock

Volume 8
Mixed Matches:
Transgressive Unions in Germany from the Reformation to the Enlightenment
Edited by David Luebke and Mary Lindemann

Volume 9
Kinship, Community, and Self:
Essays in Honor of David Warren Sabean
Edited by Jason Coy, Benjamin Marschke, Jared Poley, and Claudia Verhoeven

Volume 10
The Emperor's Old Clothes:
Constitutional History and the Symbolic Language of the Holy Roman Empire
Barbara Stollberg-Rilinger
Translated by Thomas Dunlap

Volume 11
The Devil's Riches:
A Modern History of Greed
Jared Poley

Volume 12
The Total Work of Art:
Foundations, Articulations, Inspirations
Edited by David Imhoof, Margaret Eleanor Menninger, and Anthony J. Steinhoff

Volume 13
Migrations in the German Lands, 1500–2000
Edited by Jason Coy, Jared Poley, and Alexander Schunka

Volume 14
Reluctant Skeptic: Siegfried Kracauer and the Crises of Weimar Culture
Harry T. Craver

Reluctant Skeptic

Siegfried Kracauer and the Crises of Weimar Culture

HARRY T. CRAVER

First published in 2017 by
Berghahn Books
www.berghahnbooks.com

© 2017, 2020 Harry T. Craver
First paperback edition published in 2020

All rights reserved. Except for the quotation of short passages
for the purposes of criticism and review, no part of this book
may be reproduced in any form or by any means, electronic or
mechanical, including photocopying, recording, or any information
storage and retrieval system now known or to be invented,
without written permission of the publisher.

Library of Congress Cataloging-in-Publication Data

Names: Craver, Harry T., author. Title: Reluctant skeptic : Siegfried Kracauer and the crises of Weimar culture / Harry T. Craver.
Description: New York : Berghahn Books, 2017. | Series: Spektrum : Publications of the German Studies Association ; volume 14 | Includes bibliographical references and index.
Identifiers: LCCN 2016053297 (print) | LCCN 2016058090 (ebook) | ISBN 9781785334580 (hardback : alk. paper) | ISBN 9781785334597 (ebook)
Subjects: LCSH: Kracauer, Siegfried, 1889–1966—Criticism and interpretation. | Germany—Intellectual life—20th century.
Classification: LCC PT2621.R135 Z55 2017 (print) | LCC PT2621.R135 (ebook) | DDC 834/.912—dc23
LC record available at https://lccn.loc.gov/2016053297

British Library Cataloguing in Publication Data

A catalogue record for this book is available from the British Library

ISBN 978-1-78533-458-0 hardback
ISBN 978-1-78920-836-8 paperback
ISBN 978-1-78533-459-7 ebook

CONTENTS

Preface	vii
Introduction. Kracauer on and in Weimar Modernity	1
Chapter 1. "Location Suggests Content": Kracauer on the Fringe of Religious Revival	36
Chapter 2. Reading the War, Writing Crisis	66
Chapter 3. From Copenhagen to Baker Street: Kracauer, Kierkegaard, and the Detective Novel	106
Chapter 4. Religion on the Street: Kracauer and Religious Flânerie	153
Conclusion. Criticism in the Negative Church	208
Afterword. From Don Quixote to Sancho Panza	244
Select Bibliography	255
Index	279

~: PREFACE :~

Siegfried Kracauer was one of the most striking voices to emerge out of the social and political cauldron of the Weimar Republic. His writings include pioneering works of film history and theory, sociological studies, social history, historiography, and hundreds of reviews and essays on a variety of subjects that took the measure of the kaleidoscopic nature of modern culture. In spite of his close association with and influence on well-known philosophers such as Walter Benjamin and Theodor Adorno, he remains a somewhat peripheral figure. This is unfortunate as he was among those early critics who were ready to recognize some legitimacy in popular culture, and to blend close readings of everyday phenomena and a deep engagement with contemporary philosophy—something that has become much more common today. Most readers and students who encounter him will probably first read his studies of cinema, written in English after he had fled Nazi Germany and found refuge in New York in 1941. Second in line is a selection of his Weimar essays on film and culture, published in German under the title *The Mass Ornament* in 1963 and translated into English in 1995. A number of his other writings have appeared in English, such as his social biography of Jacques Offenbach and a penetrating study of white collar workers. However, his writings on cinema are what he is most known for today, and his classic study of 1947, *From Caligari to Hitler: A Psychological History of the German Film*, remains in print decades later.

Since Kracauer is most known in film studies, where his work has had an uneven reception, he has been often perceived as a writer linked to modern mass culture, a writer embedded within modernity and part of the ferment of the interwar period. This study wants to complicate this view of him, for Kracauer, born in 1889, was already twenty-five when the First World War broke out; thus he grew to adulthood during the *Kaiserreich*, and in his intellectual preoccupations there are significant traces of debates that had begun before the war blew the old order of Europe apart. Perhaps the most important of these debates concerned secularization and the decline of religion. One motivation for this study has been to place these issues in the foreground of his development as a writer and critic, and thus to give more attention to his antediluvian baggage. This yields a portrait of Kracauer that affords more space for his writings prior to 1925. Of more significance, however, the study argues that the crisis of modernity during the Weimar Republic—whether real or rhetorical—needs to be more closely integrated with the history of religion, in both Germany and Europe. For the pre-1914 conflicts between religion and secularism were not insignificant to the conflicts of cultural modernity and the instabilities of the Weimar Republic.

As this study has had a long genesis, there are many to thank. Starting with the University of Toronto, my thanks to Modris Eksteins, Jennifer Jenkins, Derek Penslar, Jim Retallack, and, more generally, the History Department. I read the *Rites of Spring* out of general interest many years ago before traveling to Europe, so I owe to Modris a particular debt as this book led me back to school and towards the study of history. My deep gratitude to the Joint Institute of German and European Studies, and to Alan and Patricia Marchment for their support of the research needed for this book. Thanks to friends and colleagues in the History Department at the University of North Carolina at Chapel Hill where I have taught German history as an adjunct since 2015. Thanks are also owed to scholars who have helped on the way, to Eric Weitz and David Darby. Numerous archives have made research an enjoyable and less laborious task: thanks to Gudrun Schwarz and the Benjamin Archive in Berlin; Sylvia Asmus, Katrin Kokot, and the Deutsche Nationalbibliothek in Frankfurt am Main; the Bundesarchiv in Berlin; the Leo Baeck Institute in Berlin and New York; the Bayerische Staatsbibliothek in Munich; the International Institute for Social History in Amsterdam; Magdalene Popp-Grilli and the Württembergische Landesbibliothek in Stuttgart; and, most importantly, the Deutsches Literaturarchiv in Marbach am Neckar, where the Kracauer Nachlass is kept. Stephen Roeper and company at the Johannes Senckenberg Library in Frankfurt were especially welcoming. Research abroad was enabled by the hospitality of Anthony Cantor, Jenny and Sibylle Flügge, and KD Wolff. To Sibylle, I also owe much thanks for my first lesson in *Sütterlin*. My thanks to the editors and staff at Berghahn Books who have accepted this study into their substantial catalogue of books on German history and made many improvements to the book; my thanks also to the anonymous readers who read the manuscript as it made its way into publication. If some of their remarks have not found a place in the final draft it is due more to a lack of space rather than a failure to appreciate the insights and feedback they have offered and for which I am grateful. Bookstores are an important if indirect and often overlooked stimulant to study, by the simple fact of keeping history on the shelf—thanks to Book City in Toronto, the Seminary Co-op in Chicago, the Banff Book and Art Den (RIP), Labyrinth, and the excellent shop founded by Jim Munro on Vancouver Island.

Numerous friends in Toronto constituted the social glue that make extended work possible, but I send special thanks to Carla Hustak, Jen Bonnell, Scott Mackinnon, Sabrina Spatari, and the rest of the Friday night crowd at the Victory Cafe. Wanda Power, Diane Barlee, and John Vigna offered distant but valued encouragement from afar. Gratitude and much deeper debts go to those personal relations that cannot, even if they wanted to, shut out my professional self. Thanks to my sister Kelly, to Lindsay Downie and the Downie clan, and to the Craver clan. To Janet who was there from the beginning of this work and has done more to make it happen than could reasonably be expected. And to both of my parents, to whom I dedicate this work.

INTRODUCTION

Kracauer on and in Weimar Modernity

> What religion do I confess? None of all those that you
> have named. And why none? Out of religion.
> —Goethe, "Xenien," in *Goethe und die Religion*, 21

> First the Zionist Congress in Basel, then the day before yester-
> day Lourdes: again and again I come across profound adepts
> in that kind of demonstrativeness that is called religious.[1]
> —Kracauer to Werner Thormann, 22 September 1927

In the fall of 1927, Siegfried Kracauer was in Basel to report on the fifteenth Zionist Congress. By this time, Kracauer was a respected writer and editor who was known to have leftist sympathies; he also had carved out his niche as a film critic. He had shown little inclination toward Zionism, and it is uncertain why his employer, the *Frankfurter Zeitung* (FZ), chose him for this assignment. The year before, his severe criticism of a new translation of the Bible by Franz Rosenzweig and Martin Buber had angered many Jewish intellectuals. Indeed, so Kracauer later recollected, Buber had snubbed him during a chance encounter at the conference.[2] In general, Kracauer had an ambiguous impression of the congress, and though he recognized the energy and variety of the Zionist movement, his final dispatch struck a skeptical tone. Zionism, he suggested, would find it hard not to become a nationalist movement, and he could not see this as the way forward.[3]

After filing his report from Basel, Kracauer spent little time reckoning with the dilemmas raised at the Zionist conference, at least in print. He next travelled to Lourdes where he took part in a torchlight procession to the holy shrine. As he told his friend Werner Thormann, he joined the march with the consent of the pilgrims. One suspects that he was aware of some of the irony of his situation. He was a Jewish intellectual with Marxist inclinations who often compared religion to myth, yet he found himself marching among the Catholic faithful to the sacred grotto where in 1858 Bernadette Soubirous is supposed to have seen the Virgin Mary. Yet, despite the subtly mocking tone that his remarks conveyed, his letter was not meant to be derogatory. Thormann, the recipient of his card, was a devout Catholic though of a leftist stamp. Moreover, his companion in Lourdes—Elizabeth Ehrenreich, who he later married—also came from a family of Alsatian Catholics. His remarks were probably not intended to offend their religious sentiments. Rather, behind the bewilderment that Kracauer expresses when confronted with the demonstrativeness of religion, both in Basel and Lourdes, there is the attitude of the religious flâneur, an outside observer who enjoys the cultural mobility that allows him to move between religious milieus. Yet, there is also a trace of angst, as if Kracauer knows that this mobility has hidden costs yet to be recognized.[4] On the one hand, he appears to have seen his mobility as a privilege of the secular world where religious institutions could no longer compel faith, but suspected that this redrawing of the religious sphere must have consequences.

The following study investigates how these consequences were understood by Kracauer, and how they were discussed in the intellectual milieus that he inhabited. It intends to show how the postwar religious revival informed debates over culture and how the concept of culture was interrogated and recast in light of secularism and religious revival.

For Kracauer, the emergence of a secular world was an accomplished fact. Cultural modernity was accompanied by the loosening of religious dogma and the withering of religious institutions. However, for Kracauer this decline of religious authority was also problematic. A secular world that allowed the kind of mobility that he experienced on his trip in 1927 was one where both culture and religion had an uncertain status. For some contemporaries, culture was a function of religion; only in a world where religion retained its authority could one even think of a meaningful culture. For others religion was simply a cultural manifestation—a product of myth, metaphysical longings, or ethical impulses—but it had no foundational function. However, if this were so, could culture furnish its own norms and values, that is, could it become a foundation for itself? Kracauer, in spite of his repudiation of religious revival, remained ambivalent on this question. This study charts how he attempted to resolve this problem via cultural criticism.

In the early years of the Weimar Republic, the distinctions between culture and religion were less defined for Kracauer, but he appears to have put much faith in the role that culture might play in German society. In November 1918, just before the German defeat and the outbreak of revolution, Kracauer was reading one of the more aggressive tracts of German cultural particularism: *Reflections of a Nonpolitical Man* by Thomas Mann. According to his later testimony, this book had had a formative influence on him. There is some irony in the fact that on the eve of the birth of the republic, Kracauer was enthralled by this notorious defense of Germany's cultural mission. Within days an armistice would end five years of war, and, as a result, Mann's polemic would find an audience that had to respond to an altogether different situation. The armed conflict between German culture and Western civilization was over, and Mann's idea of the "culture nation" had lost. In his journal, Kracauer wrote down a one-word entry on 8 November: "Revolution!"[5] What he thought of these events is mostly a matter of conjecture, but as did many intellectuals, he probably assumed that a fundamental transformation had begun and that a cultural reformation would accompany the birth of a new political order. The critique of culture begun during the *Kaiserreich* thus continued into this uncertain age.[6] For some, the shocks of the war and revolution gave further impetus to these ideas, increasing the passion with which they were held.

In his early career, Kracauer sometimes subscribed to this view, often expressing a pessimistic but utopian strand of this "nonpolitical" idea. In a seldom-mentioned review of a 1920 publication by the philosopher Georg Burckhardt, he argued that one must turn to philosophy and religion to find solutions to the present crisis.[7] These were the disciplines that must meet the difficult task of creating a new order. He made no mention of politics, but his idea of culture clearly had political implications. Life in Germany was broken, he stated: "an order that had long rotted from the inside had collapsed, the protective circle of forms was no more; and thus, dark and nameless life-forces flooded unrestrainedly inward, shaking the foundations of the soul." To counter this spiritual catastrophe Germany had to draw on its cultural resources, but also, more specifically, on religion. "From within our breasts," he wrote, "one longs for a faith to vault over us, round and full."[8] To Kracauer, the relevance of Burckhardt's work derived precisely from the fact that it recognized the loss of this sheltering idea of culture. From this point of view, political crises were best resolved by importing culture into politics.

However, disentangling this idea of culture, especially in relation to religion, was more difficult, and the problematic nexus of religion, culture, and politics constitutes a persistent undercurrent in Kracauer's work of the 1920s. In a letter to the Frankfurt poet and essayist Margarete Susman, Kracauer explicitly privileged culture over politics. The latter, he argued, was of limited importance for it was "all the same whether one lived under socialism or communism."[9] Unless everyday existence was transformed, nothing of deep or lasting value could be achieved. To be sure, revolutionary Russia offered a compelling political model, but one had to seek its roots in the passionate Russian spirit and not simply look to the political order derived from this spirit. Similarly, he concluded his review of Burckhardt's work with an exhortation to imbue socialism with cultural ideals, though he added that these were "in the best sense bourgeois."[10] This is an odd conflation of bourgeois values and revolutionary thought; but behind these strange bedfellows, I would argue, is the idea that culture preceded politics. The deep social and political conflicts of modern Germany were to be mended neither by liberalism nor socialism, but rather by a strengthening of cultural foundations. However, this was not a strictly apolitical view of culture, but rather one that gave primary emphasis to a sound culture as a basis of political change; it suggested that the proper sphere of political transformation was in the individual not the political party, and in the street and not parliament.[11]

The idea that culture was an organizing principle for politics has a long and controversial history in Germany, one that readily becomes entangled in discussions of the German *Sonderweg*. By arguing for the precedence of culture over politics, Kracauer was thus by no means exceptional. Nor was he alone in looking to religion and philosophy as vital sources of cultural renewal. In the postwar period, particularly among intellectuals, there were numerous calls for spiritual or religious revival. This led some contemporaries to believe that the present was in fact a time of resurgent religiosity. The Catholic philosopher Max Scheler, the Protestant theologian Karl Barth, the intellectuals associated with the Free Jewish School, all spoke of the present as an age of spiritual angst that called out for a renewed religion.[12] Such convictions had deep roots, and they persisted throughout the short history of the Republic (indeed, most of these thinkers have exerted an influence up to the present). In 1928, for instance, the painter Max Beckmann, when asked for his views on politics in a special article of the *Frankfurter Zeitung*, stated that politics concerned him only if it hastened the end of this "materialist epoch." Politics, he continued, only had worth insofar as it engaged with "metaphysical, transcendent, and therefore, religious things in a new form." His response was all the more provocative as the newspaper editors had framed this article as a secularized inversion of the *Gretchenfrage* from *Faust*. Whereas Gretchen had questioned Faust regarding his position on religion, the editors used Gretchen's words, but turned them to politics. However, Beckmann refused to go along with their intentions; instead, he routed the question back to its original context, enmeshing politics in the question of religious belief.[13]

Kracauer almost joined the religious camp. He admired the work of Scheler, and in the early years of the Republic, he was devoted to the charismatic rabbi Nehemiah Anton Nobel, whom one contemporary described as an "uncanny mystical enchanter."[14] Nobel's teaching united the mystical traditions of Judaism with an extensive knowledge of German literature and philosophy, and in Frankfurt he led a study group to which Kracauer belonged for a short period. Though Kracauer may have been drawn mostly by the intellectual rigor of Nobel and his group, one cannot exclude an attraction to his charismatic religiosity. Indeed, the religious current in Kracauer's thought at this time emerges unmistakably in his letters to Susman. In early 1920, Kracauer described himself to her as a seeker of religious knowledge. "I have only gone half way down my path," he stated; "at the end stands knowledge of the divine."[15] Among the numerous projects that he confided to her, he mentioned his intentions to construct an ethical system based on religious principles.[16]

Yet, Kracauer's path soon altered. By the end of 1922, he had broken with Scheler and was in conflict with the pioneers of the religious revival. With the death of Rabbi Nobel in 1921, one of the few religious figures he admired was gone. By the end of the 1920s, his interest in religious subjects appeared to have faded, and he was engrossed by the social and political dimensions of film and mass culture.[17]

Why did Kracauer alter course and, moreover, what does this tell us about religion and secularization in the Weimar Republic? Kracauer's attitudes towards religion are not easy to pin down, for even as he repudiated the religious revival, theological concepts remained an important part of his critical attitude to culture. His intellectual trajectory, I argue, should be read as a moment of secularization, a period in which intellectual culture responded to the loss, transformation, and revival of religious thought. As used here, *secularization* means the adjustment of religion to modern societies, whether it be by way of a "worlding" of theological concepts, or a process of disintegration and reconstruction in terms of religious institutions and patterns of thought.[18] Following the lead of much scholarship devoted to this subject, secularization should not be seen as a matter of religion's decline, but rather of its reorientation. In this respect, to speak of a "moment" of secularization is slightly misleading as the term refers more to a series of moments, a complex of processes transpiring over the course of at least two centuries. Indeed, according to some historians, a truly secular society did not in exist in Europe until the 1960s, and for many the secularizing process is a subject of ongoing dispute.[19] In the 1920s, the clash between secular and religious discourse was a burning issue among intellectuals, one in which the contending parties often portrayed the present as a time of crisis. Since Kracauer registered the myriad impulses circulating in this debate, his work offers an entry point into the conflicts between religion and secular culture, as well as a means of questioning how these conflicts have been conceptualized.

The remainder of this chapter offers an overview of Kracauer's career, and a brief discussion of his importance to the issues of secularization and Weimar culture. The second chapter delves into the early biography of Kracauer in more depth, describing his situation as a Jewish intellectual amid the cultural crisis of late Imperial Germany and establishing why Kracauer allows us significant access to the tensions in his cultural milieu – for Kracauer was an assiduous reader of sociology and philosophy, as well as of polemics that tended to portray postwar Germany in crisis-ridden terms. In Chapter 3, I analyze his reading of some of these so-called war books as a means of illuminating his political opinions between the end of 1918 and 1922, a period for which there are unfortunately fewer sources. To a degree, Kracauer himself disappears for part of this discussion, but this is not entirely accidental; for, as Dagmar Barnouw has pointed out, Kracauer reflected on the process of inserting himself into the "recorded thought of others," trying to assess how his own work would be perceived when set against that of his contemporaries. Thus, his textual milieu needs to be discussed in order to reckon with how he positioned his own writing.[20] Moreover, this dovetails with one facet of my argument that draws attention to Kracauer as an exemplar of a particular kind of critical approach. In this respect, I do not suggest that he was representative of a specific attitude or point of view regarding religion and modernity; but rather that his work gave expression to the polarities that emerged in an ongoing dispute over the place and function of religion in a predominantly secular society. This is evident in his criticism of the "war books." In his essays and letters concerning this literature, Kracauer outlines one of the key motifs of his thought in the postwar period: the desire to open a critical space between the theological sphere and that of secular modernity.[21]

An early model of Kracauer's method is to be found in his posthumously published study, *The Detective Novel*, which is the subject of Chapter 3.[22] Kracauer wrote this unusual work between 1922 and 1925, and only one chapter was published in his lifetime. Scholars have recognized the transitional nature of the work, for it is here that Kracauer first combines his early philosophical interests with an investigation of mass culture. Ostensibly a study of detective fiction, the work was indebted to Kierkegaard, whose model of interrelated spheres (aesthetic, ethical, and religious) Kracauer appropriated. This importation of Kierkegaard was only "seemingly archaic," for as Hannah Arendt commented in 1932, after the war Kierkegaard was the philosopher of the day.[23] Why such a deeply Christian thinker became influential to intellectuals of different confessional backgrounds is a broad question that cannot be answered here, but some discussion of the contemporary reception of Kierkegaard is needed to situate Kracauer's use of his concepts. These concepts deeply informed his idea of critical vocation.[24]

Kierkegaard also offers a tragic frame for Kracauer's cultural-political agenda in the Weimar period. Kracauer shared an intense interest in Kierkegaard with the young Theodor Adorno, whom he met when the latter was sixteen. They probably read Kierkegaard together during the early 1920s, and it was as a symbol of this shared affinity that Kracauer dedicated *The Detective Novel* to his younger friend. Eight years later Adorno returned this gesture when he completed and published his *Habilitationsschrift*. The work, entitled *Kierkegaard: Construction of the Aesthetic*, was dedicated to "my friend Siegfried Kracauer." Adorno's book appeared on an unpropitious day in German history, the very day that Hitler came to power. Kracauer wrote a short review that he planned to publish in the *FZ*, but events rapidly intervened and Kracauer fled Germany shortly afterwards. Adorno had been eager to know Kracauer's opinion of the work, for to his mind the book was no individual achievement, but rather a testimony of their "common philosophical past."[25] The joint project symbolized by this book came to an end in 1933 and the intellectual distance dividing Kracauer from Adorno grew wider in the years of exile and emigration as Kracauer became more isolated, while Adorno drew closer to Max Horkheimer. Nonetheless, between these two works the outlines of an alternative reception of Kierkegaard appeared, one that differed considerably from the work of other writers influenced by him such as Theodor Haecker, Emmanuel Hirsch, and Martin Heidegger.[26]

Chapter 4 discusses how the critical model manifested in the detective study was influenced by, and responded to, contemporary religious trends. In the early years of the Republic, Kracauer followed developments in contemporary religious thought. Moreover, Frankfurt offered an excellent vantage point from which to observe the various efforts to reform and revive religious thought and practice. The concluding chapter explores how Kracauer's criticism continued to be influenced by the rivalry of sacred and profane in light of a controversy provoked by the 1930 publication of a polemical work by Alfred Döblin: *To Know and To Change! Open Letters to a Young Man*.[27] This chapter also shows how the critical model described in the above chapters was put into practice in the cultural politics of the late Weimar Republic.

An afterword synthesizes some tendencies in Kracauer's work that I argue are representative of a strand of thought within Weimar culture. The baroque figures of Don Quixote and Sancho Panza furnish the departure point for these concluding remarks. Quixote, of course, has become cultural shorthand for delusional romanticism; yet, for some German intellectuals Quixote was an iconic figure who symbolized the ambiguities of the "unfinished project of modernity." For Kracauer, there is a marked shift of sympathy from the flamboyant Quixote to his relatively earthbound squire, Panza. If in the early 1920s he identified with Quixote, by the end of his life it was Panza with whom he sympathized more. Yet what conceptual distance is actually traversed in the course of this move? That Kracauer identified more with Panza was not meant as an abandonment of utopia in favor of a pragmatic realism; rather, it was a matter of inflecting revolutionary passions across a different paradigm. It was also a means of questioning the meaning of utopia, its origins, and its potential for actualization.

Kracauer during the Weimar Republic

The life of Kracauer was riven by the conflicts and contradictions of modern German society. Today, much of his reputation is based on two classic studies of film history and theory: *From Caligari to Hitler* and *Theory of Film*, published between 1947 and 1960. Aside from these important texts, he is also known as one of the earliest critics to turn his attention to film, and to argue that the medium had an important sociopolitical content. Yet, though he is justly known for this work, Kracauer was polymathic in his range of interests, and he approached the problems of modern life through a kaleidoscopic lens, encompassing philosophy, architecture, sociology, and literature. He was productive in all of these areas, even though he was, by his own admission, an uninspired architect. In terms of his background and early education, there is little that anticipated Kracauer's later profusion of interests. He was born in 1889 to a family that was Jewish on both sides and that had engaged primarily in various forms of commercial trade, showing little inclination towards scholarly or artistic pursuits. His paternal uncle, Isidor Kracauer, a noted historian of the Jews of Frankfurt, and his wife Hedwig Kracauer were both exceptional in this regard. Kracauer later denied that his aunt had had any kind of intellectual influence on him, even though Adorno argued that both he himself and his friend Benno Reifenberg could remember Kracauer making just such a claim.[28] Kracauer's reasons for denying her influence are unclear. Yet, the episode shows that Kracauer was concerned with how his work was viewed by his contemporaries.

In his education, Kracauer followed a path that was part technical and part intellectual, both practical and speculative. His declared subject was architecture, but he had stronger inclinations towards literature and philosophy. While pursuing his degree, he devoted himself to the study of these latter subjects, and he began to write in his spare time. By 1919, he had accumulated several manuscripts, most of which remained unpublished during his lifetime, including the bulk of his study on the sociologist Georg Simmel with whom he established contact in 1907.[29] During the war, Kracauer maintained relations with Simmel and also with the philosopher Max Scheler whom he met in 1916; both men encouraged his philosophical aspirations. His friendship with Margarete Susman, whom he must have met no later than 1918, was also valuable in this respect. She too had studied with Simmel, and she had numerous intellectual contacts: Ernst Bloch, Georg Lukács, and Gustav Landauer were among her circle of friends and acquaintances. Moreover, she had a potentially useful connection to the press, being a friend of Heinrich Simon, the lead editor of one of the most prestigious newspapers in Germany, the *Frankfurter Zeitung* (FZ). Kracauer did, in fact, suggest that Susman should speak to Simon on his behalf, though there is no evidence that she did so or that this had the desired effect.[30]

In any case, Kracauer's access to Weimar's cultural life expanded after 1921, when he found a position as a journalist on the *FZ*. In 1924, he became a full editor, and, in collaboration with his colleague Benno Reifenberg, he helped to turn the *FZ* feuilleton into a remarkable forum for cultural experimentation. Kracauer himself appears to have thrived in this situation as his large literary output in the second half of the 1920s suggests. During this period, he wrote hundreds of articles on film, mass culture, and literature. In 1928, he published his first novel, *Ginster*; two years later there followed a much-discussed sociological study of white-collar workers.[31] In 1930, he was transferred to Berlin where he had the chance to acquaint himself with the social and cultural world of the capital.

Although Kracauer is often described as an "outsider," or in his preferred formulation, as an "extraterritorial," he was, nonetheless, well connected to contemporary intellectual life. This is true of Frankfurt, but also of Berlin and even of Paris. His letters indicate an extensive network of contacts including André Malraux, Ignazio Silone, Rudolf Kayser, Gabriel Marcel, Karl Mannheim, Hendrik de Man, Asta Nielsen, and Jean Renoir. These names suggest something of the breadth of culture that Kracauer was exposed to in these years, from the abstruse phenomenology of Edmund Husserl to the expressionist dance troupe of Mary Wigman.[32] To be sure, Kracauer expressed some antipathy to this world of literary cliques and official culture, especially in Berlin. Shortly after his move to the capital, he informed his friend and fellow editor Bernhard Guttmann that he had met just about everyone there: Döblin, Brecht, Weill, and so forth. "Without wanting to be arrogant," he continued, "I must still say that in general one gives much more than one receives."[33] However, behind this reserve to the Berlin cliques, there is a definite preference to remain an outsider, to become a privileged observer. Kracauer valued his intellectual distance; extraterritoriality meant preserving a gap between himself and his milieu, and his comments regarding Berlin should be read with this in mind.[34] This does not mean, of course, that there was not some failure of rapport between Kracauer and some of his contemporaries. He was almost certainly disappointed by the tepid reception of his novel *Ginster*, for instance. For though the work received many positive reviews, among the "literary radicals" there was no one, so one of his few admirers told him, who considered the book to be an "essential work."[35]

Similarly, in Paris, where Kracauer fled in 1933, his severe financial situation overshadowed the degree to which he still retained important social ties during his years of exile. These were critical when he later required affidavits to secure his release from the French internment camps where he was twice placed after war broke out in 1939.[36] While his connections were unable to reverse his perilous finances, there is still reason to believe that he was well known and respected among French intellectuals. Jean Paulhan, for instance, described him as one of the "best Germans," and he was angry to discover that Kracauer had been interned even as known spies roamed free all over Paris.[37] When the art historian Julius Meier-Graefe sought a closer tie to Paulhan and the *Nouvelle Revue Française*, he appears to have asked Kracauer to intercede on his behalf.[38]

Of course, these connections to French intellectual and diplomatic circles do not altogether override Kracauer's feelings of being on the periphery, nor do they negate the tangible hindrances that pushed him towards the margins of the intelligentsia. Kracauer, in spite of his close relationship with Reifenberg, was never part of the inner circles of the *FZ* around Heinrich Simon. Moreover, his relations with some of the paper's leading figures, Friedrich Sieburg and Rudolf Kircher, appear to have been cool.[39] In more concrete terms, his career was stymied by a speech impediment, and also by what many saw as his bizarre and foreign appearance. Count Harry Kessler, ever the aesthete, stated that he could scarce abide Kracauer's "hideous ugliness."[40] In April of 1925, Kracauer sent Adorno a photograph of himself with the accompanying words: "I hate images of myself—this one, every one."[41] In an age that celebrated the blonde beast—a tendency that Kracauer believed was rife among his contemporaries—his appearance was decidedly a disadvantage.[42] During the war fever of 1914, some patriots mistook Kracauer for a "foreigner," and according to his friend Viktor Klemperer, he cut his hair in an effort to look less conspicuous. The anxiety caused by his appearance is difficult to measure, but one can assume that it contributed to his sense of exclusion.[43] These impediments, together with his Jewish birth, effectively barred Kracauer from an academic career. Even those who were friendly to him, such as Meier-Graefe and Joseph Roth, found it difficult to imagine him taking on a leading public role for the newspaper.[44]

What little is known of Kracauer's sexual inclinations also suggests an outsider status. One can only speculate on the subject, but the early years of his relationship with Adorno appear to have had a strong homoerotic element. To his friend Löwenthal, he confided that his feelings toward the much younger Adorno led him to believe that at least in intellectual and spiritual matters he was homosexual.[45] This relationship will be discussed further below, but it should be noted here that Kracauer appears to have had a general inclination towards similar mentoring relationships with younger men. His intentions in these cases may or may not have been entirely platonic, but they always depended on an intensive intellectual rapport. A close collaboration that mingled the erotic and the intellectual framed his early critical endeavors, thus generating a tension between his unspoken desires and his public persona.[46] His often, but not always, muted attraction towards men, however, did not preclude marriage. In 1926 he met Elisabeth Ehrenreich, a student of music and art history, and a librarian at the Frankfurt School. They married in 1930 and remained together until his death in 1966.

After the Reichstag fire of 1933, Kracauer fled from Germany in the company of his wife to Paris, a city where his prior friendships and professional contacts would have led him to assume the potential for a stable existence. These hopes were disappointed and his emigration to France brought his career as a journalist, more or less, to an end.[47] Shortly after his arrival in Paris, he was dismissed from the *FZ* under acrimonious circumstances.[48] Afterward, the Kracauers spent much of their time fending off financial collapse, while anxiously planning their emigration to the United States and trying to help Kracauer's mother and aunt leave Germany. What time remained he devoted to a work that he hoped would become a commercial success: his *Jacques Offenbach and the Paris of His Time* published in 1937. However, the much-needed relief that this "social biography" was supposed to bring never materialized. The book sold miserably and many of his friends (especially Adorno) condemned it as a betrayal of his earlier work.[49] He would not publish another substantial work until ten years later when his study of the German cinema *From Caligari to Hitler* appeared in English. By that time, he had found refuge in New York, arriving after much struggle early in 1941. The move to the United States would become permanent, his Parisian exile constituting a threshold across which he would not pass again. To one of the few friends from Frankfurt with whom he renewed contact after the war, he wrote:

> There lies too much in between. To name only the most personal: the unthinkably terrible end of my old mother and aunt; and the long years of our first emigration in France when, with one or two exceptions, none of our German friends let some sign come our way, even though it would have been possible until '38 or '39. From this comes the differences in position, experience, point of view; and, not least, there are the human relationships that were forged in difficult times and now fulfill our present life. The past is actually past, and even if I wanted it, I cannot transform it into the present.[50]

In America, Kracauer abandoned German for the purposes of his work. His final books, *Theory of Film* (1960) and the unfinished *History: The Last Things before the Last* (1969) were written, as was the *Caligari* book, in English.

This brief overview of Kracauer's career demonstrates the degree to which he was embedded in the daily bustle of Weimar culture and its afterlife. To one observer, Kracauer was one of the "most considerable talents" on the *FZ*, a writer who had created a "new kind of journalistic genre."[51] In the sphere of cultural experimentation, he was both investigator and participant, and his work embodied numerous conflicting impulses. He was influenced by Marxism, but he was never a doctrinaire thinker and often critical of Marxism-inspired literature; he was remarkably open to the forms of "low culture" that accompanied the rise of a consumer-based society, yet he sometimes adopted a mandarin tone when discussing popular media.⁵² More relevant to this study, he remained interested in religious and theological currents, but avoided religious commitments in his own life.

How then does religion figure into Kracauer's conception of modernity and the critic's role as interpreter of social reality? Since Kracauer was an acute observer of Weimar's cultural pluralism, and because he wanted this pluralism to be reflected in his critical practice, his response to this issue is relevant to more than just the study of his intellectual development; rather his work is an entry point into the conflicted zones where religious and cultural values were contested. For Kracauer, the emergence of a secular society was a basic premise, yet, what this meant for religion was less clear. He was skeptical of attempts to subsume the functions of religion through culture, and thus he also rejected any sacralization of mass politics. Religion was to be replaced by neither a "political religion" nor a secular one.⁵³ Instead, Kracauer sometimes sought to preserve theological concepts in a modern setting, and this meant that traces of these concepts persisted in his work in a variety of forms. For Kracauer religion was besieged by the impersonal forces of instrumental reason, or *ratio*, and as a result theological concepts were detached from the life of religious faith; thus they began a period of wandering in the secular world. Here, they led a shadow existence—a form of functional negativity that, cloaked in irony and humor, undermined and interrogated the notion of a complete or fulfilled culture.⁵⁴ If some saw the religious community as a model for a secular utopia, for the establishment of a New Jerusalem, Kracauer saw theological concepts such as redemption and "waiting" as a means of demonstrating that such utopian visions were false. "Waiting" became an important quasi-theological theme in his work that occupied a middle ground between skepticism and positive religion, between secular culture and a revival of the sacred.⁵⁵ In this sense, his work sought to undermine the triumphalism of secular culture, showing it to be a form of quixoticism that foundered on the shoals of a reality that Kracauer conceived of in quasi-theological terms. To be sure, such ideas remained vaguely expressed in Kracauer's work, and they cannot be readily equated with positive religiosity. Nonetheless, they suggest the complex and ambiguous way in which Kracauer approached this issue. As Inka Mülder-Bach argued in her pioneering study of the early Kracauer, his apparent realism was always predicated on ideas of an "essentially metaphysical sort, even after 1925."⁵⁶

More significantly, Kracauer's deliberation on the fate of religion in modernity was not an isolated venture in Weimar culture. His discussions on religion and cultural crisis did not occur in a vacuum, but rather were part of an ongoing dispute with the religious and intellectual currents of his day. This suggests that attitudes towards religion, both in the later years of the *Kaiserreich* and during the Republic, were not negligible to the formation of cultural criticism, and hence, they are not negligible to an understanding of Weimar's seemingly intractable cultural crisis.[57]

Searching for the "Hollow Spaces": Between Secularization and Political Religions

Two historiographic issues inform the discussion that follows: the question of postwar religious revival and the historiography of secularization. A revived interest in religion was far from uncommon after the Great War, and the phenomenon has been the subject of increasing historical interest. Throughout Europe this resurgence took various forms, from the persistence of traditional belief that resulted in a return to the church, to spiritualist attempts to commune with the souls of the dead.[58] As a defeated power, Germany was particularly susceptible to the mood of crisis, a perception that was aggravated by the November revolution and the threat of civil war; there was then rich material upon which the rhetoric of crisis could draw.[59] In the wake of these events numerous utopian visions emerged, many of which offered alternative models of spiritual and social redemption.[60] Many attempted to move beyond a strictly materialist point of view, and even the relatively secular forms of social transformation could still be interpreted with a religious slant. In this vein, the Frankfurt writer Alfons Paquet, a fellow traveler, Quaker, and a member of the German-South Slavic Association, perceived the Bolshevik revolution as a manifestation of Russia's spiritual profundity, a depth of passion also expressed in the works of Dostoevsky.[61] Publications inspired by utopian longings spilled from the presses. *The Spirit of Utopia* (1918) by Ernst Bloch and *The Theory of the Novel* (1920) by Georg Lukács are two of the more prominent and influential publications of this kind. However, there were numerous lesser known and today mostly forgotten works such as *The Intellectual Crisis of the Present* (1923) by Arthur Liebert, or Kristina Pfeiffer-Raimund's *A Woman's Letters to Walther Rathenau* (1918).[62] Some of these utopian expressions had roots in the nineteenth century, in diverse sources such as the *Lebensreform* movements and the enthusiastic visions of technocratic progress. However, in the aftermath of war such projects took on a more radical and sometimes apocalyptic character; indeed the profusion of radical religiosity outside the churches provoked the acerbic commentary of observers such as Carl Christian Bry, who published his *Disguised Religions* in 1925.[63] Whereas to critics such as Bry these religious experiments were often distinguished by a faulty connection to reality, to some converts they appeared viable, especially in light of the political and social experiments then taking place in Russia and, briefly, in Bavaria and Hungary.

Moreover, these redemptive desires did not seem so out of place after four years of warfare and a devastating loss of life. If, as Hannah Arendt claimed, death was the "fundamental problem" confronting Europeans after 1918, then the numerous attempts to redeem existence seem warranted.[64] Aside from the massive suffering that the war caused, the Weimar Republic was also beset by a virtual catalogue of what could go wrong in modern societies. To this day the Republic remains a shorthand for crisis, whether one views it as a democratic experiment that failed, or as a social and political laboratory that succeeded in its worst imaginings.[65] In every sphere there was disruption. The economy underwent periods of depression, inflation, and hyperinflation, creating severe and nearly chronic instability; cultural affairs often assumed an extremist and militant tone; and parliamentary gridlocks plagued the political system.[66] In light of this turmoil, the constructed categories of class and gender were rendered uncertain. Historian Detlev Peukert described the resulting political and social collapse as a "crisis of classical modernity," a crisis that compounded the traumas of war and its aftermath with the darker potential lying dormant beneath the rational face of modern industrial societies. This does not mean that the Republic should be understood as doomed from the outset, or as a transitional step in a supposedly inevitable and crisis-driven march towards fascism, but rather as a period of ferment, a forum where conflicting social and political experiments were articulated.[67]

Within this classically modern setting religion occupies a somewhat anomalous position. Drawing on centuries of tradition and on long-established institutional hierarchies, religion appeared to have preserved its connections to a world prior to industry, science, and the "isms" of modern politics. At the very least, the traditional sources of religious authority could be said to have antedated these later developments; therefore, it could be argued that the core of religious belief remained immune to the vagaries and conflicts of modern society.[68] The very presence of the aged gothic churches in German towns and cities appeared to proclaim religion's deep and mystical past. On the other hand, definitions of modernity, especially those influenced by early sociology, often viewed the decline or subordination of religion as a precondition of modernity itself, thus relegating religion to the historical dustbin.[69] Indeed, for Kracauer and some of his contemporaries, the decline of religion and the accompanying disenchantments of the secularized world were often perceived as established facts, a decisive shift that had occurred during the nineteenth century. The loss of this world could be mourned, but it remained beyond recovery.[70] From this point of view, religion had to "modernize," that is, it must accept its limitations in a secular world that made greater claims on areas of authority and belief.

Yet, if the days of pilgrimages and holy tunics were supposedly over, religion still had a ghostly relationship to the modern. Thus, Kracauer sounded almost surprised to find himself in 1927 attending the Zionist congress in Basel, and then participating in a torchlight parade at Lourdes. It was as if he had discovered again Max Weber's "old gods" who still worked their magic beneath a "Janus-faced" rationalism.[71] He saw the signs of religious vitality everywhere, yet the meaning of this tenacity was less clear. Religion appeared to have a dual existence. In one sense, it represented a vanished mode of life, pushed aside by the triumphal march of reason; yet, simultaneously, it could not be denied that the disappearing idols still held their allure. As the protagonist of the *Man without Qualities* by Robert Musil remarked, "there were undeniably still a great many churches around."[72] These artifacts of the past preserved a lost social vision, a vision of the whole, of the spiritually grounded community that religion presupposed. To some this appeared as a counterweight to the modern world and a means of renewing it. The search for the new could then look backwards as well as forwards. For Adorno, this retrospective gaze to the past must be resisted as a recrudescence of the archaic in the form of the new;[73] but Kracauer, as will be seen, was not ready to disavow religious contents completely.

How then should one conceive the relationship between religion and modernity, and what role did it play in the European crisis of culture, particularly in 1920s Germany? Moreover, how was this crisis perceived, contested, and, in some sense, legitimated within intellectual milieus? A recent discussion of modernism draws attention to its penchant for images depicting violence and wounds, and herein lies some grounds for looking at the critique of religion as a contribution to the crisis-ridden atmosphere of Weimar Germany, as a means of generating a rhetoric of crisis.[74] The perception of violence in modernist art is ambiguous. It was sometimes celebrated insofar as it unleashed the supposedly regenerative power of "primitive passions." In this guise violence constitutes a purgative force that wipes the slate clean and creates something new; the sacrifices that it demands are entered into a catalogue of martyrs that list the sufferings obligatory to the creation of the new. In this regard, the sometimes violent language that infused Kracauer's descriptions of rationalization is not without significance. "Dismember," "disembody," "hollow out" (*zerreißen, entwirklichen, entleeren*) are significant words in his early writing, and the individual is often dismantled into "complexes of atoms" and "particles of soul."[75] Thus, it is secular reason that destroys and the religious vision of the whole that suffers. In its victimization and in its clear hostility to materialist worldviews, religion then finds an ally within some strands of "Janus-faced" modernity. If cultural modernism rejected the staid and materialist culture of the nineteenth century, it could find support among the faithful. Religious passion could emerge as a critique of a faded past, as something startling and originary—thus, the vision of the Christian aviator in Apollinaire's poem "Zone." In the sinking world of modernity, the poem implies, only religion retained the aura of the new. In this world of modernist experimentation, Pius X emerges (much to his own surprise, no doubt) as "the most modern of Europeans."[76] Therefore, however ancient religion was, it still preserved its originary force, a force related to the primal impulses that modernists had also sought in regenerative violence, or the unruly passions of the so-called primitive.[77] Such violence was redemptive, a creative act, and as Karl Kraus once stated "origin is the goal."[78] Thus, for some strands of modernity religion could appear in modern guise.

A rhetorical strategy that described the conflict between the secular and the religious in terms of violence did little to alleviate the prevalent discourse of crisis in Weimar.[79] Secularization was portrayed as a metaphysical catastrophe, uprooting humanity from its origins, and leaving individuals spiritually bereft. Therefore, to some observers, secularization could *only* appear as a crisis; as a result, the clash between the sacred and profane was often perceived as trauma—both by the supporters of secularism and its critics. Moreover, it was an event with consequences for the nation; for wherever rationalism and abstract reflection reared their ugly heads—in the newspapers, the state schools, the Reichstag, or cinema—the nation's spiritual vitality would soon, so it was argued, wither away. In this regard, Kracauer too was not immune to the belief that secularization had harmed the national community.[80] This is not to say that the cultural crisis of Weimar should be reduced to a critique of secularization, nor could it be said that all such critiques were intended to incriminate the Republic; but such polemics did contribute to the fevered pitch in which cultural matters were discussed. Viewing secularization as wound and crisis perpetuated a mood of spiritual turmoil, and it prodded intellectuals to search for increasingly radical solutions to a supposedly deepening malaise.

Hence, insofar as Kracauer used this language in his writing, he contributed to a more general discourse that described the conflict of sacred and profane in the starkest of terms. Such discourse could be found across the political spectrum.[81] Thus, one finds that the Kracauer of the early 1920s has some affinity for the cultural pessimism of the late nineteenth century.[82] Writing to Margaret Susman, for instance, he declared his antipathy to all things intellectual, to circles of literati, and to the hopes placed in the postwar political order. However, in spite of this hostility, his public statements were far more moderate, especially when compared with those of his contemporaries.[83] Moreover, Kracauer was ambivalent to programs that found political renewal through violence. The apocalyptic or messianic tendencies that one finds in the work of Ernst Bloch or Walter Benjamin are by and large absent, even in his writing during the economically and politically unstable years of 1918 to 1923.[84] Still, his contribution to this apocalyptic discourse should not be discounted. The discourse of secular crisis encompassed both problem and solution; the radical, sometimes violent, proposals for root and branch reconstruction correlated with the alarmist tones in which the sense of crisis had been perceived and represented.[85] Kracauer, as will be seen, was an avid participant in this discourse; he was one of many writers who sounded the alarm of cultural crisis in the Weimar era. Through most of the 1920s and the early 1930s, Kracauer resisted what he saw as a harmful overgrowth of superficial religiosity. This meant staking out a territory in the expanding discourse of sacred and profane, a linguistic territory contested by a profusion of new religions that rushed in to fill an alleged spiritual void. For some observers, the result was a form of religious dilettantism, or what the sociologist Karl Dobbelaere has called *religion à la carte*.[86] This could be described as a kind of metaphysical *flânerie*, a subject that Kracauer criticized in his 1922 feuilleton "Those Who Wait."[87] Yet, Kracauer also partook of this new religious landscape. Free to wander among any number of religious milieus, Kracauer too could on one day witness the debates between Orthodox and Reform Judaism and, on the next, tour the shrines of Catholicism. He recognized that the choice to participate in a religious community was no longer simply a matter of inner conviction or social convention, but just as often a manifestation of curiosity, or, as in his own case, a product of rational observation coupled with a vague and imprecise sense of spiritual angst.

What did these haphazard engagements with religion mean? The fragmentation of religious beliefs suggested that redemption had left the churches and synagogues and had gone out "into the street." Religious ideas circulated among spiritual consumers as if they were so many goods on the shelves of a department store. The individual who sought spiritual wholeness was now at liberty to peruse and sample these spiritual goods and then to move on when a particular product did not satisfy. Aside from the wares on offer from the established faiths, there were now numerous disciplines of the soul from which one could choose. Bry called them "disguised religions" (*verkappten Religionen*), while historian Thomas Nipperdey has referred to them as "vagabond religiosity."[88] These movements existed on the fringes of, and sometimes in opposition to, established religious traditions and hierarchies.

In regards to these phenomena there were two vital issues at stake for Kracauer. On the one hand, he was increasingly aware of contemporary desires to give collective bodies a religious meaning, and he was alarmed by the emergence of a sacred aura around the collective in nationalist, and to a lesser extent, socialist rhetoric. In part, this was a critique of what he saw as a reductive form of collectivism, but it was also due to his fear that an ill-considered plunge into a false religiosity would preclude further engagement with social realities. This aspect of his critique was on the surface directed at religion, but in the early 1920s Kracauer sometimes voiced the belief that the essence of religion was, in fact, to be found through contact with the profane. A religiosity that avoided profane reality would exclude itself from the religious sphere it sought to attain.

For this reason Kracauer, as will be seen, sometimes cited religious authorities when criticizing the religious revival. Thus, in repudiating the work of Ernst Bloch, he referred to the doubt and irony that he claimed to find in the work of Augustine and rabbinical tradition; such expressions, he argued, were both more in keeping with contemporary reality and closer to the truth contents of religion.[89] In a sense, he sought to preserve a sphere in which religious contents could survive, safe from the dual threats of encroaching rationalism and resurgent religiosity. He associated this with a position of "waiting"—a decision to remain suspended between skepticism and devotion, to neither believe, nor to conclusively deny. This was a form of reluctant skepticism that desired but still resisted utopia. A view of Judaism as the faith of a people who waits is clearly relevant here, though as a religious motif it had a wider resonance of which Kracauer was well aware. The background to his critique of religion was what Samuel Moyn has referred to as the "transconfessional religious thinking of a particular Western European moment . . . a thorough-going revolution in Weimar-era theology."[90]

The theological implications of this gesture of "waiting" constitutes an undercurrent in modernist culture as can be found in the work of Samuel Beckett, or also Kracauer's more immediate contemporary Robert Musil. Similarly, his friend Walter Benjamin conceived of a "life of deferment," an existence based upon perpetual waiting before the divine.[91] This was a theology of the unsayable; it was predicated on an unspoken anticipation of revealed truth, an event that took place outside of material reality, but nonetheless had definite consequences within it. This type of "negative theology" is not without some echoes in Kracauer's work, and similar ideas were widely discussed among his contemporaries—Barth, Bloch, Buber, Rosenzweig, and Susman among others.[92] Their writings contested common ground and, as a result, their disagreements were fought with much tenacity. Kracauer's position on religion was taken in direct confrontation with many of these writers. Indeed, underlining the differences between himself and his contemporaries on religious questions was a means of defining his own position in relation to his cultural milieu.

Still, what meaning religion had for Kracauer is unclear, and since war and immigration led to the loss of a significant portion of his papers, his early views on religion must remain obscure. We know little to nothing of his early attitudes towards Judaism outside of a brief reference to the perfunctory observances practiced among his relatives.[93] There is no evidence of a decisive break or repudiation of Judaism, but as historian Enzo Traverso has argued, there was little need for Kracauer to discuss, let alone repudiate, whatever religious beliefs he may once have held; for him religion appears to have been a truly "invisible church." Religious positions were best left unstated, and thus they never became a point of internal dissonance in his work; as he stated in a letter to Simmel, general principles are, in a certain way, "invisible" (*Unsichtig*).[94] Yet, even as religion became a less significant theme in his writing, theological concepts remained, stowed away as contraband close to the core of his critical project.[95]

If Kracauer's idea of critical vocation derives from the conflict between religious revival and secularism, what might his work tell us about Weimar intellectual culture and secularizing processes?[96] Scholars have investigated the religious and theological influences in the work of Horkheimer, Adorno, and others associated with the Frankfurt School.[97] Given Kracauer's proximity to this milieu and his recognized influence on the young Adorno, a study of this theme in connection to his work will help illuminate this important chapter in Weimar cultural history.[98] It can also expose some of the contexts of Weimar-era cultural criticism, and the degree to which it was shaped by opposing concepts of the culture/religion nexus. For the theologian Paul Tillich, religion was "the spiritual substance of culture," a view with which Kracauer would have sympathized in the early 1920s. In a brief article devoted to a lecture by Martin Buber, for instance, Kracauer expressed his agreement with Buber's argument that religion is the groundwork of all culture, not one of its more spiritual emanations.[99] However, as Kracauer devoted more attention to mass culture, he adopted a different approach to this issue; during the mid-1920s his thinking wavered between differing positions over the need of religious foundations for culture. While rejecting a flight into religious certainty, he became increasingly concerned with what he saw as the pitfalls of radical cultural agendas.

The debate over such questions has generated a discourse on culture that retains its relevance up to the present day. A recent discussion of the origins of Marxist socialism offers some context for this development. Marxism, as Gareth Stedman Jones points out, did not arise from a discussion of social justice and equity, but rather out of philosophical debates concerning the meaning of history after the disappearance of God—Marxism finding new meaning by constructing a materialist teleology.[100] Similarly, one could argue that theories of mass culture arose from the debate over the postreligious meaning of culture itself. With the disappearance of divine purpose, the meaning of history was cast in doubt; without this larger schema to legitimate it, culture too had to respond by relying on material resources to explain its values and evolution. The critic of culture then stepped into the place vacated by religious authority, or which religious authority could no longer secure on the basis of its weakened power. As Marx argued, all criticism was essentially the criticism of religion.[101]

Religion as repository of timeless values was thus no longer tenable, and nor could culture move into its position. By the mid-1920s Kracauer began to work with an idea of culture that is much more akin to our age than his own.

Culture was not a system of meanings and values derived from eternal verities, but one that was embedded within social and economic processes; it was a constructed system, and to interpret contemporary reality meant that one had to recognize one's own position within this construction. William Sewell, in a recent essay, emphasizes that definitions of culture should be understood as "a dialectic of system and practice . . . and as a system of symbols possessing a real but thin coherence that is continually put at risk in practice and therefore subject to transformation"—a view with which I think Kracauer would agree.[102]

Kracauer embraced criticism at a moment when this transfer of authority appeared to be in process, yet its implications provoked uncertainty. He was inclined to interpret the role of the critic from inside the secularization framework; but even as he repudiated religious revival, he still defended religious concepts at different points throughout the 1920s. Indeed, these concepts remained vital to him as they supported his critical stance to modern society. In this sense, he refashioned them for different purposes. Thus, while the fate of religious institutions was a secondary matter to him, this was not true of religious ideas. For this reason, many scholars of his work have recognized the stubborn persistence of the theological. Miriam Hansen argued that the Gnostic and messianic traditions in Judaism were an important influence bridging the early and later periods of his career.[103] Inka Mülder-Bach, Martin Jay, and Olivier Agard have also pointed out the presence of religious or metaphysical motifs in his work, though it is generally accepted that by the mid-1920s these motifs receded as, influenced by Marx and Weber, Kracauer began to reassess his attitudes to mass culture.[104]

If Kracauer had stopped writing before 1925, he probably would have remained mostly unknown, for it is difficult to imagine that his earlier writings would have elicited the same amount of interest as his later work. Nonetheless, I would argue that this early period was something more than a transition leading from "cultural pessimism" to a relatively progressive theory of modern culture. His perception of the critic's vocation was solidified during the earlier period: to the critic of modernity he gave the task of mediating between the social realities of a secular world and the theological concepts that continued to haunt it in new shapes and guises.

Through an exploration of Kracauer's idiosyncratic mingling of the sacred and the profane, this study will engage with questions concerning the historiography of secularization. Germany in the 1920s demonstrates many of the contradictory impulses that have been central to the debates over what was involved in this process, and even to what extent it actually occurred. Thus, when the Weimar assembly established the formal separation of church and state, some argued that it was little more than recognition of the status quo, a simple confirmation of the diminished position of the Protestant churches that had long been evident, for instance, in the shortage of trained pastors in many parts of Germany.[105] Yet, the 1920s was also an extraordinarily fruitful period in theology. Karl Barth, Rudolf Otto, Rudolf Bultmann, Max Scheler, Franz Rosenzweig, Martin Buber, Emmanuel Levinas, Romano Guardini, and Paul Tillich all wrote important works in this period, and their theological works still resonate in the present. That this happened during a time of intensive political and cultural flux does not seem accidental, and indeed, this was when the term *political religion* became commonly used to describe the conflation of religion and politics.[106] One of the most famous arguments concerning the origins of modern political principles was articulated during the turmoil of Weimar: Carl Schmitt's dictum that all modern political concepts are derived from theological ones.[107] Thus, the difficult question of what role religion should have in the postwar political order was one that was hard to ignore, especially among intellectual circles.

The decline of "social significance" that is implied by the secularization thesis has been a controversial subject. Few would argue that relations between church and state did not undergo a dramatic change in the course of the long nineteenth century, and that the same could be said for forms and patterns of religious thought and belief. However, the question of whether this means European societies became more secular before 1914 is much less certain. Evidence of the persistence of religious sentiment in the last century has led some scholars to reject the thesis of secularization altogether, arguing that it has no, or very limited, interpretive validity.[108] From the point of view of its critics, the concept is damaged irreparably by its dependence on some of the dubious assumptions that have supported sociological theories of modernization. For instance, the normative assumption that modernity can be equated with secularism, that the model of industrial-capitalist progress tends toward a secular idea of modernity, has been questioned by many including the anthropologist Talal Asad.[109] To some critics, this position derives from the intertwining of the origins of the secularization thesis and the discipline of sociology. The latter was in some respects predicated on the former, a relationship recognized by sociologist Niklas Luhmann.[110] Sociology as a field of critical discourse on society and politics, so the argument goes, was won at the expense of religion. It is to be expected that Kracauer, as a student of sociology, would have been well acquainted with some of the fatalistic views of religion that influenced the formation of the sociological discipline.[111]

However, the secularization thesis has nonetheless proved to be remarkably resilient. Karel Dobbelaere, the author of a classic study of the subject, recently revised his work in light of two decades of new research and debate, but he held to most of its central premises—in part because his statement of key arguments was more nuanced than its critics have recognized.[112] In any case, few scholars would now view secularization as a linear process in which religion was on the losing side of a zero-sum game with rational enlightenment.

Instead, historians have emphasized the reorientation of both religious institutions and beliefs.[113] Rather than dwelling on the declining "social significance" of religion, they have identified the different forms of religious practice that emerged as religion responded to the shifting conditions of modern societies. The growth of such practices accompanied the emptying out of churches and synagogues, thus complicating our notions of what secularization involved. One speaks more of the adjustments of religion or the "decline of Christendom" in order to indicate that the waning of religious institutions does not necessarily entail a decline in religious sentiments. Thus, a straightforward linear narrative has been displaced.[114]

Kracauer felt that secularization had altered the world, that modernity was a realm of disenchantment. In effect, the forces of secularization had won and "there was no simple way back."[115] Yet, Kracauer's critical project only makes sense if it is understood as a response to secularization as an ongoing and nonlinear process. As he stated in his famous essay on the "mass ornament" the process of "demythologization" was not complete.[116] Instead, it was a hesitant and perpetual process, one that moved in a number of twists and turns that were to be found in the reorientation and redefinition of theological concepts. To observe and reflect on this process, as well as to intervene in it, was the leitmotif of his critical efforts. For these reasons, Kracauer's work offers a vantage point from which to observe the problem of secularization as it was perceived during the Weimar Republic. Moreover, many themes that emerged from his attempt to expose the inner workings of disenchantment have remained important to discussions of secularization up to the present day. If one compares his work with some of the subjects that Luhmann, for instance, argued were central to the study of religion and society, Kracauer seems remarkably prescient. The emergence of a polyphonic (*polykontextural*) mode of observation, an expanded definition of culture in which religion is accorded a distinct if ambiguous sphere, a transformed perception of time and space, a recognition of the crucial role played by media—all of these themes were approached by Kracauer in the course of his work in the 1920s.[117]

A methodological consideration: it should be conceded at the outset that Kracauer rarely addressed such themes in an extended or substantial study. Rather his ideas on religion are woven into a variety of texts—fiction, sociology, and journalism—as a constantly resurfacing theme. This study suggests that the lack of a focused treatment on his part makes his relevance to a discussion of secularization more, not less, compelling. Kracauer argued that the ephemeral and chance expressions of a society afforded deeper insight into its true nature.[118] By using some of Kracauer's lesser-known writings, I hope to demonstrate the continued relevance of his claim.

"God's Policeman"? Preliminary Conclusions

Some indication of the religious underpinnings in Kracauer's work appear in the contemporary judgment of one of his friends, the Austrian writer Joseph Roth: "Dr. Kracauer... has angered me greatly. He is one of the Jehovah Jews, and Marxism is his Bible; the Eastern Jews have a good word for such men: God's policemen."[119] When Roth sent this letter, he had known Kracauer for some years, probably since the early 1920s. He had been a regular contributor to the *FZ*, and he was also close to Reifenberg who had supported the work of both writers. Their friendship was sometimes uneasy, but of course this could be said of most of Roth's friendships.[120] In any case, they remained in contact until Roth died in Parisian exile in 1939. Roth had admired Kracauer's work, and he had intervened with his publisher, Samuel Fischer, in order to promote the publication of *Ginster*. Indeed, Kracauer later credited Roth with the stimulus to begin his novel.[121] His death, Kracauer stated, had been hard for him, provoking reflections on their common struggles in Germany and their shared fate in exile.[122]

Roth implies that Kracauer is the model of someone who has found a political religion. Marx displaces the Bible; the religious zealot is transformed into an ideological fanatic. Kracauer, the "policeman of God" thus becomes the exponent of a secular religion, and from the doctrinaire believer comes the political dogmatist.

This surprising and rather idiosyncratic description of Kracauer is suggestive of the themes to be explored in this study. It is, on the surface, consistent with one of the two theories of secularization that were proposed by the French historian Jean-Claude Monod.[123] On the one hand, secularization is conceived of as old wine in new bottles, a model in which modern political forms merely appropriate religious functions. They adopt its hierarchical institutions and its sense of historical mission; hence, they mediate religious energies into a secular world view. On the other hand, secularization represents a distinct, if qualified, rupture—a position argued by Hans Blumenberg in his study, *The Legitimacy of Modernity*. Blumenberg believed that some aspects of religious thought would have hindered the secular idea of progress and, as a result, secularization meant more than just an adaptation of religious energies to secular practices. Instead, a deeper shift in terms of content had to have occurred in terms of how people thought, felt, and expressed the differences between sacred and profane.[124] Only in this way could one explain the conditions of modernity. These two theories are, of course, not mutually exclusive, as literary scholar Vincent Pecora has pointed out. Of greater significance is the investigation of how these interpretations confronted one another in specific historical contexts.[125] If we return to Kracauer as a case study, there is some reason to subscribe to the "old wine in new bottles" theory, for as his interest in Marxism and mass culture increased, the interest in religious subjects faded.

Yet, the transformation of socialism into a pseudoreligious creed is not straightforward in Kracauer's work. He was alarmed by the emergence of a political religiosity, and indeed it was probably this phenomenon that led him to conceive of a more positive valuation of reason. For if *ratio* is the villain of earlier studies such as *The Detective Novel*, after 1925 he sees in reason more than just the destroyer of religious unity, or a malignant force in the grand narrative of secularization. The "cloudy reason" of *ratio* is set against a positive, "genial" form of reason, and from this latter instrument one need not fear that it "rationalizes too much, but too little."[126] However, as will be discussed below, this more reflective rationalism was to be used not only against the old truths of religion, but also against what one critic has called a "revolutionary culturalism."[127]

What did Kracauer think religion was? Definitions of religion are, of course, a vast and intractable subject that is outside the scope of this study. Durkheim once stated that society *is* religion, a formulation that provokes as many questions as it might answer. For my purpose, it may do to accept the definition offered by Luhmann that "religion is whatever can be observed as religion."[128] The imprecision that ensues when one tries to define it is, in fact, a significant aspect of the debates to be discussed in the following pages. What remains more important, however, is not the relative validity of such concepts and assumptions, but rather how they emerged and functioned in Weimar-era discourses—how they derived from, or responded to their specific contexts. In other words, what were the social and political stakes involved in trying to decide what belonged to God and what to Caesar?

The conflict that ensued over this question was not a minor one in the context of Weimar culture. Secular viewpoints could alienate voters and galvanize religious communities. Conflicts over issues such as the separation of church and state or religious instruction in the schools were still capable of mobilizing social interests into political action.[129] Thus, when a number of independent Socialists returned to the SPD after the acrimonious split at the end of the war, it was thought expedient to alter the party's charter in order to accommodate the return of the radicals. The new charter of 1925 dropped a significant tenet of the earlier Erfurt program of 1891: the statement that religion was a "private affair." This may have been more a matter of political tactics than of secular convictions; but the move implicitly recognized the persistent struggle over religion in politics.

Given the present revival of conflicts between religion and secularism there is good reason to explore manifestations of these conflicts in different historical contexts. The ban of headscarves in France, the proposed entrance of Turkey into the European Union, and the debate over "reasonable accommodation" in Québec are just some of the issues that have stimulated a renewed interest in past historical conflicts. This has found expression in numerous publications that make it clear that the debate is not confined to academia. Charles Taylor, Michael Burleigh, Slavoj Žižek, Jürgen Habermas, Mark Lilla, and Christopher Hitchens are among those who have recently made contributions to the subject. It is certainly noticeable that some of these discussions have returned to the same textual terrain that Kracauer went over in the 1920s: Kierkegaard, Weber, and Barth, and more surprisingly, the Catholic mystery writer, G. K. Chesterton. There should be no surprise, then, that present-day discussions have been fraught with baggage from the Weimar period. In 2004, Habermas addressed this resemblance in an essay written at the invitation of the Catholic Academy of Bavaria. In part, the speech defended the legitimacy of secularization. When confronted with the argument that given what we know about the persistence of religion, European secularism was the "odd one out," he countered that "this reminds one of the mood in the Weimar Republic in Germany . . . it evokes Carl Schmitt, Martin Heidegger, or Leo Strauss."[130] Here again, we are in terrain that Kracauer would have found familiar.

Weimar's cultural crisis was never resolved; rather, it was submerged in the conformist cultural policies imposed by the Nazi regime. For Kracauer and many of his contemporaries, 1933 meant flight, exile, silence, or death; but for others, such as the *FZ* editor and archivist Hermann Herrigel, 1933 was the year of potential redemption. A friend of Kracauer, follower of both Martin Buber and the Protestant theologian Friedrich Gogarten, Herrigel's philosophical trajectory found its terminus in a theology that readily allowed one to give allegiances to God and Caesar; his faith did not conflict with his support for the Hitler revolution, as will be discussed below. The relationship of National Socialism to religion is, nonetheless, too complex to do justice to in this study, but at the very least at a time when it has become common to refer to the inability of some religions to adjust to secular modernity, it is worth considering whether secularization has been such an easy process in European history.[131]

Notes

1. I have translated what appears to be a neologism (*Angebenheiten*) as "demonstrativeness." The handwriting in this letter is exceptionally clear relative to most of Kracauer's letters, so I have taken this odd word to be intended and not a misspelling of a different word.
2. Kracauer to Hans Kohn, 4 February 1964, quoted in *Siegfried Kracauer, 1889–1966: Marbacher Magazin* 47, ed. Ingrid Belke and Irene Renz (Marbach am Neckar, 1988): 47. His objections also met with agreement, including his friends Leo Löwenthal and Walter Benjamin. For an account of his critique, see Martin Jay, "Politics

of Translation: Siegfried Kracauer and Walter Benjamin on the Buber-Rosenzweig Bible," in *Permanent Exiles: Essays on the Intellectual Migration from Germany to America* (New York, 1986), 198–216; Lawrence Rosenfeld, "On the Reception of Buber and Rosenzweig's Bible," *Prooftexts* 14, no. 2 (May 1994): 141–65, and Brian Britt, "Romantic Roots of the Debate on the Buber-Rosenzweig Bible," *Prooftexts* 20, no. 3 (Fall 2000): 262–88.

3. Kracauer, "Der Baseler Zionistenkongreß: Die Krisis in Zionismus," *Frankfurter Zeitung* (FZ), 7 September 1927 in Kracauer, *Werke* 5.2, ed. Inka Mülder-Bach and Ingrid Belke, 9 vols. (Frankfurt am Main, 2004–2012), 657–63.
4. On Kracauer and cultural mobility see Olivier Agard, *Kracauer: Le chiffonier mélancolique* (Paris, 2010), 349–54.
5. Belke and Renz, *Siegfried Kracauer*, 30. In a letter Kracauer sent to Mann in 1935, he stated that *Tonio Kröger* and the *Reflections* had "a decisive influence on my development." See Kracauer to Mann, 4 June 1935, Kracauer Nachlass (KN), Deutsches Literaturarchiv (DLA), Marbach am Neckar.
6. See Matthew Jefferies, *Imperial Culture in Germany, 1871–1918* (Basingstoke, 2003), 135–228, and Wolf Lepenies, *The Seduction of Culture in Germany History* (Princeton, 2006), 9–55.
7. Siegfried Kracauer, "Philosophie des Werks," *Frankfurter Zeitung* (FZ), 27 July 1920, in *Werke* 5.1, 89–94. The book reviewed was *Individuum und Welt als Werk: Eine Grundlegung der Kulturphilosophie* (Munich, 1920).
8. Unless stated otherwise, all translations from German texts are my own. I have translated all German sources into English except in instances where an English translation, I believe, would diminish the argument.
9. Kracauer to Susman, 11 January 1920, Susman Nachlass (SN), DLA. Some of the words in this text are not legible, but the general sense is clear. On Kracauer's opinions of Russia and the USSR, see Ingrid Belke, "Siegfried Kracauer als Beobachter der jungen Sowjetunion," in *Siegfried Kracauer: Neue Interpretationen*, ed. Michael Kessler and Thomas Y. Levin (Tübingen, 1990), 17–38. Margarete Susman (1872–1966) was a poet and essayist who worked in and around Frankfurt. She was married to the painter Eduard von Bendemann from 1905 to 1928. She studied with Simmel for a period and had numerous friends and acquaintances among the intelligentsia. After the rise of Nazism, she fled to Switzerland where she remained until her death.
10. Kracauer, "Philosophie des Werks," *Werke* 5.1, 93.
11. Kevin Repp, *Reformers, Critics and the Paths of German Modernity: Anti-Politics and the Search for Alternatives, 1890–1914* (Cambridge, 2000), and Jan-Werner Müller, *Contesting Democracy: Political Ideas in Twentieth-Century Europe* (New Haven and London, 2011), 31–32.
12. See Max Scheler, "Zur religiösen Erneuerung," *Hochland* 17, no. 1 (1918/1919): 5–21. On Karl Barth and the theology of crisis, see Mark Lilla, *The Stillborn God: Religion, Politics, and the Modern West* (New York, 2007), 268–85; on the Free Jewish School, see Nahum N. Glatzer, "The Frankfort Lehrhaus," *Yearbook of the Leo Baeck Institute* 1 (1956): 105–22; and Wolfgang Schivelbusch, "Auf der Suche nach dem verlorenen Judentum: Das Freie Jüdische Lehrhaus," *Intellektuellendämmerungen: Zur Lage der Frankfurter Intelligenz in den zwanziger Jahren* (Frankfurt am Main, 1982), 27–41. For an overview of these trends in postwar Germany, see Friedrich Wilhelm Graf, "God's Anti-Liberal Avant-Garde: New Theologies

in the Weimar Republic," *German Historical Institute London: Bulletin* 32, no. 2 (November, 2010): 3–24.
13. *Frankfurter Zeitung*, "Nun sag' wie hast Du's mit der—Politik?" *FZ*, 25 December 1928, Morgenblatt. The article solicited responses from a number of prominent individuals of different social and economic backgrounds, but with a slight bias towards intellectuals. The contributions were prefaced by the following remarks: "Certainly, many swings of opinion lie beneath the commitment of nonpoliticians to politics. Through war and revolution, the interest in public affairs deepened: so how do things stand today? . . . we intend an interesting contribution to the question, what position does politics—we do not mean some or another party position, but rather politics in general—have in the spiritual [*geistigen*] life of the nation."
14. Caesar Seligmann, quoted in Schivelbusch, 38.
15. Kracauer to Susman, 11 January 1920, SN, DLA.
16. Kracauer to Susman, 26 July 1920, SN, DLA.
17. For overviews and general interpretations of Kracauer's work, see Martin Jay, "The Extraterritorial Life of Siegfried Kracauer," in Jay, *Permanent Exiles: Essays on the Intellectual Migration from Germany to America* (New York, 1986), 152–97; Inka Mülder, *Siegfried Kracauer—Grenzgänger zwischen Theorie und Literatur: Seine frühen Schriften, 1913–1933* (Stuttgart, 1985); Michael Schröter, "Weltzerfall und Rekonstruktion: zur Physiognomik Siegfried Kracauers," *Text und Kritik* 68 (October 1980): 18–40; Gertrud Koch, *Siegfried Kracauer: An Introduction* (Princeton, 2000); Enzo Traverso, *Siegfried Kracauer: itinéraire d'un intellectuel nomade* (Paris, 1994); and Thomas Y. Levin, "Introduction" to Kracauer, *The Mass Ornament: Weimar Essays* (Cambridge, 1995), 1–30. More recently, see Agard, *Kracauer: le chiffonier mélancholique*; the essays collected in Frank Grunert and Dorothee Kimmich, eds., *Denken durch die Dinge: Siegfried Kracauer im Kontext* (Munich, 2009); and Gerd Gemünden and Johannes von Moltke, eds., *Culture in the Anteroom: The Legacies of Siegfried Kracauer* (Ann Arbor, 2012).
18. The expressions used here are borrowed from Vincent Pecora, *Secularization and Cultural Criticism: Religion, Nation, and Modernity* (Chicago, 2006), 1–6. See also Schröter, "Weltzerfall und Rekonstruktion," 18–26.
19. The vastness of the literature on secularization forbids an overview here, but see the essays collected in Steve Bruce, ed., *Religion and Modernization: Sociologists and Historians Debate the Secularization Thesis* (Oxford, 1992); Hartmut Lehmann, ed., *Säkularisierung, Dechristianisierung, Rechristianisierung im neuzeitlichen Europa: Bilanz und Perspektiven der Forschung* (Göttingen,1997); Hugh McLeod, *Secularization in Western Europe, 1848–1914* (Basingstoke, 2000); Hermann Lübbe, *Säkularisierung: Geschichte eines ideenpolitischen Begriffs*, 3rd ed. (Freiburg and Munich, 2003); and Benjamin Ziemann, "Säkularisierung, Konfessionalisierung, Organisationsbildung: Aspekte der Sozialgeschichte der Religion im langen 19. Jahrhundert," *Archiv für Sozialgeschichte* 47 (2007): 485–508. Marcel Gauchet, in his study *The Disenchantment of the World: A Political History of Religion* (Princeton, 1997) takes an even longer view of the secularizing process, arguing that the shift to the secular begins with the advent of monotheism and the division of the world into sacred and profane. For a more recent critique of the place of secularism in modernity, see Talal Asad, *Formations of the Secular: Christianity, Islam, Modernity* (Stanford, 2003).
20. Dagmar Barnouw, *Critical Realism: History, Photography, and the Work of Siegfried Kracauer* (Baltimore, 1994), 4–5.

21. On this motif, see Leo Haenlein, *Der Denk-Gestus des aktiven Wartens im Sinn-Vakuum der Moderne* (Frankfurt am Main and Bern, 1984), 133–135; Mülder, *Siegfried Kracauer—Grenzganger*, 60; and Miriam Hansen, "Decentric Perspectives: Kracauer's Early Writings on Film and Mass Culture," *New German Critique* 54 (Autumn 1991): 50. The equation of secularism with modernity is problematic, and has been the subject of much criticism. This issue will be discussed below.
22. Kracauer, *Der Detektiv-Roman: Ein philosophischer Traktat* (Frankfurt am Main, 1979). I am indebted to the discussions of this work that can be found in Mülder, *Siegfried Kracauer—Grenzgänger*, 35–48; Koch, *Siegfried Kracauer*, 15–25; David Frisby, "Between the Spheres: Siegfried Kracauer and the Detective Novel," *Theory, Culture and Society* 9, no. 2 (1992): 1–22; and Thomas Weber, "La réalité emphatique: *Le Roman policier. Un traité philosophique*, Une première interprétation de la culture de masse," in *Culture de masse et modernité: Siegfried Kracauer sociologue, critique, écrivain*, ed. Philippe Despoix and Nia Perivolaropoulou (Paris, 2001), 23–39. Agard's study of Kracauer appeared after this chapter was written. I agree with much of his reading of this key Kracauer text; see Agard, *Kracauer*, 49–71.
23. Frisby, "Between the Spheres," 3; and Hannah Arendt, "Søren Kierkegaard," *FZ*, 29 January 1932 in Arendt, *Essays in Understanding: 1930–1954*, trans. Robert and Rita Kimber (New York, 1994), 44–49.
24. Inka Mülder-Bach, "Der Umschlag der Negativität: Zur Verschränkung von Phänomenologie, Geschichtsphilosophie und Filmästhetik in Siegfried Kracauers Metaphorik der 'Oberfläche,'" *Deutsche Vierteljahrsschrift für Literaturwissenschaft und Geistesgeschichte* 61, no. 2 (June 1987): 359–73.
25. Adorno to Kracauer, 19 July 1931, in *Theodor W. Adorno/Siegfried Kracauer: Briefwechsel, 1923–1966*, ed. Wolfgang Schopf (Frankfurt am Main, 2008), 286.
26. On Hirsch see Lilla, *Stillborn God*, 281–82. On Kierkegaard reception in Germany and Europe see Jon Stewart, ed., *Kierkegaard's Influence on Literature, Criticism and Art: Tome 1: The Germanophone World* (Farnham, 2013); and Habib C. Malik, *Receiving Søren Kierkegaard: The Early Impact and Transmission of his Thought* (Washington, DC, 1997).
27. Döblin, *Wissen und Verändern! Offene Briefe an einen jungen Menschen* (Berlin, 1931).
28. See Kracauer to Adorno, 3 November 1964, *Briefwechsel, 1923–1966*, 676, and Adorno's response written on 13 November 1964, *Briefwechsel, 1923–1966*, 680.
29. These works have been collected in *Werke 9: Frühe Schriften aus dem Nachlaß*.
30. Kracauer to Susman, 20 January 1920, SN, DLA.
31. Kracauer, *Ginster: vom ihm selbst geschrieben* (Berlin, 1928); *Die Angestellten: Aus dem neuesten Deutschland* (Frankfurt, 1930). Since 1989, the study of Kracauer is greatly indebted to the bibliography put together by Thomas Levin, see Levin, *Siegfried Kracauer: eine Bibliographie seiner Schriften* (Marbach am Neckar, 1989).
32. Kracauer had limited contact with both. In 1934, when he was desperate for sources of income, Husserl wrote appreciatively of Kracauer's early sociological work. See Husserl to Kracauer, 14 January 1934, KN, DLA. Kracauer appears to have been acquainted with Wigman's sister, Elizabeth. Her surviving letters to him, preserved in KN, suggest a friendly if brief relationship. On 26 April 1925 (KN, DLA), she wrote to him inquiring whether he would be able to supply some private quarters for some of the dancers. "Is the world now so frail and beautiful?" she wrote, "Do you see that also?"
33. Kracauer to Guttmann, 16 March 1931, KN, DLA.

34. Martin Jay emphasizes this theme in his early article on Kracauer, "The Extraterritorial Life of Siegfried Kracauer," *Permanent Exiles*, 152–53.
35. Richard Gabel to Kracauer, 29 March 1930, KN, DLA. Gabel was a freelance contributor to the *FZ*.
36. Belke and Renz (*Siegfried Kracauer*, 95) have noted the interventions from the following individuals: the French diplomat Henri Hoppenot; the bookseller Adrienne Monnier; the historian Daniel Halévy; the publishers A. P. von Seggern and A. P. J. Kroonenburg; and Lucien Gaget from whom Kracauer and his wife rented rooms. The diplomat and later resistance member Pierre Viénot also appears to have supported Kracauer in this regard, as did Gabriel Marcel. See Kracauer's letter to Marcel dated September 1945, KN, DLA.
37. Paulhan to Armand Petitjean, 11 November 1939, in *Choix de Lettres II, 1937–1945: Traité des jours sombres*, ed. Dominique Aury and Jean-Claude Zylberstein (Paris, 1986), 130.
38. See Kracauer to Meier-Graefe, 24 August 1933 and 16 March 1934, KN, DLA.
39. After the war, Kracauer referred to Sieburg as the "primordial model of the opportunist, nearly its allegory." See Kracauer to Max Niederlechner, 24 March 1957, KN, DLA. Adorno alleged that Kircher detested Kracauer; see Adorno to Kracauer, 2 January 1931, in *Briefwechsel, 1923–1966*, 257–64, esp. 260.
40. Count Harry Kessler, *Berlin in Lights: The Diaries of Count Harry Kessler*, trans. and ed. Charles Kessler (New York, 2000), 456.
41. Kracauer to Adorno, 16 April 1925, *Briefwechsel, 1923–1966*, 51.
42. Kracauer counted himself as one of the admirers of the blonde beast. See Kracauer, *History: The Last Things before the Last* (Princeton, 1994), 173–74.
43. Klemperer, *Curriculum Vitae: Erinnerungen einer Philologen, 1881–1918*, II (Berlin, 1989), 183–84. See also the comments in Martin Jay, "The Extraterritorial Life," *Permanent Exiles*, 153.
44. See Joseph Roth to Bernard von Brentano, 19 December 1925, *Joseph Roth: Briefe, 1911–1939*, ed. Hermann Kesten (Berlin and Köln, 1970), 70; Meier-Graefe to René Schickele, 20 June 1931, in *Kunst ist nicht für Kunstgeschichte da: Briefe und Dokumente*, ed. Catharine Krahmer (Göttingen, 2002), 268–69. This may have contributed to his failure to secure a position in Paris following his forced emigration in 1933.
45. Kracauer to Löwenthal, 12 April 1924, *In steter Freundschaft: Leo Löwenthal–Siegfried Kracauer, Briefwechsel, 1921–1966*, ed. Peter-Erwin Jansen and Christian Schmidt (Lüneburg, 2003), 53–55. See also, Kracauer to Adorno, 5 April 1923 and 22 September 1924, *Briefwechsel, 1923–1966*, 9–18. Gertrud Koch has noted the sexual ambivalence that characterizes the protagonists in the novels, *Georg* and *Ginster*; but she cautions against reading this as a "key to his own sexuality." See Koch, *Siegfried Kracauer*, 60–65.
46. In this respect, see the discussion of the Adorno/Kracauer relationship in Heide Schlüpmann, *Ein Detektiv des Kinos: Studien zu Siegfried Kracauers Filmtheorie* (Frankfurt am Main, 1998), 11–34.
47. He still contributed articles to journals such as *L'Europe Nouvelle* and others, but he never had a stable position during his exile years in France.
48. The stated reason for his dismissal was an article that Kracauer had published in Leopold Schwarzschild's *Das neue Tagebuch*, an act that was in breach of internal protocols. However, it appears that Kracauer was fired on account of his reputation

as a leftist and a desire to deflect attacks on the paper by limiting the number of Jews on staff. See Momme Brodersen, *Siegfried Kracauer* (Reinbek bei Hamburg, 2001), 94–97.
49. Koch, *Siegfried Kracauer*, 68–69. See Adorno's letter to Kracauer dated 13 May 1937 in *Briefwechsel, 1923–1966*, 352–59.
50. Kracauer to Max Niederlechner, 21 February 1947, KN, DLA.
51. Ernst Erich Noth, *Erinnerungen eines Deutschen* (Hamburg, 1971), 208–209.
52. On Kracauer's reception of Marx, see Inka Mülder, *Siegfried Kracauer—Grenzgänger*, 56–60. See more generally, Gertrud Koch, *Siegfried Kracauer* (Princeton, 2000); Michael Schröter, "Weltzerfall und Rekonstruktion"; and Helmut Lethen, "Sichtbarkeit: Kracauers Liebeslehre," in *Siegfried Kracauer*, ed. Kessler and Levin, 195–227.
53. On the concept of political religion, see David D. Roberts, "'Political Religion' and the Totalitarian Departures of Inter-war Europe: On the Uses and Disadvantages of an Analytical Category," *Contemporary European History* 18, no. 4 (2009): 381–414; and Philippe Burrin, "Political Religion: The Relevance of a Concept," *History and Memory* 9, no. 1/2 (Fall 1997): 321–49.
54. Mülder Bach, "Der Umschlag"; David Frisby, *Fragments of Modernity: Theories of Modernity in the Work of Simmel, Kracauer and Benjamin* (Cambridge, 1986), 115–17; and Agard, *Kracauer*, 65–70.
55. Mülder, *Siegfried Kracauer—Grenzgänger*, 44–45.
56. Mülder, 18. See also the comments in Thomas Y. Levin, "Introduction," *Mass Ornament*, 13–14.
57. I am much indebted to the discussion of these issues in Pecora, *Secularization and Cultural Criticism*.
58. Stéphane Audoin-Rouzeau and Annette Becker, *14–18: Understanding the Great War* (New York, 2002), 113–34; and Jay Winter, *Sites of Memory, Sites of Mourning: The Great War in European Cultural History* (Cambridge, 1995), 119–30 and 145–77; Graf, "God's Anti-Liberal Avant-Garde"; and Kurt Nowak, *Geschichte des Christentums in Deutschland: Religion, Politik und Gesellschaft vom Ende der Aufklärung bis zur Mitte des 20. Jahrhunderts* (Munich, 1995), 205–42.
59. The concept of "crisis" in the Weimar Republic and among its later historians has been the subject of recent reevaluation; see Graf, "God's Anti-Liberal Avant-Garde"; Rüdiger Graf, "Either/Or: The Narrative of 'Crisis' in Weimar History and Historiography," *Central European History* 43 (2010): 592–615; Wolfgang Bialas, "Krisendiagnose und Katastrophenerfahrung: Philosophie und Geschichte im Deutschland der Zwischenkriegszeit," in *Geschichtsdiskurs 4: Krisenbewußtsein, Katastrophenerfahrungen und Innovationen, 1880–1945*, ed. Wolfgang Küttler, Jörn Rüsen, and Ernst Schulin (Frankfurt am Main, 1997), 189–216; and the essays collected in Moritz Föllmer and Rüdiger Graf, eds., *Die "Krise" der Weimarer Republik: Zur Kritik eines Deutungsmusters* (Frankfurt and New York, 2005). For a study that emphasizes crisis as a moment of future-oriented potential, see Rüdiger Graf, *Die Zukunft der Weimarer Republik: Krisen und Zukunftsaneignungen in Deutschland, 1918–1933* (Munich, 2008), 83–134. More generally, see Reinhart Koselleck, "Some Questions Concerning the Conceptual History of 'Crisis,'" in *The Practice of Conceptual History: Timing History, Spacing Concepts*, trans. Todd Samuel Presner et al. (Stanford, 2002), 236–47.
60. On this subject see John Willett, *Art and Politics in the Weimar Period: The New Sobriety, 1917–1933* (New York, 1996); Peter Gay, *Weimar Culture: The Outsider as*

Insider (New York, 2001); Michael Löwy, *Redemption and Utopia: Jewish Libertarian Thought in Central Europe, a Study in Elective Affinity* (London, 1992); and Klaus Vondung, *The Apocalypse in Germany* (Columbia and London, 2000).

61. See Kracauer's account of Paquet's speech on behalf of the *Deutsch-Südslawische Gesellschaft* in Kracauer, "Deutsch-Südslawische Gesellschaft," *FZ*, 14 December 1921, Abendblatt.
62. Kracauer reviewed the work by Liebert and a subsequent book by Pfeiffer-Raimund; see "Die geistige Krisis der Gegenwart" *Archiv für Sozialwissenschaft und Sozialpolitik* 51, no. 3 (March 1924) in *Werke* 5.2, 45–48; and Kracauer, "Von kommender Hochkultur," *FZ*, 7 August 1921, Morgenblatt.
63. Carl Christian Bry, *Verkappte Religionen* (Gotha, 1925).
64. Hannah Arendt in Anson Rabinbach, *In the Shadow of Catastrophe of Catastrophe: German Intellectuals between Apocalypse and Enlightenment* (Berkeley, 1997), 9.
65. Peter Fritzsche, "Did Weimar Fail?" *Journal of Modern History* 68 (September 1996): 629–55.
66. Detlev Peukert, *The Weimar Republic: The Crisis of Classical Modernity* (New York, 1992). On the cultural and social ramifications of the hyperinflation, see Bernd Widdig, *Culture and Inflation in Weimar Germany* (Berkeley, 2001).
67. Graf, "Either/Or"; and Fritzsche, "Did Weimar Fail?"
68. Nowak, *Geschichte des Christentums*, 230–35. This study's focus on the religions of the Judeo-Christian tradition should not be taken to suggest that other faiths had no presence in Europe; moreover, as will be seen, awareness of the growing popular interest in religions outside this tradition was part of the Weimar religious landscape.
69. See the study of German sociology by Harry Liebersohn, *Fate and Utopia in German Sociology, 1870–1923* (Cambridge, 1988).
70. For instance, see "Idee und Stoffgebiet der Soziologie," *Frankfurter Universitätszeitung*, 31 December 1920, in *Werke* 5.1, 108–9; and Koch, *Siegfried Kracauer*, 20–21.
71. See Peter Fritzsche's discussion of Peukert's work in "Did Weimar Fail?" 648–49.
72. Robert Musil, *Man without Qualities* 1, trans. Sophie Wilkins (New York, 1996), 25.
73. Adorno to Walter Benjamin, 2 and 4 August 1935, in *The Complete Correspondence, 1928–1940*, ed. Henry Lonitz, trans. Nicholas Walker (Cambridge, 1999), 109–10. Adorno, of course, also advises Benjamin in these letters not to neglect the theological in favor of a crude, Brecht-influenced Marxism.
74. Modris Eksteins, "Drowned in Eau de Vie," *London Review of Books* 30, no. 4 (21 February 2008): 23–24.
75. Schröter, "Weltzerfall und Rekonstruktion," 38–39.
76. Guillaume Apollinaire, "Zone," in *Alcools: Poems by Guillaume Apollinaire*, trans. Donald Revell (Hanover and London), 2–11. The poem was first published in 1913.
77. David Pan, *Primitive Renaissance: Rethinking German Expressionism* (Lincoln, 2001), 66–79; and Modris Eksteins, *Rites of Spring: The Great War and the Birth of the Modern Age* (Toronto, 1989).
78. Kraus quoted in Rabinbach, *In the Shadow of Catastrophe*, 31.
79. On the role of intellectuals in the crisis of Weimar, see the concluding remarks of István Deák, *Weimar Germany's Left-Wing Intellectuals: A Political History of the* Weltbühne *and Its Circle* (Berkeley, 1968), 222–28. Nowak also notes that among the defenders of the Republic are not the theologians of crisis, but rather

the much maligned exponents of "cultural Protestantism." See Nowak, *Geschichte des Christentums*, 212–15.
80. See, for instance, his strikingly idealized vision of the organic community in his 1921 review of Lukács's *Theory of the Novel* in Kracauer, "Georg von Lukács' Romantheorie," *Der verbotene Blick: Beobachtungen, Analysen, Kritiken*, ed. Johanna Rosenberg (Leipzig, 1992), 82–89.
81. See the comments in Graf, "God's Anti-liberal Avant-Garde," 21–24. For a nuanced interpretation of the political predilections of *Kulturkritik* see Georg Bollenbeck, "Kulturkritik: ein unterschätzter Reflexionsmodus der Moderne," in *Philosophie und Zeitgeist im Nationalsozialismus*, ed. Marion Heinz and Goran Gretić (Würzburg, 2006), 87–99.
82. Most critical writing on Kracauer draws a distinction between his earlier years when he was influenced by a conservative "cultural pessimism," and his later period as a more perceptive observer of modern culture. See Koch, *Siegfried Kracauer*; Mülder, *Siegfried Kracauer—Grenzgänger*; Hansen, "Decentric Perspectives"; Levin, "Introduction," *Mass Ornament*; Brodersen, *Siegfried Kracauer*, 28–35; Janet Ward has drawn attention to the motifs that Kracauer shared in common with cultural criticism from the right even late in the Weimar era, see Janet Ward, *Weimar Surfaces: Urban Visual Culture in 1920s Germany* (Berkeley, 2001), 183–89.
83. Kracauer to Susman, 26 July 1920, SN, DLA; and Kracauer, "Bekenntnis zur Mitte," *FZ*, 2 June 1920, in *Werke* 5.1, 70–74; concerning the political considerations that influenced the moderate tone of this feuilleton, see Brodersen, *Siegfried Kracauer*, 32–34.
84. On messianic thought in German Judaism, see Rabinbach, *In the Shadow of Catastrophe*, 27–65; Löwy, *Redemption and Utopia*, 14–26 and 200–209; and Benjamin Lazier, *God Interrupted: Heresy and the European Imagination between the Wars* (Princeton, 2007).
85. On the rhetoric of crisis see R. Graf, "Either/Or."
86. Karel Dobbelaere uses this term to describe the fragmentation of religious practice and belief. See Dobbelaere, *Secularization: An Analysis at Three Levels* (Brussels, 2002), 173–74.
87. Kracauer, "Those Who Wait," *Mass Ornament*, 129–40. On the occult and religious movements outside the church see Corinna Treitel, *A Science for the Soul: Occultism and the Genesis of the Modern* (Baltimore, 2004).
88. Bry, *Verkappte Religionen*; and Thomas Nipperdey, *Religion im Umbruch: Deutschland, 1870–1918* (Munich, 1988), 143–53.
89. Kracauer to Löwenthal, 14 January 1921, *In steter Freundschaft*, 19–20.
90. Samuel Moyn, *Origins of the Other: Emmanuel Levinas between Revelation and Ethics* (Ithaca, 2005), 12.
91. See the discussion in Rabinbach, *In the Shadow of Catastrophe*, 54; and Michael L. Morgan, *Interim Judaism: Jewish Thought in a Century of Crisis* (Bloomington, 2001), 43–45.
92. The correspondence between Kracauer and Susman is fragmentary; outside of a single letter from Susman written in 1926, only Kracauer's letters have survived, and only from 1920 to 1922. In 1925, Kracauer told Adorno that Susman had broken off their friendship because of a disagreement stemming from one of his articles, see Kracauer to Adorno, 16 April 1925, *Briefwechsel, 1923–1966*, 49.

93. See the diary entry of 17 and 18 September 1907 in Belke and Renz, *Siegfried Kracauer*, 10.
94. Enzo Traverso, "Sous le signe de l'extraterritorialité: Kracauer et la modernité juive," *La pensée dispersée: Figures de l'exil judéo-allemand* (Clamécy, 2004), 186–97; Kracauer to Simmel, 30 November 1917, in Otthein Rammstedt and Angela Rammstedt, eds., *Georg Simmel: Gesamtausgabe 23, Briefe, 1912–1918: Jugendbriefe* (Frankfurt am Main, 2008), 880–84, here 882.
95. Mülder, *Siegfried Kracauer—Grenzgänger*, 18.
96. The risk of conceptualizing the conflict between secularism and religion in terms of fixed and opposed positions should be avoided. Weimar-era debates over secularization could, as in the case of Friedrich Gogarten, lead to more positive valuations within a religious framework. See the comments in Ulrich Ruh, "Bleibende Ambivalenz. Säkularisierung/ Säkularisation als geistesgeschichte Interpretationskategorie," in *Ästhetik, Religion, Säkularisierung I: Von der Renaissance zur Romantik*, ed. Silvio Vietta and Herbert Uerlings (Munich, 2008), 29–30.
97. See the essays collected in Raymond Geuss and Margaret Kohlenbach, eds., *The Early Frankfurt School and Religion* (London and New York, 2005); and Jack Jacobs, *The Frankfurt School, Jewish Lives and Antisemitism* (Cambridge, 2015), 7–42. A collection of Frankfurt School writings on religion has also been published: Eduardo Mendieta, ed., *The Frankfurt School on Religion: Key Writings by the Major Thinkers* (New York, 2005).
98. Martin Jay argued this point in "The Extraterritorial Life of Siegfried Kracauer," *Permanent Exiles*, 162. Also, see Adorno's 1964 essay, "The Curious Realist: On Siegfried Kracauer," *New German Critique* 54 (Autumn 1991): 159–77.
99. Tillich quoted in Modris Eksteins, *Solar Dance: Van Gogh, Forgery and the Eclipse of Certainty* (Cambridge, 2012), 84; also see Kracauer, "Religion als Gegenwart," *FZ*, 21 January 1922, *Werke* 5.1, 360–62.
100. Gareth Stedman Jones, "Introduction," to Karl Marx and Friedrich Engels, *The Communist Manifesto*, trans. Samuel Moore (London, 2002), 3–187, esp. 8.
101. Miriam Hansen argued that a form of "redemptive critique" readily facilitated Kracauer's shift to mass culture and away from overtly metaphysical subjects; see Hansen, "Decentric Perspectives," 71. For a discussion of the relationship between religion and cultural criticism, see also Pecora, *Secularization and Cultural Criticism*, 25–66; a sociological view of this relationship is to be found in Niklas Luhmann, *Die Religion der Gesellschaft* (Frankfurt am Main, 2000), 309–17; and on the Marxist view of religion, see Nowak, *Geschichte des Christentums*, 110–11.
102. William H. Sewell Jr., "The Concept(s) of Culture," in *Beyond the Cultural Turn: New Directions in the Study of Society and Culture*, ed. Victoria Bonnell and Lynn Hunt (Berkeley, 1999), 52.
103. Hansen, "Decentric Perspectives," 53–55.
104. Jay, "Extraterritorial Life," 154; Agard, *Kracauer*, 65–70; and Mülder, *Siegfried Kracauer—Grenzgänger*, 18 and 57–67.
105. Daniel Borg, *The Old-Prussian Churches and the Weimar Republic* (Hanover, 1984), 6–7.
106. Burrin, "Political Religion," 321–49; Roberts, "'Political Religion' and the Totalitarian Departures"; and Michael Burleigh, *Earthly Powers: The Clash of Religion and Politics in Europe, from the French Revolution to the Great War* (New York, 2005), 1–22. Burrin offers a compelling defense of the concept, while Michael Burleigh,

who refers to the work of the Catholic political theorist Eric Voegelin, has also revived it in his work. For a brief statement by Voegelin see his "Ersatz Religions," in *Science, Politics, Gnosticism: Two Essays* (Chicago, 1997), 55–78. My own skepticism towards the concept derives from the material presented in this study as well as some of the problems inherent in the very term itself—can there be an apolitical religion, as the concept may imply? And how do we draw these distinctions without a definition of what religion is that most parties could agree upon? As will emerge below, the notion of political or secular religions that displaced "authentic" ones may obscure the fact that religion and radical politics were not mutually exclusive. For a critical view see Neil Gregor, "Nazism—a Political Religion? Rethinking the Voluntarist Turn?" in *Nazism, War and Genocide: Essays in Honor of Jeremy Noakes*, ed. Neil Gregor (Exeter, 2005), 1–21.

107. Carl Schmitt, *Political Theology: Four Chapters on the Concept of Sovereignty*, trans. George Schwab (Chicago, 2005). "Theology" and "religion" are contested words in much of the writing that will be investigated here; Kracauer does not always use them in ways that suggest he had sharp distinctions between them, though "theology" inasmuch as it suggests concepts that were freed from institutional religion is often the word of choice for Kracauer by the later 1920s. He was, as will be seen, more hostile to the idea of "new churches" or political religions, but less so the persistence of theological concepts in secular society. For the purposes of this study, "political theology" as defined by Schmitt will only be used when referring to his notion of the theological origins of modern political concepts pertaining to sovereignty, while "political religion" has a wider valence.

108. McLeod, *Secularisation in Western Europe*, 3–12. See also Rodney Stark, "Secularization, RIP," *Sociology of Religion*, 60, no. 3 (Autumn 1999): 249–73; Callum Brown, "The Secularization Decade: What the 1960s Have Done to the Study of Religious History," in *The Decline of Christendom in Western Europe, 1750–2000*, ed. Hugh McLeod and Werner Ustorf (Cambridge, 2003), 29–46; and Ian Hunter, "Secularization: The Birth of a Modern Combat Concept," *Modern Intellectual History* 12, no. 1 (2015): 1–32.

109. Asad, *Formations of the Secular*. Indeed, Kracauer's critique of a normative cultural secularism in some ways anticipates the work of Asad.

110. Luhmann, *Die Religion der Gesellschaft*, 278–85.

111. Liebersohn, *Fate and Utopia*, 1–10.

112. Dobbelaere, *Secularization*, 157–60. The study first appeared in the journal *Current Sociology* in 1981.

113. See, for instance, David Blackbourn, "The Catholic Church in Europe since the French Revolution," *Comparative Studies in Society and History* 33 (1991): 778–90; and the essays collected in Hugh McLeod and Werner Ustorf, eds., *The Decline of Christendom in Western Europe, 1750–2000* (Cambridge, 2003). On Judaism and secularism see David Jan Sorkin and Frances Malino, eds., *Profiles in Diversity: Jews in a Changing Europe, 1750–1870* (Detroit, 1998).

114. Hugh McLeod has tried to steer a middle ground between these positions, recognizing what is valid in opposing interpretive models. It should be added that some of the classic statements of the secularization thesis such as that of Dobbelaere or Owen Chadwick's *The Secularization of the European Mind in the Nineteenth Century* (Cambridge, 1975) have been aware of many of the issues raised by critics of the thesis.

115. See Koch, *Siegfried Kracauer*, 20.
116. Kracauer, "The Mass Ornament," *Mass Ornament*, 80–81.
117. Luhmann, *Die Religion der Gesellschaft*, 289–314.
118. Kracauer, "The Mass Ornament," *Mass Ornament*, 75.
119. Roth to Zweig, 30 August 1930, in *Briefe:1911–1939*, 175–76.
120. See the engaging memoir by his friend Soma Morgenstern, *Joseph Roths Flucht und Ende: Erinnerungen* (Köln, 2008).
121. Belke and Renz, *Siegfried Kracauer*, 94. See also, Kracauer to Max Tau, 13 May 1961, KN, DLA. Kracauer told Tau that Roth was his *graphologe*: "One evening in the Hotel Englischer Hof in Frankfurt, where we usually sat in the evenings, I recounted to Roth my experiences in the war, how I had peeled potatoes against the enemy and so forth. He laughed and laughed and told me I had to make a novel out of this . . . and so it began."
122. Kracauer to Walter Landauer, 4 June 1939, in Belke and Renz, *Siegfried Kracauer*, 94.
123. Jean-Claude Monod, *La querelle de la secularization de Hegel à Blumenberg* in Pecora *Secularization and Cultural Criticism*, 5–6.
124. This was not, however, viewed by Blumenberg as an absolute rupture as Pecora points out, see *Secularization and Cultural Criticism*, 59–61. See also Blumenberg, *The Legitimacy of the Modern Age*, trans. Robert M. Wallace (Cambridge, 1983).
125. Pecora, *Secularization and Cultural Criticism*, 5–6.
126. Kracauer, "The Mass Ornament," *Mass Ornament*, 81.
127. Martin Jay, *Marxism and Totality: The Adventures of a Concept* (Berkeley, 1984), 98–101.
128. Luhmann, *Die Religion der Gesellschaft*, 308.
129. Jorg Thierfelder, "Religionspolitik in der Weimarer Republik," in *Religionspolitik in Deutschland: von der frühen Neuzeit bis zur Gegenwart*, ed. Kurt Nowak and Anselm Doering-Manteuffel (Stuttgart, 1999), 195–99.
130. Jürgen Habermas, "Pre-political Foundations of the Democratic Constitutional State?" in Habermas and Joseph Ratzinger, *Dialectics of Secularization: On Reason and Religion* (San Francisco, 2006), 37–38. Habermas has also recognized the legitimate place of religion in modernity under the rubric of "postsecularism," stating that "those religious interpretations of the self and the world that have adapted to modern social and epistemological conditions have an equal claim to recognition in the discourse of modernity to the competing approaches of postmetaphysical thinking." See his "Reply to My Critics" in Craig Calhoun, Eduardo Mendieta, and Jonathan VanAntwerpen, eds, *Habermas and Religion* (Cambridge, 2013), 348.
131. On this subject see Richard Stiegmann-Gall, *The Holy Reich: Nazi Conceptions of Christianity, 1919–1945* (Cambridge, 2002); and Karen Poewe, *New Religions and the Nazis* (London and New York, 2006).

CHAPTER ONE

"Location Suggests Content"
Kracauer on the Fringe of Religious Revival

Kracauer and the German-Jewish "Hermaphrodite"

In his final work, published after his death, Kracauer argued that the temporal and spatial position one occupied in the flow of events was significant, that "location was suggestive of content." However, he probably never intended that he and his own work should be subjected to this statement; instead, he preferred to don the guise of extraterritoriality, obscuring his connections to the intellectual ferment of Weimar Germany. In the passage from which this statement comes, Kracauer confessed his deep interest in historical periods of social flux and uncertainty, periods that preceded the establishment of dominant orthodoxies: the late Hellenistic age before Christianity, the Reformation, and his own period before the rise of communism. He argued that these historical moments contained a "message" that had yet to be deciphered and that had, to his mind, eluded present-day thought. He did not identify this message concretely beyond a vague expression of humanism that he associated with Erasmus; he did argue, however, that what he had in mind was not to be found in the "contending causes" of the day but rather in their "interstices":

> The message I have in mind concerns the possibility that none of the contending causes is the last word on the last issues at stake; that there is, on the contrary, a way of thinking and living which, if we could only follow it, would permit us to burn through the causes and dispose of them.[1]

These words offer a potential entry point into Kracauer's critical work of the Weimar era, an attempt to negotiate a position that cannot be equated with the polarized political agendas of his own day, with Marxism or nationalism, with religious faith or radical skepticism. Such a position would, of course, lead to the idea of the extraterritorial that attracted Kracauer through much of his life, and in which he sought to situate himself.[2] Yet, there is good reason to not allow Kracauer the last word on this point, and to question what dimensions of the term *Weimar intellectual* was he so eager to avoid and why.

Hence, a discussion of Kracauer should also start with location, with his territorial home in Frankfurt, a city whose history of independence was part of rival historical traditions. During the Holy Roman Empire, Frankfurt had been an important site of imperial politics, and from 1562 until the French Revolution it was there that the emperors travelled in order to receive their crown. In contrast, because of the role played by the Frankfurt parliament during 1848, the city was also enmeshed in narratives of democratic tradition. Of his home city and its history Kracauer offered the following somewhat perfunctory description in *Ginster*:

> Like other cities, it exploited the past in order to generate tourism. Imperial coronations, international congresses and shooting festivals all took place within its walls which had long since been transformed into public assets . . . some Christian and Jewish families traced their origins back to the city's forefathers. Families without pedigree had brought in a banking trade that entertained connections with Paris, London, and New York. Places of worship and stock markets were only separated from one another in spatial terms. The climate is tepid; the population that does not live in the West End, and to which Ginster belonged, rarely enters into consideration.[3]

This is a rather grey portrait of the city, but it should be noted that Frankfurt in the 1920s did have an eclectic cultural life. The university attracted figures such as Karl Mannheim, Max Scheler, Paul Tillich, and Hendrik de Man. A fervid interest in sociology squared off against intellectuals wedded to the aestheticism of Stefan George.[4] The nearby cities of Heidelberg, Marburg, and Freiburg, moreover, were seedbeds of contemporary philosophy, pitting the neo-Kantian idealism of Ernst Cassirer against its up-and-coming phenomenological rivals.[5] A traffic of visiting students kept Kracauer aware of these disputes. On the level of mass culture, Frankfurt was also the home of some of the more progressive experiments in public radio, and under the guidance of Bernhard Sekles its music conservatory welcomed one of the first jazz programs in Europe.[6] Thus, if not as exciting as Berlin or Munich, Frankfurt was still not a cultural backwater.

Selmar Spier who befriended Kracauer during his school days, and later became his lawyer, offered a more positive if nostalgic image of life in Frankfurt prior to 1914. Similar to Kracauer, he would not boast of the city's charms, but for him it was still *Heimat*, and he appreciated the open-minded attitudes that seemed to distinguish the city:

> Only after the war . . . did I begin to understand what characterized Frankfurt—the tolerance that did not rest entirely on a lack of spiritedness, but rather on the old convictions of independence, that included both confessions; the

readiness to compromise founded upon the relatively good-natured character of the populace and its established affluence; the open-mindedness to the world outside its own borders, with which it had much commerce for some time; the readiness to support the arts and sciences that often derived more from genuine interest, rather than as a means of affirming that one was rich.[7]

Written many years later in Israel, these reflections may be colored somewhat by homesick memories of a vanished world, yet Spier remained suspicious of his former homeland, and his recollections of a tolerant city do accord with other Frankfurters such as Adorno. Kracauer, on the other hand, appears to have encountered more difficulties.

Kracauer was born in Frankfurt on 8 February 1889. Both of his parents were of Jewish ancestry and in Frankfurt they were part of the second largest Jewish community in Germany. Though this circumstance offered some stability in terms of communal life, by the end of the 1800s German Jews were unsettled by the conflicting movements of nationalist politics and its attendant anti-Semitism—these movements would certainly have been felt in the Kracauer household. What Paul Mendes-Flohr called the "dual identity" of German Jews was a palpable fact for many, if not most Jews. The fraught nature of this situation was given sensational expression by Moritz Goldstein in early 1912.[8] "We Jews," claimed Goldstein, "are administrating the spiritual property of a nation that denies our right and our ability to do so." Instead of persisting in the delusional belief that Jews could become full participants in German society, he called for a deliberately Jewish culture.[9] There is no mention of this affair in Kracauer's work, but he most probably knew of the outcry that it had provoked. Walter Benjamin, who would become friends with Kracauer after 1918, followed the affair's progress with intense interest, and Goldstein was not the only voice that spoke of the need for a renewed Judaism. The much-admired speeches of Martin Buber on Hasidic tradition, for instance, were published in the same year and thus added a mystical element to the debate.[10] Tradition vied with innovation, and claims were followed by counterclaims. Jews, so it was said, could neither be fully German, nor could they avoid the German part of their identity.

Contemporary discussions of religion, before and after the war, were bound to become entangled in this matrix of culture, nation, and identity. Growing up in Frankfurt, a focal point of the Jewish revival during the Weimar Republic, Kracauer would have become familiar with these discussions. It is certain that he heard the voices emanating from the Free Jewish School and very probable that he knew of the anti-Semitic gatherings that took place at the Kölner Hof hotel, near the Frankfurt train station. Among Frankfurt Jews, according to one observer, there had been an increased interest in the Zionist movement prior to the war, but, on the other hand, the Liberal-Reformers had also become more assertive. The war altered the situation for both camps.[11]

Kracauer occupied an ambiguous position in this regard, as his parents were of varying backgrounds, divided between Eastern and Western Europe.[12] On his maternal side, the Oppenheim family was long established in Frankfurt. The father of Rosetta Oppenheim, his mother, had worked there in the financial trade. On his paternal side, however, the Kracauers were relative newcomers from the East, his father and uncle having come from Silesia. As a result, his education was almost certainly influenced by the twin forces of dual identity—not only that of German and Jewish, but also of East and West.

A study of Kracauer's youth is, however, unfortunately hindered by the relative scarcity of sources before 1914.[13] After World War II, when Kracauer had settled in New York and was unpacking those of his papers that had survived the catastrophe, he expressed a desire to one day write his memoirs, a desire he unfortunately never fulfilled. If he had, the numerous gaps in his papers might have been partially compensated. His *Nachlaß* preserves a sizable number of notes, letters, and unpublished manuscripts; however, prior to 1920, such sources are on the whole very meagre. War, forced exile, and the deportation of his mother and aunt in 1942 resulted in the loss of an unknown quantity of material.[14] When he fled to France after the Reichstag fire in 1933, whatever papers he left behind in Frankfurt were lost when Nazi authorities took possession of the Kracauer apartments in Berlin. As a result, some of his early and intellectually important friendships, with Otto Hainebach and Max Flesch for instance, have left only sporadic traces; they are mentioned in his notebooks but the letters between them have been lost. Moreover, Kracauer only kept notebooks haphazardly; those written between 1903 and 1907 are the earliest written evidence that has survived in his hand. Later notebooks cover parts of the years 1911 and 1912. During the war, he was inspired by his reading of the Hebbel diaries to again keep a personal record, devoted, he said, less to daily affairs and more to his inner development.[15] However, this impetus soon faded, and by December the entries that consisted mostly of quotations from his reading dwindled to a halt.

Such limitations are only relatively less problematic for the period between 1914 and 1920. During the first years of the war while employed as an architect in Frankfurt, Kracauer devoted his time away from work to writing. In 1917, he was recruited into the foot artillery near Mainz, but after a short period he was transferred to Osnabrück where he remained for the rest of the war, employed as an architect in the German military. His vocational training probably spared him from frontline duty, but he appears to have been disenchanted with his chosen profession; instead he was much more interested in philosophy and literature. From this period come his earliest attempts at philosophical criticism. These reflections on subjects such as the limits of the natural and human sciences or the nature of the soul bear witness to his earliest influences: Nietzsche, Simmel, Bergson, and Scheler. Fragments of his correspondence with both Scheler and Simmel have survived, but only after 1920 does a more substantial record emerge; the pivotal year after November 1918 remains obscure. The most important sources for this period are his detailed and intimate letters to Margaret Susman written between 1920 and 1922, as well as his correspondence with the later critical theorist, Leo Löwenthal, with whom Kracauer had a lifelong friendship.[16] Together with some of his unpublished manuscripts, these letters offer the potential for a rough sketch of the early Kracauer. Still, some caution is needed to avoid either projecting his postwar skepticism backwards into his youth, or of assuming that there was a deep shift occasioned by the war. The truth is probably somewhere in between these positions. Even if, as Löwenthal once suggested, Kracauer became more "secular" in his outlook after he began to work for the *FZ*, it is not altogether clear what his attitudes toward religion and secularism were before that time.[17]

Of the cultural offerings of his day, Kracauer partook in many that were far from exceptional. He wrote in his notebooks of 1907 that he was impressed by *Tonio Kröger* and *Crime and Punishment*, both of which were widely read at the time. The popularity of Dostoevsky led one *Gymnasium* instructor in Munich to lament over the possible side-effects of this contagion from the East; while, according to Kracauer, *Tonio Kröger* generated a swarm of admirers for the "blonde and blue-eyed doers."[18] Aside from his interest in contemporary literature, Kracauer had also begun to read philosophy in earnest, in particular the works of Nietzsche, Kant, and Simmel.[19] To Nietzsche Kracauer maintained a skeptical reserve even as he admired his critique of the materialist culture of the past century (he appears to have thought him a "megalomaniac").[20] In general, philosophy appears to have stimulated his interest more than religious subjects, and there are few traces of religious engagement in his notebooks. An entry written on Yom Kippur in 1907 suggests that the conflict between secular philosophy and sacred tradition had been largely won by the former. He spent the holiday that year reading Elizabeth Förster-Nietzsche's biography of her brother and then reading Kant with his friend Felix Hentschel.[21] Such references are, however, quite isolated, so the conclusions one can draw from them are tentative at best.

In any case, it is clear that Kracauer was not brought up in a fully secularized or assimilated milieu.[22] The family of his father, Adolf Kracauer (1849–1918) had been closely connected to Jewish religious life in their hometown of Sagan. Kracauer's paternal grandfather had been active at the local synagogue, and his grandmother had wanted his younger brother, Isidor Kracauer (1852–1923), to become a rabbi. Her aspirations for him were not met, but Isidor did come to occupy a prominent position in the Jewish community of Frankfurt. There he became an instructor at the *Philanthropin*, a respected school that had been popular in the previous century among Jewish liberals. He was also a noted historian of the Jews of Frankfurt and had published articles on regional history.²³ Kracauer offered a critical but sympathetic portrait of his uncle in his autobiographical fiction, *Ginster*, where he portrayed him as both a fastidious antiquarian and a staunch German patriot.²⁴ Kracauer later conceded that his uncle had had some influence on his intellectual trajectory. It was because of him that Kracauer first read Friedrich A. Lange's massive *History of Materialism*, a "wonderful book towards which I have great piety."²⁵ His uncle thus offered a way not only to Judaism, but also to wider intellectual trends such as materialist socialism.

In general, the Kracauer family partook in most aspects of the German-Jewish dual identity. When Adolf Kracauer died after a long illness in 1918, the leader of Frankfurt's Liberal-Reform community, Rabbi Caesar Seligmann (1860–1950) gave the address at his graveside.²⁶ Seligmann had once argued that Jews should be receptive to modern German culture while simultaneously preserving their faith.²⁷ In 1910, he had published a prayer book to be used in the reform community; according to one contemporary, the reformed service at the Westend synagogue, where the book was used, was of the most radical kinds of Reform Judaism. The use of Hebrew, for instance, was kept to a minimum, and one prayed and sang in German.²⁸ In 1905, Seligmann had published a work that embodied this dual task of preserving Jewish identity while cultivating receptiveness to German culture, even coining a phrase from the current vogue for Nietzsche: the "will to Judaism."²⁹

Similarly, the school where Isidor Kracauer taught, and where Kracauer also studied from 1898 to 1904, sat on the cusp of a dual German and Jewish identity. According to one former student, Tilly Epstein, there were in addition to the few Christian students at the school a number of Christian teachers, particularly in the technical subjects. The mixed confessions, in general, preserved a harmonious relationship so that when the odd anti-Semitic incident (*Risches*) did occur it was not taken too seriously.³⁰ However, the secularly oriented program of the school did provoke some misgivings. The alleged weaknesses of an educational system that sat uneasily between secular modernity and religious identity had been criticized by one of the early instructors at the school who had suggested that the curriculum was emblematic of those Jews whose misfortune it was "to no longer want to be Jews."³¹ The relative emphases given to religious instruction varied during the nineteenth century, but by its end Hebrew was only offered in the school as an elective. On the other hand, this may have improved the liberal reputation of the school, for the *Philanthropin* was admired as the epitome of pedagogical liberalism in the sense intended by the Swiss romanticist educator, Johann Heinrich Pestalozzi.³² For his part, Kracauer appears to have thrived academically, even if he was bored by the manner of instruction.³³ Moreover, whatever incidents may have occurred, the *Philanthropin* must have been relatively free of the anti-Semitism that he later encountered at the Klinger Upper School which he attended after 1904.³⁴

Thus, Kracauer, from an early age onwards, would have been sensitized to his German and Jewish identities. His response to this dilemma appears to have been one of acceptance, arguing that he could not deny either his German or his Jewish background, and that it would be intellectual suicide to do so. To Löwenthal he wrote that they were both "hermaphrodites" (*Zwittern*) and this was a situation from which they could not escape. Thus, he warned Löwenthal not to turn away from European philosophy in order to follow the mystical paths of Martin Buber or Gershom Scholem (*buberisieren* or *scholemisieren*), for this would cost him his ability to "draw closer to the things of the world."[35] The figure of the hermaphrodite became a means of detaching himself from what he saw as the strictures of dogma or creed, and aligning himself to the profane world. Something of this hermaphroditic character also appeared in his novel, *Ginster*. When the protagonist finds work at an architect's office in the east end of Frankfurt, he is struck by the presence of the Jews he finds in the neighborhood: with flowing beards and kaftans, "Jews who strike one as imitations, so genuine do they appear."[36] Yet, a few pages later, as Ginster sits in his office where he leads an unsatisfying existence, he gazes out the window upon these Jews in a more complicated fashion. He perceives them as strangers, as a remote kind of other; but at the same time their affirmation of religious identity draws attention to his own feelings of displacement. Whether he thinks their religiosity is authentic is another matter, but the claim to authenticity that he attributes to them draws attention to his own tentative and undefined position.[37]

The hermaphroditic description of Kracauer's dual identity also finds an echo among his contemporaries. The philosopher Franz Rosenzweig expressed himself in comparable terms, though on the question of Judaism they were decidedly not in agreement. Still, a comparison between the two may elucidate how Kracauer responded to this issue, and how it differed from others in his milieu. Rosenzweig sometimes described dual identity in terms that would probably have been familiar to Kracauer. In letters to his mother Rosenzweig stated that if forced to choose between the Jewish and German sides of his self he knew he would choose the former, but he also knew that he would not survive the operation. In one of the last letters he wrote before his death he stated more ambiguously that "language is more than blood."[38]

The ramifications of this language of dualism might be clarified by a consideration of the distinctions between filiative and affiliative relations as proposed by Edward Said.[39] Said argues that whereas the affiliative relationship was based on invention, construction, and will, the filiative relation was grounded in the historical, cultural, and social contexts that surrounded the individual. Thus, the former was derived from ideas, the latter from social relations. There are, of course, some problems of interpretation as it may be difficult to set a border between these two categories. However, setting aside the question of how these distinctions might be made (or fail to be made) I would suggest that they can still assist one to see how Rosenzweig and Kracauer to a large extent talked past one another. Both men were influenced by a largely, but not entirely, secularized setting; but for Kracauer this meant that an affiliative relationship was no longer possible. He did not deny the influence of Jewish tradition; he accepted the filiative relationship, but the authentic religious gesture was lost to him.[40] Moreover, he tended to view expressions of religiosity on the part of others as an affiliative construction. Rosenzweig, on the other hand, perceived this relationship as essential, and he blurred the distinctions that appear important to Kracauer. As he stated in a letter to his mother, he could seek a relationship to the divine by virtue of nature and birth, by the fact of having been born Jewish.[41] Just as importantly, the process of secularization, as Rosenzweig conceived it, was more nuanced, and was not as fatal as it was for Kracauer. The test of Jewish religious authenticity was, on the contrary, demonstrated by its ability to survive successive waves of secularization, an experience that he argued Judaism had undergone.[42] Therefore, he remonstrated with Kracauer that in religious terms he possessed the "positive," a relationship between himself and the sphere of revelation that prevailed over the merely secular; Kracauer's position, he claimed, was only a matter of a tendency (*Tendenz*).[43]

The uneasy relationship between Kracauer and Rosenzweig will be discussed further below, but for the moment a couple of points should be emphasized. One, Kracauer did retain a filiative relationship to Judaism, and there is little to suggest that he ever sought to deny his Jewish background. However, this acceptance did not mean that he identified with Jewish religiosity; on the contrary, he viewed such expressions as deliberately affiliative relationships. They were a contrived kind of authenticity, and, as he warned Löwenthal, the "glimmer of authenticity" was not becoming.[44] The second point follows from the first, which is that his sense of Jewish identity was not simply a matter of external imposition, that is, he did not accept "Jewish" identity just because German society forced it upon him. As Jack Jacobs has argued in his study of intellectuals from the Frankfurt School, Jewish identity emerged out of a complex nexus of social and cultural currents, both traditional and contemporary, both internal and external. They may have been influenced by social and political anti-Semitism, but they were not determined by it.[45]

From the Revolt of Life to the Margins of Cultural Pessimism

Overall, in the postwar period the question of Jewish identity does not appear to have been a significant issue for Kracauer. Indeed, he confessed to Susman that the "Jewish question" did not excite his interest.[46] Religious or metaphysical themes are, in fact, more traceable in his engagement with philosophy, especially in his critical position towards the natural and human sciences. His earliest fragmentary expressions on these themes were often informed by the prevalent tropes of the late nineteenth-century crisis of culture.[47] For instance, he shared the common conviction that *Wissenschaft* failed society whenever it pretended to answer existential questions, for the quantifying impulse of modern thought was incompatible with the spirit of inwardness; it degraded the "things of the world" when it reduced them to categories and numbers. Philosophers, he stated in his notebooks of 1912, were deluded if they thought that a system of metaphysical knowledge could be constructed out of scientific rules: "they did not know that philosophy must be lived and suffered . . . that once again poets and prophets are needed."[48] In accord with his preference for cultural solutions to social problems, it is the prophet or artist that he valorizes; it is the quixotic individual who plays loose with empirical facts and certainly not the politician that matters. The linkage between the prophet and the artist, moreover, was based on more than their alleged superiority over the politician, for religion and aesthetics were akin to one another in so far as they both struggled to find meaning outside of the confines of scientific method.[49] There is, of course, a messianic tinge to this argument—the longing for the prophet who would give form to a meaningless and discordant present. In spite of Kracauer's subsequent repudiations of the messianic tradition, his dismissive view of contemporary culture pushed him towards it, at least for a brief moment in the early 1920s.[50]

Much of this discourse was in accord with the philosophy of life at the turn of the century. The general impulse of these philosophical trends posited a metaphysical conception of life, one that was elevated over and against rational explanation. According to Thomas Mann, by the turn of the century calls for the return to "life" had become "common currency across the nation," a movement that was evident in the influence of Nietzsche, Bergson, and Dilthey.[51] This concept of life designated what was irreducible in existence; it was the thorn in the side of any system based on abstract and scientific models. Thus, it was a counterclaim to mechanistic explanations of life as envisioned by scientists such as Laplace as early as 1814.[52] Moreover, this resistance to materialism allowed culture to assert itself as potential force against the rule of "mere" facts. The latter were the indifferent by-products of civilization and its various processes. Culture, on the other hand, was closer to the core of existence; it was what demonstrated that "life is after all always more than life."[53] This vision of the cultural struggle against a life-negating civilization found expression in Thomas Mann's notorious polemic of 1918, already mentioned above.

Yet, for Mann, even art remained susceptible to the contagion of intellect. Thus, in *Tonio Kröger* the young protagonist reflected the incapacity of the artist, forever looking in upon the flow of life that his intellect forbids him to join. Kracauer appears to have identified with this predicament, suspended between life and the artifice of the mind. In his journal of 1907, he projected Mann's conception of the struggle between life and art onto his own passions. In Tonio Kröger's love for Hans Hanssen, he found a resemblance to his own "hopeless" passion for one of his closer friends at the time, Max Flesch.[54] This conflation of aesthetic conflicts and personal ones was probably what Kracauer had in mind when he later told Adorno that the "chasm in the world" passed straight through him.[55] Isolation from the fullness of life was taken as one of the pains of cultural struggle, a component of what Simmel called the "tragic conception of culture." In one sense it was a wound, but in another, it was the mark of intellectual and cultural distinction.

The early work of Kracauer was stamped by this tragic conception of culture and its accompanying sense of mission. As Dirk Oschmann has shown, his early fictional characters were embedded within this discourse of life. Often they suffer from a surplus of intellect. They are depicted as wanderers in a spiritual and emotional void, loners in search of communal experience or a meaningful connection with life. "O Life, Life!" cries out Ludwig Loos, the protagonist of "Grace," an unpublished short story from 1913.[56] The solitary meanderings of this desperate young man are brought to an end in a melodramatic fashion—by a brief sexual encounter with a suicidal prostitute. Loos comes to a bridge at night intending to end his own life, but instead he meets a young woman intending to do the same; their chance meeting saves them both. As Kracauer explained to an acquaintance, the world was given such crude and "brutal" form in this story as only such a shocking "contact with the earth itself, the submergence in the mire" could give his character a "core" from which he could then build his way back into life.[57] The sexual favor or grace with which this tale ended offered an almost pagan conception of the world, one that had much in common with the so-called decadence of the fin-de-siècle.[58] The longed-for union with life is a return to origins; the roots of existence are recovered as Loos, through this chance moment, opens up to the fullness of life that has always surrounded him. The religious dimension of grace (*Gnade*) is readily apparent. As the sun streams down on the morning after this affair, Loos folds his hands as if to give thanks for gifts received. Yet, it is no deity but life itself that receives his offering: "He looked into the blue heaven, full of faith; he caught sight of the blooming pastures and deeply felt his belongingness with every part of thousand-fold life."[59] For Loos, the material world becomes metaphysical; he falls before it and reveres its inscrutable contingency. Thus, he confirms his acceptance of the world as he finds it. In contrast, to try to oppose life with the force of intellect meant a failure to comprehend one's natural place. As Thomas Mann had argued, this latter view was a kind of metaphysical sickness, a sign of "biological insufficiency"—aesthetically compelling, perhaps, but still a sign of decay.[60] Thus, prior to Loos's conversion, he is besieged by omens of death, and in his dreams he goes to houses stricken by the plague and even sleeps in his own coffin.[61] His return to life triumphs over this morass of aestheticism.

The concept of life expressed in "Grace" had a pagan aspect, but Kracauer also interpreted this concept as a religious one. In a letter to Simmel written near the end of 1917, he spoke of the religious function of *Leben*:

> A single idea draws itself throughout the whole, the idea that it is Life itself, that which fulfills humanity (I cannot do without this downright metaphysical concept), that ever again pushes forward the yearning to live as individuals in a truly *religious cultural community*.[62]

Thus, the individual would find fulfillment in the religious group. Such statements expressed desires for a supposedly lost religious "ground," a motive that was important to many German intellectuals (Kafka, Brod, Rosenzweig, and Löwenthal, for instance). Religion, from this point of view, was fundamental to culture. It was understood not simply as a stable and time-honored set of moral prescriptions, but rather as an innovation (or an "invented tradition") in modern life, one that in its more extreme forms wanted to purge Europe of the rational and material dross of the previous century.[63] Such thinking was not unique to German intellectuals, and one could mention here the conversion of Paul Claudel in France, T.S. Eliot's celebration of the religious writings of Lancelot Andrewes, or Apollinaire's "Zone" already cited above.[64]

Behind this revived religious sentiment, there was a sense of deliberate revolt against the prior generation.[65] The recovery of lost faith was often portrayed as redemption of venerable traditions that had been pawned off by the parental generation. For Kracauer, this conflict appears relatively muted. There appears to have been little loss of tradition insofar as his family was observant, at least outwardly. Moreover, judging by his account in *Ginster*, there was little sign of open rebellion against his parents, though his father is certainly portrayed as an oppressive presence. Indeed, the death of his father appeared almost liberating in his notebooks.[66] Among his contemporaries, however, the conflict was more pronounced. His friend Löwenthal defied paternal authority and chose to live in accordance with Judaic law, a rebelliousness that was augmented by his interest in Marx and Freud.[67] In a well-known letter, Franz Kafka, likewise, reproached his father for the loss of ancestral tradition. His discovery of the Yiddish theatre and other manifestations of Jewish culture was, in part, an attempt to reverse this loss.[68] Rosenzweig, on the other hand, reaffirmed his faith in Judaism after eight years of studying history under Friedrich Meinecke, and after an intellectual soul searching that nearly led to his conversion to Catholicism. He expressed his choice in words that resonated with the trope of recovered origins. The Jew already has a connection with the divine, he wrote to his mother, for "he possesses it by nature, through having been born one of the Chosen people."⁶⁹ Of course, Rosenzweig did not simply forsake secular thought, but he did abandon the academic career in which the older Meinecke had been mentoring him. Religious revival was thus a gesture of resistance; it was a riposte to the previous generation composed of secularists who had abandoned their faith and assimilated to a rational worldview. To return to origins, one had to reach over and beyond this declining generation.

In contrast, Kracauer appears to have kept aloof from religious movements and institutions, and, moreover, he did so in spite of the pressure from his peers. Adorno alluded to this issue many years later in the opening pages of *Jargon of Authenticity*. Kracauer, whom he designates in the text only as a friend, had been excluded from a gathering devoted to religious and philosophical questions. He was not considered "authentic" enough by the other participants, "for he hesitated before Kierkegaard's leap" of faith. Those whom Adorno numbered among the genuine were Rosenzweig, Buber, Herrigel, and the Catholic philosopher Eugen Rosenstock-Heussy.⁷⁰ Given the religious heterogeneity of this group, it appears that the authentic religious gesture mattered just as much as the confession in which it took place.⁷¹ Confronted with the pressures of such a milieu, and the fact that Kracauer did have an abiding interest in religious tradition, it is perhaps surprising that he never committed himself in a more substantial way to a religious creed.

His resistance derived from his suspicious attitude towards metaphysical systems, a suspicion that he found confirmed in the work of Georg Simmel.⁷² In a monograph devoted to Simmel, completed and partially published in 1920, Kracauer emphasized those aspects of Simmel's thought that clashed with metaphysical systems: what he called his preference for the "worm's point of view" (*Froschperspektive*). Simmel started from the concrete and minutely observed detail and then worked his way outwards, eliciting relationships to wider social and cultural contexts and only then to a more general theory of culture.⁷³ This entry point, so Kracauer argued, did not lend itself to the declaration of universal truths or systems. The totality of existence was instead perceived from the point of view of the detail, in a kind of system of the "unsystematic."⁷⁴ From Simmel, Kracauer thus derived a tendency to cling to the concrete while simultaneously confirming his resistance to generalized abstractions. In a letter of 1917, he told Simmel that he was so "completely . . . focused on the reality that lay before his eyes, so very much bound to consider how the individual detail showed itself, that he almost always could only push towards general principles—that in certain ways were *invisible*—with a bad conscience."⁷⁵ This anti-systematizing impulse may, of course, have been inherited from other sources such as Nietzsche or Kierkegaard; the revolt against system building had a number of contemporary precedents. However, in Simmel, Kracauer found this impulse joined to a close and methodical observation of everyday life, an expression of the desire to "return to the things themselves."[76]

Moreover, Kracauer was also sympathetic to Simmel's emphasis on the creative function of form, an aspect of his thought that Kracauer thought distinguished him from the other philosophers of life, particularly Bergson. The concept of form was used by Simmel in a general sense that included not only art, but also the intangible forms of sociability and politics—in essence, the whole range of human action. Both Simmel and Bergson recognized that form derived from the phenomenal stream that it then, in its own turn, influenced; but for Bergson, so Kracauer argued, the creation of form was only a residue (*Abfallsprodukt*) of the action of thought. This was rapidly dissolved in the forward movement of the élan vital. Simmel, on the other hand, gave relatively more autonomy to these emergent forms; they were, according to Kracauer, the consequence of the irreducible individual drive to project or "objectify" oneself into the surrounding world. Form was thus a "gauge" whereby the capacity of thought to channel life's ebb and flow was measured. It was the task of life to "condense" from the endless flux of experiences those forms that were then placed over and against it.[77] There is an implied freedom in this process, but Simmel tended to view this "objective culture" in an ambiguous light. For after a form was created, its original impulses were lost; the form ossified and then acquired its own modus operandi. As a result, the self-sustaining mechanisms of old forms resisted the creation of new ones that would be more in accord with their environment and, hence, more readily internalized by the individual subject. Forms, in such cases, oppressed those who lived in their shadow; they acted much like Ibsen's ghostly ideas and sentiments, a residue of the past that had a baleful and constraining influence on the present. This led to the conflict between objective forms and the subjective desires that created them—a concept that was essential to Simmel's theory of culture. Simmel described this theory as tragic, for ultimately the conflict that lay at its core was not reconcilable.[78]

Kracauer resisted the full implications of Simmel's pessimistic vision, but he was still deeply influenced by his method.[79] According to Simmel, the decisive issues of cultural conflict could be observed in the minutiae of culture just as effectively as in its more deliberate manifestations; thus, door handles and teatime were just as much the material of philosophy as the supposedly eternal forms of art. This, of course, did not mean that Simmel dispensed with concepts of totality, or that he disavowed the search for the spiritual foundations of existence. Such goals, according to Kracauer, were still important to Simmel, but one pursued them in a pointillist fashion, constructing a full picture out of a series of aperçus.[80] One could proceed towards knowledge of the "totality," but one progressed slowly, almost passively, in a patient, step-by-step fashion that held fast to the stuff of the world. To adopt a phrase of Robert Musil, the method proposed by Simmel seemed to offer that union of "precision and soul" that the protagonist of his unfinished novel thought was missing in most discussions of spiritual life.[81] The promise that one could unify spiritual content with an exactness of method was one of the reasons Kracauer and many others were drawn to Simmel before the war.[82]

However, even as Kracauer adopted the "Simmel project," he was aware that his mentor had failed to overcome the limitations of his method. One could question the need for metaphysical system building as Simmel had done, but the idea of the totality still lingered as a problem.[83] Could an unsystematic method lead to truths about the whole, and more importantly, without some generally valid premises, how could it avoid the pitfalls of relativism? These concerns raised the larger question of whether Simmel's philosophy could ever reconcile his pointillist method with his more general propositions.

After 1918, many of Simmel's former students thought that this was no longer possible. A more radical approach to philosophy was needed, and this demand was accompanied by a surge of interest in mysticism and the irrational. Against this background, Simmel appeared somewhat old fashioned, and moreover, his war-time militarism had placed his philosophy in a bad light.[84] In a 1921 feuilleton, his former student and friend Margaret Susman argued that an "abyss" had opened up between the present and the bygone age that had shaped Simmel.[85] His attempts to isolate the decisive "Ideas" or the "essentials of existence" were now exposed as a leftover of idealist and relativist thought. The significant questions of the present, she continued, were no longer those that had preoccupied Simmel, questions such as what sustained our ideas and convictions, or what was the nature of our souls? Instead, philosophy had to attend to the burning issues of the present: "what should we do?"[86] Where concrete action was required, Simmel's patient observation of daily life seemed an unforgivable kind of aestheticism that had no place in a revolutionary age. Her article, entitled "The Exodus from Philosophy," compared Simmel unfavorably to trends that strived to move beyond him. The promise of rejuvenation depended on the exodus from old ways of thinking, and among the new and vital figures of the postwar period she named Bloch, Rosenzweig, Spengler, Count Keyserling, and the lesser-known exponent of Eastern philosophy, Leopold Ziegler. All of these writers were later criticized by Kracauer in the *FZ*.

However much Kracauer may have disagreed with Susman about the "coming" philosophy, he probably would have conceded most of the points in Susman's critique of Simmel. A relativism of method and a search for the absolute were not compatible. The problem resided, according to Kracauer, in the conception of *Leben*:

> It is simultaneously the stream and the firm shore; it yields to the creations that come from its own womb, and in turn, it liberates itself from their power. Simmel's conception of life is so broad that even the truths and ideas that govern the course of life fall under its purview . . . By means of the concept of life, the totality is traced back to a single originary principle.[87]

Therefore, even if Simmel set out on his investigations from the particular, he could not avoid making foundational claims because he allowed the particular to become conflated with an "originary principle." According to Kracauer, Simmel argued that "only a person of absolute values and certainties would be able to frame the manifold, to capture the totality," but his micro-logical method would seem to exclude this as a possibility.[88] Hence, his method could not legitimate itself in the face of accusations of relativism, and his philosophy had led to an impasse. The way out of this dilemma, according to Susman, appeared in different guises, sometimes embracing the radical affirmation of relativism (Spengler) or the recovery of religious certainties (Rosenzweig).[89] Neither of these options would find a lasting place in Kracauer's work.

Instead it was Simmel's emphasis on the detail that excited Kracauer and that proved fruitful to his investigation of mass culture. His project would move beyond Simmel and break down some of the idealist distinctions that Kracauer argued had remained in Simmel's work. Even when Kracauer first heard Simmel give a lecture in 1907, he registered his reservations in this respect. In the course of an address given at the Union of Art in Berlin, Simmel had spoken on the problem of artistic style. He drew distinctions between what he called the applied arts guided by the "principle of generality," and a discrete and subjective realm of art that stirs "our inmost feelings." The former required a measure of stylization, while the latter was determined by a "principle of individuality." Kracauer was intrigued by this account of the conflict between individual and group aesthetics, but he argued that the conflict had been wrongly stated. The differences were not between art and style; instead, it was a conflict between two kinds of style, for individual works of art were stylized just as much as the objects of daily use.[90] His remark suggests that he was already beginning to blur the distinctions between high and low art, between culture for mass consumption and art for subjective contemplation. The critical analysis of culture was to cast a wide net, one that did not respect the distinctions between pure and applied art, a division that Kracauer suspected was derived from the legacy of Idealist philosophy.

This residue of Idealism was one of the reasons that many, like Kracauer, felt the need to break with some of the premises of Simmel's thought. According to Adorno, the idea of a distinct category of art, isolated from the more general category of "culture," was "undialectical."[91] Moreover, Simmel's failure to reflect more deeply on the relationship between art and culture had actually short-changed his own philosophical method. His mediation of subjective and objective culture did not penetrate into the sphere of autonomous art as it should, and thus it failed to fully comprehend either culture or art.[92] In the postwar period, when artistic movements often sought to either close the gap between art and life, or to formulate a more critical relationship between them, it was not to someone such as Simmel that one looked, but rather to those who abandoned him.

Still, in spite of these reservations there is little doubt that Simmel was a decisive influence on Kracauer. According to his own testimony, Simmel had read with appreciation one of his early essays completed in 1914 entitled, "On the Nature of Personhood."[93] Though the opening pages of his study used Nietzsche as a starting point, the influence of Simmel is clear. In a sense, the study investigates the premises of Simmel's tragic conception of culture in light of the tensions that existed both within the individual, and between him or her and the larger society. The study offers a catalogue of various types of personhood, their respective drives and different capacities, and the numerous hindrances that prevented them from "objectifying" themselves into their social setting. On this point, Kracauer referred to Simmel's tragic conception of culture, and he used it explicitly to counter Nietzsche: the fundamental human drive is not a "will to power," he argued, but rather a will to objectify oneself as an "integrated person" (*zusammengefaßte Persönlichkeit*).[94] Kracauer, as will be seen, suggests that this conflict is, at least in some aspects, resolvable, a conclusion that also derives from Simmel.

In the rhetoric of cultural crisis, the concept of the individual retained an important role. The word Kracauer used for this idea was *Persönlichkeit*, a word that was heavily laden with romantic ideals; even among some German sociologists it was seen as a last refuge of the soul, a reservoir of inwardness resisting the depredations of modern society. The individual person, in this sense, was distinguished by an insistence on the subjective as a measure of value. According to Max Weber, when compared to the bureaucratic functionary, the *Persönlichkeit* did not want to bend to systems of rules and social pressures, but rather to transcend them.[95] A contemporary study of the concept, described this type of individual in terms that distinguished it from more rational models of the self:

> ... the unique aspect and particularity of a natural being and, at the same time, the identification of its educational goals and development. This latter instance has a stronger emphasis in the word *Persönlichkeit* than in "individual." In contrast, *Individuum* and also *Person* signify something subordinate, quantifiable.[96]

This conception of personhood was also receptive to religious points of view, for the subjective relationship of the person to God could preserve itself in this sphere in disregard of a secular world governed by reason.[97] Hence, it was in accord with a philosophy that wanted to question modern rational society.

Given that Kracauer had a similar suspicion of rational system building, it is not surprising that he turned to this romantic idea of the individual in one of his earliest works. He understood the problem of how to "objectify" the person into the larger social group with reference to the contemporary terminology of community and society (*Gemeinschaft* and *Gesellschaft*) derived from the work of Ferdinand Tönnies.[98] The shift from an integral community to a disintegrating society, according to Kracauer, had rendered the status of the individual *Persönlichkeit* deeply problematic. A full discussion of how he approached this problem cannot be undertaken here, but a couple points should be emphasized. One, in his earliest work when Kracauer described personhood, he had in mind an almost organic entity that would participate with all its capacities and drives in a society that was in some sense religious. When he wrote to Simmel in 1917, as discussed above, he made this connection explicit; the individual emerges in his or her fullness only in a "religious cultural community" (*religiösen Kulturgemeinschaft*). Only in the cultural community did the individual participate with all her drives, capacities, and feelings. This desired level of social embeddedness extended from the very "core" of the self out to the "periphery" where the individual collided with the group. Social and cultural forms must allow full expression for these subjective drives, so that they had an open channel from which the core could flow outwards.[99] Kracauer's terminology on this point (*Kern, Peripherie*) was also reminiscent of Simmel. In a 1912 study, for instance, Simmel had written that "man is free to the extent that the center of his being determines his periphery."[100] It was upon this "full person" that a resolution of the cultural crisis ultimately depended.

A second point concerns the language of Kracauer's study more generally. His vocabulary was often fraught with conflicting connotations. At one point, he uses a discourse of organicism, comparing the individual to a plant that grows in accordance with natural laws. At other times, the process is one of crystallization. In both cases, the implication is that the individual is the result of natural forces that abstract *ratio* can only disrupt.[101] These images refer back to Kracauer's paganism discussed above. The crystal, moreover, was a commonly used symbol full of utopian overtones as became apparent in the postwar period: Bauhaus theorists rhapsodized over the crystal cathedral of architecture that would embrace the whole of society; the radical architect Bruno Taut imagined a fantasy of crystalline structures that would be situated in the mountains far from the spiritual pollution of the metropolis. More disturbingly, the quasi-magical crystal mine in Leni Riefenstahl's 1932 film, *The Blue Light*, could be read as a symbol of spiritual properties. Once exposed to the corrupting influences of modernity, their power disintegrates, bringing about the film's tragic ending.[102] Common to all of these symbolic or allegorical uses of the crystal is an uneasy relationship between spiritual essence and the claims of modern society, the latter often conceived of as inimical to the former. This tension is often expressed in Kracauer's language; his recourse to natural metaphors (crystals, plants, flowing channels, and emptying deltas) is in contrast to his, at times, more dispassionate references to the rules governing the "inward economy."[103] The inscrutability of the spirit sits uneasily next to economic mechanisms, as if he wanted his language to incorporate the conflict that he described in a letter to Susman: "we long to draw near to God . . . but iron sociological laws distance us from Him."[104]

Therefore, a romantic melancholy clings to his rhetoric, suggesting that there is an unresolvable conflict between individual and society, and hence between the inner core and outer periphery of the individual. This conflict took place also at the level of form and resulted in Simmel's tragic conception of culture already discussed above.[105] Cultural and social evolution was thus burdened with a pessimistic vision that Kracauer by and large accepted. "In order to be effective in the phenomenal world," he states, "everything that emerges from the soul must be affirmed by society," and to accomplish this, "inner desires are granted a form."[106] These are sanctioned forms of action, or possibilities of self-expression (Handlung- und Bewußtseins-Äußerungsmöglichkeiten); a society that cannot create them will atrophy and wither away. Over time such forms were not static, and they altered according to altered conditions. However, secularization was more destructive, and as a result the religious "complex of forms" that had once ensured a measure of continuity had lost its meaning. The political and social upheavals of the past century (he named the French Revolution and feminism), had left the spiritual nature of humanity bereft and "homeless."[107]

The cultural aftermath of this crisis, so Kracauer argued, corresponded to the failed search for formal novelty. This drive characterized movements such as Expressionism, and he lightly satirized the "dithyrambic lust for existence" that he thought typified this movement. Such desires arose from a genuine sense of loss, he conceded, but they were nonetheless unable to find an answer to it:

> Their poetry is a single hymn . . . it expresses the prevailing mood we have for a world of manifold phenomena. We have learned to love and embrace everything: the unleashed passions, evil insofar as it strengthens us and breaths the air of life; the sweetness of lust, the beauty of factories, the daily life of workers, the big city streets and the high, dark houses, the endless brick walls and tramlines, the mountains where they are near, the shadows and the light, everything, everything! And why? Because we trace life in them, naked reality, and we long for it.[108]

The problem with such art was that the more artists tried to encompass the multiplicity of life, the more they just affirmed reality as they found it.

Therefore, they precluded every suggestion of an alternative reality, or the possibility of social transformation through form. In contrast to these aesthetic designs, however, there was more critical potential preserved in the idea of the religious community. If one compares the Expressionist cityscape that emerges in the passage cited above with Kracauer's description of the Catholic town of Ulm in 1923, this point becomes clear. Against the chaotic juxtapositions of the Expressionist cityscape, the landscape of Ulm was a "world of discrete limits." At the heart of the town was the old cathedral surrounded by a jumble of medieval streets; however, in this instance the urban tangle of passageways and facades did not betray chaos, but rather a growth that had been "formed from within." The town was a genuine homeland (*Heimat*), and "embraced even the stranger in a gracious fashion."[109] Thus, the cityscape in Ulm was formed not simply by a misguided resistance to the chaos of life, but rather by the patient discovery of the forms in which its unruly flow must be channeled. On the other hand, to simply submerge oneself into the chaotic flux of experience as the Expressionists had done brought one no closer to recognition of the correct forms of life.[110]

For the early Kracauer this is what religion could provide and this explains why his study of the individual concluded with both an invocation of the religious savior and a condemnation of those movements seeking to transform society by reason alone. He saw Monism and Socialism as compromised by their reliance on abstract thought. Reason had its uses, he conceded, but rational method should not dictate to the whole of life, for it was unable to reckon with "spiritual events." Such movements remained rooted "outside of man," and on questions concerning "the regeneration of humanity, its augmentation, its liberation from nihilism . . . there is no word. On the evolution of the soul they are [both] silent."[111]

Having dismissed socialism and monism, Kracauer turned to the concept of the artistic or religious genius. These figures embodied the ideals of personhood and created the cultural forms that would restore meaning to the world.[112] One model, traditional enough, was Goethe. Kracauer argued that Goethe had possessed what he called "psychic lability," a mobility of thought and perspective that allowed him to more readily identify valid forms.[113] In the contemporary period, this breadth of vision was lost due to the forces of specialization and the consequent tendency to survey culture from the narrow perspective of one's own discipline or profession. Still, as a solution to what Kracauer saw as a deep crisis this seems far-fetched. In most situations, the recommendation that one should become as capable as Goethe was hardly practical.

His second option turned towards religious models, but not before it detoured into a Nietzschean revaluation of all values. He referred to the "originating idea of Christianity" that, in contrast to Socialism or Monism, spoke to the whole person:

Christ strived after the *inner* transformation of a helpless humanity, he turned to the Individual (*Einzelnen*), and gave him depth, meaning, value, delivered him from need; he gave to humanity new nobility. That Socialism cannot do. Nor give an ethic, nor a burning what for?[114]

Statements of this sort should not be confused with a turn toward Christianity. His reference to Christ had a more renegade source in *Thus Spoke Zarathustra*, where Christ was described as the "wheel which rolls itself." He was, according to Kracauer, "no member of one or another movement, but, on the contrary, something entirely new." Thus, he demonstrated the distance between mere politics and a genuine transformation of values. While Kracauer implied that the latter only occurred in a religious framework, it was Christ the cultural revolutionary that mattered more than Christ the Christian. Moreover, he referred to Christ as one of a species of *Wundermenschen*, a worker of miracles who could regenerate society. He was a genius of sorts, but one akin to the artistic brilliance of figures such as Rembrandt or Goethe.[115]

On this point, it is unsurprising to find that Kracauer's later critique of popular biographies drew attention to the fact that after 1918 the genre had turned towards political subjects. Consequently, the biography of the artist or prophet had declined in apparent popularity. According to Kracauer, this shift allowed for an unreflective reification of history. For whereas the artist or prophet had sought to give form to experiences and, in a sense, to shape the flow of history, the figures of political and military biographies were often the mere embodiments of historical forces. They made history into a primal element, an implacable fate that was represented by the destinies of great men. Such figures could not, of course, be numbered among the "miracle workers," and Kracauer saw this genre of literature (typified by the work of Emil Ludwig) as a retrograde attempt to give form to history while endowing it with the power of fate and myth.[116]

Kracauer found the figure of the *Wundermensch* much more viable than the "great" figures of history. Behind his predilection for such figures is his fascination with the Jewish tradition of the thirty-six *Zaddikim* (or *Lamedvovniks*).[117] These were the "just ones," anonymous individuals whose righteousness upheld the world. According to legend, every generation had thirty-six of them; their labor was unobserved by society, and their true functions remained unknown, even to each other and themselves. For Kracauer the legend was rich in meaning, and he referred to it several times in his life: in an early letter to Löwenthal, later; after he had settled in America, in a letter to the historian and Nietzsche biographer, Daniel Halévy; and in the final chapter of his book on history. With Löwenthal, Kracauer had speculated on whether Rabbi Nobel may have belonged to the *Zaddikim*.[118] For him, Nobel had been the "revelation of a genuine religious individual," someone who had a vast knowledge of literature, philosophy, and theology, but who had expressed this more in his daily existence, rather than in published works. He was, according to Kracauer, a charismatic figure whom he admired for his intellectual and spiritual leadership (charisma was, according to Weber, one of the more "effective" forms of *Persönlichkeit*).[119] In a sense, in these early years Kracauer's critical project oscillated between the poles represented by these two conceptions of the religious individual: one, the figure who performed the messianic and revolutionary task of revaluation; and two, the relatively invisible but crucial labor of philosophical inquiry that disappeared into the "interstices" of the reality that its labors preserved. However, both of these conceptions should be understood as part of the realm of these hidden *Wundermenschen*, a theme that will receive further attention in the following chapters.

During the 1920s, Kracauer's enthusiasm for the artistic genius or the secret worker of miracles subsided as he inclined towards ideology critique. Nonetheless, the *Wundermensch* represents a theme that persisted in his work: the relationship between culture and religion. On this point, Kracauer probably found some correlation again in the work of Simmel. In an essay of 1916, Simmel had argued that religion was not a discrete sphere of knowledge comparable to economics or politics; on the contrary, religion was paradigmatic, an attitude or point of view that inflected itself across the entire range of knowledge and perception. It was therefore above the conflict that existed between objective and subjective culture; it was "always an objectification of the subject and therefore [it had] its place beyond that reality which attached to the object as such or to the subject as such."[120] Such statements threw open the question of religion's relationship to culture: was it one among many resources of the cultural arsenal, or was it the groundwork of all culture? Before the mid-1920s, Kracauer almost always opted for the latter position, and he was often hostile to proponents of cultural progress, what he later called a "faith in culture" (*Kulturgläubigkeit*)—a quasi-religious or utopian belief in its beneficent role.[121]

Still, before 1914 Kracauer's thought was only slightly removed from the currents of cultural pessimism.[122] If he did not descend into irrationalism, he did sympathize with the hostile critiques of reason circulating in the later *Kaiserreich*. His suspicion of politics and his celebration of the genius readily dovetailed with the enthusiastic Führer cults so common among the youth movements of his day. His discovery of the work of Simmel undoubtedly was a turning point for him, even if this did not mean that he discarded the habitual themes of conservative cultural criticism.[123] Simmel, according to historian David Gross, represents an important shift in the development of German criticism, as it moved from reactive condemnations of modern culture to a more methodical investigation.[124] Before him, cultural criticism relied most often on moral assertions rather than attempts to understand modernity on its own terms; his work did much to confer a degree of legitimacy to the new forms of mass culture. Kracauer typifies this shift from polemic to analysis, but the overlap of pessimistic and progressive traditions should not be overlooked. For the influence of Simmel did not displace Kracauer's pessimism right away. In his notebook entries of 1911, he argued that the "will to experience" had all but vanished among his contemporaries.[125] Individuals were shuttered in the narrow mindsets of their professions, and as a result, they gave birth to a host of correspondingly narrow values, judgments and experiences (*Kastenmoralen, Kastenwertungen und -erlebnissen*). Among his contemporaries, Kracauer grumbled, there were a few individuals whom one could still admire but there were no "fixed stars with their own light." War appeared, if only briefly, as a potential antidote to this state of affairs. The experience of combat, so he mused in 1912, would galvanize those "decadent men who haunt the cafes with their burned out eyes."[126]

Such statements were by no means exceptional. As Max Rychner, a journalist and editor of the *Neue Schweizer Rundschau*, observed, anyone educated in the humanities during this time was saturated with the discourse of cultural crisis.[127] Simmel may have departed from the conventional norms of older cultural criticism, but his conception of culture as a fateful struggle between modernity and tradition was not in every respect incompatible with conservative points of view. Of course, one should not underestimate the fact that Simmel gave a different meaning to this conflict (he had shown sympathy for socialism in the 1890s), and he did not valorize tradition over and above the modern; but his description of this struggle as the "pathology of culture" was hardly optimistic.[128] As Kracauer later remarked, Simmel's response to the antinomies of culture was evasive; he simply displaced the conflict into a purely aesthetic realm divorced from its specific historical contexts. Here the conflict was neutralized and, in this fashion, he foreclosed a more far-reaching investigation.[129] Simmel still hoped that the dilemma of modern culture might be overcome, but, unfortunately, this led him to see the war as a possible solution—a judgment that did much to discredit him in the eyes of his younger admirers after 1918.[130]

The "thunderbolt" of 1914 was a crucial threshold for Kracauer. The capitulation of intellect to the "brute facts" of necessity forced him to reevaluate the place of reason, a process that lasted through much of the Republic. Of those cultural figures who Kracauer had admired prior to 1914, most supported the war effort and Kracauer, to some degree, followed their lead. He read the war polemic of Thomas Mann with sympathy, and in Mann's plea for German culture the work of Simmel also found an ambivalent echo.[131] Mann compared the culture of the nineteenth century to that of the twentieth and found that the good bourgeois sense of acquiescence towards life's imperatives was being displaced by what he called a modern "spirit in the service of desirability."[132] This "moral revolt" that vainly opposed the objective facts of the "world as it is," was a sign of weakness and decay that he argued was typical of modern civilization. There is a correlation here with the moment when for Simmel subjective culture resists the objective forces of life—but where Simmel saw the evolution of culture as a tragic but necessary process, Mann saw a fatal drift towards civilization.[133] For both writers "culture" was a domain fraught with turmoil in which the subject wages a tragic struggle with the world as they found it. That intellect should acquiesce to the latter was one outcome to this problem, and both writers argued the events of 1914 demanded this act of submission. After the war, this dilemma would be expressed again in a sensational form that captured the imagination of both Mann and Kracauer, in Spengler's *Decline of the West*.[134]

* * * * *

Thus far the discussion has situated Kracauer in the cultural currents of his milieu. We have seen that his upbringing was informed by trends in contemporary Judaism, and that he retained a sense of Jewish identity, even as he was shaped by more secular influences. Here the discourses of the philosophy of life and cultural criticism were important. The latter was also undergoing a shift, as the boundaries of conservative and progressive criticism had not yet hardened into the polarized positions that characterized cultural struggles in the Weimar period. The next chapter will deal with how the war and its aftermath influenced the themes of secularization and religious revival in his work, both during the war and in the early 1920s.

Notes

1. Kracauer, *History*, 8.
2. Jay, "Extraterritorial Life," *Permanent Exiles*, 152–54.
3. Kracauer, "Ginster: Von ihm selbst geschrieben" in *Werke* 7, 22.
4. Schivelbusch, *Intellektuellendämmerung*, 19–23.
5. See Hans-Georg Gadamer, "Die deutsche Philosophie zwischen den beiden Weltkriegen," *Neue deutsche Hefte* 195, vol. 4, no. 3 (1987): 451–67; and the remarks in Leo Löwenthal, *Mitmachen wollte ich nie: Ein autobiographisches Gespräch mit Helmut Dubiel*, (Frankfurt am Main, 1980), 54–57. On the rivalry between Cassirer and Heidegger, see Peter Eli Gordon, *Continental Divide: Heidegger, Cassirer, Davos* (Cambridge, 2010).
6. On Sekles, see Michael Kater, *Different Drummers: Jazz in the Culture of Nazi Germany* (Oxford, 1992), 17–22.
7. Selmar Spier, *Vor 1914: Erinnerungen an Frankfurt geschrieben in Israel* (Frankfurt am Main, 1961), 36.
8. Paul Mendes-Flohr, *German Jews: A Dual Identity* (New Haven and London, 1999). On this subject, also see Michael Brenner, *The Renaissance of Jewish Culture* (New Haven and London, 1996); and Shulamit Volkov, *Germans, Jews, and Antisemites: Trials in Emancipation* (Cambridge, 2006).

9. Goldstein quoted in Mendes-Flohr, *German Jews*, 46–48.
10. On the influence of Buber's *Drei Reden*, see Rabinbach, *In the Shadow of Catastrophe*, 35–36. On social and cultural currents in German Judaism, see Brenner, *Renaissance of Jewish Culture*, 11–65; and Noah Isenberg, *Between Redemption and Doom: The Strains of German-Jewish Modernism* (Lincoln and London, 1999), 1–17.
11. Paul Arnsberg, *Bilder aus dem jüdischen Leben im alten Frankfurt* (Frankfurt am Main, 1970), 196–225 and 255–59.
12. Brodersen, *Siegfried Kracauer*, 8–12.
13. An excellent selection and overview of the Kracauer papers is to be found in Belke and Renz, *Siegfried Kracauer*.
14. Both Rosette and Hedwig Kracauer were deported to Poland or Theresienstadt sometime after August 1942 and probably murdered there shortly afterward, see Belke and Renz, *Siegfried Kracauer*, 103.
15. Excerpts from the diaries have been reprinted in Belke and Renz, *Siegfried Kracauer*, 9–13 and 18–19; on the encounter with Hebbel see 28–29.
16. Much of the correspondence between Löwenthal and Kracauer has been published in Jansen and Schmidt, *In steter Freundschaft*.
17. Leo Löwenthal, "As I Remember Friedel," *New German Critique* 54 (Autumn 1991): 8.
18. See the comments of the contemporary literary scholar and state censor Josef Hofmiller in Eric Weitz, *Weimar Germany: Promise and Tragedy* (Princeton, 2007), 24; and Kracauer, *History*, 173–74.
19. See the notebook entries reprinted in Belke and Renz, *Siegfried Kracauer*, 8–12.
20. Belke and Renz, *Siegfried Kracauer*, 10.
21. Kracauer met Felix Hentschel, a student of math and physics, at the home of his aunt and uncle, Isidor and Hedwig Kracauer. Hentschel rented a room in the same building; see Belke and Renz, *Siegfried Kracauer*, 8 and 10.
22. For biographical details on the Kracauer family, see Belke and Renz, *Siegfried Kracauer*, 1–2.
23. Isidor Kracauer, *Geschichte der Juden im Frankfurt am Main, 1150–1824* (Frankfurt am Main, 1925–1927).
24. Kracauer, *Werke* 7, 46–50.
25. Kracauer to Löwenthal, 15 March 1957, *In steter Freundschaft*, 191.
26. Seligmann was a rabbi in Frankfurt from 1902 to 1937, at which time he emigrated from Germany to England.
27. Steven E. Aschheim, *The Nietzsche Legacy in Germany, 1890–1990* (Berkeley, 1992), 97–98.
28. Arnsberg, *Bilder*, 257–58; Kracauer's inability to read Hebrew was later attacked by his critics on the occasion of his polemic against Buber and Rosenzweig. See Martin Jay, "Politics of Translation: Siegfried Kracauer and Walter Benjamin on the Buber-Rosenzweig Bible," in *Permanent Exiles*, 198–216.
29. Aschheim, *Nietzsche Legacy*, 97–99. Seligmann's book *Judentum und moderne Weltanschauung* appeared in 1905.
30. Tilly Epstein, "Ein Leben im Philanthropin," in *Frankfurter jüdische Erinnerungen: Ein Lesebuch zur Sozialgeschichte, 1864–1951*, ed. Kommission zur Erforschung der Geschichte der Frankfurter Juden (Frankfurt am Main, 1997), 201–8.
31. Josef Johlson quoted in Arnsberg, *Bilder*, 107–8.
32. Arnsberg, *Bilder*, 110–11.
33. Belke and Renz, *Siegfried Kracauer*, 2–3.

34. Adorno, "Curious Realist," 161.
35. Kracauer to Löwenthal, 12 April 1924, *In steter Freundschaft*, 53–56. The hermaphrodite was a loaded image in this context, drawing attention not only to his Jewish and German dualism, but also to the ambiguous sexual overtones of his relationships to younger male companions. This will be discussed further below.
36. Kracauer, *Werke* 7, 62.
37. Kracauer, *Werke* 7, 77.
38. Rosenzweig quoted in Mendes-Flohr, *German Jews*, 84; and Franz Rosenzweig to Adele Rosenzweig, 6 October 1929, in *Franz Rosenzweig: Der Mensch und sein Werk. Gesammelte Schriften*, 4 vol., 1.2, ed. Rachel Rosenzweig and Edith Rosenzweig-Scheinmann (Hague, 1979), 1230.
39. Edward Said, *The World, the Text, and the Critic* (Cambridge, 1983), 17–24.
40. Traverso, "Sous la signe de l'extraterritorialité," 194–95; and Kracauer to Susman, 10 February 1921, SN, DLA.
41. Rosenzweig to Adele Rosenzweig, 23 October 1913, *Franz Rosenzweig: Der Mensch und sein Werk* 1.1, 129.
42. Rosenzweig quoted in Paul W. Franks and Michael Morgan, "From 1917 to 1925," in Rosenzweig, *Philosophical and Theological Writings*, ed. Paul W. Franks and Michael Morgan (Indianapolis, 2000), 87.
43. Kracauer to Susman, 20 April 1921, SN, DLA. Kracauer reported the following statement from Rosenzweig: "I myself have the positive. I live within it; I have that which you call form."
44. Kracauer to Löwenthal, 12 April 1924, *In steter Freundschaft*, 53–54.
45. Jack Jacobs, "A Most Remarkable Jewish Sect?" *Archiv für Sozialgeschichte* 37 (1997): 73–92. Also, see Jacobs, *The Frankfurt School*, 7–42.
46. Kracauer to Susman, 2 April 1920, SN, DLA.
47. David L. Gross, "*Kultur* and Its Discontents" in *Essays on Culture and Society in Modern Germany*, ed. Gary Stark and B.K. Luckner (College Station, 1982), 70–97; and Wolfgang J. Mommsen, "Culture and Politics in the German Empire," in Mommsen, *Imperial Germany, 1867–1918: Politics, Culture, and Society* (London, 1995), 119–41.
48. See notebook entry of 12 August 1912, Belke and Renz, *Siegfried Kracauer*, 19.
49. See his letter to Susman, 17 October 1920, SN, DLA.
50. Hansen, "Decentric Perspectives," 52–54.
51. Thomas Mann, *Betrachtungen eines Unpolitischen*, quoted in Dirk Oschmann, *Auszug aus der Innerlichkeit: Das literarische Werk Siegfried Kracauers* (Heidelberg, 1999), 21.
52. For a discussion of Kracauer's indebtedness to *Lebensphilosophie* and Vitalism, see Oschmann, *Auszug aus der Innerlichkeit*, 20–37.
53. Kracauer, "Georg Simmel," *Mass Ornament*, 239.
54. Kracauer, journal entry of 7 July 1907, in Belke and Renz, *Siegfried Kracauer*, 9.
55. Kracauer to Adorno, 5 April 1923, in Schopf, *Briefwechsel, 1923–1966*, 11.
56. Oschmann, *Auszug*, 38–59; and Kracauer, "Die Gnade," in *Werke* 7, 551.
57. Kracauer to Otto Crusius, 23 August 1913, *Crusiusiana* I, Bayerische Staatsbibliothek, Munich. Partially reprinted in Belke and Renz, *Siegfried Kracauer*, 23.
58. See the studies by Ralph-Rainer Wuthenow, *Muse, Maske, Meduse: Europäischer Ästhetizismus* (Frankfurt am Main, 1978); Carl E. Schorske, *Fin-de-siècle Vienna:*

Politics and Culture (New York, 1981); and Matei Calinescu, *Five Faces of Modernity: Modernism, Avant-Garde, Decadence, Kitsch, Postmodernism* (Durham, 1987), 151–224.
59. Kracauer, *Werke* 7, 574–75.
60. Mann, *Reflections of an Unpolitical Man* (New York, 1983), 12–13.
61. Kracauer, *Werke* 7, 552–53.
62. Kracauer to Simmel, 30 November 1917, *Gesamtausgabe* 23, 880–84. The italics are my own.
63. See Eric Hobsbawm, "Introduction: Inventing Traditions," in *The Invention of Tradition*, ed. Eric Hobsbawm and Terence Ranger (Cambridge, 1984), 1–14; and Brenner, *Renaissance of Jewish Culture*, 129–52.
64. Eliot said of Andrewes that he spoke with "the old authority and the new culture." See Said, *The World, the Text*, 17–18; and Apollinaire, "Zone," 2–11. The religious dimensions of Apollinaire's work are discussed in Margaret Davies, *Apollinaire* (Edinburgh, 1964).
65. Gay, *Weimar Culture*, 102–18. For a view of generational conflicts in the setting of the "Prague circle," see Scott Spector, *Prague Territories: National Conflict and Cultural Innovation in Franz Kafka's Fin de siècle* (Berkeley, 2000), 101–12.
66. Belke and Renz, *Siegfried Kracauer*, 5–6 and 29–30.
67. See the discussion of Löwenthal's early career in Jacobs, "A most remarkable Sect?" 78–87.
68. Spector, *Prague Territories*, 188–90.
69. Rosenzweig to his mother, 23 October 1913, *Franz Rosenzweig: Der Mensch und sein Werk* 1.1, 129.
70. Adorno, *The Jargon of Authenticity*, trans. Knut Tarnowski and Frederic Will (Evanston, 1973), 3–4; see also Adorno to Kracauer, 28 October 1963, *Briefwechsel, 1923–1966*, 614–15. Rosenstock-Heussy was a convert to Catholicism.
71. See the comments in Graf, "God's Anti-Liberal Avant-Garde," 5–10.
72. Dagmar Barnouw, *Critical Realism*, 22–23.
73. Kracauer, "Georg Simmel: Ein Beitrag zur Deutung des geistigen Lebens unserer Zeit," *Werke* 9.2, 278. On Simmel's influence see David Frisby, *Fragments of Modernity*, 118–19; and Brodersen, *Siegfried Kracauer*, 36–46.
74. Kracauer, "George Simmel," *Werke* 9.2, 170.
75. Frisby, *Fragments of Modernity*, 118; and Kracauer to Simmel, 30 November 1917, *Gesamtausgabe* 23, 883–84. The emphasis on the word *Unsichtig* is given in the original text.
76. This expression, coined by Husserl, was almost a slogan for the burgeoning phenomenological movement.
77. Kracauer, *Werke* 9.2, 216–17.
78. Simmel, "Der Begriff und die Tragödie der Kultur," *Gesamtausgabe*, 16 vols., vol. 12.1, ed. Rüdiger Kramma and Angela Rammstedt (Frankfurt am Main, 2001), 194–223. First published in *Logos* (1911/1912).
79. Brodersen, *Siegfried Kracauer*, 45–46.
80. Kracauer, "Georg Simmel," *Mass Ornament*, 238–40.
81. Robert Musil, *The Man without Qualities* 1, 636–54. Musil was probably more inclined to the rational side of this equation than Kracauer was at this time.
82. Liebersohn, *Fate and Utopia*, 126–30.

83. Jay, *Marxism and Totality*, 77–80; and Brodersen, *Siegfried Kracauer*, 42–43.
84. Brodersen, *Siegfried Kracauer*, 41–42.
85. Margarete Susman, "Der Exodus aus der Philosophie," *FZ*, 17 June 1921, Morgenblatt.
86. Susman, "Der Exodus"; and David L. Gross, "*Kultur* and its Discontents," 84–85.
87. Kracauer, "Georg Simmel," *Mass Ornament*, 240.
88. Kracauer, 240.
89. Susman, "Der Exodus."
90. Kracauer, notebook entry of 29 October 1907, Belke and Renz, *Siegfried Kracauer*, 11–12.
91. Theodor Adorno, "Henkel, Krug und frühe Erfahrung," *Noten zur Literatur* IV (Frankfurt am Main, 1974), 93–95.
92. Adorno, "Henkel, Krug und frühe Erfahrung," 96–97.
93. The German title is "Über das Wesen der Persönlichkeit." I have translated the German word *Persönlichkeit* as "Personhood" though this word is not quite adequate to what Kracauer intended, as the subsequent discussion should make clear. The typescript of this work is in the library of the Free University in Berlin, and reprinted in *Werke* 9.1, 7–120.
94. Kracauer, *Werke* 9.1, 16–17.
95. See the discussion of Ernst Troeltsch in Liebersohn, *Fate and Utopia*, 48–49, 68–69 and of Max Weber, 108–25.
96. Paul Kluckhohn, *Persönlichkeit und Gemeinschaft: Studien zur Staatsauffassung der deutschen Romantik* (Halle and Saale, 1925), 2–3.
97. Friedrich Wilhelm Graf, "Rettung der Persönlichkeit: Protestantische Theologie als Kulturwissenschaft des Christentums," in *Kultur und Kulturwissenschaft um 1900: Krise der Moderne und Glaube an die Wissenschaft*, ed. Rüdiger vom Bruch, Friedrich Wilhelm Graf, and Gangolf Hübinger (Stuttgart, 1989), 103–31.
98. For his later discussion of this terminology, see Kracauer, "Philosophie der Gemeinschaft," *FZ*, 30 October 1924, *Werke* 5.2, 148–54.
99. Kracauer, *Werke* 9.1, 16 and 19–20.
100. Simmel, quoted by Horst Jürgen Helle in his "Introduction" to Simmel, *Essays on Religion* (New Haven and London, 1997), xiv.
101. Kracauer, *Werke* 9.1, 19, 68, and 96–98.
102. On Riefenstahl and *The Blue Light*, see Eric Rentschler, *The Ministry of Illusion: Nazi Cinema and its Afterlife* (Cambridge, 1996), 27–51; on Taut, see *The Crystal Chain Letters: Architectural Fantasies by Bruno Taut and his Circle*, ed. and trans. by Ian Boyd Whyte (Cambridge, 1985); and Spyros Papapetros, *On the Animation of the Inorganic: Art, Architecture and the Extension of Life* (Chicago, 2012), 113–57.
103. Kracauer, *Werke* 9.1, 30.
104. Kracauer to Susman, 11 January 1920, SN, DLA.
105. Simmel, *Gesamtausgabe* 12.1, 194–98 and 204.
106. Kracauer, *Werke* 9.1, 60–67.
107. Kracauer, *Werke* 9.1, 69, 89, and 118. Kracauer appears to have had some sympathy with feminism in his early years. His notebooks record a meeting with Ellen Key, but he also appears to have associated it with the dislocations of modernity.
108. Kracauer, *Werke* 9.1, 114–15.
109. Kracauer, "Die Tagung der katholischen Akademiker I," *FZ*, 24 August 1923, *Werke* 5.1, 674–78, esp. 675.

110. Cf. his critique of modern aesthetics in "Der Künstler in dieser Zeit," *Der verbotene Blick*, 130–39 (originally published in *Der Morgen* in April 1925).
111. Kracauer, *Werke* 9.1, 115–16.
112. On this point, Kracauer was probably influenced by Simmel who had an interest in the artistic form-giving individual, figures such as Goethe, Rembrandt, George, and Nietzsche. See a more critical discussion of this aspect of his work in Kracauer, "Georg Simmel," *Mass Ornament*, 253–57.
113. Kracauer, *Werke* 9.1, 90–91.
114. Ibid., 116.
115. Ibid., 119.
116. Kracauer, "The Biography as an Art Form of the New Bourgeoisie," *FZ*, 29 June 1930, in *Mass Ornament*, 101–5. On this issue, see also Leo Lowenthal, "German Popular Biographies: Culture's Bargain Counters," in *The Critical Spirit: Essays in Honor of Herbert Marcuse*, ed. Kurt H. Wolff and Barrington Moore (Boston, 1967), 267–83.
117. Gershom Scholem, "The Tradition of the Thirty Six Hidden Just Men," in *The Messianic Idea in Judaism and Other Essays on Jewish Spirituality* (New York, 1971), 251–56.
118. Kracauer to Löwenthal, 24 January 1922, *In steter Freundschaft*, 35–36; Kracauer to Daniel Halévy, 8 October 1961, KN, DLA, reprinted in Thomas Levin, ed., "Zur Archäologie des Exils: Siegfried Kracauers Briefe an Daniel Halévy, 1935–1962," in *Siegfried Kracauer: neue Interpretationen*, ed. Kessler and Levin, 415–16; and Kracauer, *History*, 15. See his obituary for Nobel, *FZ*, 25 January 1922, *Werke* 5.1, 362–63. Löwenthal said of Nobel that he represented a "remarkable blending of mystical religiosity, philosophical insightfulness and a more or less suppressed homosexual love for young men"; see *Mitmachen wollte ich nie*, 19–20.
119. Liebersohn, *Fate and Utopia*, 109.
120. Georg Simmel, *Rembrandt: Ein kunstphilosophischer Versuch*, quoted in Helle, "Introduction," to Simmel, *Essays on Religion*, xii.
121. Kracauer, "Holzapfels *Panideal*: Zur Kritik der Kulturgläubigkeit," *FZ*, 7 February 1924, *Werke* 5.2, 14–25.
122. Fritz Stern, *The Politics of Cultural Despair: a Study of the Rise and Fall of the Germanic Ideology* (Berkeley, 1974).
123. Bollenbeck, "Kulturkritik," 87–100.
124. Gross, "*Kulturkritik* and its Discontents," 76–83.
125. Kracauer, notebook entry of summer, 1911, Belke and Renz, *Siegfried Kracauer*, 18.
126. Kracauer, notebook entry of 22 January 1912, ibid.
127. Max Rychner, "Blick auf die zwanziger Jahre," in Rychner, *Zur europäischer Literatur zwischen zwei Weltkriegen* (Zurich, 1951), 17–18.
128. Frisby, *Fragments of Modernity*, 102.
129. Ibid., 119; and Kracauer, "Georg Simmel: 'Zur Philosophie der Kunst,'" *FZ*, 4 July 1923, *Werke* 5.1, 650–51.
130. Liebersohn, *Fate and Utopia*, 157–58. On Bloch's anger towards Simmel after 1914, see Rabinbach, *In the Shadow of Catastrophe*, 51–52.
131. Gross, "*Kulturkritik* and its Discontents," 83.
132. Mann, *Reflections of an Unpolitical Man*, 11–12.
133. Beßlich, *Faszination des Verfalls: Thomas Mann und Oswald Spengler* (Berlin, 2002), 44–54.

134. On Spengler and culture see Adorno, "Spengler after the Decline," *Prisms*, trans. Sherry and Samuel Weber (Cambridge, 1981), 51–72; and more generally see H. Stuart Hughes, *Oswald Spengler: A Critical Estimate* (New York, 1952); and John Farrenkopf, *Prophet of Decline: Spengler on World History and Politics* (Baton Rouge, 2001).

CHAPTER TWO

Reading the War, Writing Crisis

The philologist Viktor Klemperer, a friend to Kracauer during his time in Munich, described the outbreak of war in autumn 1914 as a sudden rupture in their lives. For days on end every conversation turned upon the coming conflict. "One stood before the war as an eighteen-year old stands before life," so Klemperer wrote in his diary. All the philosophical and metaphysical problems that preoccupied him beforehand were no longer relevant; even to discuss them seemed "entirely out of place."[1] As a patriotic fever spread among his contemporaries, Klemperer was often with Kracauer, whom he had met the year before at a party held in the Klemperer apartments. They maintained a short and, judging from Klemperer's diary, tepid friendship. His account of this period offers one of the only portraits of Kracauer during these turbulent months. Given what Klemperer knew of his friend, he was surprised by his "sudden conversion to patriotism." In almost all their prior discussions, Klemperer recollected that Kracauer had spoken only of philosophy and aesthetics, and he had demonstrated very little interest in politics.[2] Yet the drama of 1914 had deeply unsettled Kracauer. Lonely and isolated, he seemed overwhelmed by the imperative to act, to participate in the course of grand events. According to Klemperer, Kracauer "could not be alone," and he swung wildly between moments of "analysis and spontaneous outbursts of feeling." Though Klemperer concedes that he too had succumbed to the surge of nationalist sentiment, he had recoiled in disgust when Kracauer showed him a book by Wilhelm Wundt, *The Psychology of Warfaring Nations*. To his mind, the book demonstrated that militarism had forced the capitulation of intellect, that in the conflict between life and thought, the former had won.[3]

Klemperer's testimony demonstrates that Kracauer was more involved in the patriotism of 1914 than his semi-autobiographical account in *Ginster* would suggest.[4] According to Klemperer, Kracauer was almost possessed by the war. Together they often walked into the city, and there they witnessed the first announcements of the Austrian attack on Serbia and then later the parades of recruits. With blue eyes and blond hair, young soldiers marched in the streets; one in particular caught Klemperer's attention as he seemed possessed by a glow that "he had never seen before." Since Kracauer was sensitive to his supposedly "foreign" appearance, the sight of these youths must have increased his own feelings of angst. In the commotion of those days, he had volunteered for duty, but was turned down on account of his weak constitution.[5]

However, by 9 August his war fervor had all but vanished, though the nervous agitation remained. He had been told by an acquaintance that many recruits only enlisted out of a spirit of adventure and wanderlust, that they had no sense of the "earnestness" of the moment and were not looked upon favorably by regular officers. Another friend, Ernst Crusius, argued, on the contrary, that there was a sense of deep gravitas and angst in the barracks. Perhaps, as a result of these discussions, Kracauer now clung to his own "special life" (*Sonderleben*) and repudiated his earlier enthusiasm. He would not become like those millions of "atomized masses" who were to supply the machinery of war. Moreover, he was repulsed by the sudden "coming into fashion of the love of God."[6] Klemperer (who by this time complained that Kracauer was "getting on his nerves") sympathized with this judgment. He did not understand how one could find in this communal "bloodbath" the presence of a "God who was friendly to man." The poets and the elders, he claimed, now cited religion to justify their faith in war; the horrors of the Middle Ages were being revived as intellectuals abdicated all sense of responsibility. The confused passions of these days left Klemperer "simultaneously enchanted and despairing," and Kracauer appears to have had similar feelings. His responses were volatile; he embraced the war, but seemed uncertain of his convictions. He must have overcome some of his reservations long enough to contribute some patriotic verse in support of the war as well as a reflection on "the love of Fatherland," both of which appeared as the war dragged on.[7]

For most of the war, Kracauer avoided military service by working in a number of architectural firms, but in 1917, he was finally recruited. He never experienced the frontlines, but he still described his mobilization as a "hard school." To Simmel he stated that in spite of the hardships of army training and barrack life, he had garnered valuable experiences; his desire was that this should drive his philosophy closer to "life"—that it would become more "saturated with the real."[8] Aside from this experience, the war had also given him a glimpse into the ambiguous relationship of religion and the secular world. Both of these themes would preoccupy him over the next decade.

The Influence of Max Scheler: War and Culture

> By every account we must expect an extremely religious and vital age; an age of entirely novel and difficult struggles over religion. However, for this reason it will be an age in which every given positive religion and church, must cease being a cold storage for old truths . . . For this reason no religious position of the church should allow itself to be content with mere self-assertions; on the contrary, each must labor to preserve and demonstrate its positive worth to the world. That, to be sure, is certainly a new situation.[9]

As the war drew to an end, the philosopher Max Scheler thought the coming peace would confront European society with a radically different situation. Writing in the Catholic journal *Das Hochland*, Scheler also reiterated a theme that Kracauer had drawn attention to in a short review of Scheler's earlier work, *War and Reconstruction*. In this book, he had warned against the capitalist ethos that had spread throughout Europe, replacing the concerns of the spirit (*Marienhafte*) with those of economic materialism (*Marthahafte*). The ultimate triumph of this ethos would be a catastrophe, and it was for this reason that Germany must continue to fight: defeat by Protestant England would mean a victory for the forces of materialism and the death of the spirit.[10]

Despite his patriotism, Scheler was not without pan-European sympathies, and he still viewed the struggle between capitalism and culture as a more general European problem. His nationalism emerged primarily in his belief that Germany was to play the leading redemptive role. For Scheler, as for other intellectuals such as Simmel and Werner Sombart, the war was Germany's existential moment, a moment of national assertion on the global stage.[11] "The state at war," Scheler declared, "is the state at the highest point of its existence."[12] Subjected to extreme hardship and sacrifice, a nation drew upon its deepest nature (*Wesen*), and it was on this level that the conflict between nations mattered. Hence, for Scheler, the war was neither about rival economic interests, nor about great power politics; rather, it was a struggle between the opposed values of different nations. It was a contest fought between different qualities that arose from the depths of the national essence. Indeed, a conflict that was based only upon economic or political interests could scarcely justify the death and carnage caused by the war.[13] At the end of the struggle, the triumph of German *Wesen* would be crucial in order to ensure cultural and spiritual stability during the period of postwar reconstruction.

However, as the prospect of a German victory became more distant, Scheler's nationalism was eclipsed by his concern for the common European task of rebuilding from the ruins.[14] The aggressive nationalism of his book of 1915, *German War and the Genius of War* (a book that Kracauer later referred to as "sinister"), was largely abandoned before the peace.[15] In its place there was a renewed interest in religion in general, and Catholicism in particular. Universal religion instead of national allegiance was more desirable as a means of social cohesion. For Scheler, the war that had begun as a radical cure for cultural decadence had become itself a "revelation of decadence"; it demonstrated the deep need for a renewed spiritual order.[16]

The influence that Scheler had on Kracauer in these years is unclear. Scheler's writing on the war was a mixed bag, including existential assertions, angst over the crisis of the German (and European) spirit, and hopes for a durable new order. In the early years of the war, Kracauer appreciated these attempts to find meaning in the conflict, and he appears to have found in Scheler a compelling representative of the public intellectual in a time of crisis. Yet, his admiration for Scheler is mixed with skepticism. The rough sketch of Scheler as Professor Caspari in *Ginster*, though not an accurate portrayal of their relationship, attests to some of his reservations. The two probably met during the war shortly after Scheler had given a public lecture in Frankfurt.[17] By that time, Scheler was a prominent intellectual and a public exponent of the German cause, both at home and abroad. After 1918, he emerged as an influential voice on the subject of religious renewal, and, according to Kracauer, his sophisticated theological arguments drew many back to the church.[18] Kracauer himself does not appear to have been persuaded by his Catholicism, but nonetheless Scheler played a minor role as a mentor to him. Kracauer sent him some of his unpublished manuscripts, to which Scheler responded with both criticism and encouragement, and as already mentioned, Kracauer wrote a positive review of Scheler's *War and Reconstruction*.[19]

Given the facts of their relationship, Kracauer's unflattering portrait of Scheler in *Ginster* is more of interest for the retrospective distance it places between the protagonist and Caspari.[20] The general tone of their encounter is one of skeptical indifference. Ginster attends a speech by Caspari, not so much out of interest, but because he feels obliged to have some idea of what the war was about. However, during the lecture he scarcely pays attention to what Caspari says; rather he remarks upon his penetrating stare, and he is often distracted by the comically timed outbursts of a parrot housed in a nearby zoo.[21] What he hears of the speech, however, leaves him dispirited. The insistent repetition of key words and clichés only demonstrated the emptiness of his rhetoric. Afterwards, when the protagonist meets Caspari through a mutual friend, the hypocrisy of his words is exposed, for in private Caspari admitted the war was lost even as he encouraged further struggle.[22] Ginster, who must soon report for duty, must now confront the prospect of his own death in a war that even its supporters believe can no longer be won. In this episode, there is no hint of the ambivalence reported by Klemperer; rather, the portrait of Ginster is of someone clearly unmoved by the spectacle of war and indifferent to its proponents.[23]

However, on at least one point, Scheler and Kracauer agreed. Both writers were suspicious of the strident patriotism voiced by groups such as the Pan-Germans. Some recognition of this appears in the encounter between Ginster and Caspari; Ginster remarks upon the absence of bellicose rhetoric in Caspari's speech. Indeed, he is surprised to find that the speaker drags on for over an hour without once glorifying the fatherland (Scheler had, in fact, pointedly criticized the Pan-Germans).[24] Similarly, Kracauer, in a 1915 essay, suggested that not every expression of patriotic fervor derived from true patriotism. He described "love of fatherland" as a "deep comprehension of the particular riches of the Fatherland, of its history, of its present situation and hopes for the future, and the painful suffering over all the errors that one recognizes in the constitution and daily customs of the *Volk*."[25] Such sentiments were, of course, a staple of patriotic fare, but were not nearly as extreme as what Scheler had called the "Wagnerian-heroic romanticism" of the Pan-Germans.[26]

For both Kracauer and Scheler there was a question of authenticity at stake. They both suspected that behind the conventional expressions of patriotic belligerence there was often an inner emptiness or a vague wanderlust, though Kracauer noted that one could not plumb the depths of such sentiments among a large and diverse population.[27] He argued that such sentiments could be grouped into categories that would enable one to identify some defining aspects of patriotic sentiment. To Kracauer, the majority of Germans had a superficial sense of patriotism, one that did not engage the "full and undivided soul."[28] The conventional patriotic discourse, he argued, encompassed a wide range of emotions, thoughts, and opinions, most of which lacked the stamp of authenticity. He had, of course, expressed similar misgivings during the first days of war when he was in Munich with Klemperer, and these early suspicions appear to have been confirmed by his later experiences. Scheler, for his part, warmly applauded Kracauer's essay when he received it from him later that year. Given the present state of affairs, he wrote, the analysis had an obvious "pedagogical value."[29]

On the question of religious revival, the sympathy of interests between Scheler and Kracauer was less clear. In 1921, Kracauer's sharply worded critique of Scheler's *On the Eternal in Man* demonstrated the distance between them on religious issues; yet, when and how this rift emerged is difficult to answer due to the paucity of sources from these years. Kracauer turned against nationalism in the postwar era, as did Scheler, and nationalist sentiments are mostly absent in his writings of the 1920s. Kracauer also became more interested in religion as both a social bond between individuals and as a means of giving value to a meaningless world. A letter to Susman from early 1920 even spoke of Christ as if Kracauer had experienced some kind of inner conversion.[30] In *Georg*, the protagonist does, in fact, take some hesitant steps towards the Catholic Church, though this is rapidly abandoned.[31] Outside of this scene, there is little to suggest that Kracauer ever entertained such a move himself, and he probably only intended to dramatize what he saw as a dubious search for religious certainty. Still, given the lack of sources for these years, such a move cannot be excluded outright. In general, Kracauer struck a position close to Scheler only insofar as he felt that the present crisis was not solely a question of politics or nation, but rather one of culture and religion. Their responses to this problem, however, were very different. He outlined some of his disagreements in a letter to Susman in 1921:

> I agree with him when he says that metaphysics and religion represent intentions that are essentially different in their relationships to the divine nature; in contrast to him, I deny that metaphysical intentions actually achieve their goal. On the contrary, I question the dependence of metaphysics on religion.[32]

At this point, he was clearly still engaged with religious themes, but the divergences between his views and those of Scheler, would become sharper as he read further into Scheler's book, *On the Eternal in Man*.

If Kracauer dissented from Scheler in terms of the functions of religion in modernity, he was ready to engage with phenomenological methods of investigation. As Adorno stated later, here the influence of Scheler "bore fruit in Kracauer as in few others."[33] Kracauer had concluded his reflections on patriotism by stating that "the more deeply the German soul longed after the invisible, the more solidly it rooted itself in the earthbound."[34] Phenomenology was a means of exploring precisely these connections between mental experience and material reality.

Scheler thus combined methodological innovation with an impulse to explore spheres of existence supposedly unaccounted for by the sciences. The contemporary philosopher Nicolai Hartmann claimed that it was Scheler who turned phenomenology into a "spiritual" movement combined with a deep concern for social issues, and Susman argued that it was part of the "exodus from philosophy" that should be celebrated.[35] Adorno also spoke of phenomenology as a program for those who desired to be "dazzled neither by ideology nor the façade of something subject merely to empirical verification."[36] Thus, phenomenology appeared to some intellectuals as a means of evading the limits of positivism, and thus it possessed a potential synergy with the ends of religious revival; the things of the spirit became tangible under its gaze and more directly connected to the world of daily experience.

This aspect of phenomenology, though stimulating for Kracauer at first, also led him to question its ultimate viability. The movement towards the experience of everyday existence was to be celebrated, but using it to validate religious dogma was problematic, a misguided attempt to make religion more concrete.[37] Scheler, for his part, claimed that phenomenology was an "experiential traffic with the world itself [*Erlebnisverkehr*]"; he even went so far as to describe it as "the most radical kind of empiricism and positivism."[38] Kracauer would never have expressed it in these terms, but the conjunction of a materialist means of investigating mental phenomena matches well with his later assertions that the way to the sacred lay through the profane. As Adorno stated, "the program of *Wesensschau*, the intuition of essence and especially the so-called *Bildchen-Phänomenologie*, the phenomenology of mental images" were suited to Kracauer's "long-suffering gaze."[39]

The influence of Scheler, however, should not be overstated. His brief engagement with phenomenology was significant only insofar as it confirmed his belief that the profane world was the proper site of critical investigation; the more ambitious program of uniting phenomenology with religious insight was another matter. His reservations were expressed even in the work that was most directly influenced by phenomenology: *Sociology as Science*.[40] In this work, he argues that a sociology based on phenomenological investigation would ultimately fail in its task of "sociologically reconstructing the whole of social reality."[41] Hence, the use of phenomenology to triumph over relativism was bound to fail, a position that is clear in his review of Scheler published in late 1921.[42] Kracauer argued that Scheler had tried to legitimate Augustinian Catholicism by arguing for a special affinity between phenomenology and church dogma. Kracauer responded by pointing out that phenomenology was a conceptual "factotum" and could not support any religion more than another; nor could it validate the idea of a "natural" or "originary" religion without the insertion of value judgments. Having allowed such judgements to creep into his analysis, and having denied the contingencies of his own position, Scheler had overstepped the bounds of his own method, and therefore he arrived at a predetermined judgment of religious truth.[43] His position, Kracauer told Susman, was nothing more than "disguised Catholicism."[44]

Yet the failed attempt to unite phenomenology and religious truth was in some respects a fruitful one. In Adorno's inaugural lecture before the philosophy faculty of the University of Frankfurt, he argued that Scheler had pushed phenomenology to its limits, and his efforts had exposed the gap between "eternal ideas and reality."[45] Moreover, his impulse towards materialism remained an important point of orientation for philosophy. If the attempt to analyze religious or metaphysical contents had failed, then one had to focus critical efforts elsewhere, in the material sphere. This was the direction that Kracauer took; there was no refutation of religion, but rather a refutation of specific discourses about it. He had in fact sought and, so he claimed, received support for his views on Scheler from two prominent Catholic intellectuals before submitting the article for publication. One of them, Ernst Michel, was a theologian and editor of the Catholic *Rhein-Mainische Volkszeitung*; the other was Joseph Weiger, a leading figure amongst the "new Catholics."[46] Thus, Kracauer wanted to argue his case from within a framework not fundamentally opposed to religious points of view. In a sense, he wanted to turn the materialist impulses of phenomenology against what he saw as its excesses. He set himself against the booming "philosophies of eternity with their anti-historical gestures"—precisely those trends that Scheler had argued would define religiosity in the postwar period.[47]

Strategies of Containment: Encounters with Ernst Bloch and Max Brod

In his discussion of religious revival, Scheler proposed a linkage between the cultural and political crisis of Europe and a crisis of religion. That centuries of European history had led to 1914 was an indictment of its culture, a culture that supposedly had become more secular since the French Revolution. Thus, secularization and crisis became fused in a common discourse, for if modernity was viewable as a series of crises, then secularization was implicated in these events. As a result, the calamity of war must provoke a rethinking of the relationship between sacred and profane.

Such is the impression given by the protagonist of Kracauer's second novel, *Georg*, a story of a young man adrift in the postwar years who finds work on the staff of a left-liberal newspaper. "The war will never end," he laments, in the course of investigating a fire that had destroyed an old theatre in the Ruhr.[48] The fire had broken out while the zone was still under French occupation, and many had suspected the French of sabotage. As Georg steps over the gutted stage, he broods over the postwar transformation—never again, he thinks, will he sit in a theatre and allow himself to be beguiled by fairy tales.[49] He even regrets that the fire did not burn everything to the ground. His professional lust for a story is frustrated to discover that the destruction was not the fault of the occupation authorities; the French, he is assured by the theatre director, had not caused the fire and, in fact, they had made every effort to put it out. When Georg tries to provoke the director by remarking that he saw no great tragedy in the theatre's demise, the director readily concedes the point; the fire was a blessing in disguise. The theatre was much past its prime and no longer suited modern needs. Reconstruction would follow, allowing for a modern cultural agenda.[50] Thus, the war worked its way insidiously into postwar society; the advance of the new was contingent upon the destruction of the old—a belief that was echoed in the words of the popular author, Count Keyserling: "The death of the old is already the birth of the new."[51]

The proximity of cultural progress and material destruction is a much-discussed theme in the history of Weimar and modernism, one that finds concise expression in Benjamin's well-known "Theses on the Philosophy of History."[52] Modern culture and its relationship to ideas of sociopolitical progress was a contentious and divisive issue during the Weimar years, and Kracauer read and wrote about numerous books that contributed to these debates after 1918. An investigation of his reception of these "war books" offers insight into how Kracauer conceived of the relationship between religion, culture, and politics in light of the war and its aftermath: what role should religion have in a situation of political and cultural upheaval? What place did it occupy within culture, or, on the contrary, did it lie beyond culture? And how did such questions relate to the political agendas of the present? Kracauer's approach to these questions demonstrates that the border between sacred and profane was ill-defined and vigorously contested. The precedence of religion over secular culture was no longer assured; rather, religion had to define itself anew in its shifting relationship to the secular.

"War books" should not refer only to those books for which war constituted the primary subject, or to those books that some authors intended as an overt response to it. Of course, the books discussed here do conform to these criteria, but the category needs to be expanded to include books whose reception was shaped by the contexts of their publication on the eve of, during, or after the war. Spengler's *Decline of the West* is an obvious example, but on the fringes of this category one might also include Theodor Haecker's translations of Kierkegaard that appeared in *Der Brenner* in July 1914.[53] Its publication, so Haecker stated, was a calculated intervention in the cultural and social crisis of the present. Kierkegaard had written his polemic on the eve of the revolutions of 1848, and Haecker argued that the malaise of that age bore a resemblance to his own. As a result of his efforts, Kierkegaard was probably read more often with one eye open to contemporary politics. He thus emerged as both a prescient critic of modernity and its potential antidote.[54]

War books are also distinguishable by their combative and oppositional stance. They were intended as a deliberate continuation of the cultural struggles that the war had brought to the surface, and they ensured that the postwar status quo would not go unchallenged. They proposed alternative visions to a "merely existing" present, whether this vision was one of pessimistic decline or of radical Utopia. Thus, when in 1923 Rosenzweig reviewed Max Brod's *Paganism, Christianity, Judaism*, he readily conceded its value as a war book, even as he dismissed its conception of Jewish thought.[55] The book was bad theology, he argued, but it still had value insofar as Brod had entered Judaism into the struggle against "the spirit of the present."[56] Its contrary position lent it a measure of authenticity as such books had the virtue of vigorous opposition, resisting the spiritual dearth of the present. As Kracauer wrote in a similar and symptomatic formulation, "it was not without good reason that one has compared the artist to the good soldier."[57]

Before the late 1920s, Kracauer did not take a position in these struggles that could be clearly aligned to either the left or right of the political spectrum.

Indeed, his encounter with the war literature occurred at a point when he seemed uncertain what side to take. In this period he could be viewed as an "intellectual nomad" in search of a calling; or in the terms outlined by Pierre Bourdieu, he was trying to establish his particular node in a wider cultural field.[58] His attempt conflated issues of economic security and intellectual validation. His persistent lack of a recognized position sometimes was expressed by a contradictory disdain for intellectual labor.[59] He was, as Musil wrote, among those intellectuals who seek to repudiate themselves, who resemble an "apple tree which would love to bear all manner of fruit, but . . . no apples."[60] However, his encounter with the "war books" began a reassessment of his attitudes and opinions, and by the end of the Republic his reversal is striking. In his public dispute with Alfred Döblin in 1931, he warned intellectuals not to repudiate those talents indigenous to their calling, in other words, the use of intellect.[61] This valorization of reason and the role of the intellectual was the end-point of a shift in his thought that began in the aftermath of the war.[62]

The increased legitimacy of reason mingled with his response to the messianic traditions in Judaism, a response that was more vigorous in the early 1920s.[63] He wrote to Susman in early 1921 that he set "his entire hope upon a new religious formation in which we shall all go under. One day, to be sure, the form of a founder will once again die the sacrificial death upon which new myths attach themselves."[64] This letter is puzzling because although Kracauer declares himself against "existing religions," he appears to welcome a new faith, even new myths. "We need myths," so he continued, "philosophy is long since dead, but scarce knows it. Perhaps, I will write the obituary in the form of a book." However, by 1922 he was much more skeptical of the messianic tendency, and a positive valuation of myth is no longer conceivable. His severe critique of the work of Ernst Bloch, published in that year, is a sign of this shift.[65]

Kracauer was not alone in having negative and conflicted opinions regarding Bloch. In general, *The Spirit of Utopia* provoked divergent judgments, even in the same reader. Published near the end of the war, the book was written in a highly wrought style and punctuated with feverish calls for revolution. Some readers found the book totally incoherent; the wartime censor who reviewed the work found it so devoid of practical content that he saw no harm in allowing it to be printed despite its revolutionary position. Still, the book fascinated many intellectuals, and Rabinbach remarks that with its publication Bloch became the "theologian of the German revolution."[66] In her review written for the *FZ*, Margaret Susman described the book's publication in almost rapturous tones as a "lone light" appearing before wayfarers in a storm: "a peculiar, glowing light that has arisen in the dark, severe, stormy night of the war years—a new German metaphysics."[67] Others were much less enthused; they condemned Bloch for his faulty musicology, for his arcane language, and for his "indiscriminate" religiosity. The latter point prompted Gustav Landauer to compare him with Rudolf Steiner, the leader of German anthroposophy.[68] Walter Benjamin also expressed disappointment with the work, even as he added the mitigating remark that Bloch was "ten times better" than the book.[69] Kracauer, by and large, shared this opinion: "We need men such as Bloch, but they do not show the way to religious redemption, to say nothing of politics."[70] Most of his objections appeared in his review of *Thomas Münzer: Theologian of the Revolution* and in his letters to Susman and Löwenthal, both of whom were more sympathetic to the general tenor of Bloch's work.[71] These sources demonstrate that Kracauer had become hostile to Bloch before the appearance of *Münzer* in 1922, and thus his review should be read as a more sweeping polemic against the so-called Bloch phenomena.

Both *Münzer* and *Spirit of Utopia* originated in the disillusionment caused by the war, and the utopian promise of revolution. Bloch had been horrified by what he saw as the capitulation of European culture in 1914; that even Simmel had become a militant patriot had shocked him, and led him to repudiate his former mentor.[72] Both books were also works of cultural salvage; they attempted to identify the traces of utopian longing embedded in history and cultural tradition. Such traces, Bloch argued, were signposts to the future, premonitions of the "not-yet-become"; and from these signs the present generation could orient themselves to the coming utopian order. If there was a sense to the war, it was here in this hope for a revived humanity.[73] For this reason, the destruction of the old order during the war was welcome; however, Bloch feared a German triumph which he thought would eliminate the last valid remnants of European culture. In an essay published in 1918, he had even argued that Germany must be defeated in order to uncover those "deeply buried currents of beclouded piety."[74] *Münzer*, written a few years later, was also a product of the postwar period and its revolutionary promise. Bloch later told Kracauer that it was "conceived amid the movements of 1918, amid pressures, and movements of identification that the always insufficient, private individual must undertake to put the facts in order for oneself."[75] In this study of the religious rebel, Bloch argued that the decline of the present should be measured against the glimmer of utopia, those instances of redemptive promise buried in the past. These were timeless and recoverable. If one could only identify them, they could serve as talismans for the present as it moved towards its messianic destiny.[76]

However much some may have sympathized with Bloch's intentions, his method provoked resistance. This was not surprising as his radical utopianism was matched by a stylistic readiness to experiment intended to disorient the reader. In the opening lines of *Spirit of Utopia*, Bloch distanced himself from ordinary language usage. "I am by myself," he wrote, "That I move, that I speak: is not there."[77] Language, according to Bloch, should not serve a merely discursive function; rather, it was an instrument for the recovery of "lost cultural experience," for "actualizing" redemption.⁷⁸ Thus, words were wrested from their normal patterns of usage to engender in his reader a creative form of alienation, one that would direct him or her to the missing utopian dimension. To some extent, a reader had to accept the premises of this language, and, in his rebuttal to Kracauer, Bloch suggested that Kracauer misunderstood his intentions; had he read his "logic of language" (*Sprachlogik*) the matter could have been easily resolved.⁷⁹ This was an optimistic view, for as will be discussed below, Kracauer's objections were not simply stylistic; rather he repudiated in principle the idea that language could work the kind of magic that Bloch ascribed to it.

In conjunction with Bloch's experimental language, his writing was also characterized by an extreme eclecticism. He drew together subjects and motifs from a wide array of cultural, religious, and philosophical traditions and then fashioned them anew; the legends of Mithra, Kant, Christology, messianic Judaism, the history of music, and Marxism were all juxtaposed and fused together in a manner that some critics found spurious and unconvincing.⁸⁰ The collected material was then ransacked for what Bloch called *Vor-Schein*: the anticipatory signposts of utopia, bits of the "new Jerusalem" scattered in fragments throughout the past and present. According to Bloch, "everything that is has a utopian star in its blood, and philosophy would be nothing if it did not form the ideational solution for this crystalline heaven of renewed reality."⁸¹ Kant and Hegel, for instance, were enlisted as failed attempts to shape the question that addressed final ends, what he called the "inconstruable question" that could only be answered when the "not yet" of utopian longing became actual.⁸²

The use of this eclectic cultural baggage as a means of identifying the stepping stones to Utopia endowed Bloch's thought with a teleological impulse. The historical development of aesthetics and culture were fused with revelatory tradition, and as a result, the end of time appeared to be the product of historical processes. In the concluding chapter of the book, entitled "Karl Marx, the Apocalypse and Death," mysticism mingled with hecatombs, and revolution with the task of redemption. The guiding star of Utopia flashed amidst the catastrophe, and to the just among humankind was given the task of speaking the name that would usher in the New Jerusalem:

> God exists through them, and into their hands is given the consecration of the Name, the very appointment of God, who moves and stirs in us, the presensed gateway, darkest question, exuberant interior that is no *factum* but a problem, given as a prayer into the hands of our God-summoning philosophy and of truth.⁸³

This teleological dimension of Bloch's work was one among many issues that incited Kracauer to attack his work. For Kracauer, Bloch had tried to construct a "theoretical system of the Messianic," a project to which he was vehemently opposed.[84] He even spoke of a "hatred" for Bloch and condemned his description of the messianic.[85] In his review for the FZ published in autumn of 1922, he made his position public. Yet, though he criticized Bloch for mixing politics with chiliasm, his attack was not simply a repudiation of the chiliastic tradition; rather, he wanted to show that such a fusion travestied the very idea of the messianic by reducing it to a result of human action:

> The miracle becomes regulated, the leap [of faith] becomes process, and one is blissfully referred to the dialectics of history according to Marx and Hegel. However, since the one waiting for the apocalypse does not in any way think in such historical categories, since his pathos is placed entirely elsewhere, and since the inner-historical and supra-historical are not to be seamlessly united, these constructions simply fail, as they must in the eyes of every genuinely religious individual.[86]

By conflating radical politics with religion, Bloch suggested that the appearance of the messiah was somehow contingent upon historical events, rather than being an event that transcended all history. Moreover, Kracauer claimed that Bloch, in his pursuit of the divine, had forsaken the real sphere of existence in which figures such as Münzer actually lived and acted. "The world in its entirety," he told Löwenthal in 1921, was left untouched by Bloch. By conjoining the messianic with the historical he ignored the specific qualities of both.[87]

Though Kracauer evinced no faith in the messianic order, he still wanted his critique to be understood within a religious framework, that is, not as an assault on religious tradition, but rather as an attack on the "blasphemous."[88] He defended his position to Susman by pointing out that he was not simply hostile to religion. On the contrary, he had sought the opinion of others who approached the subject of chiliasm from a religious perspective. His essay had been read by the writer Alfons Paquet, whom Kracauer described as a "thoroughly religious and honorable man." Paquet had agreed with his argument on every point, so he claimed.[89] He could also have mentioned the response of Benjamin who had expressed similar reservations concerning Bloch in his "Theological-Political Fragment." "The Kingdom of God," so Benjamin stated, "is not the *telos* of the historical dynamic; it cannot be set as a goal . . . Therefore the order of the profane cannot be built up on the idea of the Divine Kingdom."[90] If the chiliastic tradition was to retain its meaning, then it had to be understood as an "eruption" into history, not as a "terminus" of its continuous flow.[91]

To this critique, Kracauer added further grievances. Bloch, he argued, was too wedded to secular concepts and modes of expression. His persistent references to esoteric, occultist subjects and the self-aggrandizement of his verbal contortions all attested to a style that was clearly wedded to the profane sphere.[92] Kracauer did not credit Bloch's attempt to force language to create new meanings; on the contrary, he interpreted the neologisms and deliberate contortions as evidence of Bloch's egoism. In general, he was unsympathetic to such "effects of language." In an unpublished essay from 1929, he argued that this gnostic view of language only feigned a discourse of religiosity that, in fact, concealed weak religious convictions.[93] This led to a failure to think through the meaning of religious concepts in a secularized world. It also led Kracauer to question Bloch's intentions. "Does he really believe in the thousand-year millennial Reich?" Kracauer asked in a letter to Löwenthal, "is that totally concrete and real to [him], or only an as-if-Ideal?" "With Bloch," he continued, "his style derives from a lack of sincerity . . . a burning self-aggrandizement into ecstasy—all the same whether it is genuine or made up." Such rhetoric, he argued, had little to do with the utopian realms it purported to illuminate. On the contrary, they were the signs of the self-conscious writer, a deliberate flaunting of education mixed with a peculiar "wantonness" that betrayed its profane origin.[94]

Given Kracauer's far-ranging and unsympathetic critique of the *Münzer* book, it is not surprising that Bloch responded with hostility and relations between the two came to an end. Perhaps, even more surprisingly, their intellectual friendship was renewed after four years, and though strained at times, would last until Kracauer's death. The basis of this renewed rapport appears to have been a recognition that, in spite of the differences that had emerged in the *Münzer* affair, they did share common ground on subjects such as Marx and utopia. Their correspondence in the last part of the 1920s rehearsed some of their affinities and differences, and both referred to their early admiration for Lukács and his concept of totality.[95] Kracauer had read the *Theory of the Novel* with excitement in the immediate postwar years, but he later argued that criticism had to go beyond Lukács and his idealist concept of totality. A "third way" was required, one that would involve a genuine "wandering and transformation" of those truths buried in theology; it would require their absorption into the "course of historical processes" and a removal of the "mythological shell" that cloaked their "truth contents." The fate of religion in this process was unclear, but he suggested that the shift would have a deep impact on the churches and their dogma: "The formulations of the Bible are not final, the messianic still conceived of with naturalistic imagery . . . one must rob religion and leave the plundered behind to their fate."[96]

Just how this would occur, however, and what happens to religious concepts when they undergo this wandering through the profane, was not articulated in Kracauer's work—neither in the 1920s nor later in his career. His remarks that Marxist theory must be more open to theological "states of affairs" and that there needed to be a "disassociation of Marxism towards and into reality" do not fill out this picture in much detail.[97] Indeed, it seems vaguely reminiscent of a statement from a lecture by Thomas Mann that Kracauer attended in 1922. Mann had then stated that German socialism, mired in crude materialism, would not "truly rise to the height of its national task until . . . Karl Marx has read Friedrich Hölderlin."[98]

Some sense of the direction of Kracauer's thought on this issue emerges in the dispute over Lukács that Kracauer conducted with Bloch beginning in 1926. Lukács's classic statement of totality appeared in his *Theory of the Novel* wherein it was described in romanticized terms as a "golden age," a time when individuals felt no distance between themselves and the world. Such an age existed, Lukács claimed, during the Homeric period as was evident by the fact that the human form still sufficed to represent the divine.[99] In this age there was no gap between humankind and the gods, between subject and object, between form and content. The modern age, in contrast, was a time of "perfect sinfulness," an age of decline that had long fallen away from this primal unity. If in the Homeric past all the infinite parts of reality were imbued with meaning through consciousness of the whole, now they existed as a multitude of atoms, circulating the cosmos, aimless and independent from one another. In his review published in 1921, Kracauer sympathized with Lukács's vision of a fallen modernity; he described the present as a chaos that ensued after the "all-encompassing church had been dismantled piece by piece."[100] Later, Kracauer turned against this conception, recognizing that it posited the lost whole in an idealized fashion; but even then, he argued that it retained some value as a means of critiquing the present. The flaws of the sinful age could still be exposed by measuring them against the concept of a truly "fulfilled age" (*sinnerfüllte Zeit*) as a kind of ideal-type.[101] In this way, the religious concept of totality could be secularized and become part of a critical apparatus for investigating modern society.

Despite this affirmation of totality, both Kracauer and Bloch felt that the concept needed to become more open-ended, more flexible toward internal variations. In a 1924 review of Lukács's *History and Class Consciousness*, Bloch argued that the concept of totality should be "complicated with the concept of the sphere."[102] This, he argued, would eliminate the homogenous nature of the whole that results when it is understood in purely socioeconomic terms. It would allow, in Bloch's language, for the expression of "various levels of subject-object relations," and it was a consequence of "the laboriousness of founding the Kingdom that expresses itself in the temporal process as well as spatially in the creation of spheres." To Bloch and Kracauer, the Marxist reduction of reality to the economic and social realms could not reckon with the complexities of everyday experience. Bloch saw reality as possessing an "unfinished quality"; it was in the rough, crude, and still to be completed surfaces of the real (or in Kracauer's language, "the holes and tears") that the truth was to be found.[103]

The concept of spheres was thus adopted, as it would preserve this dimension of the real and prevent the model of totality from becoming homogeneous and exclusive.

Kracauer was familiar with Bloch's essay, and its content appears to have influenced him. In a letter written to Bloch in June 1926, he stated that the closing remarks of this piece had "thoroughly enlightened" him.[104] Moreover, the spatial metaphor of the spheres must have been sympathetic as he refers to this at a couple significant points in his early career. He confided to Löwenthal his intentions of writing a "gigantic Sphere-theory," and the metaphor also figures prominently in his study, *The Detective Novel*.[105] This latter work will be discussed in more detail below, but at this point I want to emphasize that this spatial metaphor was a crucial part of Kracauer's refashioned concept of totality, one that allowed him a more flexible model of social reality.[106] The spatial imagination of Kracauer the architect here overlapped with concepts that, to a reader of Kierkegaard, had definite theological implications.

Kracauer's response to Bloch's radical utopianism had, therefore, two facets: on the one hand, he was critical of Bloch's conflation of the political and the messianic, and on the other, he was not altogether hostile to the premises that lay behind this conflation. His response is a strategy of containment, a desire to coerce the unruly discourse of the messianic into different channels, leading to what he assumed would be a more fruitful engagement with contemporary realities. As his subsequent rapprochement with Bloch demonstrates, he was not simply repudiating the utopian furies; rather, he wanted to theorize a path by which the positive content of utopia could be mediated into a modern and secularized setting. This was a project of rethinking social reality; the imagination of Don Quixote had to be joined to the more prosaic observations of Sancho Panza.

Among the war books, Kracauer spoke of one as a countermodel to the early work of Bloch: *Paganism, Christianity, Judaism* by Max Brod, which appeared in 1921.[107] His positive judgment of this book of religious "confession" strikes an odd chord today. Neither as a philosopher of religion nor as a writer has Brod stimulated as much critical interest as, for instance, Rosenzweig and Bloch; even his admirers are slightly reserved in their assessment of his work.[108] Kracauer, however, argued that the book was a compelling work distinguished by its *"unconditional truthfulness, its religious intensity and its hesitant enthusiasm."*[109] He recommended it to Löwenthal as a model of how to write about "holy things" and he claimed to find in it "a confirmation of his own nature." Why Kracauer was so receptive to this book deserves some attention, as Brod's overt engagement with Judaism would seems at odds with the position on religion that Kracauer defended in his 1922 essay, "Those Who Wait."[110] Unfortunately, Kracauer did not put many of his comments on the book into print. Outside of his recommendations to Löwenthal and a positive reference to the work in his *Münzer* review, there are no other sources where he addresses the book. Nonetheless, some consideration of the themes and also the circumstances of its origin may elucidate why this work would have attracted Kracauer's interest in the early 1920s.

Brod has been described as "a spokesman of a perplexed generation," and his book attempted to show that Judaism was an answer to the social and political chaos of the postwar period.[111] *Paganism* was both a plea for a strengthened commitment to Judaism and a critique of contemporary culture and religion, both of which he argued had been complicit in the descent into war. Brod was one of many young Jewish intellectuals who resented the previous generation of their fathers, who they thought had abandoned Judaic tradition and the sense of rootedness that it had provided. In 1909, Brod heard Martin Buber speak in Prague, and he was impressed by his call for a return to Judaism, a message that was all the more urgent given the nationality conflicts of the late Habsburg Empire and the rise of anti-Semitism. By the time war had broken out Brod had not only returned to Judaism, he also had become a dedicated Zionist.

Brod's arguments concerned the status of intellectual and religious authority. His admiration for Buber meant that Brod had been appalled to find that Buber, as did many other religious intellectuals, welcomed the war in 1914, describing it as the "grace of rebirth."[112] His condemnation extended to all confessions, and he was just as harsh to what he saw as a Christian quietism, an "unofficial, inward, entirely honorable Christianity that through its indifference towards the worldly order, has in many ways enthroned every force of evil as the legal ruler of the here and now."[113] *Paganism* was a response to this alleged failure on the part of intellectuals and religious leaders, but it was also an argument about the role of intellectuals in general. The book continued a dispute that derived from his earlier plea for a more direct political engagement in the framework of religious faith, a dispute that had arisen from a clash of views between himself and his friend, the poet Franz Werfel. In 1917, Werfel had published an essay in the *Neue Rundschau*, arguing that in a "purely empirical society" the idea of religious redemption did not require political involvement.[114] To Brod this was a complete misunderstanding of what redemption meant, and his book was intended as a rebuttal to Werfel. Personal salvation, he argued, could not be separated from a commitment to secular affairs, and the war had made the perils of this position obvious:

> Beneath the bloody and hazy August sun of the first days of war, the long anticipated idea was strengthened in me: that we poets and writers had done too little, had bothered ourselves too little with the powers of reality ... for that reason I made a sharp distinction between the redemption of the world and that of the self, and I took a decisive position against "egocentrism" in which I could see nothing more than a refined emphasis on the self.[115]

Brod argued that the idea of redemption was a miraculous event that demanded a human response, even if humankind could in no way contribute to the messianic realm. He cited the story of Rabbi Simon bar Yochai whose recognition of the messianic miracle led him to practical work: "a miracle has been performed for our sake, declared the Rabbi, "therefore I shall establish a useful institution."[116] Redemption thus impelled political participation, but in contrast to Bloch, Brod was careful to stress that human action remained within the secular sphere. One could not simply leap from the everyday into revelation, and thus individuals have no actual role in bringing about redemption—a position with which Kracauer would have agreed.[117]

This distinction between a religious sphere and a secular one that existed under the sign of redemption had, so Brod argued, numerous ramifications, and many of these find an echo in Kracauer's writing. Individual freedom to act was mediated by the tension between the religious and secular spheres. According to Brod, the concept of grace (*Gnade*) allowed one "to obey one's desire in freedom, and to be of such a nature that one can yield to oneself while being in full agreement with the good."[118] In this way the individual comes into accord with the religious *Gemeinschaft* because only grace could compel individuals to love God and, in so doing, accept the frail and uncertain nature of humankind, what Brod called "noble misfortune." Similarly, without experiencing the world under the sign of the miracle, one could not achieve the highest acts of goodness in the profane world—the creation of useful institutions and the alleviation of avoidable suffering (what Brod called "ignoble misfortune"). Therefore, in spite of free will, the struggle against "ignoble misfortune" still required divine intervention: "the highest attainments were not possible through simple moral freedom."[119] Yet, individuals untouched by the "breath of God" were obliged to act in accordance with their understanding of moral obligation. The imperative to act against unnecessary suffering could not be evaded, though how one was to know if he or she inhabited a state of grace, and was thus acting with total freedom, was not clear.[120] How was a person to determine whether one's actions are due to providence or to an independent sense of moral obligation that anticipates redemption? This indeterminacy seemed to be a matter of design, because Brod argues that when God and religion "appear on the scene disorder enters the junkyard of our knowledge. Concepts are turned upside down, and all human things become nonsense, inessential, impure, evil."[121]

What Kracauer thought of this argument is a matter of speculation; but if one takes into account his response to other contemporary works that theorized the relationship between the secular and profane worlds, one suspects that he would not have been convinced by Brod's argument on this point. In his review of Martin Buber's *I and Thou*, for instance, he agreed with Buber's contention that the sphere of religion and reality mingled more often than was recognized; but he still argued that Buber had offered little to nothing in terms of how an individual could come to recognize this: how did one know when and where one spoke to the world as *Du* (Thou), as a creation of God and when as *es* (it), as one secular entity to another?[122] In general, Kracauer argued that Buber had set the bar between the secular and the profane "much too high." The realm of Thou, the realm of true reality, remains aloof from that of the "contingently existing humankind," and how the creator becomes manifest to individuals in the *Es-Welt* is not clear.[123] Similarly, the recognition of grace remained mysterious in Brod's account, yet if Kracauer thought the bar was too high, he may have found Brod's emphasis on material contingencies a more promising way of conceptualizing this problem. Engagement with the real was encouraged, but the messianic realm was kept at a distance.

Brod went further in his suggestion that a large part of modern culture had succumbed to a fusion of the material and the sacred realms, a modern form of paganism. He perceived this tendency in modern Christianity and in the culture of the late nineteenth century more generally. It was typified by a desire to find redemption in the here and now—a collapsing of the messianic into the material that deified the world as it was. He placed virtually the entirety of culture and social theory within this category: Darwinism, Nietzsche, Manchesterism, Socialism, Monism, Treitschke, and Scheler—the list goes on.[124] The latter two thinkers were of particular significance, as Brod believed their work pointed to an abandonment of the traditional Christian renunciation of the world that had, at least, the virtue of preserving the distinction between the religious and human spheres. By arguing that God was to be found in the world itself, they had veered dangerously towards paganism. Buber too was guilty of this error when he suggested that redemption could be equated with the material existence of the religious community.[125] Brod thus wanted to establish a boundary between worthy actions performed in recognition of the messianic and those actions undertaken in light of the mistaken belief that they built a bridge towards redemption.

Neo-paganism, according to Brod, erased the tension between the secular and religious spheres, confusing the material situation of the individual with spiritual redemption. The desire for personal salvation was not to be disparaged insofar as it responded to the messianic promise; but to retain its validity, the individual who sought redemption had to remain in a paradoxical tension that put the sacred in conflict with secular action. This paradox was deepened by the recognition that on the one hand, political engagement precluded the space needed for the individual reflection that would lead to a consciousness of God and, on the other, that such reflection was indispensable to a true recognition of the messianic. Hence, the individual was caught in an insoluble dilemma: either to wait passively and attend to his or her inwardness; or to pursue, in the words of Rabbi bar Yochai, the "establishment of useful institutions." Brod called this quandary the "incompatibility of the correlated." By arguing that all good deeds were, in fact, due to the intervention of God, he appears to have thought he had found a way out of this problem.[126] This dilemma had a wide cultural resonance. Max Weber's study of ancient Judaism had discussed a similar conflict between passivity and engagement, between utopian and pragmatic, a conflict that he believed was central to the Jewish worldview in antiquity.[127] Kracauer read this work, albeit with some reservations, shortly before writing his feuilleton "Those Who Wait," an essay that can be read as a response to Brod and Weber.[128] In this essay, the genesis of which will be discussed below, Kracauer sketched out an explicit position of waiting, a position that constituted a middle way between messianic utopianism and nihilist skepticism. The position is similar to that of Ulrich the protagonist of Musil's *Man without Qualities*.[129] He is also described as someone who is waiting, who has no clear profession and no clear direction in the world; rather, he seems to possess an acute if passive sensitivity towards experience, as if he were trapped in an anteroom, suspended between a belief in the need to act, and a recognition that there was in fact no concrete basis for it.

Waiting was connected to the idea of life as paradox. Brod suggested that one had to recognize and accept paradox as an essential condition. There was no point in trying to resolve it, rather one must persist within it. This had consequences in other spheres as well, and it stimulated a reconfiguration of his views on the relation between aesthetics and ethics. His reflections on aesthetic experience anticipated Kracauer's thought, especially his study of detective fiction. Brod argued that the messianic promise transfigured the world in a dual fashion; reality was undermined by a sense of "futility," but it was also punctuated by an "undeserved grace."[130] This dualism became a linchpin to his understanding of aesthetic experience:

> With this knowledge I renounced an earlier stage in which I was always astonished by the lacking parallelism between aesthetics and ethics. Here I saw the freedom of the Act; there I saw the unbidden nature of inspiration. Here lay "decency," so to say, in the street; everyone had the ability, but also the cursed obligation to be a good person; there lay no path for the citizen to follow, only for a few of the lonely chosen ones. Today I see that this "out in the street" decency was not to be equated with aesthetic dilettantism, but rather ... with honorable accomplishments, long worthy of attention, here and there, perhaps even with flashes of grace.[131]

Aesthetics thus appears to him as a kind of veil that conceals an ethical realm that approaches religious experience. That he found the latter "in the street" is suggestive of Kracauer's later argument that the way to the sacred passes through the profane; it is not in the old aesthetic forms that the path to the divine is found, but rather in the cultural ephemera of daily life. However, this connection must be stated with some caution, as Brod collapses the aesthetic into the moment of grace in a fashion that Kracauer would probably have found unconvincing. As Gertrud Koch has argued, Kracauer believed that access to the religious sphere was blocked; hence, his mode of reading the urban landscape emphasized the themes of disfigurement and negativity as a means of reading this blockage.[132] Nonetheless, Brod articulates a model for interpreting the quotidian cultural and social landscape, an attempt to cultivate aesthetic sensitivity as a means of recognizing religious "truth contents." In *Paganism*, however, Brod did not extend his analysis very far into the profane world; instead he devoted himself to interpreting religious figures who anticipated his views—such as Kierkegaard and Dante—and to the elicitation of new meanings from traditional religious texts. He criticized broad swaths of secular culture and contemporary religion, but few of these cultural manifestations were subjected to close scrutiny. Kracauer would, in contrast, turn decisively towards an analysis of the profane world.

For this reason, the connection to Brod can only be stated tenuously even if there are several themes in *Paganism* that anticipate Kracauer. There is a shared interest in Kierkegaard, part of a general wave of enthusiasm for the Danish theologian that will be discussed at more length below. Brod also discusses the music of Jacques Offenbach, for instance, as a "typically Jewish critic of the prolongation of visible ethics into invisible ones." He also refers to the dire working situation of the white-collar workers who suffer both from their economic misery and from an ideology that conceals it from them. Kracauer addressed both of these themes some years later in *The Salaried Masses* (1929) and *Jacques Offenbach and the Paris of His Time* (1937).[133] Even Brod's censure of the voluntary ethos that prevailed in the war-time military hospitals is similar to the description of this institution found in *Ginster*—both writers suggest that the zeal of civilian volunteers was deceptive, allowing them to feel they served a higher moral purpose without forcing them to confront the war as a complex moral dilemma.[134] Between the positions of Bloch and Brod, a tentative sketch of what Inka Mülder-Bach called Kracauer's "struggle on two frontiers" becomes clear. His critical project strives for an interpretation of modernity that uses theological concepts, but at the same time repudiates positive religiosity.[135] Between these frontiers Kracauer defined a space for criticism, suspended between the sacred and the profane.

Though often identified with Marxism, Kracauer's strategy of containment was also directed at the excesses of materialist theory as well. This was one of the reasons he was hostile to the later writings of Lukács. Though Kracauer conceded that the metaphysical idea of totality that Lukács constructed in the *Theory of the Novel* was untenable, he remained more sympathetic to this formulation than the later attempt to equate it with the socioeconomic role of the working classes. In response to Lukács's shift to Marxism, Kracauer commented that today the "aesthetic individual from Kierkegaard's *Either/ Or* would . . . have become a communist." Neither side of this equation could benefit, he argued; the utopian dimension of totality was lost if it excluded culture and theology, and Lukács, as Kracauer correctly argued, would fail to appease doctrinaire communists.[136]

Kracauer's fluctuating opinions concerning Lukács illuminate his attempts to draw from theologically tinged concepts while remaining rooted to a critical reading of the real. In the aftermath of the war Kracauer found the *Theory of the Novel* in agreement with his own gloomy diagnoses of postwar Germany.[137] According to a preface that Lukács wrote for the 1968 edition, the book had been written during the first years of the war "in a mood of permanent despair over the state of the world."[138] Originally, the book was to have consisted of several dialogues among a group of friends who retreated to the countryside in order to escape the "war psychosis." There they discussed the problems of cultural evolution as an indirect means of addressing the present crisis. Dropping this frame for the study did not in any way mute the political contexts; in their respective reviews, both Kracauer and Susman were quick to point out the contemporary relevance of the work. Lukács, so Kracauer stated, "looked into our historical-philosophical condition with an unheard of urgency."[139] His idea of totality, moreover, was a means of integrating culture in a larger social and political framework, one that conceived of cultural evolution in terms of changing "historic-philosophical realities." As Lukács later observed, this was in accord with the resurgent Hegelian influence in contemporary philosophy.[140]

Putting these points of agreement to one side, it is still somewhat surprising, and indicative of the postwar intellectual climate, that Kracauer with his stated resistance to metaphysical systems overlooked the seemingly obvious weaknesses of Lukács's concept of totality.[141] Aside from its romanticism, its teleological assumptions led to a narrative of decline. The present was perceived as an age of decay. From the closed "totality of life" in the Homeric period when artistic expression readily found forms commensurate to the truths they were to embody, society had entered a world of "absolute sinfulness."[142] The novel was the representative form of this fallen world; its preponderant use of irony was symptomatic of the negativity of modern art, as if it could only expose the depth of what had been lost. As Kracauer stated in his review, "irony is the self-correction of the fragmentary; it is the highest freedom that is possible in a world without God." "Not without reason," he continued, had Lukács called irony the "negative mysticism of a godless age."[143] The evolution of culture had thus led to a point where the novel could, at most, perform its critical function in terms of negative aesthetics. This would express the distance we had travelled from the "reality-become-song" of a closed culture; the arts subsequent to this decline were, at their best, stamped by a "sorrowful lightness," as in the work of Cervantes, for instance, a ghostly reminder of the epic age and its lost wholeness.[144] Later, when Kracauer referred to a "light sorrow" (*hellen Trauer*) in his review of Joseph Roth's *Flight without End*, he was almost certainly referring to these words from *Theory of the Novel*.[145]

This narrative of decline recalls Simmel's "tragedy of culture." The gap between form and content, between subjective and objective culture, was expressed anew in the alleged impossibility of "closed" cultural forms; instead culture was given a negative function that alluded to its own shortcomings in a persistently minor key.[146] Simmel, of course, had also influenced the younger Lukács, and his pessimistic strand of *Lebensphilosophie* appears as a kind of residue of this. However, even though Lukács did not point to an easy way out of the cultural-historical dilemma, he did indicate potential signs of renewal, in particular, the novels of Dostoevsky. In these works the world is "drawn for the first time simply as a seen reality," whereas in general the novel reflected the fact that "the extensive totality of life is no longer directly given . . . the immanence of meaning in life has become a problem."[147]

The cultural prestige awarded to Dostoevsky was not uncommon, especially among those inclined towards a revolutionary culturalism. As one contemporary observed, "the red Piper editions of his novels glared from every writing desk."[148] Writing in the middle of the 1930s, Kracauer offered a skeptical portrayal of this postwar "Dostoevsky cult." In a scene from *Georg*, the protagonist attends a party full of bourgeois socialists and aspiring revolutionaries. He finds among the solid furniture and glass vitrines a copy of *The Brothers Karamazov* sitting ostentatiously on a table, bound in a garish red cover strikingly at odds with its sober surroundings. The very appearance of the book in this setting was a form of provocation; the reading of Dostoevsky was practically a declaration of revolutionary faith and a testament of one's opposition to pure secularism. Just before the party ends and Georg departs, the lights that have been out all evening on account of an ongoing worker's strike come on again, and a woman begins to sing: "The messiah can dwell within us every hour."[149] The chiliastic tradition thus blends with the pseudo-revolution while the novels of Dostoevsky "glare" from the dining room table.

Kracauer believed that such revolutionary mysticism was a specialty of the "revolutionary culturists."[150] The proximity of these two traditions found expression in the work of Thomas Mann, especially in the figure of the fearsome Jesuit, Naphta, a character supposedly modelled on Lukács. For Kracauer too, at least until 1925, the theorization of culture could not be separated from theological concepts. It offered a means of guarding culture from deterministic arguments that reduced it to mere superstructure, while also curbing an excessive belief in the ability of culture in and of itself to perfect human existence. Religion constituted a challenge to both of these threats, hence Kracauer's reluctance to dispense with religious concepts entirely and his desire to find their modern and secular guise. The strategy of containment described above is again evident, barring the way to the extremes of disbelief and religious renewal. If Kracauer believed that religion could no longer function as a unifying force, this did not give unlimited license to culture to step into the void that religion left behind. The way to the sacred was through the profane, but this meant that the profane had to avoid all attempts at sacralization.

The Siren-Song of Decline: Cultural Despair and Religious Revival

Utopian and messianic literature formed one of the poles of the postwar discourse on culture; the opposing pole was the literature of cultural decline. An element of this was certainly inherent in the work of Lukács, but its most sensational exponent was Oswald Spengler. His *Decline of the West* generated wide interest, particularly, but by no means only, among intellectuals.[151] As the large number of contemporary publications devoted to attacking or, more rarely, defending Spengler suggest, *Decline* was big news; one scholar of his work described 1919, with some exaggeration perhaps, as the "Spengler year."[152] In Germany, the twin catastrophes of defeat and revolution readily lent credence to the thesis of downfall; the events of those years, moreover, appeared to confirm the dreary predictions of cultural pessimism that circulated during the last years of the *Kaiserreich* and with which Spengler's work shared some affinities. However, responses to *Decline* were not limited to those critics who specialized in the rhetoric of crisis.[153] Scientists entered the fray, commenting on how Spengler's thesis measured up to the current state of research; mathematicians joined in, as did of course, historians, sociologists, and theologians. Among the prominent intellectuals impressed by Spengler were Count Keyserling, Thomas Mann, Ludwig Wittgenstein, Hans Jonas, and Gottfried Benn; a volume of the philosophy periodical *Logos* was devoted to a discussion of *Decline*, and Theodor Heuss remarked on the intense interest it had stirred in the public.[154] Among Kracauer's contemporaries in Frankfurt, even Rosenzweig responded with appreciation, at least at first. He wrote to his friend Rudolf Ehrenberg that he had been considerably impressed by *Decline*, which he called the "greatest work of historical philosophy to appear since Hegel."[155]

Given the wide interest and controversy incited by Spengler, there is little surprise that opinions on his work diverged widely. However, even some of his detractors felt obliged to admit that in spite of his failings he had provoked a wide-ranging and potentially useful discussion. At a public lecture at Frankfurt University sponsored by the German Historical Society and the Prussian Association of Philologists, Kracauer observed that most speakers admitted that the public debate stimulated by Spengler might yield "new insights into the intellectual framework of world history."[156]

Due to his obligations as a local reporter, Kracauer became well acquainted with the debate over Decline. He wrote on Spengler no less than seven times after joining the FZ. Many of the public lectures he attended and publications he reviewed emerged at least two years after the high water mark of the "Spengler year" in 1919, which suggests that, at least in Frankfurt, the Spengler phenomenon continued to fascinate; his rapid disappearance from media attention did not mean that he was entirely "old hat."[157] Even if more people bought the book than actually read it, his general argument was widely known and as a result was difficult to ignore.

Kracauer read Spengler with curiosity and unease. He was unconvinced by the thesis of inevitable cultural decay, but he was intrigued by the debate that surrounded Spengler. In his study of Simmel, he refers to Decline, and elsewhere he described the work as "brilliant" (*geistvoll*).[158] Classical historian Eduard Meyer suggested that Spengler struck a chord among those who were "oppressed by the feeling that [they were] decadents," and Kracauer, as we have seen, was susceptible to similar misgivings.[159] Spengler thus provoked a reconsideration of some of his earlier musings on the "decadent" young men of the coffee houses, and the theme of Decline became an important reference point in his work of the early 1920s. Yet, it was more the reception of Decline that excited his interest, rather than an evaluation of its argument. The outcry it provoked and the excitement it awakened were just as important as an understanding of its central theses, for the idea of downfall could have its uses as a tool of both cultural criticism and religious revival. The gloomy harbingers of the coming catastrophe, he argued, existed in a necessary tension with the prophets of religious revival; they were, in fact, two sides of the same coin.[160] They both thrived in a mood of uncertainty that excited awe and mystery in the face of the vast riddle posed by the depths of historical time and the inscrutable nature of divine providence.

Thus, Kracauer's critique of Spengler focused just as much on the discourse generated by Decline. Writing in early 1921, he pointed out that Spengler's opponents failed to address the core issues at stake in his work. Such critiques, he argued, "remained on the surface" because they failed to recognize that Decline was a work of broad synthesis that could not be dismantled by the minute analyses of experts who stayed within the confines of their own disciplines. Having observed its subject matter "from a distance," Decline required either an equally ambitious work of synthesis to refute it, or a more sustained attack on its method. That Spengler's work was guilty of numerous errors of fact and historical judgment did not fatally damage his reputation so long as these points of attack were never integrated into arguments that would rival Spengler's model of world history.[161] Moreover, he argued that many critics hostile to the relativist implications of Decline thought that it sufficed merely to accuse it of relativism; they did not recognize that they needed to go further and propose a foundation from which they could counter this dimension of his work (a project that Kracauer at one time had also hoped to achieve).[162] As a result, rather than exposing Spengler's weaknesses, his critics had only demonstrated their own. A special issue of the academic journal *Logos* that tried to establish a firewall around Spengler was representative of this tendency. Adorno later recollected that this anthology of fastidious critiques written in a pedantic tone did almost nothing to diminish the aura that hung over Spengler and his book.[163] Indeed, the narrow points of view they represented seemed to only confirm the strength of his hypothesis; knowledge had decayed and fragmented, and the intensive specialization of the natural and human sciences, often on display in the criticism of Spengler, were signs of this.[164]

In the several articles Kracauer wrote on Spengler, there is a noticeable shift in how he thought Spengler should be opposed. In December 1921, he had argued that the Spengler thesis required a comprehensive refutation, one that only a religious or metaphysical rebuttal could provide:

> In order to root out his work and to see it for what it in truth is—a godless testimony of a godless age . . . it needs the norms of a metaphysically oriented and positive image of the world [*Weltbild*], the existence of which first offers the possibility of dissolving and annihilating [Spengler's] position.[165]

He did not offer such an alternative, but he was certainly aware of this as a potential response. In the fall of 1921, Kracauer attended a lecture that suggested religion could fill precisely this role. The lecture, entitled "Christianity and Spengler," was given by the Protestant theologian Willy Lüttge and sponsored by the Deutsch-evangelischen Volksvereinigung. Lüttge argued that there was a visible historical development towards intellectual and spiritual unity that found its highest expression in religion, and since this had prevailed in numerous cultures over successive ages, it could not be subject to the cyclical patterns of rise and fall described by Spengler. Therefore, it was possible to speak of religion as a force that transcended individual cultures.[166] On the other hand, Lüttge lauded Spengler insofar as he believed that *Decline* had undermined the "modern idols of progress." Overall, Kracauer's discussion of Lüttge is neutral; he neither affirms nor explicitly disagrees with his efforts to displace Spengler's conception of world history with a Christian one. However, given his conviction that Spengler could only be refuted by way of a comprehensive and metaphysical argument, it is probable that he at least thought Lüttge was proceeding in the right direction.

However, by 1923 Kracauer had more or less abandoned this position. He now argued that a comprehensively metaphysical or religious conception of the world was actually part of the problem, rather than a solution to cultural crisis. Kracauer's article "Downfall?" that appeared in the *FZ* in October 1923, suggested that both Spengler's *Decline* and the totalizing visions of his opponents were guilty of the same errors. All such philosophical-historical interpretations were marred by their adoption of a "birds-eye point of view" (*Vogelschau*); they reckoned with the whole of world history, yet they failed to reckon with their own position within it. As he stated: "the viewpoint of world history opens itself to them precisely in the moment in which they abandon their viewpoint over actual life."[167] This meant that they had blinded themselves to any consideration of their own historical contingency; as a result, their interpretations were invalid. On this point, Kracauer was not siding with Spengler's academic critics; instead he was insisting on the "worm's point of view" that he admired in Simmel, a view that was taken from "below to above" and eschewed totalizing perspectives.[168] According to Kracauer, both the rational means of scientific method and the abstract viewpoint of Spenglerian world history failed in this respect. For if the sciences had abandoned the real through abstraction, Spengler had committed no less an error by believing he could stand above global history without reflecting on "his own connectedness to a quite concretely defined situation."[169] Genuine historical knowledge, he suggested, could not be derived solely from abstraction; rather, it must be confronted and tested against historical contingencies. This theme persisted throughout his work and reappeared in his posthumous book, *History*, as a critique of macro-historical perspectives. This type of history, so he claimed, yielded well-constructed arguments of cause and effect, but not an account of what these events meant for living individuals.[170]

There was also a theological aspect to Kracauer's critique. Indeed, he argued, it may happen that Germany will vanish; however, "the question of decline, insofar as it is understood as a necessary historical event, is falsely put and must... remain without answer."[171] By attempting to respond to this question, Spengler had misappropriated the divine point of view, for only a God could witness history in its entirety. Therefore, judgments concerning the purpose of the world-historical process were simply outside human knowing. On this point, Kracauer quoted from Kierkegaard, arguing that God alone bore witness to the "ethical development" of "existing spirit," and only a God could exist as both spectator and participant. Individuals, on the other hand, could only observe life from the stage itself; all their theories and conclusions were of necessity limited by this fact.[172]

If anything, Kracauer argued, the world-historical perspective was itself a symptom of decline, and it mattered little whether it was used to encourage the present to accept its fate with steely resolution (Spengler), or whether it sought to build heaven on earth (Bloch). In the religious currents of the present, the "death of culture" sounded as a warning blast of the apocalyptic trumpet, heralding the birth of the new.[173] This gesture appeared in many guises, and Kracauer thought it lay behind the incessant cries for the "new man, the new society, the new art, the new religion." The discourse of decline undermined and condemned the present; it demanded the replacement of a sham decadent culture with one devoted to the unfettered spirit, to historical destiny, or to a unity with God. As the fears stemming from the "spooks of downfall" continued to "creep in," Kracauer argued, so the fervent calls for spiritual renewal became ever more strident.[174]

For Kracauer, this amounted to a psychic clutter that obscured an important intellectual issue. The twin discourses of cultural decay and religious renewal did not, so he believed, enrich the debate on social reality, for instead of provoking reflection, they choked the public sphere with dubious words of religious authenticity. Therefore, this "sphere of world-historical prophecy" had become a hindrance to a meaningful engagement with social reality and, indeed, also to the vision of a revived religion that it claimed as its goal. Instead, these discourses leapt over such realities or "chattered them away."[175] Judaism and Christianity, insofar as they welcomed this flight from the real, could thus be counted among the "vagabond religions" of the postwar period, religions that attracted what Kracauer uncharitably called the "short-circuit person," those who sought immediate refuge from the present age by way of religion.[176] Against these utopian excess and revivalist impulses, Kracauer sought instead for a "holy sobriety," a religion that made no claims for itself as such. Thus, it is entirely in keeping that he quotes Goethe again at the conclusion of his discussion of the *Decline* phenomenon:

> The hard tasks' daily perpetuation
> Requires nothing of revelation.[177]

* * * * *

Reading these postwar texts in light of how Kracauer responded to them demonstrates that he was trying to define a median course for his critical project—a position that lay somewhere between the discourses of utopian imagination and historical relativism, between the messianic and the materialist, between late imperial cultural criticism and the radical impulses of the first years of the republic. This is very much a negative position that locates itself in critical method and avoids positive statements regarding the truth or untruth of religious or metaphysical propositions. As he later wrote to Löwenthal, the "positive word is not ours."[178] However, that was in 1924, and in the first years following the war, he shows some uncertainty concerning how much one could or could not say in regards to this question—hence, his enthusiasm for the work of Max Brod. His ambivalence towards religion does not amount to a convinced secularism or a denial of religion. In the following chapters, I argue that Kracauer had to work past this ambivalence and conceptualize the place of religion in such a way that he would be free to turn to mass culture without reserve; once religion was set apart into its own sphere, the secular could become his main area of concern. The war books were a significant part of this process, as they led Kracauer into a confrontation between the intellectual baggage he had acquired prior to 1914 and an altered political and social reality.

The abandonment of religious themes in Kracauer's work should not be confused with a blanket repudiation of religion.[179] As we have seen, when he criticized Scheler and Bloch, he justified his arguments by claiming to find agreement among other religious individuals. An unpublished essay of 1929 offers an insight into how he viewed religion in light of his critical intentions. The essay was a discussion of Max Picard's *The Face of Man*, and it contained a rare personal statement of his attitudes towards theology and politics. Part of the essay consists of a letter he addressed to Picard wherein he argued that the more emotive language of theology had to be avoided: "so-called religious declarations [*Aussagen*], every declaration even, which in a direct and unbroken fashion addresses the intellect are . . . reactionary." Such language excited the passions of faith, and those who respond to it would "feel themselves . . . stirred in their souls and hold themselves to be saved." They would confuse their fervor with religious truth and, as a result, they would forgo the work of thinking through their actual position in a given social context. Hence, Kracauer decided to discuss theology only by means of "negative constellations"—a kind of "bracketing off" of religious questions.[180] Such an approach, he believed, was the only legitimate mode of religious discourse, as it corresponded to the limitations placed upon it by a largely secularized society. As he wrote to Löwenthal, what some considered religious was to his mind "blasphemous," a mode of language and conduct that was without legitimacy.[181]

Even Kracauer's increased interest in Marxism during the mid-1920s may have had a theological impetus. In 1926 Walter Benjamin received a letter from Gottfried Salomon-Delatour, a childhood friend of Kracauer who later taught at the University of Frankfurt, which offers insight into Kracauer's thinking in this period. Kracauer, so Salomon-Delatour reported, had returned home from a visit to Berlin in 1926 enthralled by his reading of Marx. Influenced by Carl Grünberg, he had embarked on a study of Marxism and the "Judaic-Christian roots of materialism."[182] Hence, his critique of religion needs to be understood in light of his belief that religion and materialism were not mutually exclusive. His claim that the truth contents of religion must undergo a kind of transformation or a period of "wandering" in modern society was an attempt to reckon with the imbrications between secular and religious thought. Still, if he implied that religion must in some sense become secular, he nonetheless refused the equation of religion with either the national community or the socialist revolution.

To secularize theological concepts meant a rethinking of the relationship between religion and culture. For Marx, all criticism was in effect criticism of religion, and this was a position with which Kracauer would have had some sympathy.[183] The very existence of cultural criticism presupposed an interpretive authority outside of religious institutions, as well as the interrogation of ideas and concepts found in religious traditions. This meant an end to the idea of a "closed culture," which is why he eventually repudiated the idea of a comprehensive metaphysical world view as a means of countering the influence of Spengler. Instead of being uniform and whole, culture was to be understood as heterogeneous, as riven with fissures and contradictions. Paradoxically, the idea of the religious totality now functioned as an effective critique of culture, as the idea of a world under the sign of redemption and perfected by divine grace, would serve to illuminate its fissures and contradictions. This was a revolutionary function as it allowed one to resist the "merely existent," to not allow empiricism to take an absolute hold over thought.

The implications of this expanded but heterogeneous definition of culture emerges in a later critique of Spengler that his friend Adorno published in 1950.[184] Spengler, according to Adorno, understood culture as a narrow domain, relegated to a mere adjunct of the material conditions of life. Culture was something that happened only *after* the material needs of society were met. For Adorno, however, culture was there from the beginning, intertwined within every aspect of human relations, and defining the nature of our material needs and interrogating them through a conjuring up of alternative states of affairs.[185] Culture was thus part of a dialectic, rather than a sphere that was separated from the material struggles of life. This meant that Spengler, rather than truly investigating the capacity of thought, simply excluded it from the core processes that determined his vision of world history. However, for Adorno and Kracauer the critical capacity of thought could serve a utopian function, confronting the contingencies of individual existence with a zone of moral and philosophical questioning. For Kracauer it meant opposition to all models of reality that presented culture as a settled affair, or capable of becoming so—whether such models were religious, messianic, or secular in origin.

* * * * *

All of the books considered in this chapter blended modernity with tradition as part of a search for a definite ground from which one could act. The recovery of the past could help to regenerate the present, not simply by its mere importation but rather by forging something new.[186] The recovery of past traditions and mysteries would regenerate the present. As Michael Brenner has argued in respect to the Jewish renaissance of Weimar Germany, the recovery of religion is at least one part "modern innovation," a partial refashioning of tradition.[187] After 1918, such refashioning seemed justified as religions had to speak for a century that had begun with visions of infinite progress and then lapsed into sudden catastrophe.

Catastrophe and violence, moreover, could be assimilated to visions of a new order. The modernist penchant for violence and destruction is a constant thread among the war books, and Kracauer too participated in this discourse. As Michael Schröter demonstrates, tropes of violence are strikingly prevalent in his writing.[188] In *Ginster*, individuals are imagined in a state of dismemberment as the violence of the war reaches into the consciousness of the home front. A visit to a baroque palace in Würzburg provokes Ginster's anger towards the cultural relics of the past, and he longs to see the archaic facades blown apart and smashed into rubble.[189] In *Georg*, as already discussed, the protagonist entertained repressed desires of violence as he visited the burned-out theatre. Schröter comments that these destructive desires are often connected with a desire for root and branch reconstruction; hence, they are the necessary precursor to a new order. In this respect, he is in accord with some of the violent imaginings of his friends, Bloch and Benjamin, both of whom considered the role of violence in the creation of the new.[190]

Still, Bloch and Benjamin opposed the war, while Kracauer was more uncertain of his position. The repudiation of the war, of course, is not the same as nonviolence. As Lukács stated, he would have welcomed the war as a means of bringing the old Hohenzollern and Habsburg monarchies to their knees; what he feared was the larger problem of "who was to save us from western civilization."[191] Bloch peppered his discussion of apocalypse with a rhetoric of violence. "Death's accomplishment," he intoned, "is thus to furnish a journeyman's test of ourselves."[192] Looking back to the work of Georges Sorel, revolutionary violence thus conferred meaning on life and on legitimate historical causes, giving them existential depth. In his 1923 revision of *Spirit of Utopia*, he wrote that "it is necessary to confront power in terms of power, as a categorical imperative with a revolver in its hand."[193] Such rhetoric was not intended to be only figurative; even if their influence was limited, they did not see culture as a safe haven removed from political events. Indeed, both writers would become entangled with the politics of revolutionary violence.[194] Thus, the critique of the world "as it is" had political implications. As Leo Löwenthal later remarked, his reading of Lukács as a young man had incited his hatred towards the "infamy of the existent."[195] One should not accept the status quo, but constantly set the utopian vision above and against it. The present situation became one of oppression, a hindrance to be overcome by the revolutionary spirit. He later described some of his own activities at the time, studying in the experimental "Torah-peutic" institute run by Frieda Reichmann, as a kind of revolutionary cult with a strong admixture of Freud and Marx.[196] Such views did not, of course, lend themselves to a pacifist mood.

If Kracauer participates in this discourse, he does with a difference. Much of the violence that appears in his work is imagined, directed towards expressing forms of violence already latent in the existing order. Such violence could be read as a means of representing a mental state of anxious passivity, as Schröter suggests. Even if the choice of figurative language is symptomatic, it does not necessarily constitute a call to arms. His approach was more ambiguous, and as Joseph Roth stated in his review of *Ginster*, the book would please neither militarists nor pacifists.[197] Violence and the vulnerability to violence become leitmotifs in his work, but they are integrated into a discourse of threatened subjectivity, an exposed inwardness at the mercy of implacable forces of rationalization.[198] Hence, violence is more often the imposition of an external force, more oppressive than liberating, and rarely celebrated as healing purgative. He would probably have been more sympathetic to the views of one French soldier who found in the war a triumph of instrumental reason and its accompanying violence: "Unbiased culture has had its day. Mankind is giving way to human materiel according to the expression the war has already made familiar. The Renaissance is bankrupt. The German factory is absorbing the world."[199]

In the aftermath of the war, a time given over to a wide array of radical imaginings, coups, and revolutions, Kracauer argued for a passive but attentive attitude towards the present, a position that he felt was truly radical in an age that glorified dynamism for its own sake. In his journalism of these years, he investigated religious currents for signs that confirmed or opposed this belief, and this subject will be further explored in the next chapters.

Notes

1. Klemperer, *Curriculum Vitae II*, 172–73.
2. Klemperer, *Curriculum Vitae II*, 29, 172, and 183.
3. Klemperer, *Curriculum Vitae II*, 357.
4. Brodersen, *Siegfried Kracauer*, 20–22.
5. Klemperer, *Curriculum Vitae II*, 179 and 183. In *Ginster* the protagonist similarly tries to avoid looking too foreign, see *Werke* 7, 16.
6. Klemperer, *Curriculum Vitae II*, 185–86 and 189.
7. See Friedel [Siegfried] Kracauer, "Auf der großen Fahrt," in Belke and Renz, *Siegfried Kracauer*, 26.
8. Kracauer to Simmel, 30 November 1917, *Gesamtausgabe* 23, 880–84.
9. Max Scheler, "Zur religiösen Erneuerung," *Hochland* 16 (October 1918): 15.
10. Scheler, *Krieg und Aufbau* (Leipzig, 1916). See Kracauer's review "Neue Bücher," *Das neue Deutschland*, 15 May 1917, *Werke* 5.1, 24–29.
11. Hermann Lübbe, *Politische Philosophie in Deutschland: Studien zu ihrer Geschichte* (Munich, 1974), 217–22.
12. Scheler quoted in Lübbe, *Politische Philosophie*, 221.

13. Kracauer, "Neue Bücher," *Werke* 5.1, 26–29; and Scheler, *Die Ursachen des Deutschenhasses: Eine nationalpädagogisch Erörterung* (Leipzig, 1917), 25 and 123–24.
14. Kracauer, "Krieg und Aufbau," *Werke* 5.1, 28–29.
15. Kracauer, "Max Scheler†," *FZ*, 22 May 1928, *Werke*, 5.3, 22–25. See also the comments in Lübbe, *Politische Philosophie*, 222–23; and Herbert Spiegelberg, *The Phenomenological Movement: A Historical Introduction* I, 2nd ed., 2 vols. (The Hague, 1965), 233; Spiegelberg points out that even in *The Genius of War* there was still a concern for the "spiritual unity of Europe."
16. John Rafael Staude, *Max Scheler, 1874–1928: An Intellectual Portrait* (New York, 1967), 87.
17. Kracauer identified Scheler as the model for Caspari in a letter to Walter Benjamin, see Kracauer to Benjamin, 7 November 1927, in Benjamin, *Briefe an Siegfried Kracauer: Marbacher Magazin* 27 (Stuttgart, 1988), 53–54; also see Belke and Renz, *Siegfried Kracauer*, 27–28.
18. Scheler, the child of a mixed marriage, had a Jewish mother. For a brief period following his father's death, both he and his mother lived with his Jewish uncle in an observant household. Scheler later fled and converted to Catholicism. His relationship to the Catholic Church, however, was uneasy. According to Kracauer, he later grew distant from the church as he thought Catholicism was a "hindrance to the development of Western metaphysics"; see Kracauer, "Max Scheler†," *Werke* 5.3, 26; and for biographical details, Staude, *Max Scheler*, 1–28.
19. Scheler's letters to Kracauer between 1916 and 1921 are in KN, DLA. Unfortunately, Kracauer's side of the correspondence has not been preserved. Though, in general, Kracauer appears to have received some encouragement from Scheler, this was not always the case. Scheler returned Kracauer's *Sociology as Science* without comment, a gesture that appears to have offended Kracauer.
20. Kracauer, *Werke* 7, 123–33.
21. Kracauer seems to have been unaware that Scheler suffered from an eye affliction.
22. Kracauer, *Werke* 7, 129.
23. See the comments in Brodersen. *Siegfried Kracauer*, 21–22.
24. Kracauer, *Werke* 7, 127; and Scheler, *Die Ursachen des Deutschenhasses*, 168–69.
25. Kracauer, "Vom Erleben des Kriegs," *Schriften* 5.1, 11–22, esp. 13–14.
26. Scheler, *Die Ursachen des Deutschenhasses*, 168–69.
27. Kracauer, "Vom Erleben des Kriegs," *Preußischer Jahrbücher* (September 1915), *Werke* 5.1, 11–24.
28. Kracauer, *Werke* 5.1, 11–12 and 18.
29. Scheler to Kracauer, 1 December 1916, in Belke and Renz, *Siegfried Kracauer*, 27.
30. Kracauer to Susman, 21 February 1920, SN, DLA. See the comments on this letter in Belke, "Siegfried Kracauer als Beobachter," 23–24.
31. Kracauer, *Werke* 7, 324–27. This scene will be discussed in more detail below. Adorno, who also was briefly tempted by Catholicism, may have provided a model for this scene. See Stefan Müller-Doohm, *Adorno: A Biography*, trans. Rodney Livingstone (Cambridge, 2005), 20.
32. Kracauer to Susman, 2 April 1921, SN, DLA.
33. Adorno, "Curious Realist," 163–64.
34. Kracauer, "Vom Erleben des Kriegs," *Werke* 5.1, 23.
35. Spiegelberg, *Phenomenological Movement* I, 228–31; and Susman, "Die Exodus."

36. Adorno, "Curious Realist," 163. Cf. his remarks on Scheler in his inaugural address at the University of Frankfurt in 1931, "The Actuality of Philosophy," *Telos* 31 (Spring 1977): 121–22.
37. Kracauer, "Catholicism and Relativism: On Max Scheler's *On the Eternal in Man*," FZ, 19 November 1921, in *Mass Ornament*, 203–11.
38. Scheler, "Phänomenologie und Erkenntnis," *Schriften aus dem Nachlass I: Zum Ethik und Erkenntnislehre*, ed. Maria Scheler (Bern, 1957), 380–81.
39. Adorno, "Curious Realist," 163.
40. See the discussion in Koch, *Siegfried Kracauer*, 11–15. In contrast to Adorno, Koch gives more emphasis to the influence of Husserl rather than Scheler.
41. Kracauer, "Soziologie als Wissenschaft," *Werke* 1, 97; Koch, *Siegfried Kracauer*, 11–14.
42. Kracauer, "Catholicism and Relativism," in *Mass Ornament*, 203–11.
43. Kracauer, *Mass Ornament*, 205–7.
44. Kracauer to Susman, 17 September 1921, SN, DLA.
45. Adorno, "Actuality of Philosophy," 122.
46. In his letter to Susman on 17 September 1921, he said he that the article had been read by both Weiger and Michel, and that both had expressed their agreement (SN, DLA). Ernst Michel was a radical voice among Frankfurt Catholics—a supporter of socialism and a member of the Academy of Labor in Frankfurt, founded by Eugen Rosenstock-Huessy. Among his acquaintances in Frankfurt were Adorno, Buber, Tillich, and Hendrik de Man; see Bruno Lowitsch, *Der Kreis um die Rhein-Mainische Volkszeitung* (Wiesbaden and Frankfurt, 1980), 36–39. Weiger was a close associate of Romano Guardini, an exponent of the influential Liturgy movement that grew out of the nearby abbey of Maria Laach.
47. Löwenthal, *Mitmachen wollte ich nie*, 92.
48. Kracauer, "Georg," *Werke* 7, 305–7.
49. Kracauer, *Werke* 7, 306.
50. Kracauer, *Werke* 7, 307.
51. Hermann Keyserling, *The World in the Making: Die neuentstehende Welt* (London, 1927), 140.
52. Walter Benjamin, *Illuminations: Essays and Reflections*, trans. Harry Zohn (New York, 1969), 253–64.
53. See Allen Janik, "Haecker, Kierkegaard, and the Early *Brenner*: A Contribution to the History of the Reception of *Two Ages*," in *International Kierkegaard Commentary: Two Ages*, ed. Robert L. Perkins (Macon, 1984), 189–222.
54. Janik, "Haecker, Kierkegaard, and the Early *Brenner*," 217–22; and Theodor Haecker, "Nachwort," *Der Brenner* 4, no. 20 (15 July 1914): 886–908.
55. Rosenzweig, "Apologetic Thinking," in *Philosophical and Theological Writings*, 95–108. On Jewish intellectuals and postwar messianic traditions, see Rabinbach, *In the Shadow of Catastrophe*, 30–32.
56. Rosenzweig, "Apologetic Thinking," 102.
57. Kracauer, "Vom Erleben des Kriegs," *Werke* 5.1, 20. Graf also speaks of a *Frontgeneration* among the religious revival, see "God's Anti-Liberal Avant-Garde," 5–10; and Stephen Eric Bronner, *Modernism at the Barricades: Aesthetics, Politics, Utopia* (New York, 2012), 21–31.

58. This expression is used by Enzo Traverso for the title of his study, *Siegfried Kracauer: itinéraire d'un intellectuel nomade*. See also Pierre Bourdieu, *The Field of Cultural Production: Essays on Art and Literature* (New York, 1993).
59. Kracauer to Susman, 26 July 1920, SN, DLA.
60. Musil, "Literature and Literati," in *Precision and Soul: Essays and Addresses* (Chicago and London, 1990), 70.
61. Kracauer, "Minimal Forderung an die Intellektuellen," *Die Neue Rundschau* (July 1931), in *Der verbotene Blick*, 247–52.
62. Kracauer distinguishes between the instrumental reason of *ratio* and one that is oriented toward humanity, see "The Mass Ornament," *Mass Ornament*, 80–81; and the discussion in Koch, *Siegfried Kracauer*, 34–35.
63. Hansen, "Decentric Perspectives," 51–54.
64. Kracauer to Susman, 10 February 1921, SN, DLA.
65. See George S. Williamson, *The Longing for Myth in Germany: Religion and Aesthetic Culture from Romanticism to Nietzsche* (Chicago, 2004).
66. Rabinbach, *In the Shadow of Catastrophe*, 53–57. For the account involving the German censor, see Peter Zudeick, *Der Hintern des Teufels: Ernst Bloch, Leben und Werk* (Moos, 1985), 69.
67. Susman, "Geist der Utopie," in Susman, *"Das Nah- und Fernsein des Fremden:" Essays und Briefe*, ed. Ingeborg Nordmann (Frankfurt am Main, 1992), 22–30, here 22.
68. Landauer quoted in Rabinbach, *In the Shadow of Catastrophe*, 226, n. 159.
69. Benjamin quoted in Rabinbach, *In the Shadow of Catastrophe*, 54.
70. Kracauer to Susman, 9 April 1921, SN, DLA.
71. Kracauer, "Prophetentum," *Werke* 5.1, 460–69.
72. See the comparison of Bloch and Simmel in Adorno, "Henkel, Krug und frühe Erfahrung," 93–97.
73. Jack Zipes, "Introduction: Toward a Realization of Anticipatory Illumination," in Ernst Bloch, *The Utopian Function of Art and Literature* (Cambridge, 1988), xi–xliii.
74. Bloch quoted in Rabinbach, *In the Shadow of Catastrophe*, 52.
75. Bloch to Kracauer, 20 May 1926, in *Ernst Bloch: Briefe, 1903 bis 1975* I, 2 vol., ed. Karola Bloch (Frankfurt am Main, 1985), 270.
76. See the discussion of *Vor-Schein* or "anticipatory illumination" in Zipes, "Introduction," in Bloch, *Utopian Function*, xxxiv–xxxvi.
77. Bloch, *Spirit of Utopia*, trans. Anthony Nassar (Stanford, 2000), 7.
78. Rabinbach, *In the Shadow of Catastrophe*, 45–46; and Zipes, "Introduction," in Bloch, *Utopian Function*, xv.
79. Bloch to Kracauer, 1 September 1922, *Briefe* 1, 266. Bloch refers to a study of language that he had written in the previous years and that has not survived.
80. See the critical remarks of Salomo Friedländer quoted in Rabinbach, *In the Shadow of Catastrophe*, 56.
81. Bloch, *Spirit of Utopia*, 171. For a passage that illustrates the formidable eclecticism of this work, see 167–73.
82. Bloch, *Spirit of Utopia*, 165–229; the passages on Kant and Hegel are on 173–87.
83. Bloch, *Spirit of Utopia*, 278.
84. Kracauer to Susman, no date (c. 1920) SN, DLA; and Kracauer to Löwenthal, 17 November 1921 and 4 December 1921, in *In steter Freundschaft*, 27–34.

85. Kracauer to Löwenthal, 16 December 1921, LLA, A 481/ 84–87, Leo Löwenthal Archiv, Johannes Senckenberg Bibliothek, Frankfurt am Main.
86. Kracauer, "Prophetentum," *Werke* 5.1, 465–66.
87. Kracauer to Löwenthal, 4 December 1921, in *In steter Freundschaft*, 31. For Kracauer, the messianic had to remain a matter of faith, not historical evidence, and such faith, as he states in this letter, he did not possess.
88. He used this word to describe Bloch's work in his letter to Löwenthal of 14 January 1921, in *In steter Freundschaft*, 19–20.
89. Kracauer to Susman, 21 July 1922, SN, DLA. Alfons Paquet (1881–1944) was a writer and journalist who had contributed to the *FZ* since 1903. He was a pacifist, and in 1933 he became a Quaker. He lived in Frankfurt until his death in an air raid.
90. Walter Benjamin, "Theological-Political Fragment," *Reflections: Essays, Aphorisms, Autobiographical Writings*, trans. Edmund Jephcott (New York, 1986), 312. As Rabinbach points out, the positive reference to Bloch that Benjamin places in this essay is highly ambiguous and it can be read as an objection to the general thrust of Bloch's thought; see Rabinbach, *In the Shadow of Catastrophe*, 59. Also, see Astrid Deuber-Mankowsky, "Walter Benjamin's *Theological-Political Fragment* as a response to Ernst Bloch's *Spirit of Utopia*," *Yearbook of the Leo Baeck Institute* 47 (2002): 3–19.
91. Kracauer, "Prophetentum," *Werke*, 5.1, 464.
92. Kracauer, "Prophetentum," *Werke*, 5.1, 465 and 467–68.
93. Kracauer, "Zwei Arten der Mitteilung," in *Der verbotene Blick*, 223.
94. Kracauer to Löwenthal, 14 January 1921, and 4 December 1921, in *In steter Freundschaft*, 18–22 and 34.
95. Bloch renewed the correspondence four years later. See his letter to Kracauer dated 20 May 1926, *Briefe: 1903 bis 1975* I, 269–71.
96. Kracauer to Bloch, 27 May 1926, *Briefe* 1, 274; Mülder, *Siegfried Kracauer—Grenzgänger*, 59–60.
97. Kracauer to Bloch, 27 May 1926, *Briefe* 1, 273–74.
98. Thomas Mann, "Goethe and Tolstoy," *Three Essays* (New York, 1929), 136. Kracauer heard Mann give this speech in connection with the 1922 *Frankfurter Goethe-Woche*; his article on the lecture appeared in the *FZ* on 1 March 1922, "Die Frankfurter Goethe-Woche," *Werke* 5.1, 379–83.
99. Jay, *Marxism and Totality*, 92–93.
100. Kracauer, "Georg von Lukács' Romantheorie," in *Der verbotene Blick*, 82.
101. Kracauer to Löwenthal, 14 January 1921, and 9 March 1922, in *In steter Freundschaft*, 20 and 42; and Kracauer to Bloch, 27 May 1926, *Briefe* 1, 274. Bloch defended Lukács in a letter to Kracauer, 6 June 1926, 275–78. On this theme in Kracauer's work more generally, see Miriam Hansen, *Cinema and Experience: Siegfried Kracauer, Walter Benjamin, Theodor W. Adorno* (Berkeley, 2011), 3–39.
102. Ernst Bloch, "Aktualität und Utopie: Zu Lukács *Geschichte und Klassenbewußtsein*," in *Philosophische Aufsätze zur objektiven Phantasie: Gesamtausgabe* 10 (Frankfurt am Main, 1969), 619. See also the discussion of this point in Jay, *Marxism and Totality*, 182–83. I have followed Jay's translation in the second passage quoted here.
103. Jay, *Marxism and Totality*, 183.
104. Kracauer to Bloch, 29 June 1926, *Briefe* 1, 281.

105. Kracauer to Löwenthal, 8 October 1924, in *In steter Freundschaft*, 63–64; and Kracauer, *Der Detektiv-Roman: Ein philosophischer Traktat* (Frankfurt am Main, 1979),11–28.
106. The sphere concept, as discussed by Mülder-Bach in her analysis of *The Detective Novel*, emphasizes a philosophical topography, but she draws attention to the importance of spatial images in his work more generally, see Mülder, *Siegfried Kracauer—Grenzgänger*, 40–41 and 61. On his spatial thinking see also Koch, *Siegfried Kracauer*, 28–31.
107. Max Brod, *Heidentum, Christentum, Judentum: Ein Bekenntnisbuch*, 2 vols. (Leipzig, 1921), translated into English as *Paganism, Christianity, Judaism: A Confession of Faith*, trans. William Wolf (Tuscaloosa, 1970). In general, I have used the English edition, but have checked all citations to the original, and in some cases, refer to the original text. In his preface to the edition of 1970, Brod noted that the translation, while faithful to the argument and spirit of the original, removed some of the more extreme expressions that he said derived from the period in which it was written.
108. See for instance Robert Weltsch, *Max Brod and His Age: The Leo Back Memorial Lecture* 13 (New York, 1970).
109. Kracauer to Löwenthal, 14 January 1921, in *In steter Freundschaft*, 19; and 13 December 1921, LLA 481/91–92, Leo Löwenthal Archiv, Johannes Senckenberg Bibliothek, Frankfurt am Main. The italicized words were underlined in the original. Thomas Mann also referred warmly, although briefly, to this work in a review of contemporary fiction appearing in the literary pages of the *FZ* on 17 April 1927; reprinted in *Franz Kafka: Kritik und Rezeption, 1924–1938*, ed. Jürgen Born (Frankfurt, 1983), 168–69.
110. Kracauer, "Those Who Wait," in *Mass Ornament*, 129–40.
111. Weltsch, *Max Brod*, 4–5. On Brod as an interpreter of Judaism, see the contemporary critique of *Paganism, Christendom, Judaism*, written by Franz Rosenzweig, "Apologetic Thinking," in *Philosophical and Theological Writings*, 95–108. For further discussions of this work, see Claus-Ekkehard Bärsch, *Max Brod im Kampf um das Judentum: Zum Leben und Werk eines Deutsch-Jüdischen Dichters aus Prag* (Vienna, 1992); and Anton Magnus Dorn, *Leiden als Gottesproblem: Eine Untersuchung zum Werk von Max Brod* (Freiburg im Breisgau, 1981).
112. Bärsch, *Max Brod im Kampf*, 53.
113. Brod quoted in Bärsch, *Max Brod im Kampf*, 55.
114. Franz Werfel, "Die christliche Sendung: ein offener Brief an Kurt Hiller," *Die neue Rundschau* 28, no. 1 (January 1917): 92–105. See also Weltsch, *Max Brod*, 16–17; and Bärsch, *Max Brod im Kampf*, 55.
115. Brod, *Heidentum* I, 184–85; the translation is my own.
116. Brod, *Paganism*, 98–99 and 104.
117. Brod, *Paganism*, 75–76 and 106–7.
118. Brod, *Paganism*, 75.
119. Brod, *Heidentum* I, 225. The translation is my own.
120. Brod, *Heidentum* I, 234–6.
121. Brod, *Paganism*, 43–45.
122. Kracauer, "Martin Buber," *Die Tat* 15, 1 (August 1923), in *Werke* 5.1, 678–85, esp. 680–84.

123. Kracauer, "Martin Buber," 682–84.
124. Brod, *Paganism*, 5–6 and 9–10.
125. Brod, *Paganism*, 37–38.
126. Brod, *Paganism*, 77–95.
127. Hans Liebeschütz, "Max Weber's Historical Interpretation of Judaism," *Yearbook of the Leo Baeck Institute* 9 (1964): 41–68; and Rabinbach, *In the Shadow of Catastrophe*, 44.
128. Kracauer spoke of his reading of Weber in a letter to Susman, on 2 May 1920, SN, DLA. The significance of this essay will be discussed below.
129. Musil, *Man without Qualities*, 276.
130. Brod, *Paganism*, 135.
131. Brod, *Heidentum*, 225–26; the translation is my own. As a recent study of the "Prague Circle" by Scott Spector has pointed out, the view of Brod as a writer who abandoned aesthetic dilettantism when he discovered religious commitment, a trajectory that is implied by this quotation, should not be accepted without some reservations. Spector points out that his earlier aestheticism was in some respects a response to the politics of national identity in the late Habsburg Empire. Moreover, the relationship between aesthetics, ethics, and religion that is posited here does not necessarily imply an abandonment of his early aesthetic interests, but rather a different interpretation of it; see Scott Spector, *Prague Territories: National Conflict and Cultural Innovation in Franz Kafka's Fin de Siècle* (Berkeley, 2000), 60–64.
132. Koch, *Siegfried Kracauer*, 20–21.
133. Brod, *Paganism*, 241 and 19–20.
134. Brod, *Paganism*, 23–24; cf. Kracauer, "Ginster," *Werke* 7, 55–61.
135. Mülder, *Siegfried Kracauer—Grenzgänger*, 45.
136. Kracauer to Susman, 11 August 1922, SN, DLA. In June 1926, Kracauer told Bloch that he had spoken with Karl Korsch in the Reichstag, and that Korsch had expressed the same reservations towards Lukács as did Kracauer four years earlier, but chose not to voice these as he did not wish to weaken Lukács's position in his struggle with the party. See his letter of 29 June 1926, *Briefe* 1, 280–85, esp. 282.
137. Oschmann, *Auszug aus der Innerlichkeit*, 81–89.
138. Lukács, *Theory of the Novel*, 12.
139. Kracauer, "Georg von Lukács' Romantheorie," in *Der verbotene Blick*, 83. Also, see the enthusiastic review by Susman, "Die Theorie des Romans," *FZ*, 16 August 1921, Morgenblatt.
140. Lukács, *Theory of the Novel*, 15–16.
141. For a general discussion of this work, see Jay, *Marxism and Totality*, 86–98.
142. Lukács, *Theory of the Novel*, 29–39, and 152. The phrase is borrowed from Fichte.
143. Kracauer, "Georg von Lukács' Romantheorie," in *Der verbotene Blick*, 84–85; and Lukács, *Theory of the Novel*, 75 and 90.
144. Lukács, *Theory of the Novel*, 58–59.
145. Kracauer; "Siberien-Paris mit Zwischenstationen. Zu Joseph Roths neuem Roman," *FZ*, 27 November 1927, in *Werke* 5.2, 704–7. Also see the comments on this article in Karsten Witte, "'Light Sorrow': Siegfried Kracauer as Literary Critic," *New German Critique* 54 (Autumn 1991), 77–94, esp. 83–86.
146. Oschmann, *Auszug aus der Innerlichkeit*, 83–84.
147. Lukács, *Theory of the Novel*, 56 and 152. On Simmel and Lukács, see Mary Gluck, *Georg Lukács and His Generation, 1900–1918* (Cambridge, 1985), 145–47.

148. Gadamer quoted in Richard Wolin, *The Seduction of Unreason: The Intellectual Romance with Fascism from Nietzsche to Postmodernism* (Princeton, 2004), 96.
149. Kracauer, "Georg," *Werke* 7, 259–69; the woman singing is Frau Bonnet, who in some respects resembles his friend Margaret Susman. See also the comments in Jay, *Marxism and Totality*, 97–98; and Emmet Kennedy, *Secularism and Its Opponents from Augustine to Solzhenitsyn* (London, 2006), 183–202.
150. Jay, *Marxism and Totality*, 100–102.
151. Barbara Beßlich, "Kulturtheoretische Irritationen zwischen Literatur und Wissenschaft: Die Spengler-Debatte in der Weimarer Republik als Streit um eine Textsorte," *Jahrbuch zur Kultur und Literatur der Weimarer Republik* 10 (2005/2006): 46–72; and Beßlich, *Faszination des Verfalls: Thomas Mann und Oswald Spengler* (Berlin, 2002).
152. H. Stuart Hughes, *Oswald Spengler: A Critical Estimate* (New York, 1952), 89.
153. On such rhetoric see Graf, "Either/Or," 597–99.
154. For general discussions of the reception of Spengler, see Hughes, *Oswald Spengler*, Farrenkopf, *Prophet of Decline*, and more recently, Beßlich, "Kulturtheoretische Irritationen." Adorno's reflections on the Spengler controversy are also of interest, see "Spengler after the Decline," in *Prisms*.
155. Rosenzweig to Rudolf Ehrenberg, 5 May 1919, *Franz Rosenzweig: Der Mensch und Sein Werk*, 1.2, 629. Cf. Rosenzweig to Eva Ehrenberg, 19 January 1925, wherein he referred to Spengler as one of his enemies, see *Franz Rosenzweig: Der Mensch und Sein Werk*, 1.2, 1019.
156. Kracauer, "Aussprache-Abend über Spengler," *FZ*, 10 February 1921, 2nd Morgenblatt.
157. Kracauer, "Aussprache—Abend über Spengler"; "Die Struktur der Weltgeschichte," *FZ*, 27 April 1921, in *Werke* 5.1, 191–93; "Ausspracheabend über Spengler," *FZ*, 2 June 1921, Morgenblatt; "Christentum und Spengler," *FZ*, 15 November 1921, Morgenblatt; "Spengleriana," *FZ*, 7 December 1921, in *Werke* 5.1, 325–28; and "Spengler und das Judentum," *FZ*, 29 December 1923, in *Werke* 5.1, 739–40.
158. Kracauer, "Sind Menschenliebe, Gerechtigkeit und Duldsamkeit an eine bestimmte Staatsform geknüpft, und welche Staatsform gibt die beste Gewähr für ihre Durchführung: eine Abhandlung" in *Werke* 9.2, 86; and "Georg Simmel," in *Werke* 9.2, 243.
159. Meyer quoted in Hughes, *Oswald Spengler*, 93–94.
160. Kracauer, "Untergang? Zum aktuellen Kulturpessimismus in Deutschland," *FZ*, 9 October 1923, in *Werke* 5.1, 704–8.
161. Kracauer, "Spengleriana," in *Werke* 5.1, 325.
162. Kracauer to Susman, 13 April 1920, and undated (probably June 1920), SN, DLA.
163. Adorno, "Spengler after the Decline," 54. According to Hughes, the appearance of *Preussentum und Sozialismus* in 1920, before the second volume of *Decline*, may have done more to damage his reputation than any of his critics on account of its pompous and reactionary tone; see Hughes, *Oswald Spengler*, 110.
164. Adorno, "Spengler after the Decline," *Prisms*, 64; and Weitz, *Weimar Germany*, 334–39.
165. Kracauer, "Spengleriana," *FZ*, 7 December 1921, in *Werke* 5.1, 325.
166. Kracauer, "Christentum und Spengler."
167. Kracauer, "Untergang?" in *Werke* 5.1, 706. Max Brod also condemned this kind of perspective; see *Paganism*, 247.

168. Kracauer, "Untergang?" in *Werke* 5.1, 706; and Kracauer, in *Werke* 9.2, 278.
169. Kracauer, "Untergang?" in *Werke* 5.1, 706.
170. Kracauer, *History*, 118–20.
171. Kracauer, "Untergang?" in *Werke* 5.1, 707.
172. Kracauer, "Untergang?" in *Werke* 5.1, 707.
173. Kracauer, "Untergang?" in *Werke* 5.1, 707; and Margaret Susman, "Geist der Utopie," in *Das Nah- und Fernsein*, 22.
174. Kracauer, "Untergang?" in *Werke* 5.1, 705–6.
175. Kracauer, "Untergang?" in *Werke* 5.1, 708. The reference to "chatter" (*zerschwatzen*) recalls Kierkegaard's condemnation of the popular press. "Chatter"—the feuilleton was the worst offender in this respect—had a malignant social influence, reducing inward reflection to inconsequential chitchat. See Allen Janik, "Haecker, Kierkegaard and the Early *Brenner*," 211–12. For an extensive study of this subject, see Peter Fenves, *"Chatter": Language and History in Kierkegaard* (Stanford, 1993).
176. Kracauer, "Those Who Wait," in *Mass Ornament*, 136–38.
177. Goethe (*Ost-Westlichen Divan*) quoted in Kracauer, "Untergang?" in *Werke* 5.1, 708. The quotation reads: "Schwerer Dienste tägliche Bewahrung / Sonst bedarf es keine Offenbarung."
178. Kracauer to Löwenthal, 12 April 1924, in *In steter Freundschaft*, 54.
179. Mülder-Bach, *Siegfried Kracauer—Grenzgänger*, 18; Haenlein, *Der Denk-Gestus*, 66–67 and 133; and Zachary Braiterman, *The Shape of Revelation: Aesthetics and Modern Jewish Thought* (Stanford, 2007), 251–54.
180. Kracauer, "Zwei Art der Mitteilung," in *Der verbotene Blick*, 222–23.
181. Kracauer to Löwenthal, 14 January 1921, in *In steter Freundschaft*, 19.
182. Gottfried Salomon-Delatour to Walter Benjamin, 5 March 1926, Gottfried Salomon-Delatour papers, 1110/8, International Institute for Social History, Amsterdam (the carbon copy of this letter is mistakenly filed with letters to the Austrian sociologist, Ottmar Spann. At the time of my visit, the archivists stated the letter would remain there as it was already catalogued.). It was to Salomon-Delatour that Kracauer dedicated his unpublished study "Das Leiden unter dem Wissen und die Sehnsucht nach der Tat" written during the war. The letter to Benjamin continues: "When I speak with him, I should like to believe that the system of drives from Fourier to MacDougall, as well as the recent impact of Freud indeed do have some legitimacy. In the past there had been monasteries for such things, today the FZ . . . God help us all!"
183. Marx quoted in Jones, "Introduction," Marx and Engels, *The Communist Manifesto*, 127.
184. Adorno, "Spengler after the Decline," *Prisms*, 53–72.
185. Adorno, "Spengler after the Decline," *Prisms*, 69.
186. This could even be said of Spengler insofar as he looked to the past in order to confirm the laws of historical evolution.
187. Brenner, *The Renaissance of Jewish Culture*, 5; and Gordon, *Rosenzweig and Heidegger: Between Judaism and German Philosophy* (Berkeley, 2005), 238–48.
188. Schröter, "Weltzerfall und Rekonstruktion," 38–39.
189. Kracauer, *Ginster*, in *Werke* 7, 42–43.
190. Benjamin, "Critique of Violence," in *Reflections*, 277–300. Also, see the discussion in Rabinbach, *In the Shadow of Catastrophe*, 58–59; and Jacques Derrida, "Force of Law: The 'Mystical Foundation of Authority,'" in *Deconstruction and the Possibility*

of Justice, trans. Mary Quaintance, ed. Drucilla Cornell, Michael Rosenfeld, and David Gray Carlson (New York, 1992), 3–67.
191. Lukács, *Theory of the Novel*, 11.
192. Bloch, *Spirit of Utopia*, 255.
193. Bloch, *Spirit of Utopia*, 242.
194. For instance, Bloch accepted the suppression of counterrevolutionary actions, such as the sailors at Kronstadt as a necessary step. See Oskar Negt, "Ernst Bloch, the German Philosopher of the October Revolution," *New German Critique* 4 (Winter 1975): 1–17. On Lukács, see Lee Congdon, *Exile and Social Thought: Hungarian Intellectuals in Germany and Austria, 1919–1933* (Princeton, 1991), 40.
195. Löwenthal, *Mitmachen wollte ich nie*, 26.
196. Jacobs, "A Most Remarkable Sect?" 84–85.
197. Roth, review of *Ginster*, quoted in Belke and Renz, *Siegfried Kracauer*, 53.
198. See his essay "Two Planes" of 1926. In this *Denkbild* the design of the city itself has a sinister component that exposes the "soft parts of the dream" to judgment "without mercy," see *Mass Ornament*, 37–39.
199. Marc Boasson quoted in Eksteins, *The Rites of Spring: The Great War and the Birth of the Modern Age* (Toronto, 1989), 222–23.

CHAPTER THREE

From Copenhagen to Baker Street
Kracauer, Kierkegaard, and the Detective Novel

> *I exist primarily, as it were, as a spy to a higher service, standing in the service of an idea, and as such I keep a lookout and spy upon the realm of Intellect and Religiosity . . . And I am no holy man.*[1]
> —Kierkegaard, "Die Gesichtspunkt für meine Wirksamkeit als Schriftsteller," 62–63

> *The romance of the police force is thus the whole romance of man. It is based on the fact that morality is the most dark and daring of conspiracies.*
> —G. K. Chesterton, "A Defense of Detective Stories," 123

> *The office of the confidence man is today one of the most important on earth.*
> —Kracauer, "Ein Hochstapler über sich selbst," *FZ*, 31 October 1926, *Werke* 5.2, 485–88

In an essay of 1924, the writer Alfred Döblin described the peculiarity of his age as a farrago, or an unshaped mass of dough in which unleavened clumps of the past blended with the ferment of modernity.[2] In this sense, *The Detective Novel*, a work that Kracauer completed in 1925, is a typical book of the Weimar era, even though it was unpublished and unknown to all but a few friends and acquaintances. Kracauer would have refused this label, just as he refused the category of "Weimar Intellectual." When Adorno wrote an essay in tribute to his friend in 1962, Kracauer asked him to refrain from mentioning the year of his birth, as he wanted to preserve his "chronological anonymity."[3] He also appears to have regularly refused information about his contemporaries when approached by later researchers, as if he feared the consequences of being lumped together with the cultural riff raff of Weimar. In contrast, he often referred to his fellow writers, such as Döblin, Jünger, and Roth, as "seismographs" or indexes of the age, even as he refused such designations for himself. Instead, he described his own position as "extraterritorial," a position without precise location or origin.⁴ Yet, the displaced or "extraterritorial" character of his study is what renders it distinctive of Weimar. On the one hand, the work constitutes an innovative experiment; it represents one of the first attempts to consider the detective genre as a socially significant form, and also it anticipates Kracauer's later reckonings with mass culture. However, the book also revisits much older philosophical controversies. Thus, *The Detective Novel* demonstrates a facet of Weimar intellectual culture remarked upon both by contemporaries and later commentators—the return of old debates that had first taken place in the wake of Hegel, in particular, the disputes between the Young Hegelians of the 1840s and 1850s.⁵ The following chapter will outline the contour of these debates in Weimar Germany and their influence on the practice of cultural criticism. Kracauer's study of detective fiction is the focal point as it demonstrates the close intertwining of theological themes with the strategies of cultural interpretation. This is most evident in his surprising conjunction of genre criticism with the work of Søren Kierkegaard. To explain why Kracauer brought together the popular with the esoteric, I will situate *The Detective Novel* amid the more general reception of both Kierkegaard and detective fiction in the 1920s; the wider implications of this work, its attempt to become a model for a sociopolitical critique of culture, and its rootedness in similar discourses on culture should then become clear.

Kracauer's interest in Kierkegaard led him back to one of the earliest critiques of philosophical idealism. Kierkegaard himself had been in the audience when Schelling launched one of the earliest salvos against Hegel in Berlin in 1841; and his own work offered an incipient existential critique of the alleged failures of Hegelian philosophy.⁶ Debates such as these did not survive unaltered during the ensuing decades, and Kierkegaard too suffered a partial eclipse of his reputation in the second half of the nineteenth century. When Kracauer started to read Kierkegaard, probably before 1914, the framework of the debate had shifted on account of the dramatic expansion of the mass media that Kierkegaard had so often railed against; yet, for Kracauer and others these media actually offered new chances for insight into the problematic nexus of culture and society.

For Kracauer and many of his contemporaries, Kierkegaard's work was a crucial link to these issues and one that drew attention to their theological implications. For just as the philosophical quarrels among the Young Hegelians had convinced Kierkegaard to reject the tradition of speculative thought, so in the 1920s Kierkegaard found his audience among those who rejected the prevailing neo-Kantian consensus. Writing in 1932, Hannah Arendt argued that Kierkegaard's popularity represented both the "atonement for and the revenge of romanticism."⁷ Her fellow Heidegger student, the philosopher Karl Löwith, expanded on this theme a few years later when in exile. He argued that German thought had never reckoned with the challenge posed by Hegel's failed attempt to encase history inside of a systematic philosophy. If history was not sacred history, but could also not be assimilated to reason, then what remained of our historical understanding, and on what foundations did it rest? Still, if Hegel had failed to answer such questions, by posing them he nevertheless had let the cat out of the bag. Those who came after him, so Löwith continued, were unable to think through the consequences of this failure. "The danger and importance of the radical philosophical and theological movement" he wrote, "of which the original Hegelians were well aware, was forgotten."[8] What followed was an antihistorical regression characterized by an unconsidered skepticism towards the bases of existence, and a strict limitation of history to the finite. This led to a philosophy shaped by what Löwith presents as a triad of economic, human, and spiritual misery—represented respectively by Proudhon, Schopenhauer, and Kierkegaard.[9] By the 1920s, Kracauer had encountered all three parts of this triad: the first in postwar utopian socialism, and the second in the so-called aesthetic decadence found in the work of Thomas Mann (*Buddenbrooks* and *Tonio Kröger*, for instance). Hence, with his study of Kierkegaard, all the components of the mid-nineteenth-century reaction had found a place in his writing. This regressive movement, so Löwith implied, had limited philosophical thought to such a degree that the problems that had occupied intellectuals of the mid-nineteenth century, had disappeared so completely that they seemed almost new again when Kant and Hegel were revisited by later generations.[10]

Placing Kracauer in this context may clarify some of the implications of his work, but there is still much to separate him from these earlier debates, and from Kierkegaard's approach to them.[11] For by situating Kierkegaard's confrontation with idealism in a modern landscape, and by merging philosophical criticism with the ephemera of pulp fiction, Kracauer was striking out into new terrain in his effort to demonstrate what criticism could and should do in modernity.[12] From this perspective, there are two aspects of *The Detective Novel* I intend to explore in this chapter. One, Kracauer's peculiar approach to modernity as a place of secular disenchantment is illuminated by this highly idiosyncratic exercise in interpretation.[13] Second, *The Detective Novel* should be viewed as an attempt at "appropriation" in the Kierkegaardian sense, that is, as an exercise in "indirect communication."[14] If Bloch exaggerated when he claimed that Kracauer was only an inferior Kierkegaard in search of his Hegel, he nonetheless correctly identified the general framework in which Kracauer understood his role as a critic.[15] Kierkegaard's attack on the foundations of idealist thought still resonated deeply for Kracauer; however, in the process of "appropriation," he altered this critique in accordance with his own perceptions of modernity and its liberating potential.

Of these differences, the most obvious is that Kracauer is more concerned with the Kantian legacy in German thought. While Hegel, the nemesis of

Kierkegaard, does appear and the specter of his "bad infinity" broods over part of the *Detective Novel*, it is primarily the Kantian transcendental subject that is Kracauer's bête noire.[16] Thus, Kracauer continued the critique of the philosophers of life who had insisted on a sphere of value that reason could not penetrate. This was a sphere where, in the words of Novalis, words that Kracauer cited, "no longer are numbers and figures the key to all creatures."[17] Still, Kracauer argued that access to this domain was blocked and only indirectly perceptible; to "render it visible" then was the uppermost problem of criticism.[18] One could not approach this sphere by either constructing a new philosophy or a *Weltanschauung*, but rather it must be intimated without systems and by means of an interpretive stance towards the real. By placing his emphasis on interpretative modes of existence and repudiating systematic thought, Kracauer was, of course, in accord with contemporary assessments of the legacy of Kierkegaard and Nietzsche.[19]

A second point of difference was that though Kracauer wanted to undermine Kantian transcendentalism, he was ambivalent to the radical subjectivism of Kierkegaard.[20] This did not mean that he was unconcerned with what he called the "existential position" of his readers, but he wanted to address these without reaffirming the autonomous subject.[21] Kierkegaard was key to this project because his redefinition of subjectivity went through the profane world, giving due recognition to the individual's contingent relationship with the real.[22] Only later did Kracauer come to believe that Kierkegaard's idea of the individual was merely "inwardness without objects"; but initially he found in Kierkegaard a potential ally, a fellow traveler who sought the transcendent in the profane.[23] For if the secular world was the site of revelation then one must seek its reenchantment rather than its abandonment. Thus, Kierkegaard portrayed Abraham in *Fear and Trembling* not as a holy mystic oblivious to his world, but rather as one who walks with both feet firmly on the earth. Only in a relationship to the contingent world, according to Kierkegaard, does the individual encounter the eternal, and as a result, the world of appearances needs closer scrutiny. In his *Concluding Unscientific Postscript* of 1846, he argued that the religious devotions of the past were typified by the monastery; the walls of the cloister symbolized the gap between the sacred and secular worlds. The modern world, however, has "gone further," and come to a point where it is "capable of holding the thought of God together with the *flimsiest expression of the finite . . . with amusement in the amusement park.*"[24] For Kracauer, the conflation of finite ephemera with the eternal meant that his instincts towards the former did not come at the expense of what he once called the "truth contents" (*Wahrheitsgehalte*) of theology.[25] The terminology he uses here is significant. He clearly wants to recognize a valid core to theological concepts, but also wants to avoid speculative judgments concerning the true and the eternal that he felt were rife within the religious revival. Instead, Kracauer circumscribes the idea of theological truth by sealing it within a subjective insight, provoked by everyday experiences that do not permit definite statements. In this sense, he preserved an element of Kierkegaard's radical subjectivism, even as he insists on a more dialectical relationship between self and the world.[26]

The third distinction is the most striking: his displacement of philosophical criticism into the realm of popular culture. The detective genre, so he argued, was a symptomatic expression of modernity, one that required philosophical and sociological analysis. The detective was the apotheosis of reason, reflecting a society where rationalism had become the absolute measure of things; moreover, the stylization of the genre produced a form of aesthetic distortion that obscured that part of reality which reason could not grasp. By investigating these areas of distortion one could interrogate the rationalist assumptions of modernity. For him the mystery genre thus became a profane theology, a cipher requiring a negative form of exegesis. The detective and his divagations remained an extension of *ratio*; but if one decoded the aesthetic distortion typical of the genre, then one could expose the distinctively modern regime of encryption and decipherment through which traces of the higher spheres might become visible.[27] For if the religious community was founded upon a sacred text that oriented the reader towards the truth of God, the fallen world reversed this relationship; instead the secular community perceives the truth of their own spiritual abasement through the creation and consumption of pulp fiction. Thus, the world of the detective becomes a world of "translatable counterimages" governed by an inverted providence. The strategy of reading images that Kracauer proposes in *The Detective Novel* is, moreover, clearly informed by contemporary currents of negative theology, as well as by a more general interest in concepts of negativity in philosophy and aesthetics.[28]

In addition to its borrowings from Kierkegaard, *The Detective Novel* also needs to be understood in light of the critical reception of detective fiction during the Weimar Republic. Defenders of the genre were quick to point out its theological significance. The genre hinted at a world beyond the quotidian reality of everyday life; it promised, but also withheld, mystery and sensation. To some writers, the suspense found therein derived not so much from its danger-filled plots, but rather from the contradictory impulses it elicited from the reader. On the one hand, the detective offers an outlet for the romantic lust for mysterious and unusual happenings, but on the other, the detective's heroic aura depends on his ability to subordinate all mystery to reason; the detective, according to one commentator, was the "adventurer of our times [*zeitgemäßer Abenteurer*]."[29] Thus, mystery is deployed only in order to show that there are, in fact, no mysteries. In this case, the detective emerges as a mere subordinate of logical process, a status that is at odds with the almost anarchic freedom enjoyed by some of the genre's protagonists. The detective, as Sherlock Holmes once stated, embodies an "impersonal thing—a thing beyond myself."³⁰ Kracauer described the detective as a neutral "counterpart to the adventurer," someone with no personal objective beyond extending their own rational processes.³¹ This emphasis on a disembodied logic diminishes the individual heroism of the detective; as a result, it generates a tension, an opposition to the illusory freedom that was opened up by the seemingly extraordinary events that typified the genre, and the seemingly unworldly powers of insight embodied by the detective.

This dichotomy of freedom and determinism also has an aesthetic counterpart. In aesthetic terms the detective novel reenchants the world, in particular the urban world of the metropolis. In the words of G. K. Chesterton, it evoked "that thrilling mood and moment when the eyes of the great city, like the eyes of a cat, begin to flame in the dark."³² The mysteries of the modern cityscape, Chesterton continued, had been mostly ignored by his fellow writers and, having done so, they had neglected a vital part of modern life. To their credit, the writers of detective stories fulfilled this forgotten task (though, Chesterton conceded, they often did so in works of poor quality), turning the city into a place of uncertainty, where "every brick has as human a hieroglyph as if it were a grave brick of Babylon."³³ However, according to Kracauer, this reinvestment of mystery into the prosaic world was deceptive. In classic detective fiction—Sherlock Holmes, Arsène Lupin, or Nick Carter—before the story ends, the detective inevitably closes the circle and all the mysterious details that beckoned as unknown ciphers are frozen into a definite and meaningful order.³⁴ They are thus degraded to the level of *ratio* and the mysterious becomes the commonplace. This process of reducing the unknown to the known was, for Kracauer as for other critics, the genre's defining characteristic. It was on this basis that Régis Messac, in his mammoth and pioneering study of 1929, distinguished detective fiction from the criminal or suspense novel.³⁵ This process is also, of course, determined by the designs of the author; the unravelling of the mystery shows us that we have not been baffled by unknowable events, but rather we have been victimized by authorial contrivance. In this way, the arbitrary ordering of the world becomes visible, and one is presented with a model of how reason fabricates the real; thus, its provisional nature is exposed in a way that anticipates Kracauer's subsequent critiques of ideology.³⁶ For Kracauer, this is analogous to the functions of the Kantian subject, a position that he argues using a passage from the French mystery writer Émile Gaboriau's *The Alibi*. Just as Gaboriau contrives a set of clues whose seeming lack of coherence defies explanation but which the detective readily disentangles, so the Kantian subject prestructures experience on the basis of its own categories and, thus, can only have knowledge of a world that it has actually created. We do not then, as readers, uncover the mystery in the company of the detective, but rather we are merely shown the once hidden workings of a system that was imposed from the outset. Thus, Kracauer describes the world of the detective story as a fabricated totality, one generated by a rationalism that ceaselessly "constitutes its own world" (*der ratio als dem welterzeugenden Prinzip*).[37]

Yet, it is not clear that mystery is, for these reasons, wholly banished. For Chesterton, the police order, or what he calls the "conspiracy of morality" is an order upheld by a "successful knight errantry."[38] In other words, there is a quixotic aspect to the everyday world; the commonplace is, in fact, the stuff of mystery and by no means in conflict with it. However, in *The Detective Novel* Kracauer muffled this point of view; just as the detective always solves the crime, the victory of *ratio* is assured, and the unknown gives way to rational certainty. Yet, this triumphalism of *ratio* does include a victim. "The object," so Kracauer writes, "suffers a radical destruction so that the transcendental subject can preserve itself as lawgiver."[39] There is then a potential site for mystery contained in the realm of the violated object; but where is this located, and how is it constituted? The detective cannot, and does not, tell us, for it is beyond his or her means to do so. Yet, by way of reading the detective's actions as an aesthetic distortion created by *ratio*, we can come to a partial and tentative recognition of this shadowy realm of objects. Hence, the "superficial expressions" of "low culture" do become imbued with an aura of mystery. As Holmes tells Watson at the beginning of one of their adventures, one must take care not to overlook common details, because it is in these minor facts that the heart of the matter resides. It is through realism that one discovers that "there is nothing so unnatural as the commonplace."[40]

This blurring of the commonplace and the mysterious is also embodied in Kierkegaard's figure of the secret agent or spy. If the detective has a talent for discerning the truth buried in the seemingly ordinary, so Kierkegaard's figure of the spy evinces a similar affinity for the prosaic. Since we are embedded within the mundane world, the absolute remains hidden from us; the ethical decisions that Kierkegaard points out in *Either/Or* are likewise concealed beneath an aesthetic veil. Similarly, the spy of God is submerged in the everyday world of appearances. He or she does not inhabit, but only stands before the higher ethical realm. Kierkegaard described these figures as morally compromised and somewhat disreputable, someone who can readily be forced to serve a higher power. The spy is no "holy man," he claims, nor is he a secular hero as is found among the protagonists of the detective genre. Moreover, there is no aura of omnipotence or of romantic freedom surrounding him; rather, the spy sinks into the quotidian world and goes incognito, a status that hides whatever relationship to authority he or she might possess.[41] Thus, the spy becomes an uncertain quantity in the world of *ratio*.

The spy or plainclothes agent in Kierkegaard is, of course, not in every sense identical to the detective, yet they have comparable functions in corresponding regimes of encryption and detection. For both Kierkegaard and Kracauer, modernity is an infinite realm of fragmentary impressions, whose meaning has been obscured by the leveling processes of reason and abstraction. Within this profusion of appearances, the detective and the spy represent a specific mode of existence, one in which interpretation becomes the primary means of resisting the forces of abstraction that blind one to the truth of one's position. As Kierkegaard puts it, the secret agents (*Geheime Agenten*) of the present have long recognized "the divine meaning of the diabolical principle of the levelling process."[42] In a regime where all experience can supposedly be defined and categorized, the spy and the detective are significant as they inhabit the border region between rational and irrational, between aesthetic and ethical. They intuit "divine meaning" in a corrupted world; they confuse appearances and disrupt fixed orders. More unsettling, they conflate the seemingly harmless things of everyday life with moral danger; they hint that the café standing to the side of the square may still be, in fact, the abyss of secret terrors; they show that one cannot move through the world with certainty when one relies only on the certainty of reason.[43] The detective is, as a result, of limited use as a guide to the modern landscape. Instead, Kracauer proposes a second figure as more representative of the modern critic. It is the sworn enemy of the detective, the so-called gentleman criminal or impostor, the genial "salon heretic" or con man, who functions in a distinctly modern fashion. It is this figure that disturbs the social order by pretending to be what he is not, and in so doing, he shows that social reality is never what it pretends to be.

This play between appearance and reality opens up a space for Kracauer's idea of criticism, but it is one that must be approached through indirect forms of communication. Aesthetic disfigurement is central to this indirect approach, and the Kracauer scholar Gertrud Koch has given due emphasis to the role that this distortion plays in *The Detective Novel*. However, Kierkegaard's concept of indirect communication emerges not only in Kracauer's attempt to read the world as if it were a distorted text, but also in the general rhetorical strategy of his work. This is observable in the style of *The Detective Novel*, which forbids clear interpretation. In his own words, the work is deliberately "exaggerated" (*absichtlich ganz zugespitzt*), and, had it been published, the surprising conjunction of "low" culture with philosophical critique probably would have struck many readers as eccentric. Kracauer appears to have anticipated these difficulties, and he did not seem alarmed by the negative comments he received from those friends and acquaintances to whom he showed the work. He could scarcely have expected otherwise, since the book appears to have been constructed precisely in order to provoke confusion. In sympathy with the intentions of indirect communication, the work opens up, or draws attention to a chasm or "gap" between the author and the reader.[44] This, in turn, demands an act of critical appropriation on the part of the latter, an act that reformulates the text in the reader's language. This process was opposed to the direct polemic or "general article" that Kracauer had likewise rejected in his letters to Gubler, his fellow editor at the *FZ*.[45] Kierkegaard had written in a similar vein in his *Concluding Unscientific Postscript*: "The highest principles for all thinking can be demonstrated only indirectly (negatively)." The "confusion of our age," according to Kierkegaard, was the result of an "excess of the didactic."[46] It is with such concerns in mind that Kracauer approached the problem of criticism. This is not to say that he never deployed overt polemic, but rather that his understanding of critical vocation placed the emphasis on indirect modes of address, on what he saw as a more pedagogically valuable approach.

Indirect communication existed in two guises in *The Detective Novel*: the genre encrypted the world and the critic deciphered the genre as a second "description of the world."[47] The distorted vision of reality that the detective novel expressed resulted from this encoding; it was a text to be read less for its literal sense, and more for the unintended meanings that could be drawn from it. In a sense, Kracauer's study anticipates the position later argued by W.H. Auden in a 1948 essay deriving from his own passion for detective stories. Auden argued that the ideal reader of detective fiction was someone such as Josef K. in *The Trial*, an individual who fails to see the interpretive task that is required of him. The Kafka protagonist, so Auden suggests, is "a portrait of the kind of person who reads detective stories for escape."[48] While Kracauer also believed that the genre was most revealing when it fulfilled its function as kitsch, the matter could not rest here.[49] For to read detective stories only for escape is precisely what should not happen; rather, they required an exegesis that K. fails to undertake in the concluding scenes of *The Trial*. Here, K. enters a cathedral and encounters a priest who reads to him the brief parable, "Before the Law." To the priest's frustration, when K. tries to understand the tale, he grasps too eagerly for a clear message; he hastily draws conclusions, and the text foils his attempts to coerce meaning from it. Shortly thereafter, he is, of course, executed by functionaries of the court. The existential stakes of interpretation then are high, and they were for Kracauer as well. Towards the end of his study, in a chapter entitled "Transformation," he offers a tentative glimpse towards the objective of his study: "If the categories of the detective novel were to be fully blown apart . . . the authentic would receive a direct language that would allow it to speak, even over the abyss."[50] Thus, if the prestructured world found in detective fiction imploded, the indirect language of a fallen world would somehow acquire the direct language that it lacks. The messianic tone of this statement is apparent, but it is less obvious how Kracauer meant this potential to be understood. Nonetheless, the task of the critic was to pursue, in an oblique fashion, this "direct language," to push past the abstract categories that concealed it—to find a remnant of the language that could speak "over the abyss."

* * * * *

Before discussing the content of *The Detective Novel*, some exploration of the reception of Kierkegaard is needed as Kracauer's intentions become clearer when his reading of Kierkegaard is situated among his contemporaries. While the book is idiosyncratic in its juxtaposition of Kierkegaardian themes and popular fiction, Kracauer was motivated by problems that were far from uncommon among Weimar intellectuals. On the one hand, the postwar surge of interest in Kierkegaard was a broad phenomenon that left its traces in art, philosophy, and religious thought, crossing confessional boundaries.[51] Hannah Arendt explained this by noting that "the differences between the confessions pale in comparison with the gigantic abyss that has opened up between a self-contained atheistic world and a religious existence in that world."[52] Thus, the problems confronting religion in modernity, the problems of redefining and reinterpreting religion in a secularized setting, were shared dilemmas that, at least to some degree, stepped over doctrinal differences—though this was certainly more the case between Catholics and Protestants. While Arendt does not mention Jewish writers specifically, Kierkegaard's work, as she was certainly aware, was read by many Jewish intellectuals of the period: Brod, Benjamin, Lukács, Adorno, Buber, and Kafka, just to name a few.[53] The interest in Kierkegaard, then, was in no way esoteric.

Moreover, the revival of Kierkegaard was a trend that some observers saw as symptomatic of the social and cultural angst that followed the war.[54] Substantial reception of Kierkegaard's work had begun in the early part of the century, and thus had its roots in the cultural crisis of the late *Kaiserreich* as well. German translations of Kierkegaard began to appear by the end of the 1800s, and he even had enough of a reputation to attract the attention of the Austrian theorist of cultural decay, Max Nordau, who included him in his rogue's gallery of social degenerates.[55] According to Arendt, the reasons for his current popularity were to be sought not only in the present malaise, but also in the resemblance between contemporary Europe and the crisis of the past century. Kierkegaard, she states, was "one of the first writers to live in a world constituted much like our own . . . a secularized world stemming from the enlightenment." Yet, his thought had come too early, and the cultural landscape in Germany had needed time to "catch up" to him. He was thus a writer of and against modernity, and his work anticipated the later crisis of culture manifested some decades later in the work of Nietzsche, Dilthey, and the "philosophy of life."[56] Such writings had worn down the conventional truths of a supposedly faded rationalism; the destruction of the war, she suggested, had done the rest. Similarly, in his later reflections on the philosophical movements of the 1920s, Hans-Georg Gadamer argued that Kierkegaard had only restated the traditional theological problem of existence as opposed to essence;

but he did so in a provocative fashion that repudiated both the churches and most of the pieties associated with religious belief. After the war, when the "problems of existence took on a renewed virulence," the Kierkegaardian critique of religion and of rationalism found a receptive audience, particularly among those who had been most affected by the prewar mood of crisis.[57] Confronted with the mass death generated by the mechanized armies of the state, the work of Kierkegaard became a "thorn in the flesh," forcing individuals to face their anxieties concerning modern society, and to reckon with their own codes of conduct that were deeply implicated by the catastrophe of war. "What our time needs," stated the Catholic theologian Ferdinand Ebner, is "Kierkegaard and once again Kierkegaard."[58]

Ebner, of course, saw Kierkegaard who was, at least nominally, a Protestant, as within the circle of Catholic belief; but the existential facets of his thought were relevant to both non-Catholics and to those who had abandoned the churches altogether. To many, Kierkegaard was valued for his devastating attacks on Hegel and the idealist tradition. According to Adorno, this seemingly decisive assault led many students to abandon altogether the classic works of idealism.[59] Having first disposed of these grand philosophical systems, Kierkegaard then forced philosophy to return to what some saw as its proper object: the subjectively existing individual and his or her relationship to absolute truth. As Franz Rosenzweig stated, Kierkegaard had placed the core of existence outside of any objectively existing system.[60] Of course, for Kierkegaard truth was closely bound to his own interpretation of Christian dogma, which via the birth of Christ posed a paradox: the eternal had become known only by entering the finite world. This meant that the individual who sought faith must risk her redemption on a "relation" with the eternal, yet this relation was both beyond thought and only attested to by a temporal event—the historical existence of Christ.[61]

This Kierkegaardian formulation of religious paradox stimulated a variety of philosophical reactions, in part because of its use as a critique of idealist philosophy. According to Hannah Arendt, for many of her contemporaries the work of Kierkegaard represented not only a turning away from Hegel or Kant, or a shift within philosophy; rather, it represented a "rejection of philosophy as such."[62] As with Nietzsche, he was understood by many as a source less of philosophical doctrines and more of a mode of existence, or in the words of Karl Jaspers, a different and "total position in thought" (*denkende Gesamthaltung*).[63] This relatively nebulous conception of philosophy readily lent itself to appropriation by intellectuals with divergent and varying agendas, and in ways which Kierkegaard may not have approved. For instance, Max Brod thought Kierkegaard confirmed his own conception of Judaism.[64] Kierkegaard, he claimed, offered a powerful statement of the "here and now" (*Diesseitigkeit*) of revelation, a moment that transformed existing reality under the sign of redemption. Indeed, he argued that this concept had received its clearest statement in *Fear and Trembling*.[65] In a sense, Brod created a Kierkegaard who justified his own conception of Judaism, just as Ebner and other Catholic thinkers sought to appropriate him for Catholicism. Later, he would become associated with existentialism or what one writer called "theology without God."[66]

Thus the reception of Kierkegaard was inflected across a varying paradigm as different intellectuals deployed his radical critique in different agendas. That Kierkegaard attracted writers as diverse as Kafka, Haecker, Jaspers, Buber, and Mann gives some sense of the multifaceted nature of his reception. Nonetheless, his strongest association was with the burgeoning *Existenzphilosophie* and, according to Gadamer, the term *Existenz* actually became more common in Germany largely on account of his influence.[67] Not everyone found this diverse reception to be unproblematic. Adorno, for instance, was suspicious of the ways in which Kierkegaard was imported into German culture. Sometimes this meant the sting of his "thorn in the flesh" was removed so as to make his writings less radical and less likely to provoke the bad conscience of his potential readers. His influence was also evident in a spiritual obscurantism that used the "qualitative leap" as a cover for all kinds of mystical points of view; or in the words of Brod: "imagination has a field day . . . for once the paradox of faith is allowed to cover up all fancies with its shield, there is no end to it."[68] Adorno lamented in 1939 that Kierkegaard had become the "house philosopher of Eugen Diederichs," the publisher known for his predilection for mystical and esoteric thought. Kierkegaard, so Adorno thought, had provoked a cultural "pandemonium" in Germany.[69]

However, Kierkegaard was also incorporated into an anti-metaphysical trend sympathetic to closer engagements with material reality, the belief that one had to push to the things themselves. This emphasis on the concrete finds a curious echo in the recollections of the Dadaist writer Richard Huelsenbeck, who mentioned Kierkegaard in connection with the *neue Sachlichkeit* of the mid-1920s: "This was the time Kierkegaard's wisdom forced attention to shift from heaven to earth and when Freud introduced the concept of dynamics into psychology. People felt that mankind was creative, and creativity encompassed both evil and good."[70] For Huelsenbeck, there is little sense of the religious aspects of Kierkegaard; the "leap of faith," the primacy of scripture, for instance, disappears into a general movement of dynamism. Kierkegaard's suspension of the ethical loses its significance as a bridge to the eternal, and instead becomes a license for aesthetic creativity. By and large, his comment suggests that Adorno was, perhaps, not wrong to fear the uses to which Kierkegaard might be put; but on the other hand, Huelsenbeck also drew attention to an important aspect of Kierkegaard reception: the emphasis on the profane world as the site of revelation. The relation to the Absolute was thus to be experienced not in metaphysical speculation or through the alleged byroads of abstract thought, but rather as something that could only be perceived through contact with the profane.[71]

To some degree, Kracauer exemplifies the rough pattern of Kierkegaard reception that emerges from these contemporary accounts. He must have first read Kierkegaard before or during the war, when his influence becomes readily apparent; in his unpublished study on the individual (*Persönlichkeit*), he describes Kierkegaard as an "excellent" observer of the conflict between ethical and aesthetic sensibilities.[72] His contempt for contemporary German philosophy, his disgust at the alleged cultural decadence of his age, his interest in the *Lebensphilosophen*—all these characteristics identify him as one of those intellectuals that Arendt saw as inclined to welcome the bracing critique of modern rationalism found in works such as *Present Age*, *Either/Or*, and the *Concluding Unscientific Postscript*.

However, Kracauer was susceptible to Kierkegaard not only because he found in him a sympathetic critic of modernity, but also because he addressed, in radical terms, the problematic relationship of the individual to the absolute. For despite Kracauer's religious skepticism, expressed both in the essay "Those Who Wait" and in his letters to Löwenthal as early as 1921, he was still situated on the cusp of religious revival, and these questions still held his interest, if not his passions. In a study undertaken during the war, for instance, he wrote of the relationship between secularism and religion in terms that assumed a fundamental incompatibility between the two: "the conditions of religious faith, in and of themselves, hinder the independence and unrestricted development of personal intellect."[73] The very title of this work, *The Suffering under Knowledge and the Longing after the Act*, is suggestive of the revolt against rationalism that Kierkegaard inspired. Such sentiments persisted in his postwar work, and they were an important context for his sociological and philosophical pursuits. "We long to approach God, as *Volk*, as humanity," he wrote to Susman in 1920, "but iron sociological laws force us to distance ourselves from Him. That is inescapable fate."[74] Kracauer's skeptical refusal of religious revival needs to be set against this wavering course between the religious and the profane. Even as he rejected a confession of faith, he still believed that religion's decline was deeply problematic; this anxiety is even more pronounced in some of his statements immediately following the war. Moreover, his turn to sociology was undertaken with a sense that one had to understand social structures in order to perceive how society prevents individuals from gaining insight into their situation. In other words, to study sociology was, in one sense, to know the enemy. This does not, of course, mean that Kracauer was not deeply interested in a sociological analysis of the present, but that this interest was multifaceted and included some contrary undercurrents.

The period of Kracauer's most intensive interest in Kierkegaard coincides with when he began work on *The Detective Novel*. Near the end of 1923, he mentioned the beginning phases of his "metaphysical" study in a letter to Löwenthal.[75] At the same time, Kracauer was very close to Adorno, whom he described as obsessed with the work of the Danish writer.[76] During parts of 1923–1924, he and Adorno traveled together, and Kierkegaard appears to have occupied much of their discussions and collective reading. Hence, there is good reason to look on *The Detective Novel*, in part, as a collaborative work, especially in light of Kracauer's impassioned statements on friendship and intellectual creation.[77] For his part, Adorno later described his own work on Kierkegaard as no "private intellectual accomplishment," but rather as a product of our "common philosophical past."[78] This collaboration, however, was uneasy, and it was complicated by the homosexual desires of the much older Kracauer. Indeed, Kracauer wrote to Löwenthal of his sufferings on account of Adorno: "I was and am very sad on account of Teddie. I believe you know that I feel an unnatural passion for this person, so that I could only explain it if I am, in fact, simply homosexual in intellectual and spiritual [*geistig*] matters."[79]

These biographical details are not extraneous to the genesis of the work, but rather a significant influence on its composition. As Heide Schlüpmann points out, the book emerged out of an almost oppressively close collaboration, one that was both intellectual and intimate. Encountering the other in philosophical discourse was a means by which the language of Kant or Kierkegaard was to be appropriated and transmuted into a "language of the body and intimacy."[80] Part of this encounter would have involved, according to Schlüpmann, recognition of the "clinging to appearances" of the individual, whereby one's image of the other person dissipates in a general and reciprocal dissolution of subjectivity—a theme that was important to the later thought of both Kracauer and Adorno. Thus, the concrete encounter with the other in philosophical dialogue became a means of exposing the false view of the subject as a well-defined entity. It revealed the bounds of the individual, and it was thus a starting point for their departure from the radical subjectivity of Kierkegaard. Schlüpmann suggests that in the early period of this relationship, Adorno became a kind of Dr. Watson to the Holmes-like detective figure of Kracauer.[81] Whether putting the relationship in these terms clarifies the intellectual indebtedness of one to the other is, perhaps, debatable; but still Schlüpmann elucidates the existential significance that Kracauer placed on intellectual partnership in the context of *The Detective Novel*.[82]

As a symbol of a very troubled relationship, it is fitting then that the book also has not fared well. Kracauer gave a reading from the work in a Frankfurt café in 1925, and he probably circulated it among his friends, but it was never published in his lifetime. A letter from Adorno in summer of that year suggests that this was due to the rupture in their personal relations. Adorno wrote that he had imagined Kracauer might one day surprise him with a publication, "but no, you will not do it, out of [your] anxiety to symbolize something that is there no more, and because you hate every lasting sign of us."[83] With its original dedication to Adorno, the book first appeared in its entirety six years after Kracauer's death, and two years after Adorno's.

These collaborative origins may explain why Adorno was the only contemporary who read Kracauer's intentions with sympathy. Based on the few surviving responses, the general attitude to the book among his friends was not positive, and Kracauer admitted that the book would have a hard time finding acceptance. "I recognize that it is difficult," he confessed to Löwenthal, "to penetrate my artificiality."[84] This artifice appears to have been intended, and as we have seen, he readily conceded the exaggerated and obsessive quality of the work. "I do not shy away from variations on *one* theme," he stated. On this point, he was referring to the complaints of his fellow *FZ* editor Hermann Herrigel, who found the chapter on the "Hotel Lobby" too repetitive and stylistically "precious." Herrigel had also complained that Kracauer's portrayal of a world fully subordinated to *ratio* was too pessimistic.[85] The sociologist Karl Mannheim had a comparable response, suggesting that the book was "oppressive" and "almost unallowable."[86] Despite these criticisms, Kracauer appears to have stuck to his original designs. In early 1925, he wrote to his friend Werner Thormann, that he had "danced the night away and brought the work to an end."[87]

Perhaps Kracauer had assumed that the popularity of detective fiction might have stirred some further interest in his readers, but his mode of analysis suggests that he must have envisioned an audience with more philosophical interests. In general, *The Detective Novel* is not an easy book to categorize. The subject matter of the work seems at odds with its difficult and almost obsessive style. When Herrigel described the book as a study in phenomenology and sociology, Kracauer rejected both labels. It was neither, he complained, and "even if it were *à la bonheur*, it would still be better than a . . . faded authenticity."[88] This reference to authenticity or to those whom he called the "concrete ones" gives some idea of, if not the audience, the second target of the book: the purported "authenticity" of the religious revival. Such claims, Kracauer suggested, demand a sign, a set of criteria to validate the work, but this is what Kracauer wants to avoid. Instead, *The Detective Novel* deploys a kaleidoscopic approach, repeating its themes from varying perspectives and incorporating them into different angles of critique. This does lend the book a repetitive if not monotonous character, and if Herrigel found reading through one chapter difficult, it is not hard to imagine how he would have responded to the entire text. Against such criticism, Kracauer responded that it was "easy" to have an idea, but it was the fleshing out that was decisive: "the eternal variation of continuously new points of view is precisely what lends intensity and engraves an image."[89] The risk of monotony then was worth taking as he thought his analysis would gain from its shifting perspectives and intensified imagery.

What then was Kracauer trying to uncover with these methods of intensification? He was certainly not alone in his conviction that the detective genre contained a hidden social content, a tentative expression of subterranean social desires. In a 1929 review of detective fiction for *Die Literarische Welt*, Heinrich Mann argued that detective stories attracted those readers disappointed by the humdrum pace of modern experience. Even the war, he claimed, could not break the monotonous and tiresome progression of days; but it was "something altogether different when criminals lock an heiress in a dungeon." Here, one finds mystery and surprise, and we find more delight in the ensuing "process of discovery" than in the "simple truth."[90] Such novels respond to "our unconsidered inclinations" and such attractions, "alongside the more rational ones, are often attached to a master of mysteries and dangers, to a deliverer from need."[91] Thus, the genre had a dual function: it disrupted the routine nature of reality, and then it furnished the redeeming hero who restored the disrupted order. This was a world in which apparent stasis alternated with puzzling and dynamic events, and the firmly ordered world of reason was juxtaposed to the apparently unexplainable.

It was only a short step to invest such terms with a theological significance. In an article by Willy Haas, the editor of *Die Literarische Welt*, this potential manifests itself in the alternation of chaos and revelation. For Haas, the detective story was a modern morality play (*Mysterienbühne*) in which the detective restored moral order to a world that had blotted out the truth with a deluge of material facts.[92] Haas described the setting and plot of the detective story in terms similar to Kracauer. The action occurs in a median zone or *Mittelgrund*; the characters act in accordance with a typology that placed them in different relations, either higher or lower, to this level—what Haas identified as the "upper," "lower," and "deepest." These levels certainly referred to moral status, but they also corresponded to levels of intellectualism. According to Haas, crimes are primarily distinguished by their "complexity" (*Kompliziertheit*).[93] Thus, they are perpetrated in the most uncommon and ingenious of fashions; the facts elude explanation and threaten to disappear into worldly chaos. In this respect, the criminal contributes to and perpetuates the prevailing disorder of the world. His collusion with chaos is a matter of natural affinity, as it is through disorder that the criminal evades detection. This, of course, is an affront not only to morality, but also to the prerogatives of reason that everywhere clarifies the nature of things and is embodied by the detective. The solution of the crime then confirms "that the world . . . is logical," that effect follows cause, which, as Haas tells us, is "not often the case in human experience." Haas goes further, however, and suggests that this function is akin to that of divine providence. The detective story then becomes "a substitute for failing religious belief. It confers confidence upon the divine Word and divine Justice."[94] In his closing remarks, Haas introduced a theme that paralleled

Kracauer's intentions. "The theological," he writes, does not and cannot "express itself openly," and thus the detective should be understood as one of its indirect expressions, a "subterranean theological symptom of the times."[95] What both writers shared then was the belief that the detective story not only contained unrecognized elements of social reality, but also that it indirectly expressed social impulses contributing to reality's construction. Thus, detective stories illuminated the society that generates and consumes them, and the decoding of these stories was a crucial task for criticism.[96]

What is unique to Kracauer is that within this task he allows for the potential recovery of a language liberated from *ratio*. Through such a language the violated world of objects might again express itself, and it is upon this premise that the potentially redemptive task of criticism rests. The language of the real constitutes a point of resistance hidden beneath the categories of abstract reason that in *The Detective Novel* appear as "mere legality," an order that is in accord with Kantian transcendentalism.[97] The detective novel is a staging ground for this struggle, but one that depends on reading the distorted images of the aesthetic sphere and decoding their correspondences to the higher or "upper" ones.[98] Where Kracauer holds out this possibility, he refers to "intentions" that are aimed towards this sphere, yet it is not exactly clear what these "intentions" are, and how they are to fulfill their liberating function. One potential source was the "fracture points" (*Bruchstellen*) that, according to Adorno, Kracauer emphasized in his reading of philosophical texts. These were the moments in a work where the writer was unable to reconcile opposing motives, thoughts, and judgments. They existed as "fissures and flaws," or a visible "wound" on the surface of the work, but a wound in which its "essential" contents became legible, even more so than in its direct statements.[99] Since such flaws were usually not deliberate, they might represent an unstated "intention towards the higher sphere"—its failure betraying, perhaps, an unfulfilled desire to reconcile the lower and the higher. In Kant's work, Kracauer suggested, the "thing in itself" constituted one such fracture point, a trace element of reality that his followers hurriedly tried to cover over.[100]

Another source for these intentions was to be found in the role of the artist. Kracauer did not elaborate on this point at much length in *The Detective Novel*, but he referred to the artistic task of "connection" between higher and lower spheres in his 1925 essay, "Artist of these Times," an essay that has much in common with the detective study. Here the artist was ensnared between rival claims. They could either represent the basic material facts of existence, or arrogate to themselves a religious status that was not in accord with their aesthetic powers.[101] In the latter role the artist acquired an almost prophetic position as aesthetics took over the functions of religion and attempted to give order to the world; the more secular the world became, the more it needed art. In *The Detective Novel*, Kracauer argued that it was a mistake to grant artists this kind of authority, but it was, nonetheless, a comprehensible one. For by "inserting intentions" into the "entangled matter" of appearances, the artist allowed them to become transparent and readable. Such intentions are derived from the artist and then infused into the forms of life.[102] Reading and interpreting these images was thus a matter of reading disfigured intentions, or of decoding those instances where contingent subjectivity displaced itself into the material world. The language of the real that might then emerge, however, still required translation, for it speaks or "stutters," so Kracauer stated, in a "foreign idiom."[103] Hence, he called his study an exercise in the "art of translation," a means of reading "translatable counterimages" and of cultivating an "inquiring existence" (*Vernommensein*).[104]

The book's argument proceeds by analyzing the typical figures and settings found in the detective genre, drawing attention to its particular modes of stylization. Against this stylized typology, the unexpressed "intentions" become more visible. The formation of types, Kracauer argued, is demanded by *ratio*, as by its very nature it seeks out the typical, or "pure quantities"; every contingency is, as a result, reduced to mere decoration.[105] In terms of setting, Kracauer argues that the representative venue of the genre is the hotel lobby, a space that functions primarily as a collecting point from which individuals can be dispersed according to their various functions (*Zweckhaftigkeit*). It is an aesthetic microcosm of the world at large, an artistic rendering of "purposefulness without purpose."[106] Kracauer referred explicitly to this Kantian concept as a means of elaborating his more general critique of the relationship between secularism and Kantian thought. For as life sinks away from the comprehensive meaning that religion once conferred upon it, society must "demand more of the work of art"; the aesthetic totality thus steps into the position vacated by religion.[107] In the case of the hotel lobby, its chaotic traffic is subordinated to an aesthetic construction that satisfies the need for spectacle, but is in itself meaningless. This he contrasts with religious space:

> The house of god, just as much as the hotel lobby, answers to an aesthetic sense that registers the requirements legitimate to it; however, if in the former, beauty has a language with which it bears witness against itself, so there [in the hotel lobby] it is mute and closed upon itself, and does not know how to find the other. In the tasteful lounge chairs the civilization directed towards rationalization comes to an end; by contrast the ornamentation on the church pews arose from a tension that conferred upon them a demonstrative significance.[108]

Here, the aesthetic totality is one of meaningless and superficial patterns, or in Kracauer's words, it degrades reality to a "mere relation of forces." It is a world ruled by abstraction, by categorical imperatives that are "no substitute for the direction that arises out of moral decision."[109] Here, he places against the world of *ratio* an ethical decisionism derived in part from the "qualitative leap" found in Kierkegaard, but also reminiscent of the work of the jurist, Carl Schmitt.[110] The theme of the decision emerges as an undercurrent in the study, placing him within a discourse on the "theological-political" problem, as will be discussed further below.[111]

The aesthetic totality Kracauer describes in the hotel lobby is complicated, however, by his Kierkegaardian model of the spheres. True to this model, humanity inhabits a median position, suspended between the lower sphere of the aesthetic and the higher or religious spheres which are "unshakably in force" in the former. They live "in time as well as in the glimmer of eternity, they cling to a perpetually untenable position between the natural and the supernatural."[112] The lower aesthetic sphere, typified by the hotel lobby, is one that is utterly secular. Compelled by logic and abstraction, it is a place where the demon of Laplace has triumphed. Nonetheless, the higher spheres haunt this reality, even if they must remain inaccessible to human thought. They surface in the denied promise of utopian fulfillment, a promise that is not yet extinguished. Existing in this suspended state between the aesthetic, ethical, and religious spheres, humanity tries in vain to satisfy their opposing claims. This ensures the preservation of the paradox, a condition that legitimates the ethical decision; for the law, according to Kracauer, only has validity insofar as it recognizes its paradoxical existence.[113] If the community should ever loosen themselves from the paradox, then they would succumb entirely to the abstract forces of the lower spheres. The world of the detective novel is one where this descent appears to be in an advanced stage. Yet, even here, in spite of this brutally regulated world, there remains what Kracauer calls "correspondences" between the higher and lower spheres. As he writes, "the crude insights and positions of the lower regions have . . . correspondences in the higher spheres; the tidings that they bring represents authenticity by inauthentic means."[114] The cosmos of the detective then is a nightmare of reason, but one in which the religious sphere retains a ghostly presence, a theological rendering of Fritz Lang's *Dr Mabuse*—everywhere present but nowhere visible.

Kracauer is also consistent with Kierkegaard in that he represents the aesthetic totality as a site of violence. Kierkegaard believed that the city was the cultural and social terminus of aestheticized cruelty; the archetypal city was Rome at the time of the martyrs, and its representative artists were Nero and Caligula.[115] An echo of this violence is to be found in the destruction of the individual perpetrated by *ratio*. According to Kracauer, the characters in detective fiction are dismembered and dehumanized; they exist only as "insubstantial marionettes," "particles of soul" and "complexes of atoms."[116] The peculiarities of character are reduced to the impersonal, part of a generalized and abstract mass of collective drives. Qualities such as love, faith, and jealousy were treated by *ratio* as "unaccented markings"—a mere "springboard for intellectual artifice."[117] The concept of the free and independent individual as formulated by Romantic writers, a concept with which Kracauer had some sympathy in his earlier work, was degraded to a collection of impulses and reactions.[118] Evidence of this destruction was to be found in the corresponding degradation of names. Whereas in the religious community names "unfolded themselves" (*die Namen sich erschließen*) in a process that reckoned with the whole person, in the secular world names were "mutilated into oblivion (*bis zur Unkenntlichkeit verstümmelt*)."[119] The world of the detective novel is thus one that always presupposes violence, a suppressed crime, committed by *ratio*, its traces left behind in language.

The institution of the law is the primary domain where the breadth of this crime becomes apparent for Kracauer. The formation of the law is a test case of the paradoxical, of the doubled and disfigured nature of reality in the detective novel.[120] Kracauer argued that law was fractured by two fundamentally opposed conceptions of itself, which he introduced with a quotation from Anatole France. On the one hand, law is absolute, "immutable, derived from God," but on the other, it is contingent, a "natural product of social life."[121] The proper destiny of humanity is to remain in the tension created by these irreconcilable positions, the latter of which offered a "distorted" or "disfigured" version of the first. For Kracauer, there is no knowledge of the law as an absolute (an echo of Kafka) because the higher spheres are beyond human reason; still this does not give us license to ignore the possibility of absolute law. The society that does so negates its relationship to the higher spheres and sinks further into the regime of *ratio*, losing all connection to the paradox and to the real.[122] In respect to the law, this means that society lapses into what Kracauer calls "mere legality." In contrast, the religious community is one where law and freedom have merged, where law is to be understood more in the sense of a way, path, or direction, a direction that we have chosen in freedom but that nonetheless reflects necessity.[123] Thus, in a religious community there would be no need of the law as an external force. In contrast the legal order of secular society claims legitimacy on account of its alleged connection to the higher spheres; but if it takes the further step of claiming to legislate *directly* on behalf of these spheres, then it oversteps its prerogatives. Just as in the fairy tale the brooms enchanted by the sorcerer continue to sweep even when the sorcerer has departed, mere legality remains oblivious to its own sources.[124] Kracauer argues that such a step is fatally presumptuous and represents the triumph of *ratio* in its Kantian guise: "the unrestrained growth of the legal principle is analogous to the expansion of philosophical systems that directly strive to extend themselves to a totality." He continues: "if the knowing and dependent self is reduced to the transcendental subject . . . then there can emerge the thought of embracing the totality within a system."[125] This means that for Kracauer the legal and epistemological are not far apart; the patterns of rule and the patterns of perception converge in a conspiracy against the real.

The descent into "mere legality" has wide-ranging consequences that Kracauer anticipated in a study written in 1919 for an essay competition. Entrants to the contest, sponsored by the Moritz-Mannheimer Stiftung, were invited to consider what form of government would best ensure the promotion of "charity, justice, and tolerance."[126] As Ingrid Belke has pointed out, the judges had intended that entrants should address the values of the Enlightenment, the legacy of 1789, and the creation of the constitutional state (*Rechtsstaat*). Kracauer, however, turned the question on its head, arguing that there could, in fact, be no permanent correspondence between a specific political order and moral ideals.[127] He also argued that philanthropic values had no specific affinity to particular state institutions and were just as well, if not better, served by a religious community. In a sense he flew directly in the face of secular rationalism, ignoring the liberal triad of liberty, equality, and fraternity. To the judges, it must have seemed as if in the first year of republican rule, he was already casting doubt on the long-term viability of democracy.[128]

Yet, his argument was not simply a matter of conservative reaction; on the contrary, Kracauer implied that if laws were mutable, as the revolution had demonstrated, then this had to be the case for all political orders, the constitutional state included. In this respect, Enlightenment precepts had no greater claim to permanence than those laws that the revolution had removed. "The manufacture of eternal justice," he proclaimed, "requires eternal revolution."[129] If this was the case then a just political order needed a flexible attitude towards its legal and constitutional forms, what Kracauer called "lability" (*Labilität*). This meant that all political arrangements must adjust themselves to changing circumstances. Indeed, Kracauer thought society should actually implement a mechanism for regular upheaval; for otherwise the community suffered under the burden of outmoded forms, customs, and laws. The influence of Simmel and the philosophy of life are readily clear. Laws were subject to an ongoing process of generation and decay, and they had their greatest validity only at the moment of origin—at the moment when they created an outlet for the spiritual forces of humanity. Afterwards, they declined and became hindrances to spiritual and moral progress.[130]

In *The Detective Novel*, the atrophy of form is equated with the decline of law into mere conventions, a process by which they lose their original ethical significance. According to Kracauer, it is the police force as a social institution that represents this decline. The police are only executors of the law and they have no part in its creation. Laws, he argues, arise from the crucible of "decision" (*Entscheidung*) and this is not the prerogative of the police.[131] As mere followers of the letter of the law, they represent what happens when the law takes on a life of its own, seeking to preserve its own power as an end in itself. The further the legal order removes itself from the original ethical decision, the more arbitrary it becomes, and then there emerges "legality without legitimacy."¹³² From this point of view, the police are only guardians of the status quo, and they are ready to forsake justice so long as their own power remains in force. It is symptomatic of this condition that they often assume the role of arbitrarily imposing the will of one part of society upon that of the other. In terms of Kracauer's philosophical critique, the police are the enemies of the real. They fulfill the same allegorical role as Kant's successors who repudiated the "thing in itself" in order to establish the absolute rule of *ratio*.¹³³

Kracauer's conception of a rift between law or "mere legality" on one side, and the cause of justice and ethics on the other, corresponds in significant ways to the work of Walter Benjamin.¹³⁴ In his 1921 essay, "Critique of Violence," Benjamin argued that one must distinguish between violence that affirms existing laws, and violence that creates new ones. The most radical instance of the latter is that of divine violence, that which holds "pure power over all life for the sake of the living."¹³⁵ This formulation sounds some alarm bells as Benjamin's distinction seems to permit the use of violence in a vaguely defined messianic context that probably had its closest affinities with the anarchism of Sorel.¹³⁶ As Derrida has argued in an extensive discussion of this text, Benjamin found something "rotten" in the law that he traced to its conservative function—that it protects the law as an entity in itself. Hence, he was at great pains to preserve the distinction between violence that preserves law and violence that founds it, in spite of its deeply problematic character.¹³⁷ Kracauer, as can be seen from the discussion above, also maintained this distinction, and as Kracauer did discuss this work with Benjamin during the planning stages, an influence from this quarter is probable.¹³⁸ Of course, some of these themes had wider currency, and we have seen that Kracauer was writing on comparable ideas as early as 1919. At this earlier juncture he referred to the religious constitutions of medieval Jewish communities for his model of lability, and this does suggest wider roots for the concept.¹³⁹

Still, the affinity to the work of Carl Schmitt in Kracauer's concept of the decision is striking. Behind these affinities is a common interest in Kierkegaard. Schmitt's formulation of the exceptional state in which sovereignty is established and exercised refers explicitly to Kierkegaard.¹⁴⁰ In the well-known example of Abraham in *Fear and Trembling*, the exception is the divine command given to Abraham to sacrifice his son; the authentic decision is arrived at when Abraham accepts this paradoxical decree. As a secularized variant of Kierkegaard's leap, Schmitt conceives of political sovereignty in terms of an "either/or" decision that takes place in an exceptional moment. In this situation, the one who decides is sovereign, and in so doing the sovereign power may assert itself over and against the normative order of law and morality.¹⁴¹

In *The Detective Novel*, Kracauer also subscribes to a critique of the law that undermines the legitimacy of the legal order.¹⁴² The moment of decision arises in an existential consciousness of paradox; in this indeterminate situation the decision creates those forms that govern social and political life. According to Kracauer, the creation of such forms is the province of the "exceptional ones" (*besonderen Einzelnen*).[143] It is they who expose the rift that divides the legal from the ethical, and the legal order from the just one. If Kracauer did not embrace the need for revolutionary violence with the same fervor as, for instance, Bloch, or even the more reserved judgments of Benjamin, he nonetheless comes dangerously close to a position that legitimated extralegal violence. He even implies that such acts may, in fact, have a closer relationship to the higher spheres of reality. Since the legal order is questioned, the criminal too has an important role to play, for insofar as his actions compel the legal order to concede its provisional and arbitrary nature, the criminal exposes those intentions that seek the higher spheres:

> The figures of the whole business of legality do not know that in transgressions against morality the displaced ethical can manifest itself, that murder must not only be murder, but rather it may signify the cancellation [*Aufhebung*] of finite, humane statutes through the higher mysteries.[144]

Insofar as Kracauer allows for the violent transgression of moral law in the service of a higher purpose, he is consistent with Benjamin and also with Schmitt's assertion that in the moment of decision "the power of real life breaks through the crust of a mechanism that has become torpid with repetition."[145] Thus, the force of "concrete life," of a contingent world made up of unrepeatable events and entities enters into the concept of sovereign power and its origins. Kracauer also uses terminology consistent with Schmitt, arguing that the legal system erroneously interprets illegal acts only in terms of rational norms (*normhafte Handlungen*) and, thus, it does not recognize their legitimate "question and claim" against the existing order.[146] In this respect, the legal order fails to reflect on the origins of its sovereignty; as a result, it cannot understand the public's "secret admiration" for the criminal who "lays bare the violence of the legal system."[147] Instead, the law leaps over the reality of every "human situation that demands an intertwining [*Miteinander*] of the law and the supralegal, of justice and of grace."[148] The cause of justice, he implies, is not identical with conventional attitudes toward the legal order.

Yet, the comparison does not hold in every respect and on at least one point Kracauer clearly diverged from Schmitt. In Schmitt's discussion of the conservative thinker Joseph de Maistre, he praised the latter for arguing that "any government is good once it is established." Schmitt approvingly glossed this statement with the remark that "making a decision is more important than how a decision is made ... the important point was that no higher authority could review [it]."[149] Kracauer's concept of lability cannot, of course, be brought into agreement with this view. Whereas for Schmitt there should be no interrogation of legitimate sovereignty, for Kracauer legitimate sovereignty cannot escape it. Every form or law, he wrote, should "at the moment of its origin raise its own shroud."[150] Of course, Schmitt could have asked how any sovereignty could be established if its claims to legitimacy were immediately challenged: would this not result in a cacophony of voices each laying claim to an existential "authenticity"?

A wider comparison that might attempt an answer to this question cannot be undertaken here, and, in any case, Kracauer did not pursue this issue further in his work. Though the issue of political legitimacy did occupy him on occasion, outside of his essay for the Moritz-Mannheimer Stiftung there are very few attempts to handle the subject. Indeed, it is difficult to see how he thought some of his ideas, such as the "intertwining of the legal and the supralegal" would emerge in practice, because he rarely discusses them in concrete terms. In *The Detective Novel*, visions of the community living in the higher sphere only emerge faintly in his allusions to fairy tales of the past, and their present-day counterparts, such as Chaplin's comical struggle against the machines in *Modern Times*.[151] The free society appears to have a chimerical quality that eludes definite description.

Yet, some sense of how his conception of the law might emerge in practice is to be found in his courtroom reporting—in particular, his coverage of two sensational murder trials, the Angerstein case and that of Lieschen Neumann. The latter involved the murder of a watchmaker named Ulbrich by three unemployed youths from the working-class district of Wedding in Berlin. In his assessment of the trial, Kracauer argued that the murder was symptomatic of the prevalent malaise.[152] He did not compare the crime to a kind of traffic with the "higher mysteries" of the supralegal, but he did perceive it in terms that are consistent with his philosophical critique. He does not deny that the perpetrators displayed character traits consistent with the crime, but he does not dwell on these factual details. In contrast to much of the press that portrayed the sixteen-year-old Neumann, in particular, as a female demon and "the Greta Garbo of Wedding," Kracauer argued that the murderers were essentially more typical than abnormal.[153] On account of widespread unemployment they had few prospects, and had surrendered themselves to the random ebb and flow of a life that lacked stability (*Haltung*). They did not, Kracauer argued, intend and plan a murder; rather they "stumbled upon it."[154] Their crime was one of a species of meaningless actions that punctuate the prevailing order, upsetting the normal stasis of everyday life. The legal system sought only to reduce the crime to a pattern of cause and effect upon which it could then pass judgment, thereby confirming its normative continuity without dealing with the deeper problems the crime had exposed. Thus, to Kracauer, the conclusion of the trial revealed almost nothing about the crime itself. Instead a chasm opened up between the act and its interpretation. This was manifest in the encounter between the courtroom examiners and Stolpe, the most violent of the three defendants. Kracauer saw in him a presumably uneducated and simple individual for whom "the encounter with the formal thought that rules over him and regulates his affairs is practically a threatening collision." In the courtroom, he is unable to logically reconstruct his crimes because, Kracauer states, he never experienced these events in a fashion "that can be assimilated to thought [*gedenkenmäßige*]."[155] Thus, his sullenness and confusion represented these events more faithfully than any logical narrative ever could.

His discussion of the Angerstein trial follows a similar pattern. Angerstein, an allegedly mild civil servant who went on a killing spree that began with his wife and claimed the lives of seven others, was put on trial in July 1925. Kracauer filed his concluding summary of the case under the title "The Crime without a Criminal."[156] Here too, the perpetrator "stumbles" onto the crime. As Kracauer reports, the psychological experts who testified at the trial suggested that Angerstein did not plan and then execute the murders; such explanations were insufficient. What Angerstein "did" appeared to be more of an "elemental event," rather than an explainable crime. The murders could not be placed into a comprehensible context, but rather they now stood "purely as an event in itself, as an isolated fact that lacks a correct origin."[157] He continues:

> Interrogations and depositions have informed us more or less of all that there was to be told. Unknown details have emerged to the surface and from a thousand statements a crude whole has been built. The image is not false, but it is also not correct. It brings to light what has, nonetheless, irrevocably decayed into darkness; it offers it to a judicial reckoning, as insufficient as it is, yet, at the same time liberating.[158]

Thus, Kracauer sharply limits the degree to which the legal order can know the truth about that which it judges. He appears to suggest that the law can tell us less about crime than crime can tell us about the law—a conclusion that runs parallel to Schmitt's view that reflections on the exceptional state of affairs can tell us more about political norms than these norms can tell us about the exception.[159]

A similar tactic is at work in Kracauer's interest in the secret affinity or "camaraderie" between the criminal and the detective. These figures resemble one another in as much as they both stand apart from the law; for, even though the detective ostensibly serves the legal system, he is not part of it.[160] Kracauer placed the detective among those "exceptional" individuals who live on the margins of society and who are engaged in the work of connection with the higher spheres. Among this group, there are the relatively legitimate figures such as the priest and hero, but there were also some ambiguous sorts: the religious zealots, enchanters, and medicine men.[161] Only insofar as they have a "relation to the mysteries" do they represent the "connectedness" (*Verbun-*

denheit) of the community, that is, insofar as their actions originate out of a "necessary vocation."[162] The detective is related to the priest in this respect, but in keeping with his modern genesis, he is more ambivalent. The detective is part hero, but he is also an abyss that represents the triumph of abstract thought. Kracauer also described the hero in very ambiguous terms:

> ... the hero also meets the danger that pressures the community from without or that originates from its own antinomies. He also breaks through the shell that encloses the space of daily life; but he does not, as does the priest, recognize the paradox, transformed and transforming, reconciled and reconciling. On the contrary, he asserts, unshakably and intransigently, the claims of the absolute in the particular, without connecting them; it is all the same whether he blindly brings about the commission of fate, or whether he wants to assist in the victory of the idea over the law.[163]

Therefore, the hero at best might bring paradox into view but without recognition; indeed, if the hero serves the community he does so almost as if by accident. The rational process drives him onwards, not the collective good. This is represented in the detective novel by the social aloofness of the detective and the uncertainty of his motives.[164] The detective is without intimate relations to the community—one must assume that sexual relationships are excluded. Thus, even a friend such as Dr. Watson exists primarily as a witness, as an occasional instrument of Holmes, rather than as a true companion. The detective may have idiosyncratic habits—cocaine use, playing the violin—but the general portrayal is nondescript. This aloofness of the detective draws attention to the importance of logical process, to the pure system of quantities and relations that Holmes stated was "beyond" himself; but it also relates him to the criminal, as will be discussed below. In general, Kracauer appears to pursue two directions in his representation, drawing attention to the detective as the agent of disenchantment, but not allowing the significance of this process to fall into oblivion. His terminology suggests that the detective is a kind of impostor of divine providence, but one who may play an indirect role in illuminating a world emptied of truth. Thus, the detective is at various times described as the "contrary of God," a "descendent of the spirit of Laplace," a "puppet of cloudy realms," someone who has "leapt out of a hole to fill an empty position"; he or she appears as a sorcerer in "pointy hat and star-spangled cloak," the "disguised figure of the adventurer."[165] These terms suggest something of the world of adventure and fairy tales that Kracauer tends, more generally, to associate with utopian promise.[166] It is not clear that Kracauer intends for the detective to partake of this aura, but at the very least, as a representative figure, these descriptors suggest that the detective occupies a numinous position—at once the representative of a fixed rational process, and a sign of possibility, referring to something beyond that process.[167]

This latter possibility becomes more evident in the final chapters as the text draws the detective and the criminal into a closer relationship. For in spite of the fact that the criminal and the detective are intellectual opponents from opposite sides of the law, they have an affinity for one other. Kracauer conceives of this as a camaraderie born out of their mutual recognition of the limitations of the police. Both figures take up an ironic position in regards to the enforcers of the law whose bumbling attempts to apprehend the criminal serve as a foil to the superior logical powers of the detective and his or her quarry. As the detective pursues the solution of the crime, this ironic position becomes more pronounced:

> If he turns to the illegal, the detective, a conscious bearer of the ethical, distances himself decisively from his starting point. His camaraderie with the criminal, his respect for those led astray out of passion exposes, at the very least, the dubiousness of the legal order, when it no longer tries to represent the paradox of existing and has fallen out of the relation [to the higher spheres].[168]

Still, one might ask, why should the detective be a bearer of the ethical? This appears problematic, especially since Kracauer has already stated that the detective initiates the process whereby "existential and ethical being" is turned into conventional legal relations. The answer, it would appear, derives from the fact that in pursuing the task of logic as an absolute, the detective violates the letter of the law. As Kracauer points out, Sherlock Holmes does not shy away from robbery or other illegal acts when trying to solve a case; Arsène Lupin is also both detective and master criminal. As the gap widens between the detective and the law, the principal of *ratio* becomes at odds with itself. In terms of his "aesthetic allegory" Kracauer states that the detective represents *ratio* as it appears to itself, that is, as the authentic "law giver"; the police, on the other hand, represent it as it appears from the point of view of "reality." From this latter position the imperfect relationship between law and justice is apparent.[169] As the detective pursues his object, he breaks the law and, thus, reopens the question of how it is constituted. Therefore, the detective can represent ethical claims against those of the law.

This does not mean that the detective is identical with the criminal, but rather that since they both have traffic with the "supralegal," they both represent a fissure within the legal order. Therefore, to maintain itself legality must obliterate the connection between the illegal act (*Widergesetzlich*) and the "supralegal" (*Übergesetzlich*). The existential community is always in a tension between law as an absolute and law as contingent, but the legal order attempts to void this tension; thus, it removes from the law its "enduring problematic being" and it removes from the unlawful any claim it might have to represent justice.[170] However, in the coming together of the two figures—the criminal and the detective—the provisional nature of the law again becomes evident.

For Kracauer, the figure that most clearly represents the instability of the prevailing order is the *Hochstapler*, the confidence man who he describes as a "gentleman-criminal." Kracauer suggests that such characters are attempts to represent the "paradox of existence"; they are "disfigurements" of existing individuals, in other words, a disfigurement of the "oriented" individual who accepts and recognizes the median position of human experience.[171] However, the gentleman-criminal is distinct from the existential individual in that the latter has a "double-life" that constitutes a personal unity, while the former represents a "rendezvous" between two different series of actions. They do not have any organic relationship to one another, but only occur by chance within fleeting time; only in vain do they "pretend to have originated from one soul." Therefore, instead of a malignant will at the root of the crime, Kracauer implied that malignant events seek out the individual and assert themselves on the same point; "respectability" and "impropriety" exist side by side, but the relationship is one of mere chance. Kracauer suggests a number of interpretations for this figure: that they are products of "pure accident," that one side of the character is a mask for the other. Moreover, through this "doubled figure" the detective genre may be "transcended."[172]

This last possibility is what most interests Kracauer, and it is this figure that has a potentially explosive role, one that might blow apart the categories of the genre and recover the language of the real. Still, it is difficult to tell what the significance of this is for Kracauer. As Gertrud Koch points out, he is often imprecise in this study.[173] In one passage, he seems to suggest that *ratio* could, in the manner of the gentleman-criminal, be turned and made to serve the cause of the real:

> Were *ratio* to be detained in some part of reality, it would be able to think of the totality as nothing other than one that aims at the ideas of God, freedom and immortality, in which the determinations of being that constitute that reality, find themselves again under cover.[174]

Yet, he also appears to foreclose this possibility. If the cosmos of the detective novel is to be transcended, then it appears to happen only negatively. The confidence man may resist the legal order and share with the detective an ironic position towards it, but Kracauer cautions us that *ratio* still "drives the whole business."[175] However, here again Kracauer has recourse to the "intentions driving to the higher spheres." These become evident in the double-sided actions of the gentleman-criminal, for inasmuch as they render visible *ratio*'s desire to master the totality, they also demonstrate its inadequacy relative to the superior power of the higher spheres. This, of course, is a theological argument that depends on the alleged existence of this higher sphere. Kracauer is hard to follow here, but these so-called intentions appear to function as a wedge driven between *ratio* and the reality it claims to encompass. Therefore, they suggest a measure of agency outside of the rational process:

> thus the higher sphere, associated with the immanent world, may connect itself to the criminal whose deed separates him from the community of the pseudo-legal. The detective then disappears, because the indifference of the rational process moves entirely to the call of the mysteries; he disappears into the criminal, who now in an inner dialectic reckons with the supralegal, or whose soul is alone the point upon which it can intervene. Instead of *ratio* exposing him without finding him, [the criminal] unveils himself in order to be found.[176]

Yet, how much freedom has been claimed in this self-exposure? It does not appear that Kracauer wants to give an answer.

This confusion arises out of a question of whether the detective's confrontation with the criminal alters either figure, and if so, what are the consequences? Moreover, does the detective effectively subsume criminality within a rational system? For as Kracauer stressed, this was the agenda that *ratio* pursues under the cover of the detective—to bring that which existed outside of the law back inside the circle of a rationalized totality. Such motives were evident in the criminological literature of his day, and having studied sociology Kracauer was probably acquainted with some of this writing. The path-breaking work of Franz Alexander and Hugo Staub, for instance, presented its mission in terms of the rational penetration of the criminal psyche: "We want to understand the criminal in order to be able to judge him correctly, so that our judgment may be just beyond question ... any disturbance of the common sense of justice has a destructive effect upon society."[177] Kracauer would certainly have objected to their belief that one could seamlessly move from rational "understanding" to "justice," and as we have seen he regarded with skepticism the attempt to logically explain criminals such as Stolpe or Angerstein.[178]

In the discussion of the "gentleman-criminal," however, it is the detective, not the criminal, whose psychological identity becomes volatile. The boundary that separates the detective from the criminal becomes less clear as the detective too becomes involved in crime; eventually, the detective simply "vanishes" into the criminal.[179] The disorientation provoked by this metamorphosis is compounded by the fact that the criminal is also identified as the "unfortunate one" (*Unglückliche*), a figure who steps from the pages of Dostoevsky into the position of the criminal. Kracauer says of this character that "no detective seeks him, but rather he emerges of his own accord; his deeds are no triumph of ratio ... he is an existence who is able to produce his own meaning." A relationship between this figure and the detective is implied, but only in an allusive fashion by way of comparison with various pairings of criminals and their interrogators from *The Idiot* and *Brothers Karamazov*: the Lord kissing the Grand Inquisitor, Ivan and Alyoscha, Myschkin and

Ragoschin. These are relations that interrogate but do not save the criminal, and Kracauer finds in them an echo of what transpires between the detective and his or her adversary.[180] Towards the end of this complicated passage, the detective appears to emerge triumphant and passes into (*eingehen*) the criminal, and one might suspect that the detective (or *ratio*) has triumphed and absorbed the criminal into the rational process. Yet, the chapter concludes with the somewhat cryptic statement that in this case the detective does not track down the connection between "figure and fact, but rather the unity of person and action unfolds itself [*erschließen sich*] in reference to the mysteries."[181] On the one hand, the attribution of a deed to a particular person is the resolution of the crime and the triumph of logic, but Kracauer presents this as inconsistent with the "unfolding" process that unites the person to his or her actions. It would seem then that the encounter with the criminal creates a process whereby the individual may recover a voice outside the rational totality.

To recover the language of the real then appears to depend on a restoration of the bonds that unite the individual and his or her deeds—in other words, the restoration of the individual who engages with reality as a "whole" person (*Persönlichkeit*). This idea of the individual is to be recovered from under the mantle of the transcendental system, but it is not identical to the radical subjectivity of Kierkegaard. Kracauer may have referred to the "dialectic of inwardness" in the Kierkegaardian sense, but he does not make the leap.[182] For Kracauer the individual who engages with reality is bound up with a process, one that he describes in terms of constant questioning and interpretation: "Reality is not a condition; it is a suspended sentence, an interrogation and an answer, a way or a process, a sanctifying process, theologically speaking, to which what is immanent must struggle since it does not rest in itself."[183] Further along, he expands on this theme: "Reality is contradiction, conflict, openness to that which opens . . . It is visible only when it is not seen; it is reality only if it remains beyond reality."[184] Reality then demands constant investigation via reading and interpretation, something that he argues the idealist system does not do; instead idealism insists on the universal validity of its *priori* judgments, and thus makes determinations that disrupt the interpretive processes that underpin our reality.[185] The individual who exists in the paradox must defer to the decisive significance of what Kracauer calls "beyond reality" or above it (*Überwirklichkeit*); the idealist system, on the contrary, must subsume everything to itself, and, thus, it negates the tension of existing in the median realm.[186] By fabricating "axiomatic images of the ideal" this system has in effect ripped asunder the "umbilical cord between the I and the world." Only in this way could the transcendental system establish itself as the "creator of objects," which it does at the cost of reducing the subject to a "logical reference point."[187]

In his conclusion, Kracauer attempted to distance himself from any stain of irrationalism, and he declared that, on the contrary, it is *ratio* as an agent of the idealist system that comes closer to an enthusiastic endorsement of the irrational. Wherever a system finds its conclusion in its own inner workings, he argues, it betrays the "here and now" and reduces the real to a mere determination in order to preserve itself. It was no matter, he claimed, whether this system was one of Kantian idealism, the "classless society," "Schopenhauer-Hartmannesque pessimism," or the popular bromide, "Have sun in your heart."[188]

To what extent Kracauer does justice to Kant in the course of his critique is a question that is outside the scope of this subject; rather, I want to draw attention to what his objections to idealism suggest about his concept of criticism. There is much in his position that is consistent with his engagement with Simmel and the philosophers of life—the "tragic concept of culture" is here reformulated as the tragedy of a paradoxical existence. Moreover, there are numerous points at which the essay reflects contemporary themes in his journalism. For instance, his identification of the real as an "openness to that which opens" is consistent with similar formulations he used in his essay "Those Who Wait." Also, his suspicion of the religious revival has a correlate in the detective study as well, most obviously in his disparaging remarks towards the "medicine-men" and "miracle workers" that flooded into the so-called danger zone. Indeed, his reference to "Have sun in your heart" (the title of a sentimental lyric written by Cäsar Flaischlen that was popular in the postwar years) was significant in this respect as he also referred to this verse in connection with his distaste for Rosenzweig's *Star of Redemption*. Of this work he wrote to Löwenthal:

> It is truly rubbish! A right proper philosophy of apotheosis that begins with the void and ends with "Have sun in your heart." I despise this sort of philosophy that makes a system out of a hymn; the most outlandish constructions applaud themselves for their own sake ... creation, revelation, and redemption are drooled over in an enthusiastic tone that moves a dog to pity.[189]

Such books were lumped in with the other baleful works of religious philosophy that Kracauer often criticized.

Given these connections between Kracauer's journalism and *The Detective Novel*, the latter study should be seen as an attempt to bring together the diverse motives and impulses in his criticism. It was not, however, a manifesto offering explicit instructions on critical practice, but a potential model of how a specific cultural formation might be read or interpreted. It could also be thought of as a cultural-political approach to what Leo Strauss later called the "theological-political problem," the issue of disentangling politics and theology in cultural discourse.[190] This entanglement is clearly related to the figure of the "gentleman-criminal" where a generalized ambivalence toward law and politics is connected to problems within idealist philosophy. I have given more emphasis to those aspects of his critique that I believe represent his critical intentions, hence, the focus on the potential "fracture points" in the detective genre that is represented by the confidence man. In the concluding section of this chapter, I want to argue the significance of this figure in relation to some further themes that will elucidate the theological impulses behind Kracauer's work of the early 1920s: the Kierkegaardian idea of the spy, physiognomy, and negative theology. Of these three, negative theology will be discussed in the following chapter, so only a brief remark should suffice here. Inka Mülder-Bach has discussed the idea of the "reversal of negativity" (*Umschlag der Negativität*) in Kracauer's work—the idea that one pursues a nihilist position to the point that there is a sudden recoil, throwing one back towards redemption. She has outlined the aesthetic and philosophical sources of this notion, to which I would also add the influence of contemporary negative theology.[191]

A comparison of the figures of detective fiction with the Kierkegaardian concept of the spy further illuminates the theological motive behind Kracauer's drive into negativity. Spies, plainclothes policemen, and secret agents appear at many points in Kierkegaard's work, most significantly in his *Point of View of My Work as an Author*, where he identified himself explicitly with the spy.[192] Still, some caution is needed as these figures are not always used in a univocal fashion. At one point, the spy is an unknown observer who detects what goes unnoticed in the world; such a person is often an outsider, compromised morally and thus easily coerced into performing the work of God (in relation to God, so Kierkegaard tells us, humanity is always in the wrong). What does this work consist of outside of observation? There is no real answer, for according to Kierkegaard, while "being" is a "system, it is a system for God." Therefore, it can have no clear meaning for the individual who serves it.[193] At other points, the "spies of God" resemble hidden points of authority that circulate unknown in society. They only appear incognito, and whereas in the past authority radiated from the individual and was worn outwardly like a badge, in the present, under the levelling influences of Hegel and the popular press, authority was distinguished by its "unknowability." The "excellent ones" go about "unknown as if they were secret police" and "covertly wear, and only negatively support, their corresponding distinctions."[194] As such they mingle with the crowds and become a hidden arm of the eternal that exists in the spectacle of the modern city.[195]

In *The Detective Novel* the figures of the gentleman-criminal and the detective have roles that appear to derive from Kierkegaard, which suggests that Kracauer read these passages closely. As already discussed, the gentleman-criminal is a volatile figure, one that threatened to erase the categories of the detective novel and expose the paradoxical nature of the law. The incognito of the gentleman-criminal thus had a potentially explosive function, for having donned social conventions to pursue his advantage, the moment of his exposure also exposes the society that accepted him.[196] Morality and the law are then revealed to be a matter of mere convention, one of the "beautiful games" that *ratio* imposes upon the real.[197] If the *Hochstapler* also has the force of justice behind him, as is the case of Maurice Leblanc's character, Arsène Lupin, then the vertigo is all the more tumultuous. Lupin actually occupied both positions—a criminal who was recruited by the bumbling police force that he had once opposed. Thus, the detective "vanishes" into the criminal.

The detective also vanished into the crowd and like the "unknowable ones" in Kierkegaard he assumed the incognito, but with a very different effect. The detective readily disappears for he is, Kracauer argued, little more than an effect of *ratio*, an apparatus designed to fill the needs of logic; even the police are more concrete, though they do not share his superior powers. Hence, the incognito of the detective needs to be distinguished from that of the Kierkegaardian spies and agents. In allegorical terms, the detective does not have a corresponding position in the higher spheres; rather, Kracauer suggests that the detective is where the allegory breaks down—he is a gap or an abyss that obliquely signifies society's exclusion from the real. The detective and his deeds become an anti-allegory that buries itself into the rational process governing everyday life. Thus, the potential of the detective is one of negative revelation, one that might lead to the "reversal" though this is only tentatively expressed.

The incognito of the disguised detective, who hides his identity in order to pursue a case, is in fact, Kracauer argues, not a true incognito. Instead, it should be seen as a distortion of its function in Kierkegaard; it signifies a sleight of hand that exists within the logical process, one in which the detective resembles an "experimenter" who has concealed his own role in determining the conditions of the experiment. Therefore, he only finds results consistent with logic, as the experimenter does not have contact with the world of the "unrepeatable" or exceptional.[198]

In contrast, in the upper spheres disguise is inconceivable. Each individual bears his or her own existence indelibly and visibly; here, the force of inwardness tolerates no potential for concealment.[199] The conditions of the "median zone" are, of course, more ambiguous, and here Kracauer sets the meaningless disguise of *ratio* against the incognito of the high ones. He makes explicit reference to Kierkegaard's interpretation of Christ's appearance as a commoner and also to Harun-al-Raschid wandering unrecognized through the streets of Baghdad. In such cases, he argues, the incognito is no disguise, but rather a "covering for the exposure to the other" (*Ummantelung zur Entblößung der andern*); it represents a "becoming-revelation of inwardness, an invitation extended to one who exists to actually be in reality—for no purpose of knowledge, [but] for a sacred meaning that binds one to it."[200] Again it is difficult to know whether Kracauer actually imagined that the landscape of modernity was inhabited by such figures. It would seem improbable, but at the very least he seems to have entertained the possibility of their secular correlate. The image of modernity that thus emerges in his diagnosis is one that possesses two ways of disappearing into the crowd and two corresponding kinds of revelation. The disguise of the detective offers a potentially negative revelation that demonstrates the emptiness of appearances, a nihilist vision that pushes one towards the "reversal" (*Umschlag*). The other rests with the hidden or "unrecognizable ones," those upon whom Kierkegaard placed the hope of redemption. Such figures have the potential to reveal the fraud that has been perpetrated by *ratio*. They inhabited the streets of the city and disappeared in the chaos of an aestheticized urbanity as a hidden source of negative revelation. For Kierkegaard, as for Kracauer, the city was the realization of aestheticism, where experience becomes surface and spectacle.[201] Reading the city, its forms and drives, its traffic and entertainments then becomes the crucial task for the critic, for redemptive potential is hidden in its interstices.

Yet, it was not clear what branch of knowledge one could look to in this task, and in spite of the growing influence of the natural and social sciences, the older traditions of conjecture remained possibilities.[202] Many of these older interpretive methods were, of course, also the specialty of the detective. According to Carlo Ginzburg, the detective novel preserves the traces of this encounter between modern science and older conjectural traditions. As Ginzburg defines them, the latter were "born of experience, of the concrete and the individual." Moreover, "that concrete quality was both the strength of this kind of knowledge and its limit; it could not make use of the powerful and terrible tool of abstraction."[203] They consisted of modes of investigation that targeted those areas remote from the sciences, such as the ephemera of daily life; they conceded that reality was "opaque" but suggested that there were still "certain points—clues, symptoms—which allow us to decipher it."[204] The most compelling case was that of the medical sciences, particularly in the area of diagnostics. While medical practice incorporated experimental methods, its results in the nineteenth century were inconsistent, and success often appeared to rest on intuitive judgments. Yet, it was generally accepted that medicine was a science based on rules of observation. As the power of the state increased and as the natural and human sciences were consolidated, the conjectural sciences were either assimilated to scientific method, or discredited. The so-called golden age of the detective novel preserves traces of this juncture; thus, Sherlock Holmes's powers of deduction did not prevent him from falling for phrenology and other such discredited pseudosciences.[205]

Of these conjectural modes, the one that Kracauer appears most susceptible to was that of physiognomy. He had a clear if ambivalent interest in a number of the practitioners of this art. During the early 1920s he had some contact with Ludwig Klages. In 1924, he told Löwenthal of a visit from Klages to the *FZ* offices during which he had his handwriting analyzed.²⁰⁶ He also was involved in the placement of an excerpt from a recent book by Klages, *Of the Cosmogenic Eros*, into the feuilleton section, and he reported on a radio lecture that Klages gave on the subject of graphology.²⁰⁷ These contacts were minor, but he had a more definite interest in the mystical physiognomists, Rudolf Kassner and Max Picard. An early essay on Kassner has been lost; but he did publish a brief account of a lecture Kassner delivered in 1927. He reported the event in surprisingly neutral terms given his hostility to occultism and esoteric lore. Though he recognized that physiognomic theory was not "free from objections," he was nonetheless impressed by Kassner's exposé, citing his discussion of movement and, for instance, his capacity to extract meaning out of the relationship between the brow and the chin.²⁰⁸ These articles do not, of course, suggest a significant indebtedness to the work of either Kassner or Klages, and given Kracauer's general antipathy to this sort of pseudoscience, it would be tempting to conclude that they represent no more than a passing curiosity. Yet, his surprisingly positive essay on Max Picard's *The Face of Man* suggests otherwise.²⁰⁹ As we have seen, Kracauer allowed a measure of legitimacy to Picard's theological mode of address, but a consideration of Picard as a physiognomist will elucidate some further implications that may be drawn from Kracauer's interest in his work.

Before he turned to writing, Max Picard, the son of Jewish parents, had studied medicine and for a brief time practiced as a surgeon. He later converted to Catholicism and wrote works of cultural criticism with a theological-philosophical bent. He was close friends with Benno Reifenberg and Wilhelm Hausenstein, and it is probably through these connections that he and Kracauer came to know one another. Picard wrote a review of Kracauer's *The Salaried Masses* under a pseudonym, and in his review of *The Face of Man*, discussed above, Kracauer refers to letters between them that have now been lost.²¹⁰ Among contemporaries who admired Picard were Thomas Mann, Joseph Roth, and Hermann Hesse, the latter describing Picard's books as standing "for themselves amidst a great silence."²¹¹ Others who knew Picard spoke of him as someone in possession of tremendous powers of insight. The deep impression he made on those who knew him contrasts with the degree to which his reputation has been eclipsed today.²¹²

Of late, however, he has emerged in the work of Emmanuel Levinas, who has pointed out that for Picard physiognomy was not just a means of reading psychological depth from surface detail, but rather was directed towards "deciphering the universe from these fundamental images or metaphors."²¹³ Picard took the biblical statement that humankind was created in the image of the creator quite literally; thus, to his mind the human face was a cipher of creation and of the eternal.²¹⁴ To look upon the face of another, he wrote, was to look upon the face of God, and when two faces looked upon one another, "eternity is in the middle and looks upon both."[215] Typical for intellectuals of this period, Picard embedded his discussion in a narrative of steady degeneration. At the time of creation, the face was radiant with the stamp of the creator, but today humankind had descended to a point where it can no longer bear the gaze of the eternal; thus, it looks upon the face no longer.[216] In his review, Kracauer quoted a line to this effect with approval. He also cited Picard's contention that at the "end of time" if God wants to warn humankind, he will do so through the "insignificant face of a simple man through whom He will reveal himself." Of such lines Kracauer wrote that "this is no metaphor, this is reality seen with unerring, ancient eyes."[217] This claim should be kept in mind when discussing what Kracauer meant by "reality" as a construction. Picard's conception of physiognomy shares a metaphysical motive with Kracauer's concept of the real. Thus, the drive to uncover the "face" of the age that Kracauer spoke of in an article of 1922 was something more than a metaphor, but rather a theological premise.[218]

Yet, it would be wrong to leave an impression that in following Picard Kracauer was leaning towards mystical speculation or pseudoscience. What attracted him to Picard's work was his attempt to approach the surface of things with a practical aesthetic sensitivity and interpret them in a fashion more akin to conjectural practices than formal logic. Kracauer, as we have seen, was well aware of the methodological limitations of these practices. Here the distinction that Ginzburg makes between "high" and "low" intuition might be useful. Klages, it could be argued, followed the "high" path leading towards mysticism; the "low" form, however, remained "rooted in the senses" and had "nothing to do with the extrasensory intuition of various nineteenth- and twentieth-century irrationalisms."[219] It is more about explaining how and why one doctor is able to give a more accurate diagnosis than another at a time when it was difficult to formulate diagnostic success into a set of prescriptive norms.

By way of conclusion, I want to return to the theme of the *Inkognito* and the unknowable ones in relation to the already mentioned legend of the *Zaddikim*, a legend that was important to both Picard and Kracauer. In *The Face of Man* Picard concluded with a reference to this legend of the thirty-six just ones whose righteousness holds up the world. Every generation has its thirty-six; according to some variations, to discover one of them would bring catastrophe.[220] Picard, following this legend, suggested that there were also thirty-six faces that performed a parallel function. It is not clear from Picard's description whether the thirty-six just faces would belong to the just ones themselves, or whether they would belong to other individuals. In the end he decides even one would suffice to ensure salvation and to preserve the redemptive link between the creator and the created.[221] We have seen above that Kracauer was also fascinated by this legend, and he included it in his final, unfinished work,

History: The Last Things before the Last. Here, in a surprising gesture, Kracauer proposed a futile quest for the thirty-six as a legitimate subject of historical investigation. However, rather than constituting an affront to the theological meaning of their incognito (the search, of course, would fail) Kracauer had a different agenda that harks back to his study of the detective genre. This was an attempt to recover meaning from the "interstices" or *Bruchstellen* of historical time, a temporality that was threatened by a "bad infinity" of endless progression that *ratio* threatened to subsume. The idea of the Just Ones itself becomes a cipher for the structure of historical time; for Kracauer they constituted the promise of fulfilled or redeemed time—a negative ground or foil to the profane. He argued that they existed outside the causes that determined most of our ideas of history.[222] From this point of view, it is perhaps not too surprising that the physiognomic motive also returns with his evocation of Ahasuerus, the wandering Jew, whose face contained the folds and lines that somehow incarnated history. Still, the reappearance of these overt theological and physiognomic motives strikes a peculiar note near the end of his career. It is as if a trusted psychoanalyst had suddenly asked to take measurements of your head; this has, perhaps, contributed to the general consensus that his final book was a failure.[223] Perhaps his proposed search for the thirty-six should not be read too literally, but instead should be understood as a touchstone for a set of problems that he associated not with history specifically, but with criticism or interpretation more generally and which remained his constant task, inflected over diverse subject matter. In a letter to the sociologist David Riesman, Kracauer tried to define his approach in a way that is very similar to what has been discussed in relation to the conjectural sciences: "the approach to a specific situation and the methods of diagnosing it must be acquired or learned in a sort of apprenticeship, like the one a student of medicine undergoes in the course of his training."[224] That he turned too emphatically towards "intuitive leaps" and against empirical means of validation in his final work, as Georg Iggers points out, weakened his arguments. It can be readily understood as a survival of his critique of *ratio* in *The Detective Novel*, a return to the scene of the crime and an attempt at playing "God's policeman."[225]

Notes

1. Most translations for the Diederichs edition of Kierkegaard were done by Christoph Schrempf who later said of his work that "the critical question is not so much whether I have accurately translated my quotations, but whether I have properly selected them." According to Habib Malik, Schrempf often departed from the original Danish, sometimes to a very considerable degree and, as a result, he has had an ambiguous influence on the German reception of Kierkegaard (See Malik, *Receiving*

Søren Kierkegaard: The Early Impact and Transmission of His Thought [Washington, DC, 1997], 313). As Kracauer and Adorno would have relied on these editions, I have in some cases used the Schrempf translation, rather than versions already existing in English.
2. Alfred Döblin, "Der Geist des naturalistischen Zeitalters," *NR* 35, no. 2 (1924); reprinted in *Schriften zu Ästhetik, Poetik und Literatur* (Olten and Freiburg im Breisgau, 1989), 187.
3. Jay, "The Extraterritorial Life of Siegfried Kracauer," *Permanent Exiles*, 152.
4. See his replies to the Döblin scholar Louis Huguet, 28 December 1958, and the Germanist Senta Zeidler, 27 August 1954, KN, DLA. Also, see his review article of Jünger's *Der Arbeiter*, "Gestaltschau oder Politik?" *FZ*, 16 October 1932, in *Werke* 5.4, 233–39.
5. Jürgen Habermas, *Der philosophische Diskurs der Moderne: Zwölf Vorlesungen* (Frankfurt am Main, 1986), 65–75; and Karl Löwith, *From Hegel to Nietzsche: The Revolution in Nineteenth-Century Thought* (New York, 1991), 115–21.
6. Schelling's lectures of 1841 popularized the attack against Hegel. Aside from Kierkegaard, the lectures were also attended by Friedrich Engels, Jacob Burckhardt, and Mikhail Bakunin. See the account of their impact in Löwith, *From Hegel to Nietzsche*, 115–21. On the significance of Schelling to modern philosophy and critical theory, see Andrew Bowie, *Schelling and Modern European Philosophy* (London and New York, 1993).
7. Arendt, "Søren Kierkegaard," *Essays in Understanding*, 49.
8. Löwith, *From Hegel to Nietzsche*, 110–14 and 120.
9. Löwith, *From Hegel to Nietzsche*, 119.
10. Löwith, *From Hegel to Nietzsche*, 120–35.
11. Mülder, *Siegfried Kracauer-Grenzgänger*, 39–44. To what extent Kracauer was acquainted with the writings of the Old and Young Hegelians is an open question. A letter to Susman suggests some familiarity with Feuerbach and Schelling, yet he readily conceded his lack of "philosophical education"; see the letter dated 26 July 1920 and an undated letter written sometime between June and July of the same year (SN, DLA). See also Weber, "La réalité emphatique," 31–35.
12. His path-breaking step in this direction seems less striking today, when philosophers such as Slavoj Žižek have made this a more common practice; but Kracauer's influence in this regard deserves recognition, as the editors of his American writings have pointed out, see the "Introduction" by Johannes von Moltke and Kristy Rawson in Kracauer, *Siegfried Kracauer's American Writings*, 21–26.
13. Frisby, "Between the Spheres," 3–20.
14. See Edward F. Mooney, "Exemplars, Inwardness and Belief: Kierkegaard on Indirect Communication," in *International Kierkegaard Commentary 12: Concluding Unscientific Postscript to Philosophical Fragments*, ed. Robert Perkins (Macon, 1997), 129–48; and Robert Poole, *Kierkegaard: The Indirect Communication* (Charlottesville and London, 1993).
15. Bloch, *Durch die Wüste* (Berlin, 1923), quoted in Belke and Renz, *Siegfried Kracauer*, 40.
16. For instance, see Kracauer, *Der Detektiv-Roman*, 118–20.
17. Novalis, *Schriften I: Das dichterische Werk*, ed. Paul Kluckhohn and Richard Samuel (Stuttgart, 1960), 344–45. Kracauer partially quotes this line in *Detektiv-Roman*, 75.

18. Koch, *Siegfried Kracauer*, 19–20; Lethen, "Sichtbarkeit: Kracauers Liebeslehre," 196–201; and Dagmar Barnouw, "An den Rand geschriebene Träume: Kracauer über Zeit und Geschichte," in *Siegfried Kracauer: neue Interpretationen*, ed. Michael Kessler and Thomas Y. Levin (Stauffenberg, 1990), 2–15.
19. See, for instance, *Vernunft und Existenz: Aula-Voordrachten der Rijksuniversiteit te Groningen 1* (Groningen, 1935), 6–11.
20. See the discussion in Schlüpmann, *Ein Detektiv des Kinos*, 10–16.
21. Kracauer to Friedrich T. Gubler, 13 July 1930, KN, DLA, quoted in Stalder, *Siegfried Kracauer: Das journalistische Werk*, 107. Gubler was a friend and colleague to Kracauer. After his transfer to Berlin, Kracauer wrote regularly to Gubler about editorial policy at the *FZ*.
22. Haenlein, *Der Denk-Gestus*, 9 and 134.
23. The phrase derives from Adorno; see his *Kierkegaard: Construction of the Aesthetic* (Minneapolis, 1989), 30–32. On the basis of his review of this book, Kracauer appears to have accepted Adorno's argument that Kierkegaard ultimately fails to reckon with the objective world; see Kracauer, "Der enthüllte Kierkegaard," in *Werke* 5.4, 486–91.
24. Kierkegaard, *Concluding Unscientific Postscript to Philosophical Fragments I*, trans. Howard Hong and Edna Hong (Princeton, 1992), 472–73. See also Pattison, *Kierkegaard, Religion and the Nineteenth-Century Crisis of Culture*, 40–41. In general, my discussion of Kierkegaard is indebted to Pattison's argument that one needs to situate Kierkegaard in the feuilleton culture of his day in order to interpret his work. The italics in the quotation are my own.
25. Kracauer to Bloch, 27 May 1926, in *Briefe 1*, 273–74. Cf. "Zwei Arten der Mitteilung," in *Die verbotene Blick*, 222–23. Here he refers to theological "contents" (*Gehalte*).
26. Schlüpmann, *Ein Detektiv des Kinos*, 14–16.
27. On this subject see Koch, *Siegfried Kracauer*, 15–25; Olivier Agard, "Les elements d'autobiographie intellectuelle dans *History*," in *Siegfried Kracauer: penseur de l'histoire*, ed. Philippe Despoix and Peter Schöttler (Paris and Laval, 2006), 141–64, esp. 149–50; and Lethen, "Sichtbarkeit: Kracauers Liebeslehre," 195–227.
28. Mülder-Bach discusses the aesthetic and philosophical contexts of his turn to negativity. See her essay, "Umschlag der Negativität," 359–73. On negativity in philosophical conceptions and politics, see Diana Coole, *Negativity and Politics: Dionysus and Dialectics from Kant to Poststructuralism* (London and New York, 2000).
29. See the discussion in Karl Lerbs, "Einleitung" to *Der Griff aus dem Dunkel: Detektivgeschichten zeitgenössisches Erzählers* (Leipzig, 1924), 15.
30. Arthur Conan Doyle, "The Copper Beeches," *The Adventures of Sherlock Holmes and The Memoirs of Sherlock Holmes* (London, 2001), 251.
31. Kracauer, *Der Detektiv-Roman*, 57. On this point see Martin Rosenstock, "Ernst Jünger's *Dangerous Encounter*—the Detective Closes the Case on the Adventurer," *Monatshefte* 100, no. 3 (Fall 2008): 392–93.
32. Chesterton, "A Defense of Detective Stories," 121.
33. Chesterton, "A Defense of Detective Stories," 120.
34. See the chapter entitled, "Prozeß," *Der Detektiv-Roman*, 131–35.
35. Régis Messac, *Le "detective novel" et l'influence de pensée scientifique* (Paris, 1929), 1–14.
36. In his essay on photography, Kracauer argued that the photographic medium could be a tool for exposing the provisional nature of existing social relationships; see

Kracauer, "Photography," in *Mass Ornament*, 61–63. On this subject more generally, see Barnouw, *Critical Realism*. Also see Kracauer, *Der Detektiv-Roman*, 97.
37. Kracauer, *Der Detektiv-Roman*, 101–5, esp. 101.
38. Chesterton, "A Defense of Detective Stories," 123. See the recent discussion of Chesterton and orthodoxy in Slavoj Žižek, *The Puppet and the Dwarf: The Perverse Core of Christianity* (Cambridge, 2003), 35–42.
39. Kracauer, *Der Detektiv-Roman*, 105.
40. Conan Doyle, "A Case of Identity," *Adventures of Sherlock Holmes*, 27.
41. Kierkegaard, "Die Gesichtspunkt," *Gesammelte Werke* 10, 62–63.
42. Søren Kierkegaard, "Kritik der Gegenwart II," *Der Brenner*, trans. Theodor Haecker (15 July 1914): 881.
43. Pattison, *Kierkegaard, Religion, and the Nineteenth-Century Crisis of Culture*, 22–23.
44. Mooney, "Exemplars, Inwardness and Belief," 139–48; and Roger Poole, "The Unknown Kierkegaard: Twentieth-Century Receptions," in *The Cambridge Companion to Kierkegaard*, ed. Alastair Hannay and Gordon D. Marion (Cambridge, 1998), 58–62.
45. Kracauer to Gubler, 28 January 1931, KN, DLA; and the discussion of this correspondence in Stalder, *Siegfried Kracauers: das journalistische Werk*, 105–8.
46. Kierkegaard, *Concluding Unscientific Postscript*, 220 and 280.
47. Koch, *Siegfried Kracauer*, 25.
48. W. H. Auden, "The Guilty Vicarage: Notes on the Detective Story, by an Addict," *Harper's Magazine* 196 (May 1948): 412.
49. Kracauer, "Spannende Romane," *FZ*, 7 January 1925, in *Werke* 5.2, 191–95.
50. Kracauer, *Der Detektiv-Roman*, 95.
51. On the reception of Kierkegaard in Germany and Europe, see Malik, *Receiving Søren Kierkegaard*, 339–92; and Poole, "The Unknown Kierkegaard," 49–75.
52. Arendt, "Søren Kierkegaard," *Essays in Understanding*, 47. I have slightly modified the translation here.
53. Malik, *Receiving Søren Kierkegaard*, 354–66 and 387; and also Bernd Witte, *Walter Benjamin, der Intellektuelle als Kritiker: Untersuchungen zu seinem Frühwerk* (Stuttgart, 1976), 58–64.
54. Pattison argues against giving too much emphasis to a "rediscovery" of Kierkegaard in the twentieth century; he argues that Kierkegaard was read before that time, though the postwar period saw a definite spike of interest in his work. See Pattison, *Kierkegaard, Religion and the Nineteenth-Century Crisis of Culture*, 177–82.
55. Malik, *Receiving Søren Kierkegaard*, 340; See Arendt's comments on the reception of his work in, "Søren Kierkegaard," *Essays in Understanding*, 44–45.
56. Arendt, "Søren Kierkegaard," *Essays in Understanding*, 45–47.
57. Gadamer, "Die deutsche Philosophie," 461–62.
58. Ferdinand Ebner, from a diary entry in 1921, quoted in Malik, *Receiving Søren Kierkegaard*, 386–87.
59. Adorno, "Fällige Revision: Zu Schweppenhäusers Buch über Kierkegaard und Hegel," *Gesammelte Schriften* 20.1, ed. Rolf Tiedemann (Frankfurt am Main, 1986), 258. The review was published in 1967.
60. Paul Franks and Michael Morgan, "From 1917 to 1925," in Rosenzweig, *Philosophical and Theological Writings*, 89.
61. Kierkegaard, *Concluding Unscientific Postscript*, 570–79.
62. Arendt, "Søren Kierkegaard," *Essays in Understanding*, 45.

63. Jaspers, *Vernunft und Existenz*, 6.
64. Brod, *Paganism*, 126–40. See the skeptical remarks concerning this subject in Rosenzweig, "Apologetic Thinking," *Philosophical and Theological Writings*, 101.
65. Brod, *Paganism*, 126.
66. Egon Vietta, *Theologie ohne Gott: Versuch über die menschliche Existenz in der modernen französischen Philosophie* (Zürich, 1946).
67. Gadamer, "Die deutsche Philosophie," 461–62.
68. Brod, *Paganism*, 235.
69. Adorno, "Wahl/Lowrie/Kierkegaard," in *Vermischte Schriften* I, *Gesammelte Schriften* 20.1, ed. Rolf Tiedemann (Frankfurt am Main, 1986), 233; and Adorno to Jean Wahl, 30 April 1939, in *Theodor W. Adorno/Max Horkheimer: Briefwechsel II, 1938–1944*, ed. Christoph Gödde and Henri Lonitz (Frankfurt am Main, 2004), 450–52. For a discussion of Marxist arguments that Kierkegaard prepared the ground for fascism, see George Hunsinger, "A Marxist View of Kierkegaard: Georg Lukács on the intellectual Origins of Fascism," *Union Seminary Quarterly Review* 30, no. 1 (1974/1975): 29–40.
70. Richard Huelsenbeck, "About My Poetry," *Memoirs of a Dada Drummer*, trans. Joachim Neugroschel (Berkeley, 1991), 168.
71. Pattison, *Kierkegaard, Religion and the Nineteenth-Century Crisis of Culture*, 22–24.
72. Kracauer, *Werke* 9.1, 32.
73. Kracauer, "Das Leiden unter dem Wissen und die Sehnsucht nach der Tat," in *Werke* 9.1, 202–3.
74. Kracauer to Susman, 11 January 1920, SN, DLA. A word in the letter is illegible but the sense is clear.
75. Kracauer to Löwenthal, 16 October 1923, in *In steter Freundschaft*, 48–49.
76. Kracauer to Löwenthal, 23 December 1923, in *In steter Freundschaft*, 51.
77. See the early writings collected posthumously in Kracauer, *Über die Freundschaft: Essays*, ed. Karsten Witte (Frankfurt am Main, 1974), esp. "Das zeugende Gespräch," 83–95.
78. Adorno to Kracauer, 19 July 1931, in *Briefwechsel, 1923–1966*, 285–88.
79. Kracauer to Löwenthal, 12 April 1924, in *In steter Freundschaft*, 53–55. The recent publication of the correspondence between Adorno and Kracauer only partly clarifies their relationship. Kracauer's letter of 5 April 1923, written when Adorno was 19 and Kracauer 34, is the most direct expression of his hopes for further intimacy. Adorno's written reply, if there was one, has not been preserved and there are no other letters between them until September of the following year. See Kracauer to Adorno, 5 April 1923, in *Briefwechsel, 1923–1966*, 9–14.
80. Schlüpmann, *Ein Detektiv des Kinos*, 15–16.
81. Schlüpmann, *Ein Detektiv des Kinos*, 24.
82. Adorno did in fact describe his relationship to Kracauer in terms that suggest its importance: "The encounter with my friend," he wrote to Alban Berg, "is in every way stimulating and important; it commands every exertion in human terms, in point of fact, it compels a revision of fundamentals." Adorno added, however, that "cheerful he is not." See the letter of 12 September 1925, in *Theodor W. Adorno/Alban Berg: Briefwechsel, 1925–1935*, ed. Henry Lonitz (Frankfurt am Main, 1997), 25.
83. Adorno to Kracauer, 25 May 1931 and 31 May 1925, *Briefwechsel, 1923–1966*, 63–64 and 72–75.
84. Kracauer to Löwenthal, 2 November 1924, in *In steter Freundschaft*, 65.

85. Kracauer to Löwenthal, 2 November 1924, in *In steter Freundschaft*, 65; on the exaggerated manner of the work, see the letter of 16 October 1923, 48–49.
86. Kracauer to Löwenthal, 28 and 29 July 1924, in *In steter Freundschaft*, 59–60. Neither Herrigel nor Mannheim appears to have read the whole work, only the chapter entitled "Hotel Hall." The word that Kracauer attributed to Mannheim is *schwül*. The closeness of this word to *schwul* (homosexual) may have been intended, but there is insufficient context to be sure one way or the other.
87. Kracauer to Thormann, 31 January 1925, Thormann Nachlaß, EB 97/145, Deutsches Nationalbibliothek, Deutsches Exilarchiv, 1933–1945, Frankfurt am Main.
88. Kracauer to Löwenthal, 2 November 1924, in *In steter Freundschaft*, 65. The omitted word was illegible in the original letter. He does, however, refer to the study as an exercise in "sociological projection" (*soziologische Projektionslehre*) in his letter to Löwenthal of 16 October 1923, 48–49. On the sociological dimensions of the study, see Frisby, "Between the Spheres."
89. Kracauer to Löwenthal, 2 November 1924, in *In steter Freundschaft*, 65.
90. Heinrich Mann, "Detektiv-Romane," *Die literarische Welt*, 23 August 1929, in *The Weimar Republic Sourcebook*, ed. Anton Kaes, Martin Jay, and Edward Dimendberg (Berkeley, 1994), 521.
91. Mann, "Detektiv-Romane," 521.
92. Willy Haas, "Die Theologie in Kriminalroman," *Die literarische Welt*, 27 July 1929, in Haas, *Gestalten: Essays zur Literatur und Gesellschaft* (Zürich, 1963), 171–78.
93. Haas, "Die Theologie in Kriminalroman," 177.
94. Haas, "Die Theologie in Kriminalroman," 177. Haas edited a special number of *Die Literarische Welt* devoted specifically to this question in which a number of writers and intellectuals were invited to discuss the modern fate of the Ten Commandments; see "Was soll mit den Zehn Geboten geschehen?" in *Zeitgemäßes aus der Literarische Welt von 1925–1932*, ed. Willy Haas (Stuttgart, 1963), 242–59.
95. Haas, "Die Theologie in Kriminalroman," 178. Haas may have known of this work, either from the above-mentioned reading Kracauer gave in 1925, or from Walter Benjamin. Kracauer spoke to Benjamin about the work and probably showed him the final draft. Benjamin may have discussed it with Haas, though I have not seen evidence of this.
96. Frisby, "Between the Spheres"; and Koch, *Siegfried Kracauer*, 25.
97. Martin Jay, following a similar line of argument, has described Kracauer as a "magical nominalist," a welcome retranslation of Adorno's description of Kracauer as "curious realist" (*wunderliche Realist*). See Jay, "Afterword: Kracauer, the Magical Nominalist," in Kracauer, *Siegfried Kracauer's American Writings: Essays on Film and Popular Culture*, ed. Johannes von Moltke and Kristy Rawson (Berkeley, 2012), 227–36.
98. Koch, *Siegfried Kracauer*, 16–17.
99. Adorno, "Curious Realist," 160.
100. Kracauer, *Der Detektiv-Roman*, 77.
101. Kracauer, "Der Künstler in dieser Zeit," in *Der verbotene Blick*, 130.
102. Kracauer, *Der Detektiv-Roman*, 22.
103. Kracauer, *Der Detektiv-Roman*, 51.
104. Kracauer, *Der Detektiv-Roman*, 9, 12 and 21–23. *Vernommensein* is attested to, he suggests, in a fashion akin to fairy tales or their modern variants; he names Chaplin and the comic figure of Pierrot (21).

105. Kracauer, *Der Detektiv-Roman*, 35–36 and 69.
106. Kracauer, *Der Detektiv-Roman*, 40.
107. Kracauer, *Der Detektiv-Roman*, 21; also see Kierkegaard, *Either/Or: A Fragment of Life*, trans. Alastair Hannay (London, 1992), 145.
108. Kracauer, *Der Detektiv-Roman*, 41.
109. Kracauer, *Der Detektiv-Roman*, 41 and 43.
110. Koch, *Siegfried Kracauer*, 18–20. Kracauer mentions Schmitt in his critical review of the intellectual circles around *Die Tat* (*FZ*, 10 and 11 December 1931), reprinted in *Mass Ornament*, 107–27), but he probably knew of Schmitt's work much earlier, if only second-hand through Benjamin. At the very least, his discussion of law and justice suggests close familiarity with Benjamin's "Critique of Violence" published in 1921. Kracauer's fascination with Kierkegaard's idea of the "qualitative leap" is referred to in a letter from Adorno, 25 July 1930, in *Briefwechsel, 1923–1966*, 237.
111. See Heinrich Meier, *Leo Strauss and the Theologico-political Problem* (New York, 2006).
112. Kracauer, *Der Detektiv-Roman*, 11–13.
113. Kracauer, *Der Detektiv-Roman*, 14–21.
114. Kracauer, *Der Detektiv-Roman*, 11–12.
115. Pattison, *Kierkegaard, Religion, and the Nineteenth-Century Crisis of Culture*, 69–70.
116. Kracauer, *Der Detektiv-Roman*, 23–25, 36 and 63.
117. Kracauer, *Der Detektiv-Roman*, 30.
118. For another contemporary description of *Persönlichkeit*, see Eva Fiesel, *Die Sprachphilosophie der deutschen Romantik* (Tübingen, 1927), 226.
119. Kracauer, *Der Detektiv-Roman*, 11. The terminology Kracauer used here is reminiscent of both contemporary phenomenology and Benjamin's theory of language. As discussed above, Kracauer was not usually sympathetic to the concept of naming as gnosis as in his critique of Bloch's *Münzer* book.
120. See Koch, *Siegfried Kracauer*, 18–24.
121. Kracauer, *Der Detektiv-Roman*, 14. The story in question is "Les juges integers," published in *Cahiers de la Quinzaine* (Paris, 1902).
122. Kracauer, *Der Detektiv-Roman*, 14–15.
123. In "Das Leiden unter dem Wissen," Kracauer cited with enthusiasm a passage to this effect that he encountered in a 1916 lecture given by Hugo von Hofmannsthal, "Das europäische Ich." The source was apparently from Tolstoi, but it has not been verified. See *Werke* 9.1, 270 and 404, n 28.
124. Kracauer, *Der Detektiv-Roman*, 67.
125. Kracauer, *Der Detektiv-Roman*, 71.
126. For an extensive discussion of this essay see Ingrid Belke, "Von Simmel zu Lenin: zu Siegfried Kracauers Schrift, 'Sind Menschenliebe, Gerechtigkeit und Duldsamkeit an eine bestimmte Staatsform geknüpft und welches Staatsform gibt die beste Gewähr für ihre Durchführung?'" *Simmel Studies* 13 (2003): 15–35.
127. Kracauer, "Menschenliebe, Gerechtigkeit und Duldsamkeit," in *Werke* 9.2, 95.
128. Belke, "Von Simmel zu Lenin," 17–18; and "Menschenliebe, Gerechtigkeit und Duldsamkeit," in *Werke* 9.2, 87–88.
129. Kracauer, "Menschenliebe, Gerechtigkeit und Duldsamkeit," in *Werke* 9.2, 118. The essay is marked by a revolutionary fervor that is at odds with his later repudiation of Ernst Bloch and indicative of his attitudes in the immediate postwar period. Here he declares his sympathy with Gustav Landauer and quotes the following passage:

"But in truth we need recurring revival, we need a readiness for shock . . . we need the trumpets of God's man Moses, who from time to time summons us to the great jubilee . . ."
130. Kracauer, "Menschenliebe, Gerechtigkeit und Duldsamkeit," in Werke 9.2, 117–21.
131. Kracauer, Der Detektiv-Roman, 66–71.
132. Kracauer, Der Detektiv-Roman, 65–77 and 92.
133. Kracauer, Der Detektiv-Roman, 128 and 77. Kracauer mentions a trajectory leading from Fichte to contemporary neo-Kantianism which at the time was centered in Marburg around thinkers such as Paul Natorp. For a discussion of this intellectual terrain, see Gadamer, "Die deutsche Philosophie," 454–55.
134. Koch, Siegfried Kracauer, 18–19.
135. Benjamin, "Critique of Violence," Reflections, 277–301, here 297.
136. Rabinbach, In the Shadow of Catastrophe, 60–61.
137. Benjamin, "Critique of Violence," Reflections, 295–300. For a reading of Benjamin's essay that argues for a "complicity of discourses" between Benjamin and Schmitt, see Jacques Derrida, "Force of Law: The 'Mystical Foundation of Authority,'" 3–67. The Schmitt/Benjamin connection has been disputed. Though Benjamin acknowledged his indebtedness to Schmitt, Derrida overstates this linkage. See Raphael Gross, Carl Schmitt and the Jews: The "Jewish Question," the Holocaust, and German Legal Theory (Madison, 2007), 246–47. The concept of "extraterritoriality" that so fascinated Kracauer also has a legal origin, referring to the state of diplomatic immunity from local law.
138. Frisby, "Between the Spheres," 3.
139. Kracauer, Werke 9.2, 118–19. The origin in Jewish tradition is also suggested by the striking resemblance of Kracauer's idea of Labilität to a short work by Kafka, "The City Coat of Arms." Herein, Kafka writes of a city existing in perpetual political and social conflict. Incorporated into its coat of arms is a giant fist that, according to prophecy, will one day smash the city with five blows. Many of the city's inhabitants long for this day, and the fist that will carry out the prophecy is emblazoned on the city's coat of arms. Thus, divine violence ends the imperfection and futility of human institutions; see Kafka, The Complete Stories (New York, 1971), 433, translated by Willa Muir and Edna Muir.
140. Carl Schmitt, Political Theology: Four Chapters on the Concept of Sovereignty, (Chicago, 2005), 15.
141. Schmitt, Political Theology, 10.
142. Koch, Siegfried Kracauer, 19–20.
143. Kracauer, Der Detektiv-Roman, 15.
144. Kracauer, Der Detektiv-Roman, 28.
145. Schmitt, Political Theology, 15.
146. Kracauer, Der Detektiv-Roman, 28–29.
147. Derrida, "Force of Law," 33.
148. Kracauer, Der Detektiv-Roman, 29.
149. Schmitt, Political Theology, 55–56.
150. Kracauer, Werke 9.2, 120–21. Indeed, he even suggested that Germany should institute a "Revolutionary Year" to take place every 30 or 50 years!
151. Kracauer, Der Detektiv-Roman, 20–21.
152. Kracauer, "Murder Trials and Society," NR 42 (March 1931), in The Weimar Republic Sourcebook, 740–41.

153. Kracauer, "Prozeß Lieschen Neumann," *FZ*, 31 January 1931, in *Berliner Nebeneinander: Ausgewählte Feuilletons, 1930–33* (Zurich, 1996), 167–69. For further press coverage, see the contemporary account written by Theodor Lessing, "Nach dem Urteil," *Prager Tagblatt*, 6 February 1931; and Kurt Tucholsky, "Die Herren Belohner," *Die Weltbühne*, 31 March 1931, in *Gesamtausgabe 14, Texte und Briefe: Texte 1931* (Reinbek bei Hamburg, 1996), 107–9. Lessing notes that Neumann had been described in sensational terms as a Garbo figure.
154. Kracauer, "Murder Trials and Society," 740. According to Lessing, the murderers claimed to have planned a robbery that through a series of unforeseen circumstances escalated into murder.
155. Kracauer, "Prozeß Lieschen Neumann," *Berliner Nebeneinander*, 168–69.
156. Kracauer, "Die Tat ohne Täter," *FZ*, 13 July 1925, in *Werke* 5.2, 272–77. See the discussion of this article in Helmut Lethen, *Cool Conduct: The Culture of Distance in Weimar Germany* (Berkeley, 2002), 206–10.
157. Kracauer, "Die Tat ohne Täter," 272.
158. Kracauer, "Die Tat ohne Täter," 273.
159. Schmitt, *Political Theology*, 14–15.
160. Kracauer, *Der Detektiv-Roman*, 88–92.
161. Kracauer, *Der Detektiv-Roman*, 18–20.
162. Kracauer, *Der Detektiv-Roman*, 20.
163. Kracauer, *Der Detektiv-Roman*, 18.
164. Kracauer, *Der Detektiv-Roman*, 51–64 and 87–88.
165. Kracauer, *Der Detektiv-Roman*, 54–57.
166. On fairy tales in his critical work, see Hansen, "Decentric Perspectives," 55–57 and 70.
167. Koch, *Siegfried Kracauer*, 21–22.
168. Kracauer, *Der Detektiv Roman*, 91–92.
169. Kracauer, *Der Detektiv Roman*, 94 and 129–30.
170. Kracauer, *Der Detektiv Roman*, 78.
171. Kracauer, *Der Detektiv Roman*, 84–85.
172. Kracauer, *Der Detektiv Roman*, 85.
173. Koch, *Siegfried Kracauer*, 23.
174. Kracauer, *Der Detektiv-Roman*, 109.
175. Kracauer, *Der Detektiv Roman*, 95.
176. Kracauer, *Der Detektiv Roman*, 95–96.
177. Franz Alexander and Hugo Staub, *Der Verbrecher und seine Richter: Ein psychoanalytischer Einblick in die Welt der Paragraphen* (Vienna, 1929), in *The Weimar Republic Sourcebook*, 735.
178. Also see Kracauer, "Der Prozeß Angerstein: Die Gutachten der Sachverständigen," *FZ*, 11 July 1925, 2nd Morgenblatt; and "Der Prozeß Angerstein: Das Gutachten von Prof. Herbertz," *FZ*, 11 July 1925, Abendblatt.
179. Kracauer, *Der Detektiv-Roman*, 96.
180. Kracauer, *Der Detektiv-Roman*, 96.
181. Kracauer, *Der Detektiv-Roman*, 97.
182. Mülder, *Siegfried Kracauer—Grenzgänger*, 40–44. The following discussion is indebted to her discussion of Kracauer's concept of *Wirklichkeit* in *Der Detektiv-Roman*.
183. Kracauer, *Der Detektiv-Roman*, 98.

184. Kracauer, *Der Detektiv-Roman*, 131.
185. Kracauer is then working with ideas about reality that are close to how Benjamin understood the work of Kafka, in the "sense that writing and reading are nothing more or less than the distillation of the world process." See Howard Eiland and Michael Jennings, *Walter Benjamin: A Critical Life* (Cambridge, 2014), 445 and 454–57.
186. Kracauer, *Der Detektiv-Roman*, 103–8 and 131.
187. Kracauer, *Der Detektiv-Roman*, 106–7.
188. Kracauer, *Der Detektiv-Roman*, 133.
189. Kracauer to Löwenthal, 31 August 1923, in *In steter Freundschaft*, 46–47.
190. Leo Strauss, "The Living Issues of German Postwar Philosophy," in Meier, *Leo Strauss and the Theologico-political Problem*, 115–40.
191. Inka Mülder-Bach, "Der Umschlag der Negativität," 368–73.
192. Kierkegaard, "Die Gesichtspunkt für meine Wirksamkeit als Schriftsteller," *Gesammelte Werke* 10, 62–63.
193. Kracauer quotes from this passage from *Philosophical Fragments* in the final chapter of *Der Detektiv-Roman*, 120.
194. Søren Kierkegaard, "Kritik der Gegenwart II," *Der Brenner* 4, no. 20 (15 July 1914): 881.
195. Pattison, *Kierkegaard, Religion, and the Nineteenth-Century Crisis of Culture*, 69–71.
196. Kracauer, "Ein Hochstapler über sich selbst," in *Werke* 5.1, 388–90.
197. Kracauer had originally intended to have the following quotation from Goethe at the beginning of his study: "I play really beautiful games with you." See Frisby, "Between the Spheres," 1.
198. Kracauer, *Der Detektiv-Roman*, 112–13.
199. Kracauer, *Der Detektiv-Roman*, 109–10.
200. Kracauer, *Der Detektiv-Roman*, 111.
201. Pattison, *Kierkegaard, Religion, and the Nineteenth-Century Crisis of Culture*, 50–71.
202. The following discussion of the "conjectural sciences" is indebted to Carlo Ginzburg's essay, "Clues: Morelli, Freud and Sherlock Holmes," in *The Sign of Three: Dupin, Holmes, Peirce*, ed. Umberto Eco and Thomas A. Sebeok (Bloomington, 1983), 81–118.
203. Ginzburg, "Clues: Morelli, Freud and Sherlock Holmes," 100–101.
204. Ginzburg, "Clues: Morelli, Freud and Sherlock Holmes," 109.
205. Ginzburg, "Clues: Morelli, Freud and Sherlock Holmes," 100 and 102.
206. Kracauer to Löwenthal, 2 November 1924, in *In steter Freundschaft*, 64–65. Kracauer wrote that Klages "noticed my inhibited nature right away, but he compensated for this with much fantasy."
207. See Kracauer to Klages, 5 May 1922, and Klages's reply on 11 May 1922. Both letters are in the Klages Nachlass, DLA. The excerpt was printed in the feuilleton of the first morning edition on 14 June 1922 with introductory remarks by Kracauer, see Klages, "Von kosmogonischen Eros." Also see Kracauer, "Ludwig Klages im Radio," *FZ*, 25 October 1924, in *Werke* 5.2, 147–48. Kracauer described this talk delivered on Frankfurt radio as "enthralling." Benjamin also knew Klages, meeting with him in 1914, and had a begrudging admiration for his work, despite many reservations. See Benjamin to Scholem, 15 August 1930, in *Correspondence*, 366–67.
208. Siegfried Kracauer, "Rudolf Kassner über Physiognomik," *FZ*, 21 May 1927, in *Werke* 5.2, 598–600.

209. Kracauer, "Zwei Arten der Mitteilung," in *Der verbotene Blick*, 219–27. See his reference to Picard in "Über den Schauspieler," *Die neue Rundschau* (September 1930), in *Werke* 5.3, 338.
210. Kracauer, "Zwei Arten der Mitteilung," in *Der verbotene Blick*, 220–21; a letter from Picard to Kracauer dated 2 October 1932 is in KN, DLA.
211. Roth to Friedrich T. Gubler, 8 October 1931, in *Briefe*, 211. Picard wrote to Hausenstein in 1930 that he had heard that Mann had reviewed the book warmly; see his letter dated 17 March 1930, Hausenstein Nachlass, DLA. The quotation comes from the end page of *Das Menschengesicht*, quoted in Siegfried B. Puknat, "Max Picard and Ernst Wiechert," *Monatshefte* 42, no. 8 (December 1950): 372.
212. Among the contributors to his Festschrift were Kassner, Gaston Bachelard, and Gabriel Marcel among others. See *Max Picard zum siebzigsten Geburtstag*, ed. Benno Reifenberg and Wilhelm Hausenstein (Zürich, 1958).
213. Levinas, "Max Picard and the Face," in *Proper Names* (London, 1996), 95.
214. Max Picard, *Das Menschengesicht* (Munich, 1929), 13–18.
215. Picard, *Das Menschengesicht* 14.
216. Here one should recall the hostility that Kracauer felt towards his own face. Unsurprising then that Kracauer noted Kassner's observation that Socrates was both the first opponent of myth and, also, the first ugly face to come down to us from antiquity. See Kracauer, "Rudolf Kassner über Physiognomik," *FZ*, 21 May 1927, in *Werke* 5.2, 599.
217. Kracauer, "Zwei Arten der Mitteilung," in *Der verbotene Blick*, 225. Cf. Charles Péguy, quoted in Walter Benjamin's "Paris of the Second Empire in Baudelaire": "One thing is certain: when Hugo saw a beggar by the road, he saw him the way he is, really saw him the way he really is, . . . saw him, the ancient beggar, the ancient supplicant, on the ancient road." See this essay in *The Writer of Modern Life: Essays on Charles Baudelaire* (Cambridge, 2006), 112–13.
218. See Kracauer, "Deutscher Geist und deutsche Wirklichkeit," *Die Rheinlande* 32 (January 1922), in *Werke* 5.1, 363–64.
219. Ginzburg, "Clues," 110.
220. Scholem, "The Tradition of the Thirty-Six Hidden Just Men," 251–56.
221. Picard, *Das Menschengesicht*, 223.
222. Kracauer, *History*, 8.
223. Martin Jay and David Rodowick argue that the book has been unjustly neglected; see Jay, "The Extraterritorial Life of Siegfried Kracauer," *Permanent Exiles*, 181–97; and Rodowick, "The Last Things before the Last: Kracauer and History," NGC 41 (Spring–Summer 1987): 109–39.
224. Kracauer to David Riesman, 8 June 1958, KN, DLA.
225. Georg Iggers, review of *History: The Last Things before the Last*, by Siegfried Kracauer, *American Historical Review* 75, no. 3 (February 1970): 816–17.

CHAPTER FOUR

Religion on the Street
Kracauer on Religious Flânerie

All genuine scholars or artists are, or should be, vagrants.
—Kracauer to David Riesman, 1 October 1958, KN, DLA

In the previous chapter, I argued that Kracauer constructed *The Detective Novel* as a tentative model of cultural criticism. It was a means of approaching layers of social reality that he thought had been abandoned by much of art, philosophy, and the sciences. To a significant degree, he framed this abandonment with reference to earlier conceptualizations of the conflict between German idealism and a theologically founded idea of the real, a conflict that he also found expressed in the work of Kierkegaard. The study was written during a time when Kracauer was becoming accustomed to his position as a journalist and editor on the *FZ*, where his duties required that he attend numerous lectures, readings, and discussions devoted to religious and philosophical subjects. *The Detective Novel* was decisively shaped by these encounters. As a journalist, he observed the various forms that postwar religious revival took, and he commented on its modes and intentions, its strivings and its alleged failures. Could such movements adjust themselves to modernity, could they give an account of modern experience that was meaningful to those who felt the loss of religious values? How he answered such questions and how this shaped his critical vocation is the subject of the following chapter.

However, before considering his writings on religion, some attention should be given to the forum in which he wrote: the newspaper feuilleton. In contrast to the critical model that was offered by *The Detective Novel*, the feuilleton afforded only limited space to deal with the themes that concerned him. That he was still able to publish in this venue a significant number of path-breaking articles that have retained their relevance up to the present is remarkable. Under the leadership of Reifenberg, with contributions from Kracauer and Joseph Roth, the *FZ* feuilleton section did in fact become an exceptional domain for cultural experimentation, publishing serialized novels by Roth among others, and a broad spectrum of literature that included everything from the letters of André Gide to the poetry of Langston Hughes.[1]

For Kracauer the feuilleton became an ideal medium for explorations based on the "worm's point of view." Indeed, what Alfred Polgar defended under the rubric of the "Small Form" was known for its exploration of the minutiae of everyday life, and its emphasis on subjective points of view.[2] Sometimes this could degrade into subjectivism run amok, but at its best, as in the work of Kracauer, Roth, Benjamin, Polgar, and others, it became an important literary form that registered the growth of the urban metropolis and its new forms of mass culture.[3]

Still, even if one wrote for a prestigious newspaper such as the *FZ*, the status of a feuilleton writer was low. As Golo Mann put it, even after 1918 a minor lecturer still "would think himself superior to a Maximilian Harden or even a Heinrich Heine."[4] Journalists and the press in general were often seen in a negative light, by both the public and by intellectuals themselves. The tradition of bemoaning the press and its baleful influence had deep roots. Kierkegaard was an early opponent whose critical tropes were sometimes adopted by later writers. The feuilleton in particular, he argued, was a force of intellectual and spiritual decay; it substituted empty "chatter" in place of inner experience. Silence was to be preferred to such discourse since the press was indifferent to the religious and existential bases of life. "Together with the passionlessness and reflectivelessness of the age," Kierkegaard wrote, "the abstractions of the press . . . give rise to the abstraction's phantom, the 'public' which is the real leveller."[5] To enter the journalistic profession was then to enter the belly of the beast; nonetheless, Kierkegaard himself was also a writer of feuilletons.[6]

Kracauer was certainly aware of the poor reputation of journalism. "What one must do in order to earn money," he complained to Susman in 1921.[7] His entry into the newspaper world was, however, a step that bore fruit for him and appears to have led to a shift in perspective. According to one of his contemporaries, the change in his career was accompanied by a "modernization" of outlook. Leonie Meyerhof-Hildeck, a journalist on the *FZ Stadtblatt* and probably an earlier acquaintance from Munich, later reported to Viktor Klemperer that Kracauer was outwardly transformed: "he is supposed to be totally *modern*, totally intellectual and totally exalted over the fact."[8] To Klemperer, it must have seemed that Kracauer had given up his past wanderings in the deserts of aesthetic musing and cultural pessimism in order to embrace the whirl of the modern. Having noted Kracauer's general disinterest in politics, he may have been bemused by his new choice of profession. Whereas before Kracauer had voiced scorn for the literati, and even for the *FZ* itself, he now was a public intellectual eager to contribute to the cacophony of the daily Weimar press.[9] Instead of the turbid prose of his unpublished philosophical manuscripts, he now devoted himself to the feuilleton written for the fleeting moment. By entering the fray of what Peter Fritzsche has called the "word-city"—a variegated play of texts that overlaid and influenced perceptions of the modern metropolis—Kracauer had entered into the "public sphere that he had sought for so long."[10] His new career, however, was not without ambiguity, and Kracauer would chafe against the lowly position of the journalist. He parodied this issue in *Georg*.[11] When the protagonist is reveling in his first newspaper publication, he tries when speaking with the paper's editor to insist on the term "essay" (*Aufsatz*), whereas the editor pointedly keeps referring to his "article"—Georg felt the latter term was not "substantial enough." However, since he does not want to alienate the editor, he eventually relents and accepts the more pedestrian terminology. The entrance into the precincts of literature then does not come easily for the writer of feuilletons.

Given the aspirations that lay behind Kracauer's critical project, he had to consider how to pursue them within the constraints of the newspaper. Criticism of this kind of writing came from a variety of quarters and addressed a variety of issues: the eclecticism of the medium, the indefinite nature of its audience, the limitations of space that required, so it was argued, a lowering of critical standards. Rosenzweig, for instance, argued that the newspaper was a decidedly plebeian venue where one addressed a vast and unknowable public, whereas he in his own writing had never written without having a precise idea of who his reader was.[12] By contrast, the journalist casts words before an amorphous mass with no idea where they might fall. As Stefan Zweig argued in an altercation with Kracauer, the newspaper was no place for serious criticism. Such critiques, however valid, would be met with the distracted attention of the average newspaper reader as they scanned columns reading stories that receive undue attention, "whether the death of a prostitute, the shooting of a sound film, stock market swings, or the creation of an iron consortium."[13] What was important one day was forgotten the next, and Zweig implied that the criteria of judgment had to reckon with this fact and be adjusted accordingly.

Perhaps even more problematic for Kracauer, his friend Susman argued, after his review of the Rosenzweig and Buber Bible, was that the newspaper was no place to write about genuine and "creative" (*sprachschöpferisch*) work. She did not reject his critique out of hand, but argued that works such as the Buber and Rosenzweig Bible could not be touched by mere "negative" criticism; to respond to them would require an equally *schöpferisch* effort and this could not be undertaken in a daily newspaper.[14] A work of religious intent was an altogether different level of discourse, and Kracauer, so she pointed out, could not engage with the work on the level it required. As Rosenzweig stated, religious messengers were not "postmen bringing yesterday's news"; on the contrary, their language was a potential vessel for divine "presence," and this presence, he argued, was the only source that could legitimate or invalidate the use of such language.[15]

Such criticisms undoubtedly had an impact on Kracauer. In his correspondence with Benjamin, he voiced his concerns over the question: Who does one write for?[16] He also recognized that most often his feuilletons would be forgotten by the time the next edition arrived. Some of his important articles, such as the essays on photography and the mass ornament, appeared over a few days and so were able to expand the limits of daily column space, but this could not help to escape the fear that newspapers were essentially ephemeral. However, he did formulate ideas of critical practice that responded to the objections of his critics. Writing to Zweig, he rejected with some vehemence the idea that critical measures should be lowered in a newspaper; on the contrary, he said, the newspaper was read by many and the importance of critical standards was thus all the more important. Even if the audience was undefined, it was of a size that was probably greater than the average readership for literary fiction, so standards had to remain in force.[17]

However, he pushed his defense further, arguing that criticism had to attend to what he described as the "existential needs" of the reader. For this reason, as discussed above, he argued for the priority of "indirect" expression, as opposed to essays seeking to persuade the reader of a particular point of view.[18] The feuilleton, he suggested, was a forum for the cultivation of a critical approach in the reader; it offered a demonstrative model that would show how to approach the multifaceted phenomena of everyday life in an interpretive fashion. His colleague Reifenberg stated that the feuilleton sought to address the "conscientious" observer, one who sought to know the present "before he criticized it," and Kracauer, who worked closely with Reifenberg, agreed with these intentions.[19] There was more value in articles that encouraged readers to dismantle the constructed realities that surrounded them, rather than just setting down guidelines. Thus, the feuilleton should not give ideological instruction, but rather offer a way of seeing how and when ideology came into play in the public sphere.

His method thus demanded an engagement on the part of the reader, the article becoming an incitement rather than an exposé. When Kracauer received a letter from Karl Vaupel, a schoolteacher and author who worked in the Ruhr region, he must have felt that his intentions had been recognized. Vaupel described Kracauer as a "born pedagogue" and applauded his articles for having demonstrated critical method, rather than lapsing into mere polemic, as in his essay "Locomotive over Friedrichstrasse."[20] Referring to this essay, Vaupel noted that Kracauer's approach always started from concrete observations and a reflection on point of view, before seeking to analyze the conditions that made both object and perspective possible. According to Vaupel, this was an instructive approach, and he found such articles to be ideal for use in his classroom. Thus, if "reality is a construction," as Kracauer had argued, such investigations were meant to show the girders and facades that put this reality together.[21]

Such indirect methods, moreover, are commensurate with his views on statements of positive religiosity, statements that, as argued above, he generally avoided. The essay or feuilleton was not a space for utopian exhortations, but a realm where the "hollow space" could be kept open, a space of waiting. In his review of a book of essays by Heinrich Mann, he alluded to this sense of language and essay form, comparing Mann's language to a "landscape broken up with crevices." Such linguistic terrain "holds darkness enough, but just as it does not deny the darkness, so it also does not dwell in it; rather it leaves the hollow spaces free."[22] Language as a landscape, cut through by fissures, was a trope by which he could indicate the necessary dialectic in language, a dialectic that swung between prevailing opacity and momentary insight.

These "hollow spaces" were the domain of waiting, an attentiveness towards the unspoken and unsayable word of redemption.[23] The essayistic mode of the feuilleton was suited to this purpose. A full discussion of some of the theological and philosophical investments that were placed onto the essay form is outside of the scope of this discussion, but suffice to note that such investments were ready at hand and Kracauer was surely acquainted with this discourse. In his book of essays, *Soul and Form*, Lukács had suggested that the critic was one who waits, and he described this task in quasi-theological terms:

> ... it is not the [the critic] who awakens [aesthetic judgments] to life and action: the one who whispers them into his ear is the great value-definer of aesthetics, the one who is always about to arrive, the one who is never quite yet there, the only one who has been called judge. The essayist is a Schopenhauer who writes his *Parerga* while waiting for the arrival of . . . *The World as Will and Idea*; he is a John the Baptist who goes out to preach in the wilderness about another who is still to come.[24]

The feuilleton too then, could make some larger philosophical claims. Even Rosenzweig, despite his dismissive view of the newspaper, conceded some ground: "Indeed even the newspaper feuilleton, however shrunk to fit the capacities of the breakfast hour, has something of the blessed oral power to banish this curse of literature: its timelessness."[25]

When Kracauer wrote about religion, the exigencies of newspaper publishing probably did influence what he thought he could and could not say in this respect. His private statements, on the other hand, are often quite blunt and furnish a different perspective to his public ones. To his friends Löwenthal and Susman, he often made his views quite plain, in part because he often sought their agreement. Thus, he wanted Susman's approval for the agenda he outlined in "Those Who Wait," and he tried to dissuade Löwenthal from pursuing

Hebrew studies at the expense of secular philosophy.[26] Taken together with his criticism of Scheler and the religious revival, one might conclude that the general trajectory of his thought led away from religious and theological concerns towards more secular pursuits. As we have seen, Kracauer himself sometimes confirmed such a view.

Yet, this does not fully account for the twists and turns that characterize his public statements on religious themes—nor do the constraints of publishing in a newspaper. The convoluted development of Kracauer's attitude towards religion is evident in his inconsistent responses to the issue of portraying religious subject matter in film. Given his later success as a film critic, it is not surprising that one of the earliest articles he wrote for the *FZ* was a review of the 1916 film, *Christus*, a dramatization of the life of Christ directed by Giulio Antamoro.[27] His article offered little in the way of actual film criticism; instead Kracauer indulged in generalizations on the national peculiarities of religious expression. Thus, he found the realism in *Christus* too crude and more appropriate to an Italian audience. "We are," he wrote, "fortunately, not yet so Americanized that we require such exhibitions to incite our piety." Germans, he continued, would not tolerate such "profanation of the holiest tenets of faith [*Glaubensgüter*]." In a short notice published the following day, Kracauer returned to this theme, but in more detail. He suggested that the lead actor was sometimes too coarse in his gestures. His bold physicality was unable to represent the sacred in a "truly comprehensible" way.[28] His main objection then is that the film has not resolved the problem of how to represent religious subject matter; he does not as a rule, however, reject such representations.

Yet, by 1926 Kracauer took the opposite position on the same question. In his review of *Ben Hur*, Kracauer voiced his reservations regarding the representation of religious contents.[29] The depiction of sacred history in the film, he argued, was "offensive" and an "evil." The filmmakers, so he claimed, seemed to think that technical expertise alone (such as the early use of color tints) could somehow bridge the gap between sacred and profane. He noted that even where they attempted a tactful gesture such as in the decision to not show the full figure of Christ, they had in fact only worsened the problem by drawing attention to the film's otherwise ambitious fabrications and general lack of taste.[30]

There are a number of questions that arise out of these two reviews. One, why does Kracauer object to the representation of sacred history in 1926, when he found it acceptable or not even worth mentioning in 1921? To what extent should one understand this objection in theological terms, that is, on what grounds does Kracauer reject these representations? Also, who is the "we" in the first article? Is Kracauer including himself in the plural form? At the outset, one must concede that Kracauer may have been influenced by the editorial policies of the *FZ*. His reviews of *Christus* appeared just days before

Christmas and the editors may have been reluctant to offend religious sentiments during the holiday season. Moreover, Kracauer would have been well aware that his readership was predominantly, though not exclusively, German and Christian.[31]

However, these facts do not entirely resolve the question of his personal identification with the views expressed. To be sure, his rejection of excessive piety and of the allegedly crude materialism of these films is consistent with his stated ideal of "holy sobriety." Moreover, there is reason to believe that Kracauer took seriously the question of offending religious sentiments. For instance, when the *FZ* was attacked publicly for offending religion and morality, Kracauer was entrusted with writing the rebuttal.[32] The attack against the paper was led by a Professor Brunner who spoke on behalf of the Interkonfessionelle Verein zur Hebung der Sittlichkeit. The group had been angered by the newspaper's support for a theatre company that had performed *Reigen*, a controversial play by Arthur Schnitzler. While conceding that the correct balance between artistic license and immorality was often difficult to determine, Kracauer argued that the paper had, contrary to the views of Brunner, always sought to find this balance without harming public sentiment; indeed, the paper had often "raised its voice against the wounding of public sensitivity in religious matters." Of course, given the collective nature of the *FZ* editorial conferences and the sensitivity of this issue, it is probable that Kracauer expressed a position approved by the *FZ* editors in common.[33] Yet, I would argue that the "we" Kracauer used here, and in his reviews of *Christus* and *Ben Hur*, was, by and large, in accord with his own views and their fluctuations at the time. For Kracauer's response to the *Reigen* affair is consistent with a pattern that emerges in his subsequent journalism on religious themes. On the one hand, he argued that religion must reckon with modernity and that this imperative precluded religious revival; but on the other hand, he never refutes religion as such—at times, he even claims to defend it.[34]

The rationale behind Kracauer's position is twofold. One, throughout much of his writing, he is reluctant to abandon religious concepts such as redemption and grace (*Erlösung, Gnade*). Though his usage of the latter term declined after the mid-1920s, redemption remained an important theme throughout his work. However, before 1925 both terms retained a critical function, particularly in his polemics against Weimar's so-called vagabond religiosity. Kracauer argued these concepts preserved viable "truth contents," and these could be salvaged from their "mythological hull," stripped of their theological language and deployed anew in a program of ideological critique.[35] This was, for instance, how Adorno understood Kracauer's intentions.[36] Of course, secularizing theological content does not amount to a defense of religion, and Kracauer was relatively unconcerned with the fate of religious institutions once their "truth contents" had been appropriated. Nonetheless, his position argued that, for the moment, religious tradition was still the custodian of a conceptual richness that could not be ignored. Any attempt to reckon with the social desires that these concepts represented meant that one had to reckon with religious traditions more generally.

Related to this point, Kracauer generally refused to allow secular culture the foundational functions that he believed religion had once possessed. This was not so much an abandonment of "revolutionary culturalism," but rather a redefinition of culture in light of the claims of religion. As he wrote in 1925, the artist only "builds the temple," but the "fundaments of faith are barred" and not his or her concern.[37] Thus, culture does have a role to play, but one with limits. Society may grant an artist the role of prophet, he argued, but the artist is never commensurate to this function. For in a secularized world the function of art was restricted to the negative. Culture could not create a meaningful and unified whole from the variegated world of appearances; rather it could only expose the failure to find such meaning. In the 1925 article "Artist of the Age," he described what he saw as the contemporary dilemma of art:

> The private soul that moves in the negative may unfold their middle core, and announce the melancholy absence of Thou in the world of appearances; the objective world as something existing cannot be seized. And the difficulties of self-expression enter into this conflict of conscience in which the artist who inquires of the middle proceeds without fail.[38]

Thus, the predominant artistic mode in modernity, as Lukács had argued, was ironic, one that recognized the loss of wholeness, and the absence of a God who could be addressed as Thou.[39] In accord with this position, Kracauer could not accept the view that religion was simply an effect of culture, a mere superstructure resting on the economic base; on the contrary, since culture did not have the resources to found a true community, religion could not be listed under its rubric. Instead, he accepted the opposite view that religion was the original condition of culture itself, and it was religion that had performed the unifying task that eluded and would continue to elude modernity.

Not only did such a position mean that culture should not and could not appropriate a religious aura, it also meant that positive religiosity was harmful to artistic expression and not to be equated with genuine religious conviction. Most often, so Kracauer believed, these expressions were merely formal, an aesthetic counterfeit of religious life. This was at the root of his seemingly "nihilist" position towards religious revival.[40] A model of what he thought was the proper relationship between religion and art emerged, surprisingly enough, in the correspondence between Jean Cocteau and Jacques Maritain.[41] Kracauer reviewed the letters between the two men in 1927 and found that the Catholic theologian and the avant-garde aesthete were in substantial agreement: there was no need to fashion a Catholic or religious art, but rather artists served God by remaining faithful to the demands specific to their artistic vocation. Thus, "the art that pleases God," so Maritain claimed, "is an art with all of its teeth."[42] Kracauer went on to note that in Germany this insight was too often neglected in the rush to "subordinate" art to religion and thus to produce a sanctified culture with a supposed access to the religious sphere. Moreover, in a "transitional society" such as Germany, the "reality-contents of art" (*Wirklichkeitsgehalte der Kunst*) were inseparable from wider "social powers." Thus, Kracauer conceived of "religious art" as a form of expression that had to avoid ostentatious piety, but could not avoid social critique. In general, he felt the religious revival had reneged on this socially critical function.

The actual extent of the religious revival in postwar Germany is, of course, difficult to determine, so it is hard to know whether or not Kracauer was in fact responding to a broad and deeply rooted cultural transformation. Historians of the Great War such as Jay Winter, Annette Becker and Stéphane Audoin-Rouzeau have argued that religion and spiritualism surged during the war, and that these impulses continued to manifest themselves in postwar practices of commemoration and personal bereavement.[43] Similarly, there was a deep and wide-ranging boom in religious practice among German Catholics after 1918, an increase that was expressed in movements for liturgical reform and greater participation of the laity.[44] Kracauer's home city, Frankfurt, was an important if idiosyncratic locus of this revived Catholicism. It was home to a large Catholic minority; after 1918, one of every three Frankfurters considered themselves to be Catholic. Between 1871 and 1925, when the population of the city more than quadrupled in size, the number who were Catholics went up from 25.8 to 31.1 percent. Thus, together with its relatively large and long established Jewish population, the city had a decidedly multiconfessional character.[45]

For Kracauer himself, evidence of the religious revival is readily found in the daily facts of his working life. His duties as a journalist compelled him to inhabit the lecture halls of Frankfurt and south Germany where he heard numerous lectures on a bewildering variety of religious, cultural, and philosophical issues. During the first half of the 1920s, he wrote on a diverse range of these subjects: church reform groups, discussion evenings devoted to Russia, Brahmanism, Chinese philosophy, anthroposophy, experiments in communal life, school reform, Buddhism, spiritual hucksters, and so forth. What united most of these diverse groups, was the common impulse of renewal—of moral, spiritual, and cultural regeneration. His second book *Georg* satirized this spiritual hunger that seemed to regularly draw considerable crowds into the auditoriums of Frankfurt:

> The followers of anthroposophy wanted to stir in him a longing for the supernatural, while the school reformers are, in the best sense, sensual and want to

develop everything from the child itself who then, perhaps, will never grow up to read Dostoevksy, concerning whom numerous lectures were held that compelled him to dissipate into a Russian, waiting upon redemption—of course, not for too long, because immediately after comes the Decline of the West, according to which he must harden himself until Count Keyserling appears who softens him anew—because Keyserling reconciles all contradictions harmoniously, one with the other, a singular harmony that lasts for precisely one hour. And so he ranged forlorn over the sea of the public sphere.[46]

Thus, setting aside the question of the actual extent of the religious revival, it is clear that there was a significant public discourse on the issue, and it is within this discourse that Kracauer positioned himself.

Of course, for Kracauer the religious revival was in many ways a personal reality. As discussed above, he was not entirely immune to its "siren call"; more importantly, the religious revival was a vital issue to a large number of his friends and intellectual acquaintances. Some of these figures, such as Susman, Löwenthal, Rosenzweig, and Thormann, have already been mentioned; others will emerge in the course of the following discussion.

Adrift on the Seas of Religious Revival

Kracauer's position towards the religious revival had already become confrontational when he published his sharply negative review of Max Scheler's *Of the Eternal in Man* near the end of 1921. By that time Scheler was an intellectual "star of the first order"; Kracauer, on the other hand, was a scarcely known journalist at the beginning of his career.[47] Hence, the essay's harsh and almost disrespectful tone must have been surprising. Kracauer almost certainly intended to have this effect, as he had shown a draft of the essay to Susman before publication, and her comments would have alerted him to the fact that some might find the essay too aggressive. Though in the end he proposed the addition of some mollifying references to Scheler's intellectual stature, the effect was no less unsettling and the published review earned him a private rebuke from Rosenzweig.[48] The abrasive and ironic tone that he adopted when discussing religious issues did much to alienate Kracauer from his more religious-minded friends. As Ernst Simon pointed out to him, even if he claimed to respect those he criticized, "admiration does not take well to irony."[49]

However, despite this sharp tone, Kracauer did not want to be understood as irreligious or anticlerical. As he wrote to Susman, he did not sympathize with the radical skepticism of a Max Weber.[50] This was one part of the argument contained in his 1922 article, "Those Who Wait." This essay outlined a tripartite approach to the problem of religious revival and secular society.

Between the religiosity of figures such as Rabbi Nobel, for instance, and the deep skepticism of someone such as Weber there were those who waited and watched. These were the ones who were deeply affected by the loss of religious certainty; they would have welcomed faith, but they could not justify it in intellectual terms. Moreover, they believed that faith could not be compelled, and the result was that they occupied a position of indefinite waiting. Kracauer described this state as a "hesitant openness," but he did not elaborate on this point at much length—what are these people actually waiting for? Nonetheless, he clearly intended that this suspended state should not be understood as a merely passive "wait and see" with no object in mind, even if the final resolution was outside of our understanding. Such a position should not cause undue despair, he argued, at least not for those who were still "exerting themselves" (*die Sich-Mühenden*).[51]

The question then becomes what did the efforts of "waiting" involve, and how did Kracauer envision this state of endless anticipation? At least part of the answer resides in the formation of a critical vocation. Active waiting involved the deciphering of the present, and *The Detective Novel* was a way of putting this stratagem into practice. Modernity was akin to the "danger zones" described in the opening chapter of this study.[52] This was the space where the swarms of enthusiasts, miracle workers, and religious adventurers ran rampant. Amid this "flood of heretics" the process of *ratio* was embodied in the profane black mass celebrated by the detective and his "unwilling helper," the criminal. The solution of the mystery, however, did not unveil the real; rather it reduced it to the ready-made categories of idealist thinking. Similar to the man in Kafka's story "Before the Law," none of these heretics and adventurers is able to push their way through the door and find access to the truth. The critic was no exception to this rule; but Kracauer accepted this limitation and confined his task to seeking out and identifying the door and its gatekeepers.[53] These were to be found wherever theological impulses ran aground on the shores of the secular, where the utopian confronted the material bases of the real. If access to the religious sphere was blocked, then criticism would expose this blockage. We could not know redemption, but we could know a world that waited for it. Furthermore, we could recognize the erroneous ideology that held human society to be a knowable and ever-fixed order. Exposing ideology would provoke an unmediated encounter with the negative and launch humankind on a vaguely defined and uncertain path to redemption.[54]

Kracauer outlined this concept of the critical vocation in a letter to Susman in early 1921, a letter that anticipates the programmatic agenda of his essay, "Those Who Wait." Referring very little to specific political events, the letter still conveys what Kracauer saw as the uncertain mood of the newly born republic. The instability of those years provoked a sense of anxiety that compelled him to take a position, to define himself vis-à-vis the numerous discourses of revolutionary transformation. It is on account of these discourses, that his response, one of renunciation and waiting, acquires a measure of radicalism; for during a period when almost everyone followed a program or party line, or spoke of the "new man" and the new order, "waiting," so he implied, was a form of resistance. If as the protagonist of *Georg* proclaims, everyone must have a position (*Halt*), then waiting might be described as an antiposition.[55] Yet, it still offered Kracauer a sufficient foothold from which he could contribute to the cultural-political struggle. In his letter to Susman, he described his response to the contemporary spiritual resurgence:

> To be sure, a tremendous historical moment is at hand—I sense it, it stirs me to my very fingertips, I cannot sleep because of it ... The quest for meaning echoes powerfully as it does throughout the centuries. Within Catholicism it begins to stir, and Protestant idealism as well is everywhere inflamed. Settlements have been founded, such as that of Eberhard Arnold's at Sannerz bei Schlüchtern that seeks to start a new life on the basis of a Christian-communist foundation. The same goes for Judaism; many live again within the law and seek to devote themselves inwardly to form.[56]

Clearly, Kracauer was affected by this spike in religious sentiments. His response was anticipated by his earlier admiration of the charismatic Frankfurt Rabbi, Anton Nobel, as discussed above.[57] Of course, it is not clear that the charisma of someone such as Nobel would have been able to draw him into a religious existence. In the same letter to Susman, he casts suspicion on those movements that depend on "charismatic personality." Such movements, he claimed, could not generate ideas or concepts that transcended the personal; thus, they could not bring about the "transformation of thought ... for which we all longed." His remarks on this question were more specifically directed at Protestant and mystical sects, but he also conceded that in spite of his admiration for Nobel, he could not follow his model. Similarly, he could not find his way to the certainty (*Haltung*) claimed, for instance, by Rosenzweig and Rosenstock-Huessy. It would be "romanticism," he asserted, to come to an "affirmation and dedication to the "Law" ... only out of knowing, out of insight." Without faith such actions lacked authenticity. Having thus repudiated the believer's path, he could see only one valid position:

> I see only one way to follow *!!Waiting!!* To be passive, to watch and to know, to live right and virtuously ... perhaps, the words of Lao Tzu are valid here: nothingness moves the world. Please write to me: can you follow Judaism as does Rosenzweig? Can you follow Catholicism? No, that I know. You are a mystic. Perhaps we all must be one; it is, at the end of the day, our fate![58]

Surprisingly, he argues that Rosenzweig had confirmed his views in a discussion, though he added that Rosenzweig still maintained that what for Kracauer was only "tendency" was for himself a definite "positive." This he defined as a *Mitleben*, an always present "dwelling" within the religious sphere: "I live in it. I have that which you call form."[59] Kracauer later responded to such claims of authenticity with the idea of the "short-circuit man." According to Kracauer, these individuals sought refuge from a meaningless world by fabricating a religious certainty. They are, so he claims, often indistinguishable from "genuine believers" and their psychology and motives are more difficult to recognize.[60] Kracauer seems divided at this point between attributing some authenticity to religious sentiment and rejecting it altogether. Though he mentions "genuine believers" one suspects that he did not believe that many such existed. He warns against being so presumptuous as to shine a light into the "spiritual depths of others," but he seems to do precisely that when he then argues that the "short-circuit men" can only reach the religious sphere in part: "their faith is not borne by the full breadth of their self, and for that reason the truth of religion does not draw entirely near; it is more a will to faith rather than a lingering within it, more a hasty interpretation than an accomplished fact."[61]

Kracauer seems unable to concede the possibility of faith, a fact that may have derived from his perceptions of what I would call a religious flânerie. Everywhere, he claimed, the religious traditions of the world are sampled as if they were goods in a department store. "No confession of faith is too remote," he mused, "we mix Buddhism, Confucianism and Mohammedism as if we were shuffling cards."[62] Even those who appeared earnest had wavered at times, or had undergone crises of conversion, as was the case with men such as Scheler, Rosenzweig, and Rosenstock-Huessy. His inability to concede ground on the question of religious authenticity provoked a rupture between him and the advocates of religious revival. From their point of view, Kracauer was among the "inauthentic" and, according to Adorno, this meant his exclusion from any serious discussion of religion.[63]

The difference between the authentic and the inauthentic was carried over into different interpretations of waiting, its meaning and its occupations. At the close of his letter to Susman, Kracauer offered some idea of what direction his own work was to take in light of this position. He imagined a project that would reevaluate words such as "I," "time," and "Eternity"; however, he stressed that he could not give these concepts a new meaning (*Sinn*) for he did not possess it. Instead, the drive to interpret these terms anew was a preliminary or anticipatory gesture: "I stand outside the door, and only know that here is the entrance. Is that enough, to point to the entry way? But perhaps someone else opens the door!"[64] This then was to be a project that observed certain limits. In contrast to the man who seeks the law in the Kafka tale, Kracauer assumes from the outset that one cannot pass over the threshold.

How Susman responded to Kracauer's overture is not known as her half of the correspondence has been lost; but she probably would have had little difficulty in sympathizing with his views. Indeed, she might have found very little that was striking about them. Her own writing covered similar terrain, and it was this aspect of her thought that was admired by Ernst Bloch, for instance. Before the war, he had written to her in gratitude for her striking demonstration that Judaism was an "unconcluded" religion:

> Judaism is the religion of waiting . . . the relativity that poisons all religiously ungifted devotees of religious forms, has become in Judaism a motive of religion itself; it is ever heretical, because it is always longing, being partway in the beyond [Darüberhinwegsein], and mystical.[65]

Thus, there is potential agreement on waiting as recognition of the perpetually inconclusive nature of the world and of a longed for but not actualized redemption. Certainly, the idea of "waiting" was one that Kracauer could have derived from Jewish tradition. However, as a means of investigating how this theme took shape in his work, some further consideration of his engagement with the religious currents of his day is needed, including the religious revival in Christianity.

* * * * *

What Kracauer thought or felt in regards to the Christian and Jewish faiths was sufficiently vague to elicit speculation concerning his actual religious allegiances. In the circles around Rosenzweig, Kracauer was sometimes suspected of having Catholic or Protestant sympathies. At one point, Rosenzweig remarked that his work "smelled of Catholicism," while his friend Hans Ehrenberg stated that Kracauer was a lowly offshoot of recent trends in Protestant theology. According to Ehrenberg, Kracauer hid his "inner impotence" with a "cloak à la Barth," though he "naturally" did not want to suggest that Kracauer was comparable to Barth in intellectual terms.[66] His loyalty to Lutheranism, so Rosenzweig later suggested, was probably one of the reasons behind his attack of their translation of the Bible: "Comical people, these Jews, who work themselves up in the spirit of a Bible-thumping Protestant matron!"[67]

Yet, there is not much to suggest that Kracauer ever thought of himself as a Protestant, and, moreover, his responses to the Protestant revival after 1918 suggest that he had many reservations towards Protestantism. These stem from two main sources. One, the Reformation was tainted from his point of view by its role in destroying the stable order offered by medieval Catholicism, thus inaugurating the destructive process of secular emancipation. "The decisive turn in the German spirit (and that of Europe overall) since the Reformation," so he argued in the pages of *Die Rheinlande*, "now consists in the fact that it has forfeited the unconditional truth and absoluteness of the holy teaching of the church." As a result, the "cosmic unity" of the past had been "blown apart."[68]

In the immediate postwar years, Kracauer undertook a study of these events, reading works on the Reformation by Dilthey and Ranke as part of his attempt to reckon with the meaning of a secularized world. In the latter, Kracauer claimed to have been impressed by the words of the Protestant leader Zwingli, to the effect that "one could not bring heaven to earth."[69] On the other hand, he thought that Luther's support of the princes during the Peasants' War had had a devastating effect on the course of German history. However, neither Luther nor Zwingli, he believed, could be counted as true revolutionaries; indeed, Kracauer suggested a fundamental incompatibility of revolution and the German spirit:

> To the German, revolution is not the final goal; indeed, one notices this today. "Society" does not mean the same thing for him as for the western nations; he is so barbaric and stupid in all his political affairs. When his nature is absorbed into society, he just feels a shudder; he is only beautiful when he is an inwardly, metaphysical individual.[70]

For Kracauer, Protestantism then is associated with a fatalist decline from the organic unity of the Middle Ages to the fragmented and stoic world of individualism. The liberation from the Roman church is paid for with an incurable inner restlessness, and the individual now had to confront an impenetrable world with the limited resources of culture and science.[71] In this view, an organic communal totality is displaced by the idea of society as a perpetual cultural project. The rise of idealist thought was to be understood as a flawed attempt to reckon with this problem—though Kracauer was careful not to attribute the triumph of idealism to the Reformation alone, noting the influence of the Enlightenment as well.[72]

It is surprising to find Kracauer paying homage to an almost romantic vision of medieval Catholicism, even if he discarded the ideal of a "closed culture" early in his writing career. Still, in the early 1920s, this concept exerted an almost magical aura that seemed to obscure the difficult problems of emancipation and secularism. That a closed culture of this sort implied a potentially oppressive degree of cultural and religious homogeneity did not unsettle his crude vision of organic harmony. Indeed, Kracauer seems oblivious to this as a problem at all, and part of the reason for this may be that he simply did not associate the emancipation of Jews and other minorities with the rise of secular culture. Indeed, in his essay for the Moritz-Mannheimer Stiftung he suggested that some values such as charity and tolerance could be best ensured in the framework of a church-led society.[73] The state, on the other hand, was inevitably limited; it could legally emancipate Jews, but it could not compel their social acceptance. Therefore, legal equality did not translate into social equality, and while institutional changes were not negligible, only a comprehensive transformation of social values would decisively alter the situation. In this respect Kracauer implied that the religious community could be a more effective agent of change than the constitutional state.[74]

If the state was unable to affect a social and cultural transformation, then the locus of attention shifted to the individual, and it was here that Kracauer detected a more intractable dilemma in Protestant theology. Kracauer accepted the view that the Protestant insistence on the individual's direct relationship to God coincided with the emergence of the rational and autonomous subject. However, the latter had the effect of undermining belief in any "absolute meaning" that transcended subjectivity. The disappearance of meaning meant that abstract thought could insert itself between the subject and "concrete reality." Thus, the "German mind" was no longer held in the "custody of the designed world," but rather it presumed for itself the "middle point" of existence. Therefore, "the ideas cherished by the free-floating 'I' further displace the world-sheltering myth."[75] Under the reign of this modern individual, religion also suffers; God is reduced to a mere "idea," a formal concept dependent upon the judgments of the rational subject (*Vernunftsubjekt*). This overweening subjectivity led to two kinds of individualism: the levelling and "atomizing" individualism of the Enlightenment and the Romantic ideal of an unfolding personal essence.[76] Though superficially these concepts were at odds, they resembled one another in that neither of them facilitated contact with the objective world of things. Thus, to recover the real, one had to dismantle the idealist influence that had found a home in Protestant theology.

Yet, Kracauer was also aware that the need to overcome idealism was alive in contemporary Protestantism itself.[77] After 1918, the work of Barth, Jaspers, Thurneisen, and Gogarten had initiated a wide-ranging critique of both liberal and orthodox theology. These writers tried to restore Protestantism to what they saw as its fundamentals, that is, to the individual's relationship with an absolute and unknowable God. This meant removing all mediations between God and the individual, including the allegedly noxious overgrowth of idealist philosophy. While Kracauer was sympathetic, he did not believe that idealist thought could be so readily deleted.[78] In a 1925 article discussing contemporary religious trends, he argued that the repudiation of idealism had, in fact, been pursued to such an extreme that the new theology had harmed their attempts to reclaim the real.[79] By emphasizing that only through faith in God could one enter reality, they had eliminated all other factors. When compared to Catholicism, Kracauer believed that the new Protestant theology allowed no room for "creaturely contingency." Moreover, he argued that their reinvigorated concept of the individual subject was still built upon idealist constructions; essentially, the new theology had not advanced far beyond the old. Instead, they had mistaken the recovery of Protestant origins with an overcoming of idealist thought, yet, it was by no means clear that the latter followed from the former. To Kracauer, in a review of work by Karl Jaspers, what resulted was a rigid "negative religiosity," a "world view that no longer viewed the world."[80]

However, in spite of these reservations, Kracauer sympathized with some aspects of Protestant thought. By rendering visible "those deep shadows that idealism did not see and did not want to see," the new theology had performed an important task.[81] Just as importantly, Kracauer believed that Protestantism retained a rebellious core that might serve as a bulwark against the encroachments of state power. In two articles written in 1933, he drew attention to what he saw as the stubbornly nonconformist aspects of the Protestant tradition. Given the situation in Germany at this time, this was a potentially useful legacy. In the resistance of Barth and other theologians to the Nazi church reforms of that year, Kracauer argued that one could trace the unruly "spirit" of the Reformation. "While the Vatican had made its peace with Hitler," he wrote, Protestants had met Nazi ideology with "open resistance."[82] Such claims were almost certainly exaggerated for tactical purposes, and for this reason, his earlier judgments concerning Luther's political role during the Peasants' War were put aside. It is also worth noting that in the same article Kracauer mentioned Gogarten as an opponent of the Nazi threat to church independence. Yet, Gogarten had a much more ambiguous relationship with both the German Christians and the National Socialist state.[83] Kracauer, already in Paris, may not have known of his contradictory positions in this regard. Therefore, he may have drawn on his impressions of his work prior to 1933, or he may have chosen to make tactical use of his reputation to counter more dangerous opponents. This was indeed the main point of the article that reviewed a recent pamphlet published by Barth, *Theological Existence Today!* This work, Kracauer stated, represented a challenge that went far beyond the conflict between church and state; for Barth could hardly repudiate Nazi church policy without likewise repudiating the ideological premises of the total state.[84] Of course, Kracauer also believed that the current nationalist frenzy did, in fact, have a distinctly Protestant stamp, but nonetheless he seized upon Barth's intervention in church policy as a potential means of challenging Nazi claims to absolute power.[85]

Thus, on the one hand, Protestantism emerged as a resistant force towards the powers of the state, and on the other, it harbored tendencies that supported, or could support, accommodation to Nazism. This was a conflict of direction that he almost certainly was aware of firsthand through his connection with Hermann Herrigel, a fellow editor on the *FZ* who was responsible for the university page (*Hochschulblatt*) in which many of Kracauer's essays first appeared.[86] Not much concerning their relationship is known, but according to Kracauer, initially they had a good rapport. The two men often discussed "the most difficult of philosophical questions" well into the evening hours, and Kracauer told Susman that they shared the same fundamental position (*Grundposition*), readily finding agreement on the work of writers such as Lukács and Count Keyserling.[87] As already mentioned, Kracauer also sought the opinion of Herrigel regarding his detective study, a fact suggesting that he valued his opinions. Of greater interest, however, is his claim, in a letter to Susman, to speak both for Herrigel and himself when he articulated the position expressed in "Those Who Wait."[88] Given the scant number of sources that attest to this collaboration, the issue of Herrigel's potential influence must be stated with caution, but as he does appear to have been a significant figure for Kracauer at this early stage in his career, some attention should be devoted to this largely forgotten writer.[89]

Herrigel may be thought of as a kind of religious flâneur, a notion I want to use more widely in connection with Kracauer's reading of postwar religiosity. The use of this term should not suggest that in some way his religious opinions and judgments were superficial, resembling the passing judgments of the casual window-shopper on the street; rather, he represents a fluid and mobile religiosity, one that sought ways to accommodate faith in modern culture and that was open to experimentation in the religious sphere. Herrigel was a devoted observer of trends in religion and philosophy, as is evident in two of his works from the 1920s: *New Thinking* published in 1928, and two years later, *Between Question and Answer: Thoughts on the Cultural Crisis*. Moreover, he wrote numerous essays on religious and philosophical themes, not only in the *FZ*, but also in journals such as *Die Rheinlande*, *Die Tat*, and *Die Kreatur*. As this list suggests, Herrigel was also deeply engaged with questions of religious revival. He was a member of the Evangelical church, and he was close to Friedrich Gogarten whose ministry he sometimes visited.[90] However, his circle of friends and acquaintances was broad in terms of confession, and it overlapped considerably with Kracauer's milieu—for instance, Ernst Michel, Alfons Paquet, Werner Thormann, and Martin Buber. A Friday evening *Stammtisch*, to which Kracauer referred in a letter to Thormann, would probably have included Herrigel.[91]

As a student, Herrigel had been impressed by the work of the neo-Kantian philosopher Paul Natorp, yet, Herrigel was no simple neo-Kantian. He was, in fact, deeply critical of the attempt to revive idealist thought, and by the end of the decade he had become an avid supporter of the so-called new thinking—a term that he probably derived from Rosenzweig, whose work he also admired.[92] These interests led him to Davos in 1929 where he witnessed and reported on the famous quarrel between Ernst Cassirer and Martin Heidegger. While his account was by and large even-handed, he was clearly more sympathetic towards Heidegger and his departure from Western philosophical traditions.[93]

Herrigel was a stimulating discussion partner for Kracauer because of his critical attitude towards idealism and his deep interest in the fate of religion in modernity. Herrigel was a vigorous proponent of what he called the "realistic spiritual movement"—an umbrella term encompassing the religious revival. He promoted this idea in a special number of the *FZ* university page in 1928, wherein his own work appeared alongside an essay by the cultural philosopher Eberhard Grisebach, a discussion of Gogarten, and shorter excerpts from the work of Rosenzweig and Rosenstock-Huessy.[94] These writers, so the editors remarked, sought to overcome idealist influence, a critique that Herrigel had put forward as early as 1922. In this earlier essay, published in *Die Tat*, he claimed that idealism had hindered the connection to the real, a connection crucial to any religious view of the world. Therefore, the influence of idealism needed to be countered by what he called "transcendent critique," a process of thinking through the system of abstract thought to its end. This method would isolate the absolute limit that separated humankind and God, the negative from the positive.[95] Such ideas are not without some affinities to Kracauer's work of the early 1920s, but this should not obscure some of the differences between the two—these were already apparent in Herrigel's negative response to the *Detective Novel*. Even though they shared common reference points to mutually recognized problems, their motives and intentions differed considerably. This was certainly the case in terms of statements of positive religiosity. In contrast to Kracauer, the idea of God was for Herrigel both a condition of the "negative world" and a necessary part of any critique of idealism.[96] From this point of view, he was predisposed to misread *The Detective Novel* as a purely negative representation of reality excluding any positive valuation of *ratio*, or any positive consequences whatsoever. Kracauer grumbled to Löwenthal "as if that was what I had meant."[97]

For both Kracauer and Herrigel, the postwar period was a period of flux in terms of their attitudes to religion and politics. That is, they both were flâneurs of a sort, but for Herrigel the search for different forms of belief tended towards a more closed system of thought: Protestant nationalism, and afterwards, the German Christian movement.[98] Indeed, there is good reason to believe that after 1933 he became an enthusiastic supporter of the Nazis.[99] By his own admission, he was deeply impressed by the theology of Hans Schomerus, a strong exponent of the German Christian movement, and he also had ties with the *völkisch* theology represented by figures such as Wilhelm Stapel.[100] During the Third Reich, he edited the journal *Christliche Besinnung Heute*, which was a forum for his views. The journal was, however, eventually banned by Nazi authorities in 1939.[101] His accommodation to National Socialism appears to have been assisted by his belief in a so-called middle order, a layer of reality that he argued was suspended between the symbolic and the factual and that was only valid in faith. From this point of view, God was to be sought for only in the sacred words of belief; the material world, on the other hand, could be left to politics. To be sure, he did not want to separate these realms absolutely, but he believed that politics would "mistake its task" if it became a mere instrument for the "work of God." The state then should not interfere in the religious development of the individual, but politics was another matter. In a letter to Martin Buber written in 1936, Herrigel argued that to his mind the current political order had struck a good balance between these claims. It did not invade the space between the private person and God; rather, through the *Führer* principle the movement placed more emphasis on "personal responsibility and decision." It allowed for freedom in religious cultivation, and action in politics—and politics, so he argued, "cannot wait."[102]

This concept of politics as a sphere that does not tolerate passivity does suggest some of the differences that would later separate Kracauer from Herrigel. To be sure, the admiration of the *Führer* principle does not sit comfortably next to the critical stance taken in "Those Who Wait." Yet, it should be noted that Kracauer was not without some sympathies towards the *Führer* principle in the early 1920s when he appears to have been closest to Herrigel. At this time, he published two essays on the theme of political authority: "The Essence of Political Leaders" and "Authority and Individualism." These essays did not propose an uncritical acceptance of authoritarian rule, but some of his remarks do tend towards a murky concept of authority and its uses.[103] "The soul of the leader," Kracauer stated, "embraces at once beginning and end, his actual realm is the way itself; he is the *Master of the way*." Such a leader, he continued, "resembles the artist."[104] These remarks were probably influenced by the sense of ongoing political and cultural crisis that afflicted the early Republic, in particular, the violent confrontations over political legitimacy between right and left. Kracauer, however, is careful to separate himself from a simple glorification of state power and stability for its own sake. More at issue for Kracauer is the foundation of a political legitimacy that would moderate the extremes of both individualism and authoritarianism. This would, moreover, draw from what he saw as the positive side of utopian ideals, joining them to a political pragmatism that neither affirms existing political realities nor lapses into arbitrary state rule.[105] Still, these essays are worth considering in reference to Herrigel, because Kracauer's definitions of sacred and profane politics become blurred in ways that anticipate Herrigel's more dubious formulations. Kracauer even outlined a role for the intellectual: the "wise one." This figure was complementary to the *Führer*, an individual who combined the qualities of the idealist and the realist, and who identified the communal goals that the leader would then bring to fulfillment: "the wise one and the *Führer* find completion . . . the one who espies the final goal and longs for the way, and the other stepping onto the path and mastering it; in such fashion the affairs of God are best served in our world."[106]

In the work of Herrigel, religious flânerie emerges as a project beset by many risks. His interests in religion are eclectic and permitted a good degree of experimentation. According to one student of his writing, outside of his desire to challenge the idealist consensus, Herrigel did not have a firm and consistent philosophical point of view until after the 1920s.[107] The attempt to define the boundaries that separated the sacred from the profane, and to identify the claims legitimate to both, led Herrigel to accept radical experimentation in politics and culture. Positive religiosity thus legitimated political extremism. As Hausenstein, his former colleague on the *FZ*, warned him in 1934, his "religious theses" had given too much precedence to contemporary "ideas of the world," by which Hausenstein meant the current political order.[108] For Herrigel, a search that led from the idealism of Natorp and Cassirer to the "new thinking" eventually led to support for the German Christians and the Nazi state—perhaps, as a solution to the very religious eclecticism that distinguished his interests in the 1920s. This conclusion to his intellectual trajectory is a sobering comment on the limits of Weimar's religious pluralism, all the more so as Herrigel's interest in Jewish religious thought was probably exceptional. That he finally chose a movement that sought to end this religious eclecticism suggests that the religious experiments of the 1920s were a deeply ambivalent phenomenon.[109]

* * * * *

As with contemporary Protestantism, Kracauer found Catholic thought to be in a similar state of flux, and marked by a deep unease towards modern society. His review of the correspondence between Cocteau and Maritain, discussed above, demonstrates his interest in Catholic thought.[110] Wherever the church tried to reckon with quotidian reality and not demand the "positive word" of faith, Kracauer appears to have felt that it could maintain its relevance in modernity. However, during the course of the 1920s his belief altered, and he became more suspicious of the Church's direction as it attempted to negotiate the political instability of these years. The desires for an authentic Catholic culture, he would argue, overshadowed the desire to connect with the real.

His ambivalence towards Catholicism has a parallel in his novel *Georg*. Dispirited by the world around him, Georg visits the Jesuit priest, Father Quirin. The young man confesses his anxiety to him; he tells him of the endless parade of religious and political reformers whose points of view he presents in a leftist newspaper. He declares his admiration of Catholicism, and says he grasps the "facts of dogma." When the priest affirms his views of modern society, he is almost surprised to find agreement so readily with a Jesuit; "Faith is easy," he thinks. Yet, as their discussion continues it is this sense of ease that begins to disturb him. He declares his inability to accept the doctrine of papal infallibility, to which Quirin simply replies that everyone has a moment when the facts of faith appear in their true nature. Georg is disappointed that his attempt to create a barrier between himself and his entrance to the church provokes no friction. As Father Quirin speaks more at length, however, Georg's position becomes clear; when he hears the words "Lord's Supper" a chain of reflections is triggered in his mind:

> The word appeared foreign to him, it came from a world that he did not know, shoved itself before him and grew and grew. The Lord's Supper—faith was hard. One must remain at one's post; the railway strike was still not at an end ... Georg stared towards the floor and lost himself in the dull expanse, as if he were drifting alone over a frozen sea, toward evening.[111]

Within a few moments Georg thus progresses from a belief in the "ease of faith" to recognition of its overwhelming difficulties. Whereas to "grasp" the "facts of dogma" was easy, to know them in the light of religious belief was another matter. That this does not preclude his entrance to the Church surprises him; "whereto, whereto," he asks himself towards the end of his interview. As he takes leave of Quirin, the priest tells him that there exist "many ways."[112] Thus, in a sense Georg leaves his office just as much a flâneur as when he entered. "The way," as Kracauer had declared in 1926, is "through the profane," and Georg is distracted by thoughts of the strike, of the political conflicts of the present.[113] To emphasize this direction Kracauer frames Georg's thoughts in language that may be interpreted as a profanation of biblical language; whereas in the Book of Genesis, "the spirit of God floated upon the water" (*der Geist Gottes schwebte auf dem Wasser*), Georg, bereft of faith, "swept ... alone over a frozen sea" (*schweife ... einsam über einen zugefrorenen See*), not towards holy communion, but merely towards an inscrutable evening.

Yet, in the subsequent chapter of *Georg*, the protagonist finds himself nonetheless impelled to defend a positive estimation of Catholic thought. Georg becomes the center of a political intrigue in the *Morgenboten*—the newspaper for which he writes—on account of an article he has written on contemporary youth movements.[114] He declares his hostility to this phenomenon, refusing to see in groups such as the *Wandervogel*, with their interminable wanderings in guitar-wielding packs, the future of Germany. He contrasted their rampant individualism to the Catholic youth movement. In the latter, he argued, there was greater sense of responsibility and less emphasis on personal will as a supreme value. This position places Georg in conflict with the prevailing editorial line of the paper, which is generally unsympathetic to clerical politics. However, because his sympathy for Catholic youth suits the momentary tactical needs of the head editor, Dr. Petri, Georg survives this mishap.[115] Following immediately after Georg's disillusioning attempt at conversion, this episode demonstrates the poles of Georg's and Kracauer's position towards both

Catholicism and religion more generally: he profanes it, but he also confirms its value as a means of criticizing the more dangerous political tendencies in German society.

Kracauer's qualified defense of Catholicism is probably due to the atypical radicalism that distinguished some of the Catholic milieu in Frankfurt.[116] Among his friends and acquaintances were two of the more left-leaning Catholics whose record on social questions and anti-Semitism was probably exceptional. Werner Thormann, whom Kracauer must have met at the latest by 1923, was a journalist and editor, first of the *Rhein-Mainische Volkszeitung* (*RMV*) and later of the *Deutsche Republik*, a voice for the Catholic circles around Joseph Wirth.[117] His family had been active in Frankfurt politics for several decades and had long registered their opposition to Prussian hegemony and militarism. Thormann also had many connections in Catholic politics, including Wirth and Ignaz Seipel. In general, he appears to have had a contrarian personality; he was cosmopolitan in terms of art and culture with a pronounced interest in French literature. He regularly used the *Du* form of address with younger friends, a practice that apparently extended to Kracauer. Under his editorship, both the *RMV* and the *Deutsche Republik* were critical of the rising tide of nationalist politics; according to one study of the *RMV*, the paper was one of the only ones in Germany to consistently and strenuously oppose anti-Semitism.[118]

Ernst Michel, who also wrote for the *RMV*, was likewise among the most radical voices in Frankfurt Catholicism.[119] Like Thormann, Michel professed views that placed him on the fringes of the Center Party and even of the Church itself. His insistence on the increased role of the laity within the church and his belief that they should have greater independence in political questions led to the placing of his work, *Politics Out of Faith* on the Catholic Index. Similar to Thormann, his interests were eclectic; his doctoral thesis was a study of Montesquieu and, for a short period, he worked as a reader in the Eugen Diederichs and Teubner publishing houses. Of his relationship to Kracauer not much, however, is known. As mentioned above, Kracauer claimed that Michel approved of his essay on Scheler before publication, and Kracauer appears to have been a regular visitor to the Friday evening gatherings at the Café Laumer where those influenced by Michel often met. Here they came into contact with other radically minded individuals (Heinz Blankenberg names, for instance, Adorno, Horkheimer, and Tillich). In the case of Thormann, on the other hand, there is a patchy correspondence that suggests that their friendship was durable and survived into their mutual exile in New York. When Kracauer's financial position became precarious following his flight from Germany, Thormann published his work in the *Deutsche Republik*. However, shortly afterwards he too would follow Kracauer into Parisian exile. In a condolence letter written to Charlotte Thormann after her husband had suddenly died in 1947, Kracauer spoke warmly of their common struggles, of the assistance that Thormann had offered him, and of the fact that his mother and aunt had spoken warmly of both Thormanns when Kracauer was in Berlin.[120]

Thus, personal connections to the leftist Catholic milieu may explain, in part, why Kracauer was a receptive observer of Catholic intellectual currents. The significance of Scheler's work has already been discussed, but his contact with Catholic thought was much more extensive. Through his reportage on the Catholic youth movement, or perhaps through Thormann and Michel, Kracauer met other Catholic intellectuals in the early 1920s, including Joseph Weiger, a priest from nearby Mooshausen. As we have seen Kracauer claimed to find affirmation from Weiger for his Scheler article, and there has survived parts of a brief correspondence between the two men from the years 1921–1922.[121] The letters from Weiger suggest they had cordial relations and that he appreciated Kracauer's work. Nonetheless, it does appear that Weiger had more reservations regarding Kracauer's polemic against Scheler than Kracauer had indicated in his letter to Susman. Indeed, Weiger also wrote an essay on Scheler, defending him from his more severe critics. Though Weiger did not mention Kracauer by name, Kracauer may have understood this as a rejoinder of sorts, and he appears to have asked why Weiger did not send his essay to him.[122] Weiger responded somewhat evasively, arguing that he doubted Kracauer would have found anything new in what he wrote so he thought it not worth sharing with him. One suspects, however, that Weiger believed Kracauer would recognize that doctrinal matters had discouraged him from pursuing their differences too much further. Weiger took some pains to stress that he felt he felt an "inner affinity" for Kracauer and his work, and their basic positions on Scheler were not far from one another. Yet, he added that he must view Scheler from a position of faith and as a "fellow believer." Moreover, he argued that for Catholic intellectuals, Scheler had to be applauded for the sheer fact that he was one of the few Catholic philosophers not devoted to "scholastic rationalism."[123] This, he argued, compensated for his problematic forays into "intuitionism" and phenomenology, both of which he found problematic.

Still, in spite of these differences of opinion, Kracauer would have had good reason to think that his work was not viewed by Catholic intellectuals as hostile to their faith. Moreover, he could look at his essays on Catholicism as taking part in a conversation with progressive voices in the Catholic camp. Aside from Weiger, he also received signs of agreement from Romano Guardini, a close collaborator with Weiger, a prominent theologian and leader of the Quickborn youth movement. Kracauer probably met Guardini when he attended a conference of Catholic academics in Ulm in 1923. An undated note from Guardini in the Kracauer papers probably dates to this period. Guardini expressed agreement with the words Kracauer had written in regards to the Catholic "middle" (*Mitte*). This concept was, he stated, a decisive entry point for his own work.[124] The letter was written in Lake Como, where Guardini was at work on his *Letters* that investigated the challenges posed to culture and religion by technology. Thus, Kracauer's writings interested precisely those voices in Catholicism who were most engaged with the problem of mediating the differences between religion and modern society. To Kracauer, this was a problem that theology could only ignore at its peril; hence, he sympathized with Catholic attempts to wrestle with the chaotic material of reality without recourse to a flight into dogma.

As an outside observer of the Catholic world, Kracauer thought this median position could be fruitful. His report on the Ulm conference of Catholic intellectuals took care to stress his position as an outsider, but one who had more than just a casual interest in Catholic thought. The article appeared in the university page, and the editors included some brief remarks to frame its intentions.[125] According to this preface, the essay was the work of someone who was not a Catholic and did not want to propound a Catholic position; rather, the article wants to bring to light an "emergent spirit," for which the "coming of a better future has been formed." This spirit was identified with that of German youth and, especially *"those individuals of the inner middle and the morning."*[126] To what extent Kracauer agreed with these words is a matter of conjecture, of course, but this was a position that was in accord with his general attitude towards Catholicism. It allowed him to address the currents of religious reform from the more general perspective of "emerging spirit" rather than issues specific to Catholic doctrine.

However, the specific address to youth should not obscure Kracauer's interest in the wider domains of Catholic theology. This emerges in his discussion of the "Catholic middle" that he described in terms that closely resemble his discussion of the "median zone" in *The Detective Novel*. Kracauer mentioned this concept in his account of an address given by Ildefons Herwegen, a theologian and the abbot of an important locus of the incipient liturgical movement, Maria Laach.[127] Herwegen, according to Kracauer, had demonstrated the formidable "capacity of regeneration" that resided in the Catholic Church. In particular, Kracauer admired the commitment to the real; what he understood to be one of the core tenets of the Catholic world view. Thus, he drew attention to Catholicism's direct engagement with material contingencies, rather than venturing into the fraught terrain of dogma. Still, the supernatural and the material were not to be understood as opposing principles, for the "life of individuals is only actual life [*wirkliches Leben*] when it has its place in the supernatural." Kracauer did find the definition of these realms somewhat vague, but overall he suggested that the Catholic idea of the "middle," as described by Herwegen, represented a viable approach to modern reality:

> If [the life of the real] is to become truly actualized, it must not only take part in the supernatural, it must also remain persistently aware of its creaturely existence; it must, as it were, be suspended, from the contingent into the absolute. In other words, it only gains reality and concreteness as a life of the Middle—more precisely, the provisory *Mitte*—that neither betrays heaven to earth, nor seeks to deny its earthly heritage.[128]

Thus, both heaven and earth, sacred and profane could press their claims, and this meant that one could not ignore social problems. Indeed, the published version of Herwegen's speech makes reference to industrial culture and the social question. These gestures, however slight, appear to have made an impression on Kracauer, allowing him to find points of agreement with Herwegen while avoiding areas of potential divergence that might have risked alienating Catholic readers.[129] A critical discussion of Catholic dogma, for instance, could compromise his support for the liberal wing of Catholicism. In comparison, three years later at a subsequent conference in Recklinghausen, Catholic liberals were in the minority. As a result there was little benefit to be gained by withholding criticism, and indeed, Kracauer then singled out Herwegen for his rigid dogmatism.[130]

In the long run, the efforts of Michel and Thormann, of course, did not triumph over the conservative factions of the Church, and if Kracauer hoped his interventions would have some effect, he was ultimately disappointed. The impulses he admired at the Ulm conference in 1923 were unable, so he later argued, to fulfill their intentions.[131] This was the case, he claimed, in regards to the liturgy movement led by Guardini. Kracauer understood this movement as a revival of Catholic symbolism, one that would attempt to wed symbols and rituals to the world of everyday experience. Thus, the movement drew from the traditional repertoire of Catholic liturgy, but it also wanted to invest everyday objects with spiritual value. It was in this sense that Herwegen had spoken of the tools of the engineer as symbols of "higher divine thoughts"; they were still practical objects, of course, but they also possessed the "glimmer of mystery."[132] To allow such objects to become illuminated by the light of truth required a renewed "symbolic capacity," a sensitivity to the place of objects in a divine order embracing the totality of human relations. This revived symbolic power created a *Mitleben*, a second dimension of life that accompanied the individual through all his or her actions, and that embraced the whole person.[133]

Kracauer found this idea sympathetic, but he clearly doubted that the liturgical movement could resolve what he saw as the "antinomian tensions . . . between religion and culture." Guardini, so he argued, had conceived this problem in the wrong way. He seemed convinced that traditional religious symbols could annex the real and, thus, absorb the material of everyday life into the corpus of Catholic teaching; he wanted to "wrest a properly understood religious 'culture' from the conditions of a bad 'civilization.'"[134] Such an approach, Kracauer thought, was not viable if one insisted on using only the resources of Catholic tradition. However, his criticism was muted at the time, because he chose to wait for a forthcoming book in which Guardini promised to deal with the subject at more length.

However, when *Liturgical Education* appeared in the following year Kracauer was clearly disappointed, and his review of the book revisited his earlier objections.[135] He recognized that Guardini was aware of the problems posed by his insistence on traditional ritual, and he conceded that the author had removed himself from the "romantic" visions of medieval Catholicism. Thus, he guarded against the potential for a renewed symbolism to lapse into a pseudoreligious "cultural pageantry" (*Kulturspielerei*).[136] Still, even if one could isolate liturgical form from aesthetic contamination, Kracauer argued that other problems were more fundamental. For if one followed the path of liturgical education recommended by Guardini then much would "depend on how one judged the present and what consequences one drew from this judgment." In other words, from the outset everyone had to reckon with their own contingent position in a world of fragmentary culture, so how could a renewed liturgical practice build upon this foundation? In the course of his refutation, Kracauer drew explicitly from the work of other Catholic writers, in particular, those who had spoken out against Guardini and the Quickborn movement that he led. This group of young Catholics, such as Robert Grosche and Albert Mirgeler, had opted for a different path. According to Kracauer, every "isolated individual" first had to come to terms with themselves "as an individual [*Einzelnen*], that is, as a whole person in a suspended state." Only on this premise could one envision a "common life within form." Hence, there was an emphasis on the radical isolation of the individual and his or her decision in a contingent situation, where law appears uncertain and culture in ruins:

> Of course, wholeness of the person and obedience towards the law condition each other reciprocally; however, it is another matter, whether or not, in a time of lawlessness, one takes one's first steps in accordance with the law, or, in recognition of the situation, tries to penetrate to the source from which the law originates.[137]

This is the territory that concerned Kracauer in *The Detective Novel* and also writers such as Schmitt and Benjamin. In these zones, Kracauer argued, the forms of belief and traditional ritual could only help one so much. He did not mean to repudiate the viability of traditional forms, but only to point out that one could not "work outwards from them, but rather [one] must struggle with them as individuals who do not know, or do not yet know, how to efface their individual existence."[138] The important point for Kracauer is that these young Catholics refused to seek solutions that involved stepping outside of their own concrete situation—whether it was by way of dogma or by abstract thought. In their insistence on the real, Kracauer saw one of the more vital forms of Catholicism.

Thus, Kracauer's review of Guardini is notably interventionist. Whereas his assessment of the 1923 conference described the multifaceted range of Catholic opinion with some approval, the later review explicitly supported the more radical strands of modern Catholicism. In the course of his critique, Kracauer referred to a book edited by Ernst Michel entitled, symptomatically enough, *Church and Reality*.[139] The volume comprised essays drawn from issues of *Die Tat* devoted to the present state of Catholic thought, including contributions from Guardini as well as from his critics. One of the latter, Albert Mirgeler, contributed a sharply worded polemic against the Quickborns and their concept of "creative obedience" (*schöpferischen Gehorsams*).[140] The movement, according to Mirgeler, was clothed in "lovely words" that could not disguise the realities that it failed to address. While Mirgeler conceded that Guardini and others in the movement were devoted to the problem of overcoming the gap between Catholic doctrine and modern reality, the movement was still mired in the unreal: "instead of recognizing the demands that the present situation of the church, economy, and family ... place upon the personal decision of every individual, one abstracts from them on the basis of the adored and praised means of idealism."[141] By supporting voices such as Mirgeler, as well as the views originating from the RMV, Kracauer was attempting to intervene within Catholic circles in order to support the stance taken by his kindred spirits in the Catholic camp.

By 1929, it was abundantly clear that the Church would no longer tolerate the views of Michel and those who sympathized with him, but Kracauer's disenchantment with Catholicism was clear long before. After 1923, Kracauer followed the subsequent conferences of Catholic academics with some alarm, attending two of these conferences in a professional capacity. In August 1925 he published a polemical article on the meeting held in Innsbruck.[142] Compared with what had transpired two years earlier in Ulm, Kracauer found the general tendency of the conference was to avoid discussion of social and cultural realities and to insist on the precedence of religious dogma. He explained this in part as a consequence of the time elapsed since the inflation years, the memory of which had cast a shadow over the Catholic academics who gathered at Ulm. In those conditions, one could not ignore social questions; but after a couple years of relative stability, the same individuals, with some exceptions, were now content to address such issues purely from a doctrinal point of view. Hence, according to Kracauer, the conference in Innsbruck did not resonate very far outside of Catholic circles as had the conference at Ulm. Indicative of this was the accompanying display of Catholic art. Aside from a few pieces of interest, Kracauer thought that most of the work was only striking on account of its consistent mediocrity. The point of view propagated at the conference seemed unable to recognize that "a coffeehouse scene by Van Gogh could have more religious meaning than a badly painted image of a holy subject"—in other words, "art with all its teeth."[143] Kracauer shared this position with his friend Thormann whose essay on the issue appeared in *Church and Reality*. To counter the claims of religious art, he quoted the admonitions of the romantic poet Joseph von Eichendorff: "We want no dogma on the stage, no moral theology, not even in allegorical covering; we desire nothing other than a Christian atmosphere that we breathe unconsciously and that lets the higher hidden meaning of earthly things themselves shine through in their purity."[144] In contrast, the art displayed at the Innsbruck conference, so Kracauer stated, had ignored the "things themselves" and tried to hide the fact with a veneer of religious piety. To his mind, this art unfortunately served as a barometer for the general mood at Innsbruck. The only voices that reckoned with social and political realities were liberal figures such as Goetz Briefs, or surprisingly enough, the former Austrian chancellor, Ignaz Seipel, whom Kracauer described as the only speaker to "take true steps into the realm of the practical and the profane."[145]

Thus, as a rule Kracauer was receptive to Catholic intellectual currents that embraced the profane world. This meant that they did not look upon the world as irredeemably hostile to religion, and that they did not insist upon the absolute need to displace secular existence through the "assertion of a clerical universal-culture."[146] In this respect, Kracauer appears to have foreclosed the potential of traditional religious forms to accommodate modernity; or at the very least, he argues that they must incorporate a reference point outside of themselves and in the profane world. To be sure, this is a secular point of view, one that sees adjustment to secular modernity as the only way to unite church and reality. Part of the problem is that Kracauer does not really address the question of what makes religion religious. For himself the answer rested on a conception of the real as a dialectical process, a perpetual encounter between a drifting subjectivity and the shifting phenomenal world; it also derived from his acceptance of negativity, a willingness to hold out in an improvised position that did not recognize an absolute truth. His approach was to elaborate a critical model that would attempt to extract some form of truth from the material bases of existence. As for religion, he seems to have felt that the churches could still be cajoled into a deeper engagement with modern life, and that this step toward secularization was essential. Afterwards, what remained of the churches would, as he said to Bloch, be left to their own devices.

Yet, in spite of this dire prognosis for the churches, Kracauer was ready to ascribe to them a measure of validity when compared with the "vagabond religions." Indeed, Kracauer may have argued that the churches were hamstrung by their misunderstanding of secular culture, but this did not mean that he privileged secularism in an uncritical fashion. Indeed, his hostility towards the new religions was at its most severe in those cases where he believed a presumptuous secularism had united with a kind of religious neopaganism. Such movements seemed to blur the lines of sacred and profane, often seeking a new kingdom in the here and now.[147] According to Nipperdey, such movements had grown in strength during the last decades before the war of 1914, and they continued to attract adherents through the postwar years; many of the movements and figures he discussed remained active during the Weimar era. Such movements were a response to the loss of stability brought by modernization. Social and political transformations weakened the older patterns of belief, but at the same time, these disruptions provoked an increased desire for spiritual fulfillment. Often these movements brought together an "emigration from the church and a general interest in religiosity"; thus, rather than a retreat from religion they represented a gap between popular religious practice and traditional religious institutions.[148] Nipperdey also points out that these movements were not opposed to modern society as a rule; rather they should be understood as a rejoinder to modern skepticism. They sought to reinvigorate a fallen world that had been destroyed by relativism and abstract thought.[149]

For Kracauer the model of a revived or new religion was misconceived. In an article written for *Die Rheinlande* in 1922, he had argued that it was "presumptuous and not a little romantic to dream of a new church in our situation . . . such may come or it may not, but one cannot make it happen; indeed, one must not even want to make it happen."[150] The numerous spiritual seekers that Kracauer saw as rampant symptoms of postwar malaise readily created new homes for their religious longings, or they saw the old abodes with new eyes. "No region is too far afield," he complained in a later article on cultural pessimism, "we play catch ball with India, China, Japan, and dispose of continents and cultures . . . we measure the centuries with the speed of light. World history, always only world history, sounds the solution."[151] Against this rush into religious flânerie, Kracauer asserted his gesture of radical waiting; to counter the revival one had to withdraw into a life of "much skepticism . . . restful waiting (better too long than too short) . . . the veneration of the unsayable." So he wrote, in a long polemical letter to Löwenthal that he concluded with an ironic allusion to Luther—"Here stand I."[152]

Kracauer argued that the struggle between religious sobriety and religious excess took place at that point where there was no authority to distinguish the "legitimate from the illegitimate."[153] This was where the critical model of *The Detective Novel* could best be deployed: an indirect form of address that countered the "direct" mode of positive religion. This was the approach that informed his polemical reading of the Catholic academic conference in Innsbruck. Herein he speaks of the "inverted sacrifice of the intellect" that must be undertaken from the religious side. The religious individual of today must ascend into the present conceptions of the profane, which are at present so powerful among the masses, because another possible way to the transformation of social structures is not and is never to be hoped for. Perhaps, this indirect method that gives to the world what belongs to the world, recommends itself more than the direct method which alone wants to grasp the positively religious; but in any case this direct method requires completion through the indirect.[154]

The indirect method then was seen as a necessary step, but not a fundamentally irreligious one. Yet, how was this indirect and invisible form of religious expression to be distinguished from the "vagabond" religions of the present that, likewise, plunged into the profane world?

Kracauer sometimes distinguished this modern wandering religiosity more by its waywardness and the seeming haphazardness of its convictions, rather than by its contents. The growing interest in religions from other parts of the world, Asia in particular, caused some misgivings for Kracauer, but not because he objected to their doctrines. Instead, it was what the alleged infatuation with different religious traditions demonstrated about contemporary European culture. Thus, in a scene from *Ginster*, this fascination is portrayed as mere whim, undertaken without conviction. The daughter of one of Ginster's employers, Berta, draws his attention to a book on the Buddha that she first states is in accord with her own views, but then one moment later, she dismisses the book out of hand.[155] Since the religious flâneur has no necessary connection to the beliefs that he or she professes, spiritual wisdom is as easy to put down as to pick up. In this case, it is much more the European attitude to other religions that is at issue, rather than the religions themselves. Thus, Kracauer found in a work by Leopold Ziegler, *The Eternal Buddha*, the lingering traces of Christian thought and European philosophy; Ziegler's Buddha, he noted, was one that was shaped by Kant and Nietzsche and responded to the dilemmas raised by their work.[156] In contrast, he praised Thomas Zenker for his work on Chinese philosophy, noting its caution in regards to drawing analogies to "Western thought" and thus obscuring the specific nature of Chinese concepts. This was something that he felt was often not the case among historians of philosophy.[157] This did not mean, however, that Kracauer believed that interest in the religions of China, India, or elsewhere was a dead end. It was not a matter of making Europe a fortress for the secular inheritors of the Judaeo-Christian tradition, but rather a way of questioning how such traditions were perceived and appropriated. Wherever he thought that the interest in other religions veered towards disengagement from social reality, he remained critical.

Kracauer was also unremittingly hostile to every religious or spiritualist movement that blurred the distinctions between *Wissenschaft* and faith, between culture and religion. The extent of his numerous interventions in this area forbids a comprehensive discussion, so the argument will confine itself to a few instances. In Kracauer's campaigns against the "vagabond religions" some labelled him a dogmatist, and certainly his persistent attacks on figures such as Rudolf Steiner and Count Keyserling do resemble an effort to assert dominance over fringe movements. Thus, he attacks one of Steiner's followers, Friedrich Rittelmeyer, by pointing out that he was once an admirer of the Protestant theologian Johannes Müller. He accused Rittelmeyer of obscuring his connections to Steiner in order to entice listeners who might otherwise have dismissed him if his actual beliefs were known. He also publicized a lecture given by Ernst Michel, attacking the allegedly pernicious influences of Steiner and his followers. Even his obituary of Steiner is tinged with malice. "How fast this spook will be forgotten," he wrote to Adorno in 1925.[158]

Thus, his pugnacious attitude towards the vagabond religions was bound to generate some hostile responses. This was the case with one of his regular targets, Count Hermann Keyserling. Keyserling was born into a family of Baltic aristocrats living in the Russian empire in 1880. He studied geology and philosophy, and during his youth he travelled widely. These journeys and the impressions he derived from them constituted the material for his work of 1919, *The Travel Diary of a Philosopher*.[159] During the 1920s, he established the so-called School of Wisdom, an educational experiment founded on supposedly universal and democratic principles. The school attracted some renowned speakers including Max Scheler, Leo Baeck, Carl Jung, and Rabindranath Tagore. His public persona, as a representative of pan-global cultural aspirations, and of Franco-German rapprochement also attracted some skeptical ire. Joseph Roth satirized him and his readers in his 1929 novel, *Right and Left*. The admirers of Keyserling, Roth implied, were those who had disconnected the reality of life from their ideals. Thus, they talked peace, but worked for war; they preached humanity, but profited from its destruction. They were "the wealthy, the cultured and pan-European, the industrialists who produced poison gas in their factories and read Keyserling at home."[160]

When Kracauer attacked the School of Wisdom in 1921, he provoked a discussion in the pages of the *FZ* that included a sharp rebuttal from Otto Flake.[161] Flake was an Alsatian writer, close to the circles around René Schickele with whom he had collaborated on a journal devoted to Alsatian culture in 1902.[162] He was also a friend of Kurt Tucholsky and a contributor to *Die Weltbühne*, and thus was known as a writer of the left. Still, he was later one of the 88 signatories of the notorious statement in support of the Hitler's regime in October 1933. In the 1920s, Flake had been a vocal supporter of Keyserling, though not an altogether uncritical one. His objections to Kracauer's polemic derived, in part, from the use of the word *Sinn*—a term that Keyserling and Flake invested with more meaning than Kracauer was willing to allow.[163] According to Flake, Keyserling thought it legitimate to speak of an eternal "sense" or "mind" that oriented individuals in a world of appearances. Why then, so Flake asked, could this not become a source for new religiosity?[164] To Kracauer this was an essentially false proposition; he had argued that the notion of an "eternal essence" was without content, a fact that he argued was demonstrated by the educational agenda of the school. Keyserling had boasted of the fact that he had no fixed program to speak of and that there were no underlying premises that guided him; students developed according to their own path towards this "eternal essence." The avoidance of dogma appeared attractive; yet, Kracauer asked, without some form or content how were the students to come to a point where they could evaluate and interpret their experiences without falling prey to whatever dogmas or ideologies prevailed around them?

Flake countered by arguing that Kracauer had misunderstood what Keyserling meant by *Sinn*, and that he had done so on account of his own dogmatic rigidity. *Sinn*, Flake countered, was no empty term, but rather it was to be understood as a fundamental strata, an "indestructible ground" that was the condition of all appearances in the world. This concept, he claimed, was readily comprehensible to both the religious believer and the philosopher, and it was from this premise that Keyserling sought to connect appearances to the eternal, and thus provide an "abstract anchoring" (*abstrakte Fixierung*) for human action.[165] This was the "core of the religious," he stated, and there was no reason why one could not "salvage" it from religion as "a new religiosity . . . a relation—desirous of meaning—of the creature to the fundament, or the eternal relation." Moreover, if Kracauer insisted that this terminology required more content, or that *Sinn* could only be delivered by the "contents of faith," then he was nothing more than a dogmatist to whom one might respond with Spinoza that "thought consists in having liberated God from moral attributes—here philosophy begins."[166]

However, what was at issue in the dispute between Kracauer and Flake was not a question of religious dogma, but rather a clash between different modes of religious flânerie. Kracauer did not want to privilege one confession over another or to place philosophy beneath religious doctrine; he was pointing out that dogma presented a problem to Keyserling's ideas on education. As he noted, Keyserling often quoted from Christ and Buddha, but he gave no sense of how his students should respond to a statement such as "He who is not with me is against me." Any concept of *Sinn* as an "indestructible" ground must then offer valid means for distinguishing and deciding between similar contents of faith, to say nothing of political judgments. Otherwise, his school would simply devolve into ideological eclecticism: Catholics would become Catholics, Buddhists would become Buddhists, and Bolsheviks would become Bolsheviks. Recognizing this problem did not mean that Kracauer thought a fundamental grounding could only be derived from a religious creed, but rather that it could not serve the unifying cultural purposes that Keyserling and Flake intended. Moreover, he added that he did not deny the existence of some kind of essential base identified by the word *Sinn*; but he argued that it must reckon with the boundaries of knowledge. From this point of view, he argued that it could only be partially known by way of its profane manifestations:

> To be sure, *Sinn* is not the content itself, it is of the beyond, it is behind content und appearance. However, our human constraints are precisely such that we are unable to push away "name and form" and proceed directly to *Sinn* itself; on the contrary, the unsayable *Sinn* must be received in the shell of appearance. It would be presumptuousness if we wanted to slip past the vessel in which the spell of *Sinn* reveals itself to us, if we sought to unburden ourselves of the veiling form through which alone God is manifest.[167]

Keyserling, so Kracauer thought, had stepped into regions about which nothing could be spoken, and in order to do so, he had resorted to an abstraction that betrayed his idealist premises. Rather than opening onto a "new land" of religious insight, Keyserling, he argued, remained stuck in a morass of idealism and mysticism.

Though Kracauer did not use a harsh tone in his rebuttal to Flake, he was not yet done with him. Kracauer appears to have been intrigued by the conflict of identity that emerged in Flake's work, a condition that he attributed to his Alsatian origin. A subsequent book by Flake, *The Modern-Antique Idea of the World*, drew some sympathy from Kracauer, yet overall he was puzzled by what he saw as Flake's tentative mode of religious flânerie: "What does Flake want then? The position of a mystic without the flight from the world, the religious approach to life without God and religion?"[168] He was confused by this attempt to find a "new religion" rising out of the ashes of modern Protestantism—a "new kind of paganism" that accepted the relativity of appearances in the world, but still tried to unite "what cannot be united." Kracauer found that this new paganism falsely erased the distinctions between "the creature and the created, and thought [and] existence." In general, culture and religion were forced into too close of a relation. By doing so, Kracauer implied that Flake had ignored the distinct claims of both.[169]

This was a point on which Kracauer indeed was dogmatic: if religion and culture had legitimate claims then they must be recognized as distinct spheres and not collapsed into a neopagan fusion. In a 1922 article on culture, he suggested that the gap had widened because the confessions were "no longer able to hold within themselves the image of the world [as experienced by] German individuals." Yet, this did not mean that culture had stepped into the breach; on the contrary, "our culture lacks the strong structures of form possessed by the confessions, and it appears questionable whether or not it is able to imagine such forms."[170] If culture were to fulfill its legitimate potential, he argued, it must not pretend to the functions of religion.

This position emerged clearly in his dispute with the cultural philosophy of Rudolf Maria Holzapfel and his followers. Holzapfel, though more or less forgotten today, enjoyed some influence before and after the Great War.[171] His magnum opus *Panideal* was published in 1901 and brought out again in a revised edition by Eugen Diederichs in 1923. The second edition was accompanied by some fanfare, including a collection of essays written by his acolytes (also published by Diederichs) and eventually a biography.[172] Among his professed admirers were Arthur Schnitzler, Christian Sénéchal, Romain Rolland, and Ernst Mach. Holzapfel had, in fact, studied for a short time under both Mach and Richard Avenarius. Later, Mach supported Holzapfel during periods of financial difficulty, even contributing an introduction to the original edition of *Panideal*.[173] Beyond this small number of intellectuals, he appears to have attracted readers among the young, particularly those who were dissatisfied with the philosophy taught in German and European universities. One follower, the cultural philosopher, Hans Zbinden, later wrote that Holzapfel had been a "decisive experience" in his life. After his encounter, he devoted "all his passions" to the promulgation of his world view.[174] Another disciple, Otto Hausherr, enthused over his mentor in a lecture given at the invitation of the Deutschen Freistudentenschaft in Hamburg and Berlin. According to Hausherr, the discoveries of Holzapfel meant that the waiting was over. The accomplishing of tremendous tasks was not only "dreamed of in fiction, full of longing—it is a consummated act. It is Rudolf Maria Holzapfel, the great investigator of the soul and the creator of the *Panideal*, who has given us the solution to those problems that we have recognized as decisive for the formation of a new intellectual culture."[175]

Undoubtedly, it was the alleged influence among younger students that provoked Kracauer to attack Holzapfel early in 1924. His work on the *FZ* university page meant that he was often occupied with issues pertaining to German youth. In the eyes of the editors, this was all the more urgent given the rise of a political extremism that had only abated slightly after the Munich putsch attempt of the previous autumn. Erich Troß, Kracauer's colleague on the university page, had written to Thormann, also in early 1924, speaking of the need to counteract the "siren-tones" of the Hitler movement, especially among younger voters. To counter these influences, the *FZ* editors were planning a special number of the university page to coincide with the election campaigns of that year. By such measures they sought to lead the young away from extremism and back to the path of "holy sobriety."[176]

Therefore, Kracauer's polemic was an attempt to define the relationship of religion and culture in light of these political intentions. He wanted to instill a more sober sense of what it was possible to accomplish via cultural means.

In the case of Holzapfel, he argued that an inordinate faith in culture had exceeded its possible bounds, for culture was always a "work of human labor," and as such it was subject to the same contingencies that influenced all human existence. Therefore, instead of imagining that it was given to individuals to actualize an ideal perfection of culture, arbitrarily and according to their own estimation, the individual must recognize that, on the contrary, "the imperfection of human conditions confirms that culture neither today nor tomorrow, nor even at some final point, signifies finality."[177] To demonstrate his position Kracauer gave a short theoretical sketch of the individual's relation to culture. This he argued proceeded from recognition of the "exact place" (*richtigen Orte*) someone occupies in a contingent situation, a position, however, that has roots outside of oneself. One does not set one's own foundation, so the individual must concede his or her "created existence" (*Geschaffensein*), and acknowledge the dependency that stems from this. This "negative" insight forbids the idea that an individual has the resources to "press the seal of Caesar upon the world." Indeed, "to accept culture as the last word and the highest value is forbidden to individuals once and for all." Such a position, Kracauer suggested, would be the equivalent of Münchhausen pulling himself out of the swamp by his own hair. However, culture does not become insignificant as a result, and Kracauer argued that its critical functions should be affirmed; nonetheless, one had to avoid the cultural optimists just as much as the pessimists.[178]

Behind Kracauer's refutation of Holzapfel there was a definite theological dimension. To Kracauer, the "possibility" of culture only exists if it "stands perpetually in question." This meant that "the consciousness of human *limits* alone demonstrates to the individual the place that is appropriate to him." Elsewhere he spoke of the "expropriation" of God, and he positioned his critique by alluding to the author's alleged antipathy towards religion in general. His essay opens by drawing attention to the time Holzapfel spent traveling abroad, gaining experiences that led him to conclude that the diverse forms of life were too complex to be accounted for by religious dogmas. Thus, religion was to be absorbed by the categories of cultural philosophy, a conclusion that Kracauer implied was blasphemous: "Yes, even *Religion!*" he exclaimed, "Because for Holzapfel it is readily understood that it would be annexed by the Cathedral of Culture."[179]

Readers of Kracauer's article responded to the religious dimension of his argument. The writer and cabaret artist Klabund wrote to the *FZ* to express his agreement with Kracauer, bluntly calling *Panideal* a "blasphemous" work.[180] The supporters of Holzapfel also drew attention to the issue of religion. Wladimir Astrow, one of his followers and later his loyal biographer, wrote an extensive rebuttal. Astrow claimed that Kracauer had misread his master on many points, but in particular, he had misunderstood his attitude toward religion. Moreover, he argued that Kracauer, by referring to concepts such as grace, betrayed a religious orthodoxy that would lead to a quietist position: "Neither Moses nor Christ desire of men and nations that they should leave the future to God alone . . . and lay their hands in their laps."[181] Astrow stressed that for Holzapfel religion was not a subject of attack, but on the contrary, he sought the "spiritualization of religious feeling."[182] Kracauer responded by claiming that this formulation was vague to the point of emptiness, and moreover, did not escape his primary objection that religion was reduced to a function of culture—perhaps, the highest function of culture, but derivative nonetheless. That Holzapfel proposed an "Academy of the Exceptional" to instruct and educate the cultural geniuses who were to establish the coming religion only aggravated the matter for Kracauer, who clearly recognized an affinity between this proposal and the "School of Wisdom" led by Keyserling.[183]

One may concede that Astrow was correct in his assumption that Kracauer was asserting the authority of traditional religious concepts in this respect; yet, he did so in a fashion that was not intended to increase the authority of religious institutions. He plainly stated that to interpret theological concepts one had to move from "above to below," a procedure that he equated with an orientation towards "last things." To demonstrate his point, he referred (somewhat surprisingly) to the definition of conscience offered by the nineteenth-century theologian Franz von Baader: "a knowing certainty of the existing knowledge of God" (*Gewiß-wissen des Erkanntseyn von Gott*).[184] This is a puzzling reference in this context, and it appears that Kracauer wanted to suggest that a conviction of faith can stand on its own as such, that is, within certain bounds that do not aspire to empirical certainty. Holzapfel, in contrast, submerged religious convictions into a science of culture. To Kracauer, von Baader trumped Holzapfel as the former accentuated the antinomies of existence that the latter tried to resolve through a misplaced faith in the perfectibility of culture. In contrast, for Kracauer the individual must persist in his "negative knowing" and in the "perpetual tragedy of his position." If the individual was

> to step out of the merely tragic realm into the associations of confessional life as a Jew or Christian, then he admittedly may still act in the world, but he does not enter and work through it; he may be certain of redemption, however, he will never build towards his own redemption.[185]

The interpretive validity that religion retained was thus not to be found in the institutions themselves, or even in their dogma, but rather in the theological contents that they preserved—the hidden meaning in words such as grace, redemption, and immortality. Here resided the authority that Astrow thought Kracauer had given to religion; but for Kracauer, this was an issue that had to be confronted in terms of individual interpretation not dogma.

Thus, there are two movements that emerge in Kracauer's critique of Holzapfel. On the one hand, he insists upon the historical specificity of the individual; he or she must work within the confines of contingent reality—the "worm's point of view" that he spoke of in connection to Simmel. However, he also insisted that one had to interpret the material world in reference to concepts derived from "above to below." Holzapfel, to his mind, failed on both counts; he shorted the claims of the material world, and he also betrayed God to culture. Yet, one might ask how Kracauer reconciled these two seemingly contradictory positions; or if he chose not to reconcile them, what justified his approach?

In this respect, Astrow drew attention to Kracauer's deployment of the concept of grace. In his use of the term, Kracauer seems to allow it a quasi-redemptive force, but he does not openly state this. In general, *grace* is not a common word in his vocabulary, but it does appear in a number of significant places, first as the title of his early unpublished short story already mentioned. In this instance, the act of grace manifests itself in the form of a redemptive sexual encounter with a prostitute. Their chance meeting dissuades both of them from their suicidal drives; spiritual fulfillment and brute physicality are thus united under its rubric. Further, in his programmatic essay "Artist of this Age," Kracauer again alludes to grace in connection to the moment of artistic creativity, when the artist successfully discovers forms that give to their materials the "grace of self-witness," when the impenetrable nature of the world is given meaningful content.[186] In the Holzapfel polemic, grace appears again, but in an unclear fashion. He condemned Holzapfel for moving the "idea of a perfect culture into the middle-point" of life, and thereby denying creaturely existence its "allotted share of *grace*." The former is of a secondary order, he claims, for the perfect culture will always flee from those who attempt to realize it. As a function of grace, it appears only to those who do not desire it.[187]

It is difficult to see what place the concept of grace is supposed to occupy in Kracauer's critical venture, and given the scarcity of its use, it is tempting to consider it as simply idiosyncratic, a residue of his theological concerns that disappeared as he became more enmeshed in the critique of ideology. Yet, I would argue that the theological concept of grace, as of redemption, had more significance for him. Grace, in the references mentioned above, might be understood as that "flash" of insight that Walter Benjamin discussed in his theses of history, "a memory that is seized as it presents itself in a moment of danger."[188] Thus, the necessity of the present and the past overlapped in a reciprocating moment of historical recognition; the historian, in this instance, answers to both and evades a purely chronological sense of time. It is to this alternative structure of time that Kracauer appealed when, much later in his life, he wrote to the historian Henri-Irénée Marrou that it indeed would be surprising if in the course of secularization "the humanly impenetrable tangle of the 'time of nature' and the 'time of grace' had dissolved into thin air without leaving a trace."[189] Grace, so his letter implied, becomes the moment when the "antinomies" of time are recognizable. Kracauer would not deal with these themes at any length until he began his final work on history, but he clearly had begun to formulate such ideas much earlier, mentioning an essay on the subject to Löwenthal in 1922. "There is today," he lamented, "a deep lack of understanding for the uncanny nature of history."[190]

This uncanniness is something that Kracauer thought was best observed from the point of view of extraterritoriality.[191] The "extraterritorial" has clear affinities to the outsider, and also to the flâneur. Kracauer's position as a German Jew, of course, also tended towards this self-conception of "extraterritoriality." Therefore, it is significant that in the same letter where Kracauer informed Löwenthal of his plans for an essay on history he also spoke of a renewed interest in Judaism, or at the very least, a recognition that he had not broken with some dimensions of it. In this letter, Kracauer discussed his recent encounters with the work of Thomas Mann and Martin Buber. Mann he had heard lecture on the subject of Goethe and Tolstoi.[192] Buber he had met at his home in Heppenheim, but unfortunately there is no record of their conversation. However, shortly before this meeting, Kracauer had written on a lecture given by Buber, in the course of which Kracauer described his position in terms similar to his Holzapfel critique: culture was not a precondition of religion, but rather the other way around.[193] In any case, Kracauer declared himself to be more inclined towards Buber and a renewed interest in Jewish tradition than towards the cultural politics of Mann. In his letter, he seemed almost surprised by this fact. "Evidently," he wrote Löwenthal, "one cannot just push Jewishness aside."[194]

Still, this was not an uncritical encounter. Kracauer's upbringing in a partially secularized Jewish milieu appears to have been a dispiriting experience, marked by ambivalence towards Judaism. Nonetheless, he laid claim to a deep sense of Jewish identity and history. In 1921, he wrote to Susman:

> To be sure, I also feel the riddling nature of the history of the Jewish people in all its depth, but would you just once be able to explain to me what specifically Jewish spirit is—without fabrications—and what remains of the Jewish religion ... when one removes it from the "law."[195]

Judaism almost presents itself to Kracauer as more of a historical identity rather than a confessional one. Indeed, an occasional remark regarding Jewish texts betrays a definite antipathy. He found the Hebrew Bible both "too moralizing and too foreign"; he even referred to it as a "Jewish book for robberbarons" (*jüdisches Raubritterbuch*).[196]

Yet, this is only side of the story, as his remarks to Löwenthal suggest. Two years later, he reported to Susman his plans to read Talmud (at the time he was also reading Augustine) and that, having met again with Buber, he found they agreed on many subjects.[197] Even his relations to Franz Rosenzweig have more ambiguity than the later dispute over Rosenzweig and Buber's translation of the Bible would suggest.[198] He was unreceptive to *The Star of Redemption*, though this was just as much on account of its allegedly hidden idealism as its religiosity. To his mind, the book was a work of reinvigorated "idealism," a new species of thought that wanted to create a science of God.[199] "I feel uneasy with this type of pathos, saturated with Talmudic understanding," he explained, "because I fear that the whole thing runs into a philosophically allegorical interpretation such as that practiced by Philo."[200] Further discussion of the validity (or lack thereof) of Kracauer's criticism would be out of place here, but suffice to say that he felt the book was not a good argument for religious revival. Hence, he was out of step with one of the most significant movements in contemporary German Judaism.

Kracauer's hostility towards the *Star of Redemption* did not, however, preclude a wider exchange of ideas between himself and Rosenzweig. A small number of letters suggest that they debated a number of themes relevant to Kracauer's conception of religion and history. Thus, even if Kracauer was unable to accept the tenets of religious faith, or enter into a sustained dialogue with contemporary Jewish thought, it does not follow that the encounter, or the dispute, with Judaism left no important traces in his work.

The early signs of disagreement between Kracauer and Rosenzweig are clear in their divergent attitudes to Max Scheler. Rosenzweig recognized that Kracauer's critique of the Catholic philosopher implied a more sweeping repudiation of religious revival.[201] Moreover, Rosenzweig was alarmed by the withering tone of Kracauer's remarks, and he addressed this point in a brief letter to Kracauer. He also argued that Kracauer's criticism had not hits its mark, because he had failed to appreciate the fullness of meaning residing in the word "to wait." "There was," Rosenzweig stated, "also in 'waiting' . . . a living value in which one makes out the beautiful double meaning of the word (not simply to wait upon one thing or another, but on the contrary, to wait as an appointed watchman), not simply that waiting with constrained hands—hands constrained behind one's back."[202] The criticism may have stung, especially the implication of quietism; but on the basis of his essay on the religious revival discussed above, Kracauer was by no means penitent.

However, in spite of this inauspicious beginning, a measure of rapport did develop between the two men. In 1922, Rosenzweig asked Kracauer to give a number of lectures on contemporary religious trends at the Free Jewish School. The following year, Rosenzweig responded appreciatively to Kracauer's article, "Creative Dialogue" and a brief correspondence between them followed.[203] There were, it should be noted, other motives for Rosenzweig to foster relations with Kracauer: one, he hoped that by doing so he might draw some of the writers from the *FZ* to his school, and he also hoped that he might be able to help Kracauer overcome some of his inhibitions, in particular, his speaking impediment.²⁰⁴ Nonetheless, this was a relationship in which Rosenzweig clearly saw himself as the intellectual superior. Thus, after reading Kracauer's review of Buber's *I and Thou*, he described Kracauer as a "wren," even though he conceded, to his annoyance, that he was not entirely in disagreement with him.²⁰⁵ Given these circumstances, the relationship was likely to be fraught. Kracauer was over thirty years old when they met, and while he recognized that Rosenzweig had a deeper knowledge of religion and philosophy, he probably found it difficult to accept a subaltern role.²⁰⁶

Two further letters from Rosenzweig to Kracauer have survived, and these give some idea of the points of contention that existed between them.²⁰⁷ Without Kracauer's part of the correspondence, the context is obscured and one can only guess the content of his replies, but there are some clear indications of the problems that were addressed. Rosenzweig attempted to correct a number of errors of which he thought Kracauer was guilty.²⁰⁸ While he stated his agreement with Kracauer insofar as he too found the present times chaotic and spiritually vacant, he argued that it was meaningless to say of an age that it was either near to or far from God; the divine could cross any distance, and thus such judgments had no relevance. Though it may be true that modern society with its nationalist passions prevented many individuals from finding a relationship to the religious sphere, this was not sufficient reason to make a distinction between a fallen present and an ideal past. In this respect, the medieval period was no haven of religious immediacy, for feudalism too had its own constraints, to say nothing of the barriers that the medieval church had put in the way of true faith. For Rosenzweig, this view of the world as distant from God was thus theologically flawed; for God did not enter into a world that was foreign to him, he claimed, but rather into one that he had created.²⁰⁹ In the new theology that he identified with Karl Barth, the world appeared as a place that God seemed to have forgotten; while in his own conception the autonomy of the world preserves the divine relationship, as an actualization and confirmation of the world as God's creation. As we have seen, Rosenzweig believed, at times, that Kracauer had been unduly influenced by the new dialectical theology, so these barbs directed towards reformed Protestantism were probably intended to steer him away from these cloudy waters. Insofar as this also meant a repudiation of the "blithe cultural theology of the last decades," this message may have struck home for Kracauer; for as we have seen, he was skeptical of any fusion of culture and religion. According to Rosenzweig, Judaism when properly understood was a "metahistorical" religion; it stood "in a critical tension with culture and history."²¹⁰ Thus, Judaism could be viewed as an embodiment of the "extraterritorial" relationship to culture and history.

This assertion of a critical distance to culture may have evoked some sympathy from Kracauer. His adoption of the "extraterritorial" point of view has some affinities to this, but as is clear from these letters, there were also differences between them that would have influenced how extraterritoriality was to be understood. For Kracauer, extraterritorialism had meaning as an historical identity, but not as a confessional one.

The main differences that existed between Kracauer and Rosenzweig emerged in a discussion of "prophetic speech" and its significance. In his first letter, Rosenzweig had addressed this problem by agreeing with Kracauer's fears that its current usage was often inappropriate. This would only change, he argued, when it was recognized that prophecy was nothing "exceptional" (with the exception of the Hebrew prophets of the Old Testament). Prophecy, he elaborated, was not derived from the qualities of the individual, and thus it was not dependent on the rare occasion of genius; rather it was an intervention of God communicated and constituted through language. Hence, wherever there was language, prophecy was possible, and language, as he pointed out, was "not at all 'exceptional'" but rather "universal to all."[211]

Given the mollifying tone of Rosenzweig's following letter, Kracauer must have objected to this idea of prophetic speech with some vehemence.[212] "I ought not to abandon you any longer to your fears," Rosenzweig wrote, though he thought it should have been clear to Kracauer that he "did not mean such harsh things." Kracauer appears to have believed that Rosenzweig had removed any room for human agency. Rosenzweig denied this, stating that what he said of prophecy applied only to the specific case of prophetic speech. To be sure, the prophetic was solely the province of the divine; it was something that human agency could not influence. However, since this was not the only way that God related to his creation, it did not necessarily bear on other spheres. Moreover, to say that the human is always dependent on the divine does not say anything against human agency; rather, it is what makes possible the "relation" existing between the transcendent realm of God and the contingent realm of the human.

It is difficult to imagine that Kracauer would have accepted this answer, as parts of these letters would have awakened his ingrained suspicion that logical and religious concepts were being forced together. In the first letter, Rosenzweig had described the potential for a "becoming absolute" (*Absolutwerden*), a situation where an "age" or "nation" might become an absolute value.[213] One could know the absolute, but one had to relinquish forms of knowledge that sought demonstrations and proof; strictly speaking, it did not depend on evidence, and it was beyond the distinctions of rational and irrational. Its subject was the "not yet there." "Therefore," continued Rosenzweig, "logically spoken (in the sense of the new logic) it comes not to a question of evidence, but one of the probationary [*Bewährung*]." He concluded this part of the letter by noting that what he said was no matter of subjectivism, for one could actualize "mathematical, rigorously adhered to, objective ideals." After having read Kracauer's "essay on dialogue," which he interpreted as a logical investigation, he believed that Kracauer could go further into this domain.

For his part, Kracauer would probably have taken the mention of a "new logic" as a sign that Rosenzweig was still ensnared in idealist thought. He may have sympathized with the notion of the "not yet there" as a lingering but unknown utopian promise, but he would almost certainly have rejected these references to new forms of logic that could somehow account for this realm. He had tried to persuade Kracauer that the "new logic" would avoid the problem of "subjectivism," and would be able to find a way across the gap between the absolute and the particular, but it seems improbable that Kracauer would have found this position convincing, having already argued against it in the work of Ernst Troeltsch.[214]

However, if we accept that he was unreceptive to much of what Rosenzweig had written, what motivated him to undertake this debate over prophetic speech in the first place, that is, what did he want to salvage from the idea of prophecy? Some idea of this can be found in his review of the film *The Street*, directed by Karl Grune. The review was entitled "Film Image and Prophetic Speech."[215] The review appeared a year after his dispute with Rosenzweig, but it is probable that these discussions informed the essay. The divide between prophetic speech and cultural expression emerges in an oppositional form, serving a negative function that clarified the distance between a language fully commensurate with experience, and the failed intentions of culture. Art could only orient itself towards the desired reconciliation of cultural form and existential need, but it could not bring this union about. In a sense then, the limitation of human agency argued in Rosenzweig's letter was preserved here.

Thus, in spite of the better known conflicts between Kracauer and the leading figures of the Jewish revival in Frankfurt, there is reason to think that his argument with the revival was significant to his later work. His subsequent dispute with Buber and Rosenzweig over the publication of their Bible translation has received considerable attention from scholars, so I will not go over the details of this dispute here.[216] It will suffice to mention that Kracauer's most serious objections were that Buber and Rosenzweig had fallen into a linguistic archaism, a mode of expression that no longer spoke to the spiritual or material needs of the present; the language was out of the step with the status of Hebrew in Germany in the 1920s. More seriously, he suggested that it also betrayed *völkisch* tendencies. The merits and demerits of this critique have also been discussed at length, Martin Jay taking a more favorable position towards Kracauer, while the recent work of Peter Eli Gordon has pointed out that his position was a distinctly minority one.[217]

Given Kracauer's position on the Bible translation, it is improbable that he would have accepted Rosenzweig's metahistorical construction of Judaism. However, this is not due solely to its alleged *völkisch* tendencies, but rather because it would have conflicted with his claims for a more indeterminate kind of "extraterritoriality." The metahistorical, in some respects, resembles the extraterritorial insofar as they both suggest a point of view that is grounded in distance; but for Kracauer this perspective remained outside of positive religiosity or a fixed political agenda. The religious flâneur must refuse both a secular and a metaphysical home; hence, Zionism could not solve what Kracauer saw as the enigma of Jewish history, nor could religion offer a safe haven in the world.[218] Rosenzweig's argument that a "collective" (*Tum*) could become absolute would have had little resonance for him in either a material or metaphysical sense.[219] In contrast, he had an affinity for the Jewish wanderers, buffeted by events and the history of persecution, figures that exposed the deceptions behind the ideals and ideologies that surrounded them. These could be found in the writings of Joseph Roth or in lesser known works such as *Fischbein Lays Down His Arms* by Matwej Roesmann, or *A Little Prophet* by Edmond Fleg. The former was the story of a Jewish trader in Russia who is unable to adjust to the demands of the revolution and is eventually executed; the latter told the story of a young man negotiating the religious currents of Judaism and Christianity.[220] In this book, a Jewish youth in Paris first is tempted to convert to Catholicism in order to marry the woman he loves; but a sympathetic priest, recognizing his lack of true faith, refuses to convert him. He then enters the Zionist movement, studies the work of the Jewish prophets, and comes closer to his ancestral religion; after these episodes he joins the Pathfinders before finally proclaiming his vocation as a "pathfinder of humanity." Of this work Kracauer wrote: "in our German-American climate, such a youth, who is more for the messiah of peace than for the ocean-wide journey, would certainly go to ruin. He breathes the atmosphere of the hothouse, closed off from the outside, and has no contact with the profane—an overly sensitive youth, who will later find life unbearable."

This sympathetic predilection for the stories of Jewish wanderers recalls Kracauer's somewhat jarring evocation of the "wandering Jew" towards the end of his unfinished work on history. To Kracauer Judaism is predisposed to historical flânerie, a situation that he also experienced as he travelled in 1926 from the Zionist conference in Basel to the torchlight processions in Lourdes. The position of the flâneur accords with the one who waits, the one who reads and interprets and points to the incompletion of human intentions and desires.[221] The flâneur does not possess what sits behind the glass, and knows that it should never be possessed, just as Kracauer never grasps for a religious creed. In theological terms, modernity is the place of "love at last sight," a scarcely perceived glimpse that cannot be recovered outside of a split second in the here and now.[222] The flâneur does not find the absolute, but tries to decipher those points where the "time of nature" and the "time of grace" are still entangled. In this case, the problem with the flâneur is not one of restlessness; it is not the flâneur who endlessly looks that is the problem, but the one who claims to have found an end to looking. The religious flâneur who searches for stable essences beneath the world of appearances forsakes the critical potential inherent in flânerie. For to give up wandering and come to rest is to take up residence in the society represented in the *The Detective Novel*, one that tries to escape from the contradictions of existence. As a result they sink into the unreal, into ideology as Herrigel did when he embraced the German-Christian movement.

For Kracauer, a secularized theology was a potential point of resistance, a means of trying to prevent the lapse into ideology and myth. To his mind, religious institutions had failed to confront this problem, and the new religions were more of a danger than a solution. Religion was slowly barring the door between itself and a true engagement with the real. By 1926, when he attended a subsequent Catholic Academic conference, the trend towards a restorative Catholicism was increasingly evident. One of the speakers was a supporter of the Rembrandt-Deutschen, an extremist conservative group inspired by Julius Langbehn. The year before in 1925 he had heard a lecture on the conversion of the Jews.[223] Thus, it was not only the provocations of modern society that compelled his turn toward the critical interpretation of culture and history, but also a disenchantment with contemporary religion.

Notes

1. "André Gide an Walther Rathenau," *FZ*, 8 September 1928, Abendblatt; and "Auch ich singe Amerika" and "Hausknecht," *FZ*, 16 December 1928, 1st Morgenblatt.
2. Polgar, "The Small Form," in *The Vienna Coffeehouse Wits, 1890–1938*, ed. and trans. Harold B. Segel (West Lafayette, 1995), 279–81.
3. Andreas Huyssen, *Miniature Metropolis: Literature in an Age of Photography and Film* (Cambridge, 2015).
4. Golo Mann quoted in Mendes-Flohr, *Divided Passions: Jewish Intellectuals and the Experience of Modernity* (Detroit, 1991), 44–45.
5. Kierkegaard quoted in Allen Janik, "Haecker, Kierkegaard and the Early Brenner: A Contribution to the History of the Reception of *Two Ages*," ed. Robert L. Perkins (Macon, 1984), 211–13.
6. George Pattison, *Kierkegaard, Religion, and the Nineteenth-Century Crisis of* Culture (Cambridge, 2002), 25–49.
7. Kracauer to Susman, 25 January 1921, SN, DLA.
8. Viktor Klemperer, *Leben sammeln, nicht fragen wozu und woran: Tagebücher, 1918–1924*, vol. 1 (Berlin, 1996), 887. The emphasis is indicated in the original.
9. Kracauer, letter to Susman, 26 July 1920, SN, DLA: "I hate the literati and all that goes around under the title of *Geistiger* und *Intellektueller*."
10. Peter Fritzsche, *Reading Berlin 1900* (Cambridge, 1996); and Kracauer, "Georg," in *Werke* 7, 320.
11. Kracauer, "Georg," in *Werke* 7, 286.

12. Rosenzweig to Herrigel, 9 January 1925, *Franz Rosenzweig: Der Mensch und Sein Werk. Briefe* 1.2, 1014–15.
13. Stefan Zweig to Kracauer, 26 August 1930, KN, DLA.
14. Susman to Kracauer, 22 March 1926, KN, DLA. As Susman's letter to Kracauer was written before his review had appeared, it is possible that he may have shown her the essay prior to publication as he had done with his essay on Scheler. However, their friendship appears to have soured in the interim. See Kracauer to Adorno, 16 April 1925, *Briefwechsel, 1923–1966*, 49.
15. Franz Rosenzweig, "Scripture and Word: On the New Bible Translation," in Martin Buber and Franz Rosenzweig, *Scripture and Translation*, trans. Lawrence Rosenwald with Everett Fox (Bloomington, 1994), 42.
16. Walter Benjamin to Kracauer, 18 January 1927, *Briefe an Siegfried Kracauer*, 37.
17. See Kracauer to Zweig, 24 September 1930 and 2 October 1930, KN, DLA.
18. Kracauer to Friedrich T. Gubler, 13 July 1930 and 28 January 1931, KN, DLA, also quoted in Helmut Stalder, *Siegfried Kracauer: Das journalistische Werk in der 'Frankfurter Zeitung' 1921–1933* (Würzburg, 2003), 107.
19. Reifenberg quoted in Stalder, *Siegfried Kracauer: Das journalistische Werk*, 100. Stalder demonstrates the close collaboration between Kracauer, Reifenberg, and Roth as they formulated a critical agenda for the *FZ* feuilleton.
20. Karl Vaupel to Kracauer, 30 January 1933, KN, DLA. Vaupel (1896–1968) was a schoolteacher and education reformer. He published numerous pedagogical works including *Kinder im Industrieland* (1933), a book that he sent to Kracauer with his letter of 30 January. Kracauer responded warmly to both the letter and the book. He intended to circulate it among his fellow editors with an eye to printing an excerpt in the *FZ* at a later date. Hitler's ascent to power interrupted these plans.
21. Kracauer, *The Salaried Masses: Duty and Distraction in Weimar Germany*, trans. Quintin Hoare (London, 1998), 32
22. Kracauer, "Der Schriftsteller Heinrich Mann. Zu seinem Prosa-Band: *Das öffentliche Leben*," *FZ*, 3 July 1932, in *Der verbotene Blick*, 263–68.
23. "Hollow space" or *Hohlräume* was a term that resonated with negative theology; on the use of this terminology by Bloch and Benjamin, see Howard Eiland and Michael W. Jennings, *Walter Benjamin: A Critical Life* (Cambridge, 2014), 479.
24. Georg Lukács, "On the Nature and Form of the Essay," in *Soul and Form*, trans. Anna Bostock, ed. John T. Sanders and Katie Terezakis (New York, 2010), 32. Kracauer had read this book: see Kracauer to Susman, 11 August 1922.
25. Rosenzweig, "Scripture and Word," 41.
26. See his letter to Susman, 20 April 1921, SN, DLA, and his letter to Löwenthal, 12 April 1924, in *In steter Freundschaft*, 53–55. Löwenthal credits Kracauer for having exerted a "decisive" influence on his later development. See Löwenthal, "As I Remember Friedel," 8–10.
27. Kracauer, "Die heilige Geschichte im Film," *FZ*, 23 December 1921, in *Werke* 6.1, 12–13.
28. Kracauer, "Volks-Lichtspiele," *FZ*, 24 December 1921, in *Werke* 6.1, 14.
29. Kracauer, "Ben Hur. Zur Aufführung in Frankfurt," *FZ*, 23 October 1926, in *Werke* 6.1, 264–66. See also, "Ben Hur in Frankfurt—Vorbericht," *FZ*, 22 October 1926, in *Werke* 6.1, 263. Cf. the Frankfurt School and the reluctance to name or describe God in Martin Jay, *The Dialectical Imagination: A History of the Frankfurt School and the Institute of Social Research, 1923–1950* (Berkeley, 1996), 56.

30. Kracauer, "Ben Hur," in *Werke* 6.1, 266.
31. The *FZ* did, of course, have foreign subscribers, and it was certainly well read by the Jewish population in Frankfurt, see Modris Eksteins, *The Limits of Reason: The German Democratic Press and the Collapse of Weimar Democracy* (Oxford, 1975), 24–28 and 122–32.
32. Kracauer, "Kunst und Sittlichkeit," *FZ*, 2 May 1922, in *Werke* 5.1, 411–15.
33. Eksteins, *The Limits of Reason*, 27 and 122–24.
34. Mülder, *Siegfried Kracauer—Grenzgänger*, 45; and Zachary Braiterman, *The Shape of Revelation: Aesthetics and Modern Jewish Thought* (Stanford, 2007), 252–54.
35. Kracauer to Ernst Bloch, 27 May 1926, in *Briefe* 1, 272–75.
36. Adorno to Benjamin, 4 March 1938, in Lonitz, *Theodor W. Adorno and Walter Benjamin: The Complete Correspondence*, 248–53, esp. 249. In this respect, Adorno compared Kracauer to Scholem and Theodor Haecker.
37. Kracauer, "Der Künstler in dieser Zeit," in *Der verbotene Blick*, 132.
38. Kracauer, "Der Künstler in dieser Zeit," in *Der verbotene Blick*, 138–40.
39. Kracauer, "Georg von Lukács' Romantheorie," in *Der verbotene Blick*, 84.
40. Braiterman, *The Shape of Revelation*, 252–55.
41. Kracauer, "Die Künstler und der Weise," *FZ*, 29 May 1927, in *Werke* 5.2, 609–11.
42. Maritain quoted in Kracauer, "Die Künstler und der Weise," 610.
43. Audoin-Rouzeau and Becker, *14–18: Understanding the Great War*, 114–34; and Winter, *Sites of Memory*, 119–44. Still, statistics concerning the withdrawal from church membership do suggest large-scale disaffection, with almost two and half million Germans abandoning the Protestant Church and a further half million leaving the Catholic fold. See the statistics cited in Richard Overy, *The Dictators: Hitler's Germany, Stalin's Russia* (London and New York, 2005), 279.
44. Erwin Iserloh, "Innerkirchliche Bewegungen und ihre Spiritualität," in *Handbuch der Kirchengeschichte: Die Weltkirche im 20. Jahrhundert*, vol. 7, ed. Hubert Jedin and Konrad Repgen (Freiburg, 1979), 301–37. For a further overview see Nowak, *Geschichte des Christentums in Deutschland*, 205–42; and on the revived postwar religiosity, see Graf, "God's Anti-Liberal Avant-Garde."
45. See the census data in Heinz Blankenberg, *Politischer Katholizismus in Frankfurt am Main, 1918–1933* (Mainz, 1981), 4–9.
46. Kracauer, *Werke* 7, 320–21.
47. Hans-Georg Gadamer, *Philosophische Lehrjahre: Eine Rückschau* (Frankfurt am Main, 1977), 69.
48. Kracauer to Susman, 17 September 1921, SN, DLA; and Rosenzweig to Kracauer, 12 December 1921, KN, DLA, partially reprinted in Belke and Renz, *Siegfried Kracauer*, 36.
49. Ernst Simon to Kracauer, 17 May 1926, KN, DLA. Ernst Simon (1899–1988) probably met Kracauer in 1920 through Löwenthal. He studied religion and philosophy and was active in the Free Jewish School. A proponent of Zionism, he immigrated to Palestine in 1928 and taught at the Hebrew University.
50. Kracauer to Susman, 16 June 1920, SN, DLA.
51. Kracauer, "Those Who Wait," in *Mass Ornament*, 140.
52. Kracauer, *Der Detektiv-Roman*, 19.
53. Kracauer to Susman, 20 April 1921, SN, DLA.
54. See his concluding remarks in "Photography" in *Mass Ornament*, 59–64; and Mülder, *Siegfried Kracauer—Grenzgänger*, 86–102.

55. Kracauer, *Werke* 7, 321.
56. Kracauer to Susman, 20 April 1921, SN, DLA. After studying philosophy and theology, Eberhard Arnold (1882–1935) turned to evangelical work with the Salvation Army. In 1920, he founded a Christian commune at Sannerz. The membership grew to the point that a larger farm was sought, but after 1933 the commune was persecuted by the NSDAP and eventually disbanded. It has since become known as the Bruderhof movement and is still active in the United States.
57. See his obituary notice, "Rabbiner Dr. Nobel†" *FZ*, 25 January 1922, in *Werke* 5.1, 362–63. In contrast, though Kracauer was impressed by Buber, he said they lacked a genuine rapport; see his letter to Löwenthal, 1 March 1922, in *In steter Freundschaft*, 38–39.
58. Kracauer to Susman, 20 April 1921, SN, DLA.
59. Kracauer to Susman, 20 April 1921, SN, DLA.
60. Kracauer, "Those Who Wait," in *Mass Ornament*, 136–37.
61. Kracauer, "Those Who Wait," in *Mass Ornament*, 137–38. Translation slightly modified.
62. Kracauer, "Untergang?" in *Werke* 5.1, 704.
63. The reference is to the opening pages in Adorno, *Jargon of Authenticity*, 3–4.
64. Kracauer, 20 April 1921, SN, DLA.
65. Bloch to Susman, undated letter probably from 1911, in Susman, *Das Nah- und Fernsein*, 79.
66. Rosenzweig to Martin Buber, 11 October 1922, in Rosenzweig, *Franz Rosenzweig: Der Mensch und sein Werk*, 1.2, 836–37; and Hans Ehrenberg to Franz Rosenzweig, 11 May 1926, *Franz Rosenzweig Collection*, reel 7, "Luther und die Schrift," Leo Baeck Institute, New York. See also, Rosenzweig to Rudolf Ehrenberg, 3 March 1922, *Franz Rosenzweig: Der Mensch und sein Werk*, 1.2, 755–56.
67. Rosenzweig to Martin Buber, 28 April 1926, *Franz Rosenzweig: Der Mensch und sein Werk*, 1.2, 1092–93. I have slightly modified the grammar in translation.
68. Kracauer, "Deutscher Geist und deutsche Wirklichkeit," in *Werke* 5.1, 366. *Die Rheinlande* was edited by Wilhelm Schäfer who would become a popular writer with a strong *völkisch* stamp. He never joined the NSDAP, but pursued similar cultural-political goals in his work.
69. Kracauer to Susman, 11 January 1920 and 16 June 1920, SN, DLA.
70. Kracauer to Susman, 16 June 1920, SN, DLA.
71. Kracauer, "Georg von Lukács' Romantheorie," in *Der verbotene Blick*, 82–83.
72. Kracauer, "Deutscher Geist und deutsche Wirklichkeit," in *Werke* 5.1, 365–69.
73. Kracauer, "Menschenliebe, Gerechtigkeit und Duldsamkeit," in *Werke* 9.2, 88.
74. Kracauer, *Werke* 9.2, 93–94.
75. Kracauer, "Deutscher Geist und deutscher Wirklichkeit," in *Werke* 5.1, 364–65.
76. Kracauer, "Deutscher Geist und deutscher Wirklichkeit," in *Werke* 5.1, 366.
77. On Protestantism in the 1920s, see Friedrich Wilhelm Graf, *Der heilige Zeitgeist: Studien zur Wissenschaftsgeschichte der protestantischen Theologie in der Weimarer Republik* (Tübingen, 2010).
78. See the opening remarks in his article, "Protestantismus und moderner Geist: Ein Vortrag Gogartens," *FZ*, 3 April 1924, in *Werke* 5.2, 51–55.
79. Kracauer, "Zur religiösen Lage in Deutschland," *Gemeindeblatt der Israelitischen Gemeinde Frankfurt am Main*, reprinted in *Werke* 5.2, 157–58.

80. Kracauer, review of *Psychologie der Weltanschauungen*, Karl Jaspers, in *Archiv für Sozialwissenschaft und Sozialpolitik* 51(March 1924), in *Werke* 5.2, 48–51, esp. 51.
81. Kracauer, "Zur religiösen Lage in Deutschland," in *Werke* 5.2, 158.
82. Kracauer, "Deutsche Protestanten im Kampf," *L'Europe Nouvelle* (18 November 1933); reprinted in *Werke* 5.4, 474–77. Kracauer does not appear to have had a good perspective on the post-1933 situation of either church in Germany, and may not have been aware that Gogarten had accepted the new state in 1933.
83. On Gogarten see Graf, *Der heilige Zeitgeist*, 265–328.
84. Kracauer, "Deutsche Protestanten im Kampf," in *Werke* 5.4, 476–77. Also, see Kracauer's discussion of the Protestant theologian Günther Dehn, in Kracauer, "Theologie gegen Nationalismus," *FZ*, 14 January 1933, 5.4, 344–49.
85. Kracauer, "Theologie gegen Nationalismus," 346.
86. Herrigel edited the *Hochschulblatt* until his forced departure from the paper in 1934; see Günther Gillessen, *Auf verlorenem Posten: Die Frankfurter Zeitung im Dritten Reich* (Frankfurt am Main, 1986), 151 and 330.
87. Kracauer to Susman, 17 October 1920, and 22 November 1920, SN, DLA. Susman may have introduced Kracauer to Herrigel. At the latest they had met by July 1920. See Belke and Renz, *Siegfried Kracauer*, 34.
88. Kracauer to Susman, 20 April 1921, SN, DLA.
89. For a brief biography and overview of Herrigel and his work, see the introduction by Günther Schulz and Ursula Schulz, *Hermann Herrigel, der Denker und die deutsche Erwachsenenbildung. Bremer Beiträge zur freien Volksbildung* (Bremen, 1969), 7–14.
90. Schulz, *Hermann Herrigel*, 8–9.
91. Kracauer to Werner Thormann, 22 September 1927, Thormann Nachlaß, EB 97/145, Deutsche Nationalbibliothek, Deutsches Exilarchiv, 1933–1945, Frankfurt am Main.
92. Hermann Herrigel, *Das neue Denken* (Berlin, 1928), 219–44. Rosenzweig was skeptical of Herrigel as an interpreter of the "new thinking," and he noted with some irony that Herrigel appeared to have only read his explanation of the *Star of Redemption* and not the full book itself. See his letter to Richard Koch, 2 September 1928, in *Franz Rosenzweig: Der Mensch und sein Werk*, 1.2, 1197.
93. Hermann Herrigel (H.H.), "Denken dieser Zeit: Fakultäten und Nationen treffen sich in Davos," *FZ*, 23 April 1929, Abendblatt. See the discussion of this article in Peter Eli Gordon, *Rosenzweig and Heidegger: Between Judaism and German Philosophy* (Berkeley, 2003), 289–91. For a more extensive study of the altercation between Cassirer and Heidegger see Gordon, *Continental Divide: Heidegger, Cassirer, Davos* (Cambridge, 2010).
94. See the section *Für Hochschule und Jugend* in the *FZ*, 30 July 1928, Abendblatt.
95. Hermann Herrigel, "Zur Kritik des deutschen Idealismus—Vorrede eines ungedruckten Buches," *Die Tat* 14, no. 2 (May 1922): 114–21.
96. Herrigel, "Zur Kritik des deutschen Idealismus," 121–22; and *Das neue Denken*, 94–97. This section of the Herrigel's book derives largely from his 1922 article in *Die Tat*.
97. Kracauer to Löwenthal, 2 November 1924, in *In steter Freundschaft*, 65.
98. On the history of the German Christians, see Doris Bergen, *The Twisted Cross: The German Christian Movement in the Third Reich* (Chapel Hill, 1996).

99. The Herrigel Nachlaß (HN) is kept at the Württembergische Landesbibliothek (WL), Stuttgart. The papers are not yet catalogued and his letters from the 1920s have not survived. Only correspondence from after the Nazi ascent to power remains, though he clearly had a relationship with Gogarten since the early 1920s. According to some sources, Herrigel, perhaps under the influence of Gogarten, increasingly identified with the position of the German Christian movement. According to Gillessen, Herrigel took a sympathetic position to the movement in his journalism, a position that was not in accord with the other editors of the *FZ*; for this reason he was eventually forced out of the editorial conferences. Rudolf Kircher was one of the editors who appears to have pressed for his removal. Moreover, Heinrich Simon reported to Reifenberg in 1933 that in questions of race Herrigel was in favor of a position close to the NSDAP (see Gillessen, *Auf verlorenem Posten*, 147 and 151). In that year, Paula Lewin, who appears to have been a friend from Frankfurt, wrote to him in astonishment concerning a rumor that he had joined the party (Paula Lewin to Hermann Herrigel, 23 May 1933, HN, Ordner no. 1, HN, WL). There is no response in his papers, and I have not confirmed whether he did in fact join the NSDAP. Adorno, however, returns to this issue in 1963, and he numbered Herrigel among the "authentic" ones who he attacked in the opening passages of his *Jargon der Eigentlichkeit*. In a letter to Kracauer, he stated that Herrigel, out of "sheer concreteness" (*lauter Konkretheit*), had become a "fervid Nazi." See Adorno to Kracauer, 28 October 1963, *Briefwechsel, 1923–1966*, 614.
100. See Wolfgang Tilgner, *Volksnomostheologie und Schöpfungsglaube: Ein Beitrag zur Geschichte des Kirchenkampfes. Arbeiten zur Geschichte des Kirchenkampfes* 16 (Göttingen, 1966). Herrigel states his admiration of Schomerus in a letter to Gottlob Lechter, 3 August 1935, Ordner no. 1, HN, WL.
101. Among the subscribers to *Christliche Besinnung heute* were Martin Buber and Wilhelm Hausenstein, both of whom cancelled their subscriptions due to economic reasons. However, this may have been an alibi on both counts (Hausenstein to Herrigel, 3 November 1936, Ordner no. 3, HN, WL and Buber to Herrigel, 22 August 1938, Ordner no. 5, HN, WL). Buber's disagreement with Herrigel over the relationship of politics and religion is discussed in Maurice Friedman, *Martin Buber's Life and Work: The Middle Years 1923–1945* (New York, 1983), 189–90.
102. Herrigel to Martin Buber, 19 November 1936, in Buber, *Briefwechsel aus sieben Jahrzehnten II, 1918–1938*, ed. Grete Schaeder (Heidelberg, 1973), 622–24. Herrigel's receptivity to the work of Carl Schmitt is also evident here.
103. Kracauer, "Autorität und Individualismus," *FZ*, 15 February 1921, in *Werke* 5.1, 167–73; and "Das Wesen des politischen Führers," *FZ*, 12 June 1921, in *Werke* 5.1, 211–20.
104. Kracauer, "Das Wesen des politischen Führers," 214–15. The italics are in the original text.
105. Kracauer, "Autorität und Individualismus," and "Das Wesen des politischen Führers," 215–20. The accent, however, is unmistakably on authority. In "Authority and Individualism" he writes, "More dangerous, because more seductive, is the repudiation of authority in favor of the inherent significance of the individual."
106. Kracauer, "Das Wesen des politischen Führers," in *Werke* 5.1, 220. On ideas of political leadership in modern Germany, see Walter Struve, *Elites Against Democracy: Leadership Ideals in Bourgeois Political Thought in Germany, 1890–1933* (Princeton, 1973).

107. Schulz, "Einleitung," *Hermann Herrigel*, 8.
108. Wilhelm Hausenstein to Herrigel, 20 July 1935, Ordner no. 1, HN, WL.
109. Graf, "God's Anti-Liberal Avant-Garde," 7–11.
110. Also, see Kracauer, "Zur religiösen Lage," in *Werke* 5.2, 156–58.
111. Kracauer, *Werke* 7, 326.
112. Kracauer, *Werke* 7, 327.
113. Kracauer, "The Bible in German," in *Mass Ornament*, 201.
114. Cf. Kracauer, "Eine Woche der Jugendbewegung," *FZ*, 13 November 1921, in *Werke* 5.1, 297–303.
115. Petri is a rough and by no means flattering portrait of the *FZ* lead editor, Heinrich Simon.
116. On Catholicism in Frankfurt, see Blankenberg, *Politischer Katholizismus*.
117. On Thormann, see Bruno Lowitsch, *Der Kreis um die Rhein-Mainische Volkszeitung* (Wiesbaden and Frankfurt am Main, 1980), 28–30; and Blankenberg, *Politischer Katholizismus*, 13 and 109–10.
118. Lowitsch, *Der Kreis um die Rhein-Mainische Volkszeitung*, 85–128.
119. Lowitsch, *Der Kreis um die Rhein-Mainische Volkszeitung*, 37–39; and Blankenberg, *Politischer Katholizismus*, 89–94.
120. Kracauer to Charlotte Thormann, 25 May 1947, Thorman Nachlaß, Deutsche Nationalbibliothek, Deutsches Exilarchiv, Frankfurt am Main.
121. Only the letters from Weiger have survived.
122. Weiger to Kracauer, 29 December 1921, KN, DLA. The essay in question is probably "Neue Menschen und katholisches Erbe: Ein Versuch über Max Scheler," which appeared in the April 1922 issue of *Die Tat*. It appears that Kracauer may have known of this essay earlier, as Weiger wrote to Kracauer explaining why he did not send his own Scheler essay to him. Kracauer may have been given the essay by Rosenzweig who, in response to his attack on Scheler, had sent him a piece written by a "Catholic writer" that Rosenzweig suggested contained what he thought Kracauer had "missed." Rosenzweig said the essay was given to him by Michel who was the editor of the special issue of *Die Tat* in which the essay appeared. See Rosenzweig to Kracauer, 12 December 1921, KN, DLA.
123. Weiger to Kracauer, 29 December 1921, KN, DLA.
124. Romano Guardini to Kracauer, no year (24 September), KN, DLA. The year is not indicated but the reference to Ulm suggests that it was written on 24 September after the conference that took place from 10 to 16 August 1923.
125. Kracauer, "Der Tagung der Katholischen Akademiker, II," *FZ*, 6 September, 1923, in *Werke* 5.1, 685–91. Kracauer's copy of this article in KN, DLA attributes this brief text to Erich Troß, a fellow editor on the *Hochschulblatt* in the mid-1920s. Nothing is known of the relations between the two men, but they must have worked closely in these years. Kracauer kept copies of all his articles for the *FZ* in a scrapbook with annotations; see Levin, *Siegfried Kracauer: eine Bibliographie*, 13–29.
126. "Der neue Werden," *FZ*, 6 September 1923, in *Werke* 5.1, 691.
127. Kracauer, "Die Tagung der katholischen Akademiker I," *FZ*, 29 August 1923, in *Werke* 5.1, 674–78. Ildefons Herwegen (1874–1946) served as Abbot from 1913 until his death. In 1933 he argued for an opening of the Church to National Socialism. On the history of Maria Laach during the Weimar Republic and under the Third Reich, see Marcel Albert, *Die Benediktinerabtei Maria Laach und der Nationalsozialismus*. Kommission für Zeitgeschichte 95 (Paderborn and Munich, 2004). The

published version of Herwegen's speech entitled "Das Mysterium als die Seele katholischen Wesens," can be found in Ildefons Herwegen, *Lumen Christi: Gesammelte Aufsätze* (Munich, 1924), 107–38.
128. Kracauer, "Die Tagung der katholischen Akademiker I," in *Werke* 5.1, 675–76.
129. Herwegen, "Das Mysterium als die Seele katholischen Wesens," *Lumen Christi*, 127–29.
130. Kracauer, "Die Krise im deutschen Katholizismus: Zur Recklinghauser Sondertagung des Verbands katholischer Akademiker," *FZ*, 3 January 1926, in *Werke* 5.2, 331.
131. His disappointment corresponds with the views of some Catholic assessments of this period as well; cf. with the polemically titled essay by Walter Dirks, "Das Defizit des deutschen Katholizismus in Weltbild, Zeitbewußtsein und politischer Theorie," in *Religion und Geistesgeschichte der Weimarer Republic*, ed. Hubert Cancik (Düsseldorf, 1982), 17–30. For a more general account of Weimar Catholicism, see Thomas Ruster, *Die verlorene Nützlichkeit der Religion: Katholizismus und Moderne in der Weimarer Republik* (Paderborn, 1994).
132. Herwegen, "Das Mysterium als die Seele katholischen Wesens," in *Lumen Christi*, 128.
133. Kracauer, "Die Tagung der katholischen Akademiker II," in *Werke* 5.1, 685–86.
134. Kracauer, "Die Tagung der katholischen Akademiker II," in *Werke* 5.1, 686.
135. Romano Guardini, *Liturgische Bildung: Versuche* (Berg Rothenfels am Main, 1923).
136. Kracauer, "Liturgische Bildung," *FZ*, 20 June 1924, in *Werke* 5.2, 90–91; also cf. Kracauer, "Zur religiösen Lage in Deutschland," in *Werke* 5.2, 156–57.
137. Kracauer, "Liturgische Bildung," in *Werke* 5.2, 91.
138. Kracauer, "Liturgische Bildung," in *Werke* 5.2, 91.
139. Ernst Michel, ed., *Kirche und Wirklichkeit: Ein katholisches Zeitbuch* (Jena, 1923).
140. Albert Mirgeler, "Jugendbewegung vor dem Ende: Eine Abrechnung mit Romano Guardini und dem Quickborn," in Michel, *Kirche und Wirklichkeit*, 180–85.
141. Mirgeler, "Jugendbewegung," 183.
142. Kracauer, "Das Religiöse und das Profane. Zur Tagung der katholischer Akademiker," *FZ*, 25 August 1925, in *Werke* 5.2, 289–95.
143. Kracauer, "Das Religiöse und das Profane," 289 and 292.
144. Thormann, "Die Aufgabe des katholischen Dichters in der Zeit," in Michel, *Kirche und Wirklichkeit*, 146.
145. Kracauer, "Das Religiöse und das Profane," in *Werke* 5.2, 292–93.
146. Kracauer, "Das Religiöse und das Profane," in *Werke* 5.2, 292.
147. Nipperdey, *Religion im Umbruch*, 143–53. Also see Martin Green, *Mountain of Truth: The Counterculture Begins, Ascona, 1900–1920* (Hanover, 1986).
148. Nipperdey, *Religion im Umbruch*, 149.
149. Nipperdey, *Religion im Umbruch*, 151–52.
150. Kracauer, "Deutscher Geist und deutsche Wirklichkeit," in *Werke* 5.1, 371.
151. Kracauer, "Untergang?" in *Werke* 5.1, 704.
152. Kracauer to Löwenthal, 16 December 1921, Leo Löwenthal Archiv/A 481, Johannes Senckenberg Bibliothek, Frankfurt am Main.
153. Kracauer to Löwenthal, 16 December 1921, Leo Löwenthal Archiv/ A 481, Johannes Senckenberg Bibliothek, Frankfurt am Main.
154. Kracauer, "Das Religiöse und das Profane," in *Werke* 5.2, 291.
155. Kracauer, "Ginster," in *Werke* 7, 68–69. In light of Kracauer's notoriously gendered conceptualization of the cinema audience in "The Little Shop-Girls Go to the

Movies," one might suspect a gendered representation of the casual and unconsidered encounter with Eastern philosophy; however, this does not appear to have been the case.
156. Leopold Ziegler, *Der ewige Buddho. Ein Tempelschriftwerk in vier Unterweisungen* (Darmstadt, 1923); and, Kracauer, "Europasien," *FZ*, 23 June 1922, in *Werke* 5.1, 438–45.
157. Kracauer, "Chinas Philosophie," *FZ*, 11 December 1927, in *Werke* 5.2, 707–9.
158. Kracauer, "Dr. Rudolf Steiner in Frankfurt," *FZ*, 19 January 1922, Abendblatt; "Welt-Erlösung," *FZ*, 9 May 1923, Stadtblatt; "Anthroposophie und Christentum," *FZ*, 28 October 1923, in *Werke* 5.1, 718–20; "Zum Tode Rudolf Steiners," *FZ*, 18 April 1925, in *Werke* 5.2, 228–32; and Kracauer to Adorno, 16 April 1925, *Briefwechsel, 1923–1966*, 47. On Steiner, see Nipperdey, *Religion im Umbruch*, 145–46.
159. Hermann Graf Keyserling, *Reisetagebuch eines Philosophen* (Darmstadt, 1919).
160. Joseph Roth, *Right and Left*, trans. Michael Hofmann (New York and Woodstock, 1992), 223.
161. Kracauer, "Von der Schule der Weisheit," *FZ*, 6 October 1921, in *Werke* 5.1, 289–96; see also the contributions from Kracauer, Flake, and Erich Mosse in "Stimmen zur 'Schule der Weisheit': Schlußwort," *FZ*, 20 October 1921, Morgenblatt; partially reprinted in *Werke* 5.1, 295–96.
162. The journal was entitled *Der Stürmer*, but there is no connection to the journal of the same name later edited by Julius Streicher.
163. I have not translated *Sinn* in this discussion as the variability of its meaning was at the root of the disagreement between Keyserling, Flake, and Kracauer.
164. Otto Flake, "Stimmen zu 'Schule der Weisheit.'"
165. Flake, "Stimmen zu 'Schule der Weisheit.'"
166. Flake, "Stimmen zu 'Schule der Weisheit.'"
167. Kracauer, "Von der Schule der Weisheit," in *Werke* 5.1, 292–93 and 296; and "Stimmen zu 'Schule der Weisheit.'"
168. Kracauer, "Otto Flake: *Das neuantike Weltbild*," *FZ*, 12 December 1922, in *Werke* 5.1, 539–41.
169. Kracauer, "Otto Flake: *Das neuantike Weltbild*," 540.
170. Kracauer, "Die Krisis der deutschen Kulturpolitik," *FZ*, 24 March 1922, 2nd Morgenblatt. This article reported on a speech given by Gertrud Bäumer.
171. He is not entirely forgotten. A Web site is devoted to his work and a number of his books are still in print.
172. Hans Zbinden, ed., *Ein Künder neuer Lebenswege: Einzelbilder zur Seelenforschung Rudolf Maria Holzapfels* (Jena, 1923); and Wladimir Astrow, *Das Leben Rudolf Maria Holzapfels* (Jena, 1928).
173. Ernst Mach, "Vorwort" to Holzapfel, *Panideal: Psychologie der sozialen Gefühle* (Leipzig, 1901), vii–viii.
174. Hans Zbinden, *In Strom der Zeit: Gedanken und Betrachtungen* (Berlin and Munich, 1964), 289–93.
175. Otto Hausherr, "Die Möglichkeit einer neuen Kultur," in Zbinden, *Ein Künder neuer Lebenswege*, 20.
176. Erich Troß, letter to Thormann, 3 April 1924, Thormann Nachlaß, EB 97/145, Deutsche Nationalbibliothek, Deutsches Exilarchiv, 1933–1945, Frankfurt am Main. Kracauer and Troß seemed to have agreed on the need to bring a "holy sobriety" into German political culture.

177. Kracauer, "Holzapfels *Panideal*," in *Werke*, 5.2, 17.
178. Kracauer, "Holzapfels *Panideal*," in *Werke*, 5.2, 16–17.
179. Kracauer, "Holzapfels *Panideal*," in *Werke*, 5.2, 17–19 and 23.
180. Klabund, "Zu Holzapfels Panideal," *FZ*, 20 February 1924, Abendblatt.
181. Wladimir Astrow, "Holzapfels *Panideal*: Eine Erwiderung," *FZ*, 19 March 1924, 2nd Morgenblatt.
182. Astrow, "Holzapfels *Panideal*."
183. Kracauer, "Holzapfels *Panideal*," in *Werke* 5.1, 19–20 and "Duplik" *FZ*, 19 March 1924, reprinted in *Werke* 5.1, 24–25.
184. Kracauer, "Holzapfels *Panideal*," 20–22. His knowledge of von Baader was shared with and perhaps derived from both Löwenthal and Benjamin, both of whom studied his work, Löwenthal submitting a doctoral thesis on von Baader in 1923.
185. Kracauer, "Holzapfels *Panideal*," 17.
186. Kracauer, "Der Künstler in dieser Zeit," in *Der verbotene Blick*, 132.
187. Kracauer, "Holzapfels *Panideal*," in *Werke* 5.1, 18. Emphasis is given in the original.
188. Walter Benjamin, "Über den Begriff der Geschichte," in *Kairos: Schriften zur Philosophie* (Frankfurt am Main, 2007), 315. Kracauer expressed misgivings about Benjaminian conceptions of redemption and reconciliation. See Kracauer to Adorno, 7 June 1931, *Briefwechsel, 1923–1966*, 282. Nonetheless, they persisted in Kracauer's work, reemerging in the subtitle to his *Theory of Film* and, of course, in his final work, *History*. On Benjamin's influence, see David Rodowick, "The Last Things before the Last: Kracauer and History," 109–39.
189. Kracauer to Henri-Irénée Marrou, 18 May 1964, KN, DLA.
190. Kracauer to Löwenthal, 1 March 1922, in *In steter Freundschaft*, 38.
191. Martin Jay, "The Extraterritorial Life of Siegfried Kracauer," *Permanent Exiles*. In his letter to Marrou of 18 May 1964 (KN, DLA), Kracauer referred to the "antinomy at the core of time."
192. Kracauer, "Die Frankfurter Goethe-Woche. Die akademische Feier," *FZ*, 1 March 1922, in *Werke* 5.1, 380–82.
193. Kracauer, "Religion als Gegenwart," *FZ*, 21 January 1922, in *Werke* 5.1, 360–62.
194. Kracauer to Löwenthal, 1 March 1922, in *In steter Freundschaft*, 39.
195. Kracauer to Susman, 10 February 1921, SN, DLA.
196. Kracauer to Susman, 2 May 1920, and 2 April 1920, SN, DLA.
197. Kracauer to Susman, 17 January 1922, SN, DLA.
198. Matthew Handelman, "The Forgotten Conversation: Five Letters from Franz Rosenzweig to Siegfried Kracauer, 1921–1923," *Scientia Poetica* 15, no. 1 (2011): 234–51.
199. Kracauer to Susman, 10 February 1921, SN, DLA; and Kracauer to Löwenthal, 16 December 1921, LLA/A 481, Leo Löwenthal Archive, Johannes Senckenberg Bibliothek, Frankfurt am Main.
200. Kracauer to Susman, 10 February 1921, SN, DLA.
201. Kracauer, "Catholicism and Relativism," in *Mass Ornament*, 203–211.
202. Rosenzweig to Kracauer, 12 December 1921, KN, DLA.
203. Rosenzweig to Kracauer, 31 March 1923, KN, DLA.
204. Rosenzweig to Rudolf Hallo, December 1922, *Franz Rosenzweig: Der Mensch und sein Werk*, 1.2, 861.
205. Rosenzweig to Buber, 16 July 1923, *Franz Rosenzweig: Der Mensch und sein Werk*, 1.2, 912.

206. Kracauer to Löwenthal, 4 December 1921, in *In steter Freundschaft*, 33–34.
207. Rosenzweig to Kracauer, 25 May 1923, and 6 June 1923, KN, DLA. On these letters, see Handelman, "The Forgotten Conversation," 244–48.
208. Rosenzweig to Kracauer, 25 May 1923, KN, DLA
209. Rosenzweig to Kracauer, 6 June 1923, KN, DLA.
210. Mendes-Flohr, *German Jews*, 82–83.
211. Rosenzweig to Kracauer, 25 May 1923, KN, DLA.
212. Rosenzweig to Kracauer, 5 June 1923, KN, DLA.
213. Rosenzweig to Kracauer, 25 May 1923, KN, DLA.
214. Kracauer, "Crisis of Science," in *Mass Ornament*, 214–18.
215. Hansen, "Decentric Perspectives," 52–54. His first review of the film appeared as "Die Straße," *FZ*, 3 February 1924, Stadtblatt; the second as "Filmbild und Prophetenrede," *FZ*, 5 May 1925, Morgenblatt. He also included parts of it in his longer essay, "Künstler in dieser Zeit," in *Der verbotene Blick*, 134–37.
216. See Martin Jay, "Politics of Translation," *Permanent Exiles*, 198–216; Martina and Walter Lesch, "Verbindungen zu einer anderen Frankfurter Schule: Zu Kracauers Auseinandersetzung mit Bubers and Rosenzweigs Bibelübersetzung," in Michael Kessler and Thomas Y. Levin, eds., *Siegfried Kracauer: neue Interpretationen* (Tübingen, 1990), 171–93; Traverso, *Siegfried Kracauer*, 34–44; Lawrence Rosenwald, "On the Reception of the Buber and Rosenzweig's Bible," *Prooftexts* 14, no. 3 (1994): 141–65; and Gordon, *Rosenzweig and Heidegger*, 239–41.
217. Kracauer, "The Bible in German," in *Mass Ornament*, 189–201; Jay, "Politics of Translation," 213–16; and Gordon, *Rosenzweig and Heidegger*, 239–41.
218. Kracauer, "Der Stand der zionistischen Bewegung: Eindrücke vom Baseler Zionistenkongreß," *FZ*, 20 September 1927, in *Werke* 5.2, 675–76.
219. Rosenzweig was not a strong supporter of Zionism; indeed, his views of it were mostly negative though there is some debate over his later position on the subject. See Paul W. Franks and Michael Morgan in Rosenzweig, *Philosophical and Theological Writings*, 93, n. 11.
220. Kracauer, "Privatschicksale in Sowjetrussland," *FZ*, 31 May 1931, in *Werke* 5.3, 536–39; and Kracauer, "Ein pariser Junge," *FZ*, 14 August 1927, in *Werke* 5.2, 645–46. Matjew Roesmann's novel was translated from the Russian and was published by the Bruno Cassirer Verlag in 1931. *L'enfant prophéte* by Edmond Fleg (1874–1963) appeared in France in 1926, and it was translated into German the following year.
221. See the comments on this theme in regards to the work of Karl Mannheim in Dirk Hoeges, *Kontroverse am Abgrund: Ernst Robert Curtius und Karl Mannheim—Intellektuelle und 'freischwebende Intelligenz' in der Weimarer Republik* (Frankfurt am Main, 1994), 36.
222. Walter Benjamin, "The Paris of the Second Empire," in *The Writer of Modern Life: Essays on Charles Baudelaire*, trans. Howard Eiland, Edmund Jephcott, Rodney Livingstone, and Harry Zohn (Cambridge, 2006), 77. On the flâneur more generally, see 66–96; and Anke Gleber, *The Art of Taking a Walk: Flanerie, Literature and Film in Weimar* (Princeton, 1999).
223. Kracauer, "Die Krise im deutschen Katholizismus," in *Werke* 5.2, 330; and "Das Religiöse und das Profane," in *Werke* 5.2, 292.

CONCLUSION

Criticism in the Negative Church

> Has film displaced the old Gods, the cinema the gothic dome, the Moorish synagogues and the mosques of Allah? I think film is an idea, a primal element of the mind, as old as every God and, perhaps, even an older God in a new house. Film is . . . a matter of the eyes and, I believe, it is as old as our eyes.
> —Leo Hirsch, "Der platonische Film," 67

> As for film, it was always just a hobby for me, a means of making certain sociological and philosophical statements.
> —Kracauer to Wolfgang Weyrauch, 4 June 1962, in Belke and Renz, *Siegfried Kracauer*, 118–19

By the end of the 1920s, Kracauer as the foregoing chapter shows, had some grounds for suspecting that religious points of view were not always able to mesh with aspects of modern culture. His belief that modernity was essentially secular meant that conflict was inevitable, but as we have seen, he did not in every case argue that religion was fated to disappear. Still, by the end of the Weimar Republic, his statements on religion became increasingly pessimistic about the role it might play in modern society—but why should modernity have posed such intractable problems for religion, and just what was modern about secular culture? Many intellectuals, of course, had devoted considerable efforts to dissecting the nature of modernity, its origins and consequences. In 1930, Max Rychner offered a skeptical perspective on the question in a lead article for the *Neue Schweizer Rundschau* (NSR), a journal he also edited. Of the modernists, Rychner spoke with some suspicion, as if they were simply cultural provocateurs: "From where comes this modernist fear that the world might stand still if the trend is not constantly whipped and spurred onwards by clichés?"[1] Was the modern then a creation of criticism? Or was it the product of an augmented historical consciousness, an anxiety over the vast expanses of empty time and the world's "infinite multiplicity"?[2] Kracauer was among the many critics who tried to integrate these diverse phenomena into a critique of modernity. Infinite multiplicity and empty time were drawn together in what Kracauer called the "negative church." In a chapter of *The Detective Novel*, he used this phrase to describe the hotel lobby, but the description has a wider relevance. The hotel lobby was the place where *ratio* declared its rule, a site where reason without purpose rendered itself aesthetically, demonstrating its pervasive power. The depiction was stark, an exaggeration perhaps, but the power it portrayed was nonetheless real for Kracauer. If one were to find some means of orientation in the world then one had to learn how to interpret the distortions and disfigurements that prevailed in the negative church.

A "negative church" is, however, different from a *negated* one. It required the church as a foil. The house of God had not vanished, but had turned against itself and become its own negative image. It was displaced, but it remained as a phantom presence. This reference to a church in reverse was not a trope that Kracauer abandoned, though he was uncertain of the choice of expression. The published editions of the study in both the *Schriften* and *Werke* are based on a corrected typescript that originates from the 1920s. In this text Kracauer described the hotel lobby as a "counter-image" (*Gegenbild*), instead of a "negative church." However, when he selected the chapter entitled "The Hotel Lobby" for publication in 1963, he did not retain the corrections that he made in the 1920s—corrections that also can be found on a second Weimar era typescript of this chapter.[3] Therefore, Kracauer appears to have reversed his original decision to strike this expression from the text, thus making his work more theologically suggestive.

For in the imagined and allegorical edifice of the negative church the functions of ritual referred to their opposites. Whereas the church of the past was where the community gathered for the purpose of representing and creating its link to the higher spheres, in the negative church individuals coagulated in spaces that were without purpose. Such locations were just transit points, places that existed only as conduits of a meaningless social traffic. Its sole purpose was the preservation of its own system. Images of the sacred were now images of the profane, and "those who waited" found solace in the cults of distraction. Kracauer was well aware of the attractions of this negative reality where kitsch took the place of redemption, and thus removed the melancholy sorrow from life. With this in mind, it is of interest that Kracauer enjoyed working in such places. Just as Ginster enjoyed spending time in railway stations, Kracauer later confessed that he had always worked best in such places, in cafes and hotel lobbies where he was saturated by the "inarticulate noise" that his criticism tried to decipher.[4]

By the middle of the 1920s, the "inarticulate noise" that interested him most was film, and thus it is surprising that he speaks so casually in regards to the importance that film had for his work as a whole. However much his status as a film theorist has been contested, his name is nonetheless firmly connected with the formation of film studies and the critique of mass culture.[5] Yet, his statement that film was only a means to an end need not be seen as a serious repudiation of its central relevance to his work; rather, it allows us to situate his interest in a more general framework of investigation, one that sought to decode the ephemera and fragments of culture, to ascertain something of the tenuous relationship between truth and appearances.[6]

Thus, Kracauer may have expressed himself differently than the contemporary essayist Leo Hirsch, quoted above, but he would have agreed with his general argument that the problem of film aesthetics belongs to a wider and older philosophical frame of reference. Film was certainly modern, but for Kracauer it crystallized a set of problems that were not in every respect new; indeed, film was the historical guise by which certain problems had become apparent.[7] On account of the photographic medium, the surface order of things acquired an objectivity, or outward expression, that provoked further investigation into the relationship between a chaos of appearances, modes of representing them, and the elusive contents of truth. The crisis of reason, of science, of the modern subject, of history—such labels identified the seemingly inescapable intellectual drive to put all certainties to question.[8] After the disruptions of war and revolution, as Kracauer struggled to find a foundation for his critical ambitions, the fear of relativism had been one of his primary concerns, for it vitiated every claim to truth, leaving in its wake a formless anarchy of opinions. There was indeed no absolute, merely perspectives, and as Paul Valéry wrote in his reckoning with the postwar intellectual malaise, "every point of view is false."[9] World history, relativism, the siren songs of religious revival, the arrogance of science—all these forms, customs, and patterns of thought argued for some means of clarifying the relationship between culture, society, and truth. To some, however, such ways of thinking represented the burdens of intellect rather than its means; they led the individual to an insoluble conundrum, trapped, to quote again from Valéry, between "order and disorder."[10] Between these two poles, Kracauer situated his hopes for criticism.

The objective of this study has been to show how Kracauer responded to this dilemma by conceptualizing a specific form of critical practice, and how this practice was informed by the discourses of secularization and religious revival. Kracauer's criticism sought to define a space between a materialist skepticism, on the one hand, and religious or metaphysical determinations of truth on the other. It was framed around the potential for a tentative or "hesitant openness," the operative space of a "liberated consciousness."[11] Historian Dagmar Barnouw has discussed this potential in relation to Kracauer's concept of the "secular openness" of history, its "incompleteness" (*Nicht-Vollendung*).[12] Kracauer directed his critiques against a resurgent religiosity, but nonetheless, such concepts do have their correspondences in contemporary religious discourse, and this correspondence should not be underestimated when reckoning with his work. As we have seen, Kracauer believed that the utopian longing for redeemed time was often conflated with historical teleology. This conflation was engendering a confusion that seemed to characterize modernity, producing a situation where, as Valéry wrote, the historian was beset with the same problems as the prophet.[13] For Kracauer, the hopes that accrued around both the idea of redemption and of historical teleology could not be fulfilled. Conclusive and meaningful statements about either were forbidden, and they were both characterized by a "fundamental ambivalence" of interpretation.[14] From this ambivalence, however, an idea of freedom arose, and it is here according to philosopher Andrew Benjamin that Kracauer's belief in a "liberated consciousness" comes into effect. Wherever interpretation displays an ambiguity that derives not simply from the relative nature of scientific knowledge but rather from recognition of the incompleteness of existence "under the sign of redemption," it is at this point that the possibility of a momentary and distorted glimpse of the truth arises. It is the "here" with which Kracauer concluded his Kafka essay, a point where, in Kafka's words, one may see a star "adjacent" to the sun but which still outshines it—a place where Kracauer tells us we must remain waiting with "unconfirmed longing for the place of freedom."[15]

In this respect, Inka Mülder-Bach notes the recurring motifs of escape and recapture that appeared in his work of the 1920s. The individual oscillated between moments of free interpretation and a stasis of meaning imposed by the rationalized world.[16] In his Weimar writings, the "sinister edifice" of the latter almost always triumphed, and the desire to seize the elusive "truth contents" of religion was repeatedly foreclosed by a reentrenched *ratio*. Thus, the threshold of the absolute could be recognized, but never crossed. "As if," so he wrote to Bloch, "the reality of truth lies at exactly that point past which we have just proceeded (and, to be sure, at the point just ahead of us as well)."[17] However, in Kracauer's final work, there were glimmers of hope. Here Kracauer suggested that the so-called interstices of history offered a real chance of escape.[18] The desire to position himself within these interstices led him to disavow all definitions and labels that assigned him a fixed place in history. The designations of "Weimar Intellectual" or even of "film critic" jeopardized the insights that could be gained from chronological anonymity. It was as if in order to search for the "gold of time" one had to avoid being *exclusively* defined by it.[19]

"Chronological anonymity," then, was a way of remaining in a paradox, of holding out the possibility of redemption while denying its potential for historical actualization. On this point, Kracauer was not always consistent; thus, he admonished Adorno for not giving substantial content to the idea of utopia, but he hardly attempted to do so in his own work.[20] Though, as Gertrud Koch warns, one should not reduce Kracauer's writings simply to a kind of "revelatory critique," the tropes of redemption and utopia persist throughout his work, even if he tried to modify them to a materialist project.[21] What is striking about Kracauer, especially when compared to his contemporaries, is that the adjustment to secular modernity did not result in an unqualified support for utopian political agendas; nor did he allow himself to speak of utopia and redemption as an ersatz religion or a political theology. His position is caught between contrary motives, and in this respect he does resemble the figure from Jean Paul's *Selina* mocked by Schopenhauer—someone who clings to concepts that cannot be rationally accepted out of anxiety over death. However, for Kracauer it was not so much the matter of death that required redemption, but rather the problem of suffering. Adorno described Kracauer as a "man without a skin," one for whom the problem of suffering was decisive: "What pressed for philosophical expression in him was an almost boundless capacity for suffering."[22] Modernity in much of his writing is typified by suffering and violence: the protagonists of his books fantasize about destruction even as they suffer from the violence of their age; the world of the detective novel is conceived of as one of atomized individuals, reduced to a collection of aimless drives. The consequences were not just a matter of literature; his critique of detective fiction was also consistent with his perception of the bewildering violence that he encountered in the course of the murder trials of Angerstein and Lieschen Neumann. Kracauer believed that the explanations put forward in the course of these trials ignored the most important issues; his criticism was a means of giving "philosophical expression" to the suffering that was effaced by such explanations. Such expression was not to be equated with the supposedly limited explanations of science, with aesthetic reconciliation, philosophical or religious palliatives. Moreover, suffering seemed to be an inescapable outcome, an accompaniment to the dismantling of social and cultural forms and the imperative of creating new ones.[23] A photograph in the *FZ Stadtblatt* strikingly illustrated this premise: over the heading "Victims of the New Sobriety" a photograph appeared of two severed heads lying in a rubble heap of stone and masonry.[24] Upon closer inspection it is clear they are the heads of two sculptures destroyed in the course of building renovations—the masonry ornaments of the past, relinquishing their place to wide expanses of concrete and glass. Through their destruction, the traces of thought, expression, and desire that they preserved are banished into oblivion.[25] The utopian hope that "nothing should go lost," expressed in his final posthumously published work, included this suffering that inhered in cultural and social transformation just as much as the material suffering caused by violence.[26]

To what extent then was Kracauer still fundamentally indebted to theological concepts, and does this justify discussing his thought with reference to "political religion"? By way of an answer to this question, I want to consider a controversial pair of essays he wrote in the last years of the Republic. Both of these essays, "What Should Mr. Hocke Do?" and "The Minimal Requirement of Intellectuals," were provoked by the publication of a much-discussed work by Alfred Döblin in 1931.[27] With the rise of Nazism as a threatening background, this debate concerned the possibilities open to intellectuals, what they could and should do when they felt themselves trapped between the extremes of right and left but still felt drawn towards action. Kracauer's essays illustrate how his critique of religion became less overt, and his work became more concerned with the exposure of ideology. In the fallout from his clash with Döblin, theological motives reappeared, but in a different guise that illuminates the stakes behind his practice of criticism. In his writing from the later 1920s onwards, he connects himself increasingly to Marxist theory, while religious themes recede from view; yet, his idiosyncratic variant of revolutionary theory never becomes a political religion. Indeed, the remnants of theology make this impossible, and hence his work suggests the limitations of the concept. Finally, I shall consider these conclusions briefly in relation to a quixotic dimension in Weimar culture, an obsession with the critical reading of the modern landscape that led to the interpretation of windmills as giants, but also more problematically of giants as windmills.

Döblin: To Know and to Change

Appearing in 1931, at a time of deepening political and economic conflict, the publication of *To Know and to Change! Open Letters to a Young Man* by Alfred Döblin provoked heated discussions. On account of the success of his 1929 novel *Berlin Alexanderplatz*, Döblin had become an important literary figure. This was one of the reasons that a young student by the name of Gustav René Hocke wrote to him in the name of Germany's wayward youth.[28] Aside from his literary fame, Döblin also had a reputation of personal integrity derived from the circumstances of his life. He worked as a physician, primarily serving the poorer denizens of Berlin from his office in Lichtenberg; he was also a member of the union of Socialist doctors and the Gruppe 1925, a collection of left-liberal and socialist intellectuals that included Bertolt Brecht. As a radical both in his art and life, Döblin thus challenged the divide between thought and action.[29]

Politics and confessional identity were a dilemma with which Döblin also struggled in the 1920s. He was the son of Jewish parents, but he appears to have had a weak connection to Judaism as a confession. Later, he married a Protestant, and thus furthered his distance from the faith of his parents. Nonetheless, the shock caused by outbreaks of anti-Semitism in the 1920s spurred his engagement with Zionist politics.[30] He refused, however, to visit Palestine, arguing that the natural home of European Jews was in Poland, where he visited in 1924 in search of an authentic Jewish identity. Despite these involvements, he still remained aloof from Judaism; yet, as one commentator has argued, there is a definite "religious undercurrent" in his work from an early age onwards.[31] Sometimes he exhibited an aggressive atheism, but he was still reluctant to accept the purely materialistic attitudes of Marxism. The spiritual and intellectual potential of humanity, he wrote, was "explosive material . . . we are able to have positively messianic hopes."[32] By 1935 he was immersed in the religious writings of authors such as Kierkegaard and the fourteenth-century Dominican mystic Johannes Tauler. Five years later, while in exile in Paris, he shocked many of his Jewish and socialist friends by converting to Catholicism; only twenty-seven years before, he had defended the German army's destruction of the cathedral at Reims.[33] Thus, Döblin was, in some respects, representative of the collision between secularism and religious revival that interested Kracauer, an exemplar of the religious flânerie that emerged as a postwar form of religiosity.

Though Döblin discusses religion in *To Know and to Change*, it was not the impetus for the book. Instead, it was the question of political action and how individuals were to find a direction in the fraught political atmosphere of 1931 Germany. The book consisted of a number of letters in which Döblin offered advice to a hypothetical young intellectual who wanted to contribute to social reconstruction, but who was alienated by the current political climate. The letters were addressed then to a broad intellectual community of German youth, though the hypothetical individual was, in fact, Hocke whose letter to Döblin was also reprinted at the beginning of the volume. Hocke had been perplexed by a lecture that Döblin gave the year before in Bonn. At the time, Döblin had spoken on socialism, but in a fashion that had left Hocke confused as to what political direction one should pursue. In response, he addressed an open letter to Döblin in the pages of *Das Tagebuch*, asking for both clarification and guidance:

> Because for us . . . nothing can be more binding than the word of a leader who has helped us to shape the spiritual face of the age, we turn to you out of inner need . . . because you are just, we have trust in you; because you abhor dogmas, we may readily believe in you.[34]

Clearly, Hocke wanted his appeal to be understood as a collective yearning for moral leadership, not just a solitary cry of angst. Among his contemporaries, this was a controversial step. While Döblin received a number of such letters, not everyone welcomed Hocke's intervention.[35] In his memoirs, Hocke recollected:

> Overnight, I had become a sort of celebrity. A few friends embraced me, others walked far around me. A couple of deadbeats no longer greeted me. Extreme

right-wing students felt it an evil that I had addressed Döblin, a Jew, as a leader in the intellectual forum of the nation . . . One person reproached me for romantic "Indecisionism"—an awkward word ... it soon became a slogan.[36]

The range of reactions that Hocke provoked would find its correlate in the acrimonious and mostly dismissive reception of the book. If Hocke had intended to elicit practical instruction in politics, it had the opposite effect: that of exposing the deep angst that many intellectuals felt when they confronted the growing politicization of everyday life in Germany.

Indeed, the reception of *To Know and to Change* was probably more negative than that given to Hocke's original letter. Hocke had received a few gestures of support, but Döblin felt bereft of attentive readers and attacked from all corners. "O this madness, to want to help in this land," he lamented in the pages of *Die neue Rundschau*.[37] Döblin was not exaggerating, as some scholars of his work have remarked. Hocke noted that the "echo in the press" was significant, but hardly supportive:

My teacher Ernst Robert Curtius wrote . . . that Döblin was an "enemy of education" even if he was otherwise of a good sort. The big bourgeois papers took up his pedagogical action with mixed feelings. Every party responded sourly because Döblin had warned of the increasing one-sidedness of humanity.[38]

Hocke was undoubtedly correct in his assessment that given Döblin's rejection of all party allegiances, he was bound to provoke animosity from many sides. Yet, the issues that the work and its reception raised went deeper, as his comments likewise suggest. When it appeared, the book was, in fact, widely reviewed by both literary journals and the larger newspapers; it also led to two roundtable discussions in *Die Literarische Welt* and *Die neue Rundschau*.[39] The impact of these discussions left some with ambivalent feelings. One of Döblin's few supporters, the music critic Viktor Zuckerkandl, expressed dismay over the level of the discussion in *Die neue Rundschau*: "It says nothing, is without character, wretched . . . It is a demonstration of the rarity of intellectual freedom in Germany and, following from that, its readiness to be provoked to unfruitful anger."[40] If Kracauer later referred to Döblin as a "nucleus of the manifold trends that obtained under the Weimar Republic," it was probably episodes such as this that he had in mind.[41] Kracauer was, in fact, among the less severe critics of *To Know and to Change*, and he welcomed the public discussion he thought the book would inaugurate.

Why were so many critical of Döblin? His advice to Hocke and to disenchanted youth more generally was to hold themselves aloof from party politics, but to align themselves "next to" the working classes.[42] In keeping with his socialist leanings, Döblin argued that one could not position oneself with those who held political and economic power. Bourgeois politics, moreover, were reflected in bourgeois culture, and Döblin suggested that young intellectuals should distance themselves from the prescribed paths of cultural edification. Bourgeois ideals embodied the spirit of German servility, a trajectory in German thought and education that led back to Luther and was perpetuated by Goethe, Wagner, Nietzsche, and George.[43] Hence, the politics of the bourgeois parties were a dead end for Döblin. However, he was just as skeptical of the parties on the left, arguing that they had misinterpreted the works of Marx, and had merely turned "class struggle" into an institution, one that served the party rather than humanity. To recover the original impulses of socialism, one had to reach back to the promise of "liberation" preserved in a primordial "Ur-communism" that had long since been obscured by the extraneous theories of doctrinaire Marxists. "Reality," he warned, "had no obligations to follow some theory."[44] While he had sympathy and interest in the Soviet experiment, their turn to brutal "state capitalism," he argued, was unmistakable and quite foreign to true socialism.

This repudiation of theory, of course, did not mean that Döblin did not have one of his own. This had been formulated in his earlier essay, *The I over Nature*, and again in a largely ignored work of 1933, *Our Existence*.[45] In general, Döblin rejected the notions of structure and superstructure, arguing that these concepts led to a false understanding of the role of the spirit and to ignorance in regards to actually existing reality.[46] Doctrinaire Marxism had mistakenly privileged the economic and material existence of humanity at the expense of thought; in this sense, he argued, it was not even in accord with Marx himself.[47] Instead, Döblin proposed what he called a "dialectic Naturism" wherein thought occupied a determining role alongside nature; thought both shaped material conditions and was shaped by them. Ultimately, he argued that "the transformation of consciousness and of the will preceded the transformation of [our] situation and of being."[48] He attempted practical advice in this regard: one should work in a factory to gain knowledge of proletarian conditions; or one should regenerate the domain of private life in order to prepare the way for a new social consciousness. This latter would involve the "dismantling of the public sphere" that, in any case, was too contaminated by the bureaucratic institutions of the capitalist state.[49]

Thus, Döblin was trying to resolve a quandary that was perceived by many intellectuals: should they direct their critical energies to the transformation of social conditions as a means of transforming consciousness, or vice versa? As we have seen, Kracauer's position on this question fluctuated during the 1920s, and in his Picard review of 1929 he conceded some ground to a position very similar to that of Döblin. The direct route of transforming thought, feelings, and perceptions was legitimate, Kracauer had argued, and he had framed this position in theological terms. At the time, his editor, Max Rychner, had found the article still too full of revolutionary phrases, and he gave scant attention to

Kracauer's theological positioning. Rychner was similarly dismissive of Döblin, and he heaped his scorn on what he saw as Döblin's intellectual "vandalism."[50] Rychner was suspicious of the presumably subordinate role that intellect would play given the hostility to traditional education that was evident in the book. In contrast, Rychner remained more sympathetic to the revived humanism advocated by his friend Ernst Robert Curtius, and he reacted harshly to what he saw as a narrow definition of the spirit implied by Döblin's broadside against German cultural traditions.

Yet there was a common motive between Döblin, Rychner and Kracauer, in so far as they all wanted to defend intellect against any kind of rigidly materialist determinism. They thus took a position that gave considerable weight to the transformation of consciousness as a precondition to social and political change. This is true of Döblin just as much as Rychner, even if their approaches differed considerably. Moreover, as was the case in Kracauer's review of Picard, there is in *To Know and to Change* a religious and metaphysical undercurrent. While dialectical thought, Döblin argued, should in no way bind itself with the religions of the past, there were still "powerfully effective ingredients preserved" in the latter that should not be ignored. In his naturalist conception of reality, he described God as "devoured" and "absorbed" into the world. "It is childish of us to demand religion and norms," he remarked, for "we incorporate religiosity from head to toe!"[51] The social and political tasks, for which the present generation was accountable, were indeed to be understood as religious ones, but ones framed within a secular world.[52]

Kracauer's review of *To Know and to Change* did not address the book's recurring strain of religiosity. Rather, he considered the polemic in light of the intellectual predicament from which the book derived. In general, he argued that Döblin had correctly reckoned with the problems that confronted contemporary youth who were politically motivated but without direction.[53] Döblin, he felt, was justified in warning Hocke against the working-class parties, for their attachments to abstract theory, their economic determinism, and their misconceived collectivism were all hindrances to effective social and political engagement. These insufficiencies left many who wanted to work towards socialism in an intellectual cul-de-sac. As a result, they either retreated into a purely inward position, or fell prey to the prevailing and often dangerous radicalism. In 1931, this, of course, meant Nazism. To Kracauer, the position represented by Hocke was a "hole" or "gap" that accommodated every kind of social and political idea:

> [His] letter is already a sign of that fearful neutrality that has spread through Germany. Out of an impotence that penetrates and castrates nearly every manifestation of public life, this neutrality no longer seeks to somehow bring balance between contending forces, but instead simply dispenses with confronting them dialectically.[54]

However, in terms of answering the question that Hocke had posed to Döblin, Kracauer was in some disagreement. Döblin, he noted, responded to the latter as a "doctor and physiognomist" and by implication not as a politician or social theorist. Thus, if Döblin had advised that one must stand next to the working classes, Kracauer argued that this position was undialectical. It did not reckon with how the encounter with proletarian reality would influence the intellectual's position. Indeed, it was not clear what would arise from this encounter and how it would generate the consciousness that anticipated socialism. If one concentrated one's energies on reclaiming the private life of individuals and smaller groups for the purposes of socialism, how did this relate to the wider social and political realities whose influence could not be ignored? One could carry out the "dismantling of the public sphere" in their own lives, but this did not mean that the process of dismantlement would continue to spread "without interruption" in society more generally. He did not repudiate Döblin's advice in its entirety, but he noted that in the current situation it could lead to an ideology where "in the name of socialism one does not concern oneself with it, that involuntarily demands more romanticism than enlightenment, and does not so much activate self-reflection, but [instead] awakens contemplation."[55] How Hocke and company would ever emerge from their predicament was thus difficult to ascertain. Still, Kracauer concluded the review with an acknowledgement of what the book had accomplished and an invitation to further discussion.[56]

Kracauer referred to Hocke's quandary as the *Gretchenfrage*, which draws attention to some of the unstated assumptions regarding religion and secularization that informed his critique. In his subsequent essay, "The Minimal Requirement of Intellectuals," this dimension is further clarified. His essay was one of the most substantial contributions to the discussion of *To Know and to Change* that took place in *Die neue Rundschau* (a circumstance that certainly displeased Döblin, who disagreed with much of its content).[57] His argument tried to define and legitimate the role of the intellect and its critical tasks. Mentions of the Nazis or the KPD were sparse in this discussion, but they were certainly a menacing presence that informed this debate; indeed, the hostility towards intellectuals associated with Nazism influenced Kracauer's desire to redefine intellectual goals.[58] Briefly stated, Kracauer argued that the "Herr Hockes" of the present must deploy their intellectual capacities, and, more specifically, deploy them in what was their proper task: "the destruction of every mythical existence ... the dismantling of natural forces."[59] This meant the exposure of ideology and the readiness to "throw radically into doubt all preconceived positions." In terms of method, one had to test all concepts and ideas against the "results of revolutionary theory ... and then in accordance with this reckoning, lay out what still remains of these concepts." The "revolutionary theory" was a Marxist-inspired dialectics, but one which he intended to be more flexible than the doctrinaire variety that guided the working-class parties. For he stated that the confrontation of theory and inherited ideas was by no means predetermined in favor of the former; it was possible that "under some circumstances" the latter retained "a measure of reality" that then provoked a "correction" of theory. Socialism, however, still maintains a privileged place in this conception—an arbiter over society's final destination, even if its content is subject to potential modification.

The confrontation of theory and the accumulated mass of opinions, ideas, and concepts was the point where the question of religion reinserted itself into the debate. Kracauer prefaced his claims regarding the legitimate destructive role of the intellect with a short anecdote recounting a discussion he had with a young man whose situation resembled Hocke in most respects. The youth was in his twenties, intellectually gifted, and inclined towards the goals of socialism. He understood these in the broad "primordially human" sense that Döblin had intended, but at the same time, he was unable to align himself with any of the working-class parties. These he saw as just one part of the chaotic Weimar system. Moreover, Kracauer stated that whenever their discussions drew close to that "sphere of religious reality and the rights of the existential individual who was aligned with it" the young man began to speak with a "passion that in no way stemmed from the intellect."[60] His conversation partner, so Kracauer suggested, was particularly wedded to what he called "uncontrolled contents," and if he "naively" wanted to place these over and above revolutionary theory, he was then no different than those who embraced a nationalist mythology.[61] Under the term "uncontrolled contents" Kracauer suspected resurgent religious passions, but not only this. The term also suggests a nebulous array of potentially irrational and anti-intellectual sentiments. What is at issue, however, is neither the religious sphere, nor its existential claims, but rather a particular attitude towards it. This will be discussed further below.

The debate initiated by Döblin, however, did not end here for Kracauer. His account of the allegedly uncritical position that some youth were taking towards certain "spiritual possessions" did not go unchallenged. The model for the young man described by Kracauer readily recognized himself, and he wrote Kracauer to protest against the way in which he had represented their disagreement. The young man was a mostly forgotten writer named Egon Vietta.[62] He was primarily a writer of plays and essays, though he also penned two short novels, *The Angel of This Side* and *Corydon*. He had trained as a lawyer, but had wide interests in contemporary literature and philosophy. Today, he is remembered less for his plays and fiction than for his essays, including an important early article on the work of Kafka. He was also a vocal admirer of Hermann Broch (with whom he had a substantial correspondence), one of the earliest German interpreters of Sartre, and a supporter of Heidegger before and after the war. His book-length study of Heidegger was an attempt to rehabilitate the disgraced philosopher after 1945.[63] Later, he was also in contact with Carl Schmitt and, thus, more generally engaged with intellectual trends that emerged from the war deeply entangled by their relationship with Nazism.

These biographical details are of interest here, as his relationship to Kracauer appears to have turned on a disagreement that placed the legitimacy of the intellect on one side along with Marxist theory; and on the other, a growing attraction to the philosophy of Heidegger and his radical critique of the humanist tradition. The surviving correspondence between the two is small, covering the years 1930–1931. They probably met after Kracauer was transferred to the Berlin office of the *FZ* in 1930. Kracauer, the older man by fourteen years, appears to have played a mentoring role to Vietta, who had just published his first novel in 1929 and a short pamphlet entitled *The Collectivists* in 1930. Vietta solicited Kracauer's opinions on his work, and indeed, he even credits Kracauer for the stimulus behind the *The Collectivists*.[64]

Nonetheless, their brief correspondence is characterized by numerous disagreements. The letters also suggest a degree of intellectual intimacy that allowed for direct and open criticism of each other's views. Kracauer appears to have tried to influence Vietta, encouraging him to consider the motives that resided in Marxist theory, and to discourage his growing fascination with Heidegger. Vietta's inclination towards the latter, already apparent in *The Collectivists*, became more pronounced by 1931.[65] However, alongside his enthusiasm for Heidegger, Vietta was also discovering numerous authors whom Kracauer admired or had admired in the past: Kierkegaard, Scheler, Stendhal, Kafka, and Ortega y Gasset. Vietta also was impressed by Kracauer's work, in particular *Ginster* and *The Salaried Masses*, but he argued that some of the premises behind these works were in contradiction to some of the positions adopted in his journalism. Near the end of 1930, shortly after publishing *The Collectivists*, he wrote to Kracauer to express his reservations. While he admired *Ginster* with his "body and soul," he believed that his own work was developing in a way that was contrary to Kracauer.[66] In particular, he objected to Kracauer's position regarding collectivism and its relationship to "last things." By this term, Vietta referred to his belief in a dimension of reality that was not reducible to the determinations of reason—a kind of prerational substratum. On this point, he implied that Kracauer appeared to restrict the independence of this reality, and he had bound it too closely to ideology:

> You still always think that the last things will be taken as a pretext to avoid concerning oneself with pressing necessities. I hold that both of these are fully separate and only by chance thrown into the same pot . . . why should it not be possible in the completion of one's daily labor to hold open a view to the final, the eternal, or whatever one calls it . . . [67]

He was puzzled by this since he believed that Kracauer had, in fact, expressed a similar position in parts of his work (the last chapter of *The Salaried Masses*, for instance), but he felt that it was at odds with much of his journalism. In the latter, Vietta was suspicious of Kracauer's interest in dialectical theory and his support for socialism. Indeed, he felt that there was a noticeable divide between Kracauer's artistic and journalistic work. Given these positions he found Kracauer's intentions uncertain: if a space was to be "held open" for "last things" then he thought one had to investigate it more explicitly than Kracauer had done. For his part, Vietta had pursued this subject in his pamphlet, *The Collectivists*. Here the terminology of "last things" was displaced by that of "other reality," a formulation derived from his attempt to work through the ideas of Heidegger, whose *Sein und Zeit* had made a strong impression on him.[68] As Vietta later told Döblin, Kracauer had flat out rejected this concept; but Vietta remained firm in his convictions that the "worn out foundations" of socialism were incompatible with any meaningful conception of the spirit or reality.[69]

Kracauer responded in a fashion that demonstrates his propensity to mix indirect and direct forms of communication. In his letter to Vietta of January 1931, he warned his friend not to be deceived by the apparent differences in his artistic and intellectual work; on the contrary, he claimed, they formed a coherence that was quite deliberate.[70] He did not elaborate on his intentions in any detail, but claimed the differences in his work were not a matter of "doing something different with one hand than one does with the other"—a common reproach against journalists. He also argued that Vietta had misunderstood his attitudes to socialism and collectivist thought. He had not argued that one must become a collectivist, but rather that one must reckon with the "factual motives" that push towards collectivism. These must then be incorporated "dialectically" in one's work.[71]

Vietta was probably dismayed by Kracauer's assertion that his cultural-political intentions were in accord with his artistic ones, for he still believed that Kracauer had not reckoned fully with the potential clash between his adherence to dialectical theory and his desire to "hold open" a space for "unverifiable" contents. In this respect, Vietta was not alone, for his attitude to some of the collectivist experiments emanating from the Soviet Union caused misgivings among his friends and readers alike, though for very different reasons.[72] According to Bloch, many were confused by the apparent contradictions in his work.[73] For instance, he had attacked the Soviet writer Sergei Tretjakow, condemning his conception of literature as too doctrinaire, and his understanding of individualism as deeply flawed; but simultaneously, he also chastised Brecht's *Three Penny Trial* for its adherence to an "individualist position."[74] Though these attacks on leftist writers may have confused some of his readers, Kracauer was not trying to play two hands at once. During this period he was in fact attempting to think through a reorientation of concepts such as "collectivism" in light of the transformed conditions of modernity. As he wrote to Hans Flesch, a Frankfurt radio programmer, the popular conception of "collectivism" was derived too heavily from notions originating from the Soviet experience and from contemporary innovations in the theatre (Brecht is probably meant here). "On the contrary," Kracauer argued, "... the collective represents no fundamental innovation." There were earlier conceptions of the collective to be found even in the works of Goethe and Schiller. This was a minor but by no means insignificant example, he claimed, as these authors were often associated with notions of individual genius that were held to be inimical to collectivist thought.[75] The merits of this argument are not at issue here, but it does show that Kracauer wanted to construct an alternative configuration of the individual and the social group, one recognizing the claims of both. The project, however, was never fulfilled, and at the time he wrote to Flesch he confessed that his thought on the matter was still in an incipient stage. The lack of a clear statement on the subject may be why Vietta and others found Kracauer's position confusing.

Such notions of the collective and the individual were not unrelated to Kracauer's theological motives. A renewed idea of the collective that avoided the crudities of the Soviet model was needed, so he argued. Against these vulgar constructions, he asserted the claims of what he called the "hollow spaces," the gap held open for the "everywhere and nowhere Verifiable-Utopian."[76] As he wrote to Bloch, who was deeply upset by Kracauer's essays on Tretjakow and Brecht, he was still committed to a "revolutionary Marxism"; but he nonetheless insisted that the visions of Brecht, and at least some of the views of Tretjakow, were hindrances to any truly utopian project.[77] His loyalty was more to his own dialectical method, rather than to what he saw as the party line on questions of philosophy, religion, or social theory. Indeed, Kracauer claimed he was working with a "real dialectic" that did not simply mingle the transcendent realm with the material one in an unconsidered way. On the contrary, this was a dialectic that arose out of a "labor of enlightenment" achieved through the "exposure of the self" (*Selbstentäußerung*); it was a process that truly opened the "hollow space" in which utopian longings could still dwell. His language on this point is loaded with theological implications. *Hohlräumen* has already emerged in his writing as the undefined place where the "unspoken positive" might one day be pronounced, while *Selbstentäußerung* also has the religious connotation of self-mortification.[78] Such motives, however, were almost never stated openly. Given that Kracauer preferred to leave such motives unstated, Vietta's recognition of these suggests that he was actually one of Kracauer's more sensitive readers.

Yet, Vietta and Kracauer found it difficult to bring their views into agreement. After the publication of his essay in *Die neue Rundschau*, the differences between them sharpened considerably. Kracauer had implied that "uncontrolled contents" or, what Vietta called the "other reality," was bound to the religious sphere. Vietta disputed this position and, in a letter to Döblin, claimed that he had not once mentioned religion to Kracauer—that the choice of the word had been entirely his. Further, he explained:

> I myself had never, by the way, spoken of a religious reality. That is more than misleading. Kracauer chose this adjective. I am, just as you are, for the most extreme here and now position, as wide-reaching as it is in Heidegger's investigations, where all religious haziness is exposed as illusory. *Uncontrolled contents* need not be religious. To me it seems that the historical role of the creative does consist of such uncontrolled contents, but only a few religious communities have taken over the error that Kracauer persists in, that everything is to be controlled by God himself.[79]

Writing to Kracauer, Vietta used the term *geistig* to indicate these contents, and he stressed that the *geistig* was in no way "identical with intellect, even less with religion or myth."[80] He also tried to reverse Kracauer's arguments by pointing out that his dialectics were not a privileged method of philosophical or social analysis. If Kracauer wanted to challenge all received opinions and values, then he must submit his dialectics to the same test. If he refused then he was simply a dogmatist and had no right to challenge the dogmas of others.[81]

Kracauer's response to Vietta's rebuttal took a similar form to his earlier letter. In general, he referred only to points of method and not to content. Thus, he found Vietta's attempt to undermine the legitimacy of dialectical thought to be an empty and relativist argument. It did not suffice, he claimed, to simply point to the relative premises of one's opponent and by so doing think that one had voided their argument. If Vietta, as a "pupil of Heidegger" wanted to refute him, he must state his own premises and proceed from there. This seems to miss the point of Vietta's attack, but Kracauer had already conceded the "historical contingency" of intellectual positions in his *Rundschau* article. From his point of view, that the critic was enmeshed in historical contingency was a basic fact and not a decisive means of argument in and of itself.[82]

Kracauer also argued that Vietta had ignored the framework of his statements.[83] He was not speaking in "empty space," and he had never intended his remarks to apply to intellectuals in general; rather he was referring only to those who felt themselves drawn to socialism in the sense that Döblin had defined it. The legitimacy of socialism as a goal was not a subject of discussion and would naturally have required further analysis. The title of the article supports Kracauer's claims, and it went unnoticed by Vietta and also by Döblin. Kracauer was only concerned with the "minimal" demands to which intellectuals were answerable. He did not mean the essay to be a comprehensive summation of their general social position. Indeed, the only point where he refers to this task is at the point where the essay abruptly ends. As soon as he mentions the possibility of a more expansive understanding of intellectual vocation, he terminates the discussion, as if he only wanted to suggest further possibilities rather than state them explicitly.[84]

Thus, in a fashion that is consistent with the notion of "indirect communication" Kracauer left Vietta to his own interpretive devices. He did not dispute content, but only asked that he be read with some effort made to understand his intentions. The only point in his letter where he deviates from this is his insistence that dialectics was not "philosophy in the old sense," and he did not mean to use intellect as a weapon against the *geistig*; indeed, he did not acknowledge the distinctions that Vietta drew in regards to these two terms. Most importantly, Kracauer declined to expand on what he meant by "uncontrolled contents" and how these related to the intellect. However, I would argue that this is consistent with what he understood by this term. Such contents were "unverifiable" and thus did not permit of positive statements. To speak of them would begin the slide towards those forms of ideology that most benefit from the abandonment of intellect.[85]

Given Vietta's continued progress towards a Heideggerian position, one imagines that he must have been frustrated with Kracauer's refusal to concede some validity to his arguments. Since Kracauer insisted that intellect was a "practical instrument," Vietta probably felt justified in thinking of it as something different in nature from the spirit, and he looked to this *geistig* realm in order to conceptualize "uncontrolled contents." This was very much in line with his understanding of Heidegger, and in *The Collectivists* Vietta quoted from *Sein und Zeit* on this point. The intellect was the tool of *das Man*, the word Heidegger used for the technocrat, the functionary, the one who avoids situations where "existence is forced into decision."[86] Thus, the confrontational boundary that separated the philosophers of the Frankfurt School from those influenced by Heidegger is already to be glimpsed in this debate. By repudiating Vietta's concept of the "other reality," Kracauer already participates in the Frankfurt School's general hostility to Heidegger's fundamental ontology. By 1931, Kracauer was already arguing against what he saw as its illegitimate annexation of death and nothingness—an attempt to revalue the void, and to construct, according to Adorno, a "metaphysics of death."[87]

Secularization as Translation: Kracauer and Vietta

What implications are to be drawn from this debate between Vietta and Kracauer? At the root of their disagreement is a dispute over the meaning, extent, and consequences of secularization. The outlines of this dispute emerge more clearly if one looks at secularization as a form of translation, an idea discussed by Vincent Pecora in his study of cultural criticism. *Translation* is one of a number of terms used to conceptualize one of two lines of thought that have emerged on this question. On the one hand, secularization is viewed as a "carrying over," or "worlding" of religious concepts and institutions, and it is in this sense that the term *translation* emerges for Pecora.[88] The second, in contrast, suggests that secularization represents a more substantial break with religious thought, that is, that it generates its own content and cannot be fully understood if it is thought of only as a simple transference of religious concepts into a secular framework. Pecora is interested in how cultural criticism has shuttled between these two interpretations, and the devil does emerge in the details of his study, demonstrating that neither interpretation has been able to fully reckon with religion's persistence. Drawing on the work of Habermas, Blumenberg, Löwith, Said, and Talal Asad, his work suggests that constructions of the "secular" are unable to extricate themselves entirely from religious concepts and values. These often are incorporated into the secular, and persist there in a sometimes antagonistic relationship. Ultimately, Pecora wants to open up the question of the nature of secularization, as well as the role of cultural criticism in disseminating it; what results is a model that blurs the border between religious and profane, suggesting a secularizing process that is "messier, more paradoxical" and "clearly ongoing."[89] He draws conclusions that are relevant to Kracauer's early work, pointing out that the secular is no "neutral" concept, but rather it comes "with certain historical and religious strings attached." Therefore, the idea that criticism is normatively secular, as suggested by Said, overlooks its religious motives and the ways that it responds to religious patterns of thought.[90] For Pecora, Kracauer is situated more within the second of his interpretive frameworks, and is thus aligned with Blumenberg's argument that secular modernity represents a substantial shift from religious views of the world, a shift that conceived new relationships between humanity and history, and that looked upon modernity as "an infinite yet open-ended and not inevitable progress."[91] As David Roberts argues, this is a shift that generates new "sources of discontent, but also its own sense of possibility and responsibility."[92] Kracauer's conflicts with the religious revival and his rejection of messianic ideas of utopia or culture are in accord with this view of modernity as a definitive shift.[93]

Still, I would argue that the concept of secularization as translation does have relevance for Kracauer's work, though I agree with Pecora that Kracauer sees more of a break between the secular and the sacred. In this sense, translation should be understood as representing a more fundamental alteration, that the original contents are, in fact, transformed in their move from one language to another. We have seen that Kracauer referred to his detective study as an example of the "translator's art," and in his Döblin polemic he spoke explicitly of the transfer of "valuable contents" from the mythical shell of religious tradition into a modern and secular context.[94] Yet, the result was not simply a product derived from these religious contents, as Löwith later suggested in his *Meaning in History*, nor was it a self-foundation of the secular that had fully dispensed with its religious genealogy.[95] Rudolf Pannwitz's condemnation of contemporary German translators suggests something of the change that is being addressed here. German translators, he argued, did not properly allow their own tongue to be decisively moved by the language they translated from; hence, they prevented their translations from having any contact with that point where a language can transform itself, where the native tongue has the capacity to "expand and deepen" itself.[96] Of course, this analogy does not say anything concrete about what happens to religious contents that undergo this process, but it does suggest how it might be viewed as a means of conserving (or extending) what was considered valuable in religious traditions, while also generating new potentials.

Still, the analogy to translation cannot avoid the issue of derivation. What a translation owes to its own language and what it owes to the language of the other is not readily resolvable. If the analogy is used for religion, it readily loses precision. Hence, the argument between Vietta and Kracauer has no discernible resolution. In his *Neue Rundschau* essay, Kracauer had argued that "since the violent move from one form of society to another does not take place in a day, some especially valuable contents must be put into storage. Otherwise one gets in the way of the movers." With this in mind, he claimed that "packing is an art."[97] Though the rhetoric has an unmistakable revolutionary tone, Kracauer is still frustratingly vague in terms of what happens to the contents thus put into storage. Moreover, he does not speak here of secularization as "negation" or transformation, but more as a displacement and one that still leaves the final destination of displaced contents unmentioned. This, I would argue, was a deliberate choice on his part and one that was consistent with his general avoidance of theological language and a preference to speak around this issue rather than to it. Vietta, on the other hand, in spite of his secular intentions still had a demonstrable predilection for rhetoric steeped in the language and imagery of religion, as one of the few studies of his work has demonstrated.[98] Religious motifs pervade his novel, *The Angel of This Side*—the figure of the eponymous angel becoming a catalyst of secular revelation. Such imagery was meant to suggest the profanation of religious concepts; Vietta intended to stimulate a deepened relationship with the everyday rather than a transcendent flight from it.[99] Kracauer appears to have appreciated this direction in Vietta's work. "I do not think," he wrote to Vietta, "that you want to change from an angel of the here and now into a collectivist."[100] Nonetheless, Kracauer may have recalled this predilection for religious imagery when he suggested that Vietta's reception of Döblin and Heidegger reflected a persistence of religion and myth, rather than a manifestation of the *geistig*.[101] Vietta had once written to Kracauer that "scarcely have I eliminated God and the Church, then there emerges considerations in regards to the individual, to the concept of the nation, [and] to socialist doctrine."[102] Vietta probably intended to similarly eradicate collectivist thought; his statement suggests that he viewed religion in terms of nebulous social energies that could migrate from one social or political form to another. As a result of such statements, Kracauer may have come to the conclusion that his younger friend was among those who "naively" toyed with metaphysical constructions and thus did an injustice to the profane. This was not a trivial issue to him as he clearly believed that such sentiments might find their political niche in Nazism. Here the unsheltered soul would finally feel at home.[103]

Secularization and Modernity: Politics, Culture, and Religion

Were figures such as Vietta in search of a political religion? There is no clear answer, and his exchange with Kracauer tends to render problematic the relationship between political and religious convictions. As Philippe Burrin has pointed out, the concept of political religion has been fraught with polemical overtones ever since its first use in the 1930s. One of its early proponents, Eric Voegelin, associated the phenomena with a specific philosophy of history that viewed the Enlightenment as a crucial stage in a general movement of social and cultural decline. The religious societies of the past had been gradually eroded by secular Gnosticism, and the Christian community displaced by the idea of the collective. The final result, according to Voegelin, was the triumph of "anti-Christian religious movements" such as National Socialism.[104] Similarly, Raymond Aron argued that secular religions are "doctrines that in the souls of our contemporaries take the place of a vanished faith, and that locate humanity's salvation in this world, in the distant future, in the forms of a social order that has to be created."[105] These definitions stress the functional equivalencies between political religions and their supposedly more apolitical counterparts. Thus, the social forms of the religious community, its hierarchical structures, and the belief in a transcendent but distant purpose were all appropriated for political ends.[106]

This was a potential that Kracauer, in general, rejected and feared. As we have seen, he condemned Bloch's *Thomas Münzer* for what he saw as its confusion of chiliastic religiosity and political revolution. Even after he reconciled with Bloch he still contrasted his own dialectical method with Bloch's allegedly uncritical mingling of spheres that could not be united. Similarly, he criticized Holzapfel's theory of cultural perfectibility, as he felt it arrogated to culture a function that only religion could perform. There is a reasonably consistent adherence in his work to the idea that the existential needs of the individual were best approached through indirect discourse and not by means of an agenda that uncritically equated "last things" with political ends. In this sense, his *Münzer* review anticipated his final work on history; messianic redemption was not to be accomplished in time, but rather outside of it.[107] This could in no way be equated with political utopia, or with cultural progress. By stressing this distinction, Kracauer attempted to pull the rug out from under any political movement that claimed to represent an absolute form of salvation. In this sense, he was aware of the potential for political ideologies to take on a religious aura, and he believed that such phenomena had to be resisted.

If Kracauer's work suggests that a functional interpretation of political religion has some validity, his writing also suggests the need for some qualifications. For Kracauer, it was still clear that however much politics tried to appropriate religious energies and structures, or at least in some of its forms resembled them, ultimately politics and religion were based on different social desires, and one could not simply displace the other. This meant that politics and religion still occupied different spheres of engagement, and, at least in principle, religious belief and radical politics were not mutually exclusive; hence, he preserved the space for the "unverifiable." Similarly, in his 1929 essay on Picard, the economic sphere has legitimate claims that do not crowd out those of theology; hence, revolutionary theory could still be entertained without conflicting with a religious point of view. It is for this reason that Kracauer in spite of his hostility to religious revival still argued that religion was not merely ideology, and not a branch of culture.[108]

Thus, there is no reason to assume that radical politics must always displace religion. As historian Neil Gregor has recently argued, there is abundant evidence to the contrary, and it is clear that religious belief did not necessarily preclude a commitment to the political programs of the 1920s and 1930s.[109] Political religions did not just step into a void, sometimes they entered into a partnership. As a result, if political religion is to be useful as a conceptual model, it needs to be sensitive to the fact that the ideologies of these decades did not simply push aside religious institutions, nor did they simply appropriate social energies that had been left homeless by secularization. On the contrary, religious faith could be open to the political extremism of Europe between the wars. Thus, in 1937, the future Pius XII responded with astonishment that the 800,000 Germans in Romania, many of whom were Catholic, could believe that the "Nazi doctrines condemned in the recent encyclical [were] compatible with the Catholic faith."[110] This, of course, cuts both ways. Thus, some of Kracauer's Catholic friends were both devout believers and staunch leftists, arguing that the laity should be more politically independent of the church. However, their embrace of radical politics, though ineffectual in the crisis of the early 1930s, did not facilitate the spread of political religions but rather it resisted them—hence, why Kracauer wrote in support of the efforts of reformist Catholics such as Ernst Michel and Goetz Briefs.

Recognizing that political religions do not always uproot the traditional varieties should serve as a caution towards the more tendentious interpretations that may arise when one adopts a linear model of displacement based on comparisons.[111] Such interpretations have arisen where a comparative approach is employed that does not take fully into account the possibility that individuals might identify themselves as both a Christian and a Nazi, or a socialist and a believer.[112] Moreover, such approaches do not convincingly account for the ambiguous terrain where religions themselves become political just as politics become religious. This is a significant issue for, as Burrin points out, it is just as probable that political religions were successful precisely in those countries where the process of secularization was relatively weak. Hence, the presence of a vital and politicized religious culture may in some instances have aided the establishment of radical political ideologies.[113]

This does not deny the fact that religious institutions and beliefs often struggled against Nazism or Communism; but it does point out that if we want to know why these movements attracted so many adherents, including those who considered themselves to be religious, one needs to be aware of the potential synergy between politics and religion. In the case of Kracauer's colleague, Hermann Herrigel, religious belief appears to have presented no barrier to his acceptance of the Nazi state and a reinvigorated idea of the *Volk*. Indeed, some have argued that the Protestant radicalism of the early postwar period may have facilitated the spread of *völkisch* politics.[114] In other words, some may have accepted Nazism because of their religion, not in spite of it. What this point raises then is that religions may be political, and that in assessing the genealogies of fascism and socialism both secular religions and traditional ones need to be considered as potential tributaries to these movements. In the 1920s and 1930s, it may be the case that the "complicity of discourses" was a significant contributor to the rise of ever more radical visions of politics and society.[115]

The politicization of religion, moreover, raises the difficult issue of how we legitimately distinguish between the "religious" and the "political": to what extent might an idea, a pattern of thought, or social organization be derived from either religious or political models? This question is complicated by the fact that the terrain of political religion is often viewed as a one-way street; that is, political religions appropriate from the treasure horde of religion itself. The possibility that religion borrows from politics, or politicizes itself, is less often part of the discussion. This is an unstated assumption in the term *political religion*, which suggests that normally religion would be apolitical—a conclusion that few would probably accept. Burrin's account points towards this grey area when he mentions the "politicization of elements inherited from

Christian culture," a direction that is derived from Voegelin's work.[116] He cautions, however, that a phenomenological definition of what is actually religious is a potentially irresolvable question, and that it may be best to accept the "metaphoric nature" of the concept and place more emphasis on the adjective rather than the noun.[117] Moreover, disputes over precisely this question often help us to define what is at stake in arguments over the meaning of secularization. As one critic stated, "at the heart of many disputes about the definition of secularization ... lie differences about the very notions of religion and the sacred."[118] Thus, if there is no clear line between the religious and the profane one can nonetheless see why these determinations were significant in a particular discourse. In a sense, one must adopt the tentative definition offered by Luhmann that "religion is what can be observed as religion" and then reckon with how such perceptions worked in different social and political contexts.[119]

From this point of view, it is remarkable how often conflicts over the definition of the religious and secular arose in Kracauer's work. In the early 1920s, this was manifest in his disagreement with Scheler over the alleged affinities of phenomenology and Catholicism, as well as his clash with the religious revival in Frankfurt. The issue emerged again in his critique of Holzapfel. He collided with numerous friends and acquaintances over this issue as well, including Rosenzweig, Buber, Susman, and Ernst Simon. By the last years of the Republic, religious themes were less overt in his work, but as the dispute with Vietta demonstrates, he was still concerned with the boundaries of sacred and profane. This was the crux of his dispute with Vietta: were "uncontrolled contents" to be understood as essentially religious or metaphysical in nature? Or were they *geistig* in a different sense, as argued by Vietta? Thus, Kracauer's work demonstrates the complicated, uneven, or "messy" process of secularization and its persistence in the interwar years. This is a process that defines the secular not as a sphere that eliminates religion, but rather exists in a persistent tension with it. Thus, the concept of the "secular critic" needs to reflect this, by reckoning with the religious determinants that have informed its history.[120] This conclusion does not deny that Kracauer viewed secularization as intrinsic to modernity, but rather it complicates our understanding of this process and how it was reflected in his writing. In his 1922 discussion of the work of Ferdinand Tönnies, he argued that the enlarged sphere for public opinion was locked into a zero-sum game with religion; matters that once were the privileged domain of theologians and spiritual leaders were now discussed openly by the general public.[121] As a journalist then, he was well aware of the potential for conflict between what were the premises of his own occupation and religious belief. Similarly, his sociological work placed him on the side of the profane, observing religion more as an object of research rather than a source of spiritual authority.[122] Likewise, his vocation as a critic reckoned with his own complicity with the secular. His affirmation of theological language in his Picard essay of 1929 is thus not so much an anomaly, but rather an indication of the twisting directions of the secularizing process.

Here we might recall the work of Niklas Luhmann and his view that secularization is a nonlinear process that does not displace religion, but rather exists in tension with it. Secularization, he claims, derives from social structures that allow for *"polykontextural* observations ... in which the contextual frameworks of the observer are no longer identical with those of being or of God."[123] Religion then becomes one mode of perception among a multiplicity of perspectives. Kracauer—with his background in architecture, sociology, and literature, his reliance on the form of the essay as a means of concrete situation analysis—represents a kind of intellectual mobility that seems to have adjusted to this new mode of observation. Indeed, many in his intellectual milieu (Adorno, Benjamin, Haas, Mannheim, Musil, for instance) demonstrated this polymath sensibility. Often writing against the constraints of their disciplines, often chased into exile, they came to embody the "intellectual mobility" that Edward Said argued was decisive for the emergence of what he called "secular criticism."[124] In contrast with Said, however, the intertwining with religious discourse, at least in the work of Kracauer and many of his contemporaries, should be recognized.

For Kracauer two problems resulted from this *polykontextural* structure of the secular: an expanded idea of culture and a proliferation of different modes of analysis that sought to reckon with it. According to Luhmann, the expansion of culture resulted in a "doubling" of phenomena, a "redescription of descriptions that oriented one to the world."[125] In the course of the nineteenth century these "doubling" discourses resulted in a number of analytic modes that eventually became (at least in some cases) synonymous with terms of reproach: historicism, positivism, relativism.[126] The result was what Luhmann calls a "symptomatology" that sought to elicit from every artifact a different level of meaning. This could involve on the one hand the augmentation of the secular, the increased incorporation of our experiences of the real into one or another system of knowledge; on the other hand, it could view the surface appearances of culture and nature as a means of decoding lost origins, what the painter Franz Marc identified as a "second sight" that found hidden meanings in the material world. This faculty, so Marc believed, would be the basis of a "new Europe."[127] Such impulses ran parallel to the ideas of the philosophers of life and their "laborious efforts" to establish a "cult of immediacy, authenticity, genuineness and identity."[128] Enlightenment in rational terms is not the desired result, and as Luhmann suggests, the rational pursuit of a "symptomatology" may, by way of its failure, still yield a form of secular religion. In this case, the religious reconstitutes itself at that point where the limits of human reason are recognized. The "inscrutability" of God becomes the inscrutability of the system, embodied in the fact of the "unavoidable opaqueness of the system to itself."[129] Here again we are in the territory reckoned with in *The Detective Novel*; it is the "negative church" of the modern where the workings of *ratio* find their total fulfillment. Similarly, this is the world Kracauer found in the work of Kafka, not just in the famous Kafkaesque nightmare of a world bureaucratized and rendered rational but without purpose, but also in the language that Kracauer had described as an opaque surface that obliterates the world in order to recover a fragment of the truth.[130] The will to truth was to be found in this "holding out in the negative," not in the perfection of culture or in aesthetic constructions that sought to redeem the real by its own power; culture's true function was one of method, a means without a clear end. Hence, why Kracauer was so often hostile to the idea that culture could annex religion. On the contrary, even if the truth contents of religion had to be pried away from myth, they must be prevented from finding a new home in a closed culture.

Of religious concepts, redemption remained the one to which Kracauer referred most often and most consistently throughout his life. The critic did not, however, secure redemption or take steps towards it; rather he or she exposed the myths that tried to mask an unredeemable social reality. Under *ratio* this reality was violent, one under which the atomized individual could possess no meaningful subjectivity. In its worse guise, during the war, the opacity of *ratio* demanded total subordination.[131] No longer was individual fate disposed of by the inscrutability of chance; instead, the state imposed its own inscrutable command over the fate of the individual; it did so in accordance with rationally prescribed goals and means, but with no sense of "last things." Suffering under reason thus became confused with suffering under fate. In Max Brod's words, the modern had confused "noble" and "ignoble" misfortune.

In *Ginster*, when the protagonist reflects on the son of one of his mother's friends, burned alive in action on the Eastern Front, or on the death of his close friend Otto, he can only marvel at the fact that he is still alive while they are dead.[132] After his mobilization, when some recruits to an artillery regiment are suddenly transferred to the infantry, he knows they have passed from the camp of the elect to that of the damned.[133] The random actions of the army thus embody the opacity of the modern in its most destructive guise, a "monstrosity" in the words of his friend Joseph Roth; or Max Weber's disenchanted gods working their magic under the guise of modern *ratio*.[134] Against these implacable forces, the Chaplinesque Ginster does not really resist. Indeed, part of the novel's irony stems from the fact that Ginster survives the war not because of any gesture of resistance, but rather through a collusion of passivity and chance. He survives because the opacity of the modern is just as indifferent to his life as to his death. The world of emancipated *ratio* finds its material fulfillment in the seemingly random destructiveness of war—a sinister version of Kantian "purposefulness without purpose."[135] Thus, the inversions that characterize the negative church become visible in the ritualized workings of reason, a kind of "black mass" in which *ratio* is the only celebrant. It displays itself as an impenetrable surface, blocking access to a reality that it can never itself discover.

How effective was Kracauer's criticism? By 1930 one could surely argue that the need for cogent discussions of the social and political situation in Germany and Europe was urgent. Many commentators have since argued that the showing of intellectuals in this regard was remarkably poor. Instead of attempts at even-handed analysis, they delivered screeds that represented the interests of their respective parties or cliques; few mounted a spirited defense of the Republic.[136] The *FZ*, setting aside the feuilleton department, was not exceptional. One of Heinrich Simon's last ill-fated gestures was to throw his support behind the 1930 merger of the rump Democratic Party and the Young German Order—this entity performed miserably in the election campaigns that followed. In this kind of editorial environment, Kracauer was limited; but still given the shocks of the Great Depression and Nazism's dramatic electoral success, a cultural critical approach that wagered so much upon the "reversal of negativity" appears to be both too subtle and too ambitious.[137] His emphasis on interpretation and indirect method sought an existential shift in the individual; such intentions were far-reaching and probably exceeded the bounds of what could be done in this particular journalistic environment. Yet, if the approach aimed at too much, it may also have been too refined. Vietta and others, for instance, displayed frustration over what they saw as a wavering of position in Kracauer's writing. A further letter that Kracauer received in the fall of 1931 from one of his readers asked pointedly why the *FZ* did so little to openly refute anti-Semitism.[138] The disinclination towards open polemics may have been intended to have a more decisive pedagogical effect, but such aims probably required more engagement than most readers were willing or able to give. Thus, while his approach may have intended to help his audience to navigate the ideological swamp that aggravated the Republic's final years, did it not also forsake the smaller political victories that might have been won by a more quotidian approach to politics?

One need not condemn Kracauer's efforts in order to still find his response to the crisis problematic. His work does not amount to a "desertion" of the Republic, but nor is it a bold and overt defense. Nazism was ready to use parliamentary means to undo democracy, however, the opponents of Nazism were less likely to pursue democratic options to defend either the Republic or the values it claimed to represent. Kracauer appears to have remained fixed upon what he believed could be accomplished within the sphere of his critical method. To a remarkable degree, he seems to have possessed what Coleridge described as a "negative capability," the capacity to persevere in a state of perpetual crisis that negated most of the traditional footholds that culture and politics could provide; he wrote without any recourse to a stabilizing notion of truth—neither the materialist idea of progress, nor the second Jerusalem.[139] Still, given his portrayal of modernity as a space of social violence, as a crisis provoked by an inevitable secularization, his pedagogical intentions might appear too subtle to be effective. To be sure, he was often identified as a "man of the left," but his position, often stated obliquely, was unclear to some—hence, the confusion between himself and Vietta and the accusations brought against him by Bloch that his political attitudes were too obscure, a blend of directionless radicalism and intellectual complacency.[140] Kracauer's wager was that truly meaningful change would come only if individuals were able to read their situation in a radically different way—a strategy that he had begun to develop in *The Detective Novel* and that led to the dialectical situation-analyses he proposed in the "Minimal Requirement of Intellectuals." In 1922, Kracauer had implied this kind of strategy in connection to the gesture of radical "waiting", conceived as a form of engaged preparedness, directing one's energies towards tasks not yet recognized. His critical agenda needed time, however, and by 1933 time was something that the Republic could not afford, confronted with a political movement that made no secret of its readiness to use force.

In his riposte to Döblin and Hocke, Kracauer spoke of the "frightening neutrality" that prevailed in Germany, particularly among German youth, and he clearly intended that his work should oppose this trend.[141] Given the general trajectory of events in Germany, his hopes clearly were not met; but even in the smaller intellectual circles that he addressed, he probably had a limited impact. The debate provoked by Döblin, which some felt had only demonstrated the "pitiful" state of German intellectual culture, was echoed by more general assessments. "It is a type of madness," wrote the French diplomat and writer Pierre Viénot, "to live in a world without law, and the fear of this madness wards off destruction—but what does one do if this madness is actually there?"[142] In other words, can one actually hold out in chaos? In answering his question, Viénot, who lived in Germany from 1925 to 1930, argued that many Germans persisted "with courage and a raw will to survive . . . virtuousness, manly fortitude, a shrewd attentiveness to the state of affairs, self-confidence and even joy in risk . . . in short, a type of heroism stands at the top of the table of values in modern Germany." Nonetheless, he could not entirely exclude from this "heroism" a distinct "pleasure in chaos" and a widespread "fatalism." He was stirred by the resilience displayed by many Germans in the face of material and spiritual want, but he noted with misgivings that these qualities were now found just as often among the supporters of Hitler and the communists. Germany, he contended, was increasingly becoming a land where morals "had no positive content," that is they "gave no answer to fundamental ethical questions, because they lacked . . . a positive norm."[143] Whether or not one accepts Viénot's emphasis on normative morality, he nonetheless identified a view common among the German intelligentsia: that morality had become entangled by the habit of making a virtue out of uncertainty and hesitation. In different ways, both Kracauer and Döblin had recognized this predicament.

In contrast to the possibilities set out in their works, however, one could embrace "chance" as an almost metaphysical premise, as did Ernst Jünger in his 1929 work, *The Adventurous Heart*.[144] Such responses were precisely what Kracauer hoped to fend off with his criticism, and after 1933 he began to lose faith in this project. After his forced migration, he seemed to distance himself from his past cultural political interests. Writing to his friend Fränze Herzfeld in 1933, he lamented over the fact that the whole German "nest of literary vermin" with all its "hateful" problems had followed him to Paris.[145] It was as if he had already begun to distance himself from the intellectual quagmires and controversies of Weimar; or perhaps, it would be better to say that he had begun to pursue similar problems, but outside of a specifically Weimar context.

The focus of Kracauer's work had centered on problems that he believed were most especially felt by intellectuals and professionals, but also the "white collar classes."[146] It is difficult to determine to what extent Kracauer correctly reckoned with the concerns of this imagined readership. As Mülder-Bach points out, if there is continuity in his work during the Weimar years, it is his preoccupation with these segments of society, from those who refuse religion and nihilism in "Those Who Wait" to the "unsheltered" masses who were the basis of his sociological work of 1931. This was the readership he wanted to address, which is why he refused the offer to write for *Die Weltbühne* despite the fact that many friends and admirers thought that he would be more at home there. However, this was precisely what he wanted to avoid; he preferred to write from the mainstream, from a position where he was not entirely at home.[147] As his concluding remarks in *The Salaried Masses* demonstrate, Kracauer was alarmed by the political consequences that might arise from this part of German society, spiritually adrift, their existential needs, by and large, untended.[148] This was a pool of discontent from which the extremist parties could readily draw. As Vietta wrote to him in an admiring letter, the white collar classes were the "the point of least resistance in the bourgeois dam."[149] Later in 1931, Vietta wrote Kracauer again from his home in Schopfheim, expressing some of the angst of this tenuous position, trapped amid competing forms of radicalism: "I am once again in a reality shot through with demonstrations, dealings with communists. It is difficult to speak of these things ... besides, collectivism will carry the world just as Christianity once did."[150] Recent studies of voting patterns during the last years of Weimar have suggested, however, that this anxiety over the white collar workers was exaggerated and that they remained relatively immune to Nazism, at least until 1933.[151] Thus, his diagnosis would appear to have been only partially on the mark. Whether the problems of secularization and the attractions of religious revival were as significant as Kracauer argued is a question that is outside the scope of this study; rather, I have wanted to show how these rival discourses functioned within a specific intellectual milieu and how they related to a particular idea of criticism's potential, and a discourse of crisis in which the fate of religion played a significant part.

However, Kracauer and his milieu were not unique in thinking that such questions mattered. When in July 1937 the exhibition *Degenerate Art* opened in Munich, the curators of the exhibit devoted an entire room to the alleged outrages that art had perpetrated upon religious feeling during the years of the Republic. One of the first works that confronted visitors to the exhibit was a large expressionist crucifixion by the sculptor Ludwig Gies. This work had already provoked controversy fifteen years earlier in Lübeck, and then again in Munich. Indeed, the head of the Christ figure had been struck off from the sculpture when it was placed in a Lübeck Cathedral; the piece was restored but later removed. The message was clear: the Republic that allowed religion to be insulted by Bolshevists, Jews, and the "party system" was now at an end. A new era was beginning in both German politics and art, and presumably, in religion too.

Notes

1. Max Rychner, 'Was ist Modern?" *NSR* 23, no. 9 (September 1930): 641–44.
2. On this point Rychner quoted Peter Meyer, a member of the Swiss Werkbund member, who argued that what was different about modernity was "historical consciousness"; technological innovation was constant and gradual, but the contemporary sense of the past represented a rupture.
3. Kracauer, "The Hotel Lobby," *Mass Ornament*, 175; and *Detektiv-Roman*, 38; and the editors' remarks in *Werke* 1, 389–90.
4. Kracauer to David Riesman, 30 June 1958, KN, DLA.
5. On the fraught reception of Kracauer's film theory, see the discussion in Patrice Petro, "Kracauer's Epistemological Shift," *New German Critique* 54 (Autumn 1991): 127–38. Also, see the introduction by Leonardo Quaresima in the revised edition of Kracauer, *From Caligari to Hitler: A Psychological History of the German Film* (Princeton, 2004), xv–xlix.
6. For an argument that Kracauer's final work represents a significant break with his earlier thought, see Inka Mülder-Bach, "History as Autobiography: The Last Things before the Last" *NGC* 54 (Autumn 1991): 139–57. Petro comes to a more moderate conclusion that there is a "shift in emphasis" that does not exclude continuity in his general concerns; see Petro, "Kracauer's Epistemological Shift," 137–38.
7. See on this topic, Barnouw, *Critical Realism*, 53–103.
8. Rychner, "Was ist Modern?" More generally, see John Burrow, *The Crisis of Reason: European Thought, 1848–1914* (New Haven: Yale University Press, 2000); Jacques

le Rider, *Modernity and Crises of Identity: Culture and Society in Fin-de-siècle Vienna*, trans. Rosemary Morris (New York, 1993); and Eksteins, *Solar Dance*.
9. Paul Valéry, "The Intellectual Crisis II," *The Athenaeum* (2 May 1919): 279.
10. Paul Valéry, "The Spiritual Crisis I," *The Athenaeum* (11 April 1919): 184.
11. Kracauer, "Those Who Wait," *Mass Ornament*, 138; and "Photography," *Mass Ornament*, 62–63.
12. Dagmar Barnouw, "Vielschichtige Oberflächen: Kracauer und die Modernität von Weimar," in *Denken durch die Dinge: Siegfried Kracauer im Kontext*, ed. Frank Grunert and Dorothee Kimmich (Munich, 2009), 23.
13. Valéry, "The Spiritual Crisis I," 183.
14. Andrew Benjamin, "Denaturing Time," paper presented at the colloquium *Provisional Insight: Siegfried Kracauer in the 21st Century*, Monash University, 2008 (accessed 7 June 2010 at http://www.arts.monash.edu/film-tv/colloquia/provisional-insight/2008/podcast/#benjamin).
15. Kracauer, "Franz Kafka" *Mass Ornament*, 278. It was this final sentence that deeply impressed the young Dolf Sternberger when he read this essay; see Sternberger to Kracauer, 11 September 1931, KN, DLA.
16. Inka Mülder-Bach, "History as Autobiography," 147–48 and 155.
17. Kracauer to Ernst Bloch, 29 June 1926, *Briefe* 1, 280–84. Here I follow Gail Finney's translation of this letter included in Mülder-Bach, "History as Autobiography," 147.
18. Mülder-Bach, "History as Autobiography," 155–57.
19. The phrase comes from André Breton, *Break of Day* (Lincoln, 1999), 3 (originally published as *Points du jour* in 1934).
20. This subject is discussed in Martin Jay, "Adorno and Kracauer—Notes on a Troubled Friendship," *Permanent Exiles*, 196–97.
21. Koch, *Siegfried Kracauer*, 17–18.
22. See Schopenhauer, *Parerga und Paralipomena II: Sämtliche Werke* 5 (Frankfurt am Main, 1986), 316; and Adorno, "The Curious Realist," 161.
23. Schröter, "Weltzerfall und Rekonstruktion," 38–39.
24. *Frankfurter Zeitung*, 6 July 1930, Stadtblatt.
25. For a discussion of Kracauer's interpretation of architectural ornamentation, see Henrik Reeh, *Ornaments of the Metropolis: Siegfried Kracauer and Modern Urban Culture* (Cambridge, 2004).
26. Kracauer, *History*, 136.
27. Döblin, *Wissen und Verändern!*
28. A number of useful sources on the origins and reception of *Wissen und Verändern!* can be found in *Alfred Döblin, 1878–1978*, ed. Jochen Meyer (Marbach am Neckar, 1978), 296–314.
29. For a discussion of Döblin's political writings, see Wulf Koepke, "Döblin's Political Writings during the Weimar Republic," in *A Companion to the Works of Alfred Döblin*, ed. Roland Dollinger, Wulf Koepke, and Heidi Thomann Tewarson (Rochester, 2004), 183–93.
30. Klaus Müller-Salget, "Döblin and Judaism," in *A Companion to the Works of Alfred Döblin*, ed. Roland Dollinger, Wulf Koepke, and Heidi Thomann Tewarson (Rochester, 2004), 233–46.
31. Müller-Salget, "Döblin and Judaism," 239–40.

32. Döblin, *Wissen und Verändern*, 37–38.
33. Müller-Salget, "Döblin and Judaism," 239–240; and Koepke, "Döblin's Political Writings," 184.
34. Hocke in *Das Tagebuch* 11, no. 27 (5 July 1930), partially reprinted in Meyer, *Alfred Döblin*, 297–98; the letter was reprinted in its entirety at the beginning of Döblin, *Wissen und Verändern*, 13–16.
35. See the excerpts of letters reprinted in Meyer, *Alfred Döblin*, 301 and 303.
36. Gustav René Hocke, *Im Schatten des Leviathan: Lebenserinnerungen, 1908–1978* (Munich, 2004), 72.
37. Döblin, "Vorwort zu einer erneuten Aussprache," *Die neue Rundschau* 42, no. 1 (1931): 100–103.
38. Hocke, *Im Schatten des Leviathan*, 72. See also, Wolf Köpke, "Alfred Döblins Überparteilichkeit: Zur Publizistik in den letzten Jahren der Weimarer Republik," in *Weimars Ende: Prognosen und Diagnosen in der deutschen Literatur und politischen Publizistik, 1930–1933*, ed. Thomas Koebner (Frankfurt am Main, 1982), 318–29.
39. See the bibliography compiled by Louise Huguet, *Bibliographie Alfred Döblins* (Berlin and Weimar, 1972). *Wissen and Verändern* received 39 reviews by her count; among the reviewers were Gertrud Bäumer, Rudolf Arnheim, Walter Benjamin, Hendrik de Man, Axel Eggebrecht, and Béla Balázs (327–30).
40. Zuckerkandl to Döblin, 6 July 1931, quoted in Alfred Döblin, *Schriften zur Politik und Gesellschaft* (Freiburg im Breisgau, 1972), 495–96. Zuckerkandl's own contribution to the debate also appeared in *Die neue Rundschau*; see Zuckerkandl, "Alte und neue Bildung," *Neue Rundschau* 42, no. 1 (1931): 94–99.
41. Kracauer to Louise Huguet, 28 December 1958, KN, DLA.
42. Döblin, *Wissen und Verändern*, 58–59 and 81–82.
43. Döblin, *Wissen und Verändern*, 49 and 68–75.
44. Döblin, *Wissen und Verändern*, 118.
45. Köpke, "Alfred Döblins Überparteilichkeit," 323.
46. Döblin, *Wissen und Verändern*, 105–7 and 119.
47. Döblin, *Wissen und Verändern*, 42. Also, see Koepke, "Döblin's Political Writings," 189–90.
48. Döblin, *Wissen und Verändern*, 123.
49. Döblin, *Wissen und Verändern*, 166–170.
50. Max Rychner, "Anmerkungen: Döblin warnt: Weg von den Gebildeten." *NSR* 24, no. 5 (1931): 321–25. Though Rychner evinced a minimum of respect for Döblin as an individual, his tone was more than a little condescending: "Nietzsche once wrote that thoughts that come on pigeon's feet will one day conquer the world; he did not yet so clearly perceive that thoughts that come with dogs' noses will undertake the conquest of Germany" (322).
51. Döblin, *Wissen und Verändern*, 104 and 136–39.
52. Döblin, *Wissen und Verändern*, 94.
53. Kracauer, "Was soll Herr Hocke tun?" *FZ*, 17 April 1931, *Werke*, 5.3, 486–93.
54. Kracauer, "Was soll Herr Hocke tun?" *Werke* 5.3, 486–87. Kracauer also described Chaplin as a "hole" (*Loch*), a figure that represented the predicament of the individual after the destruction of Kantian subjectivity. See his review, "Chaplin," *FZ*, 6 November 1926; reprinted as "The Gold Rush" in Kracauer, *Der verbotene Blick*, 291–93.
55. Kracauer, "Was soll Herr Hocke tun?" *Werke* 5.3, 493.

56. The roundtable in *Die neue Rundschau* may already have been foreseen when Kracauer wrote his review; the final line certainly made a direct appeal to continue the discussion in another venue, and he was at that time acquainted with the editor of the *Neue Rundschau*, Rudolf Kayser.
57. Döblin and Kracauer did know each other during his time in Berlin, but there does not appear to have been much rapport between them. When Kracauer was approached by the Döblin scholar Louise Huguet, he confessed that he did not "feel attracted by his personality, by his cast of mind. But I greatly appreciated his 'Alexanderplatz' and, with reservations, his fecund, sprawling, almost vegetative imagination." See his letter to Huguet, 28 December 1958, KN, DLA.
58. Kracauer, "Minimalforderung an die Intellektuellen," *Die neue Rundschau* 42, no. 1 (July 1931); reprinted in Kracauer, *Der verbotene Blick*, 247–252, here 251. Also, see Koepke, "Döblin's Political Writings," 188–90.
59. Kracauer, "Minimalforderung an die Intellektuellen," *Der verbotene Blick*, 249.
60. Kracauer, "Minimalforderung an die Intellektuellen," 248.
61. Kracauer, "Minimalforderung an die Intellektuellen," 250.
62. Egon Vietta was the pen name of Karl Egon Fritz (1903–1959).
63. Egon Vietta, *Die Seinsfrage bei Martin Heidegger* (Stuttgart, 1950).
64. Egon Fritz to Kracauer, 20 October 1930, KN, DLA. In his published writings, Vietta appears to have avoided his original surname. In the DLA, however, his letters are sometimes filed under "Vietta" and sometimes under "Fritz." In the Kracauer papers his letters are filed under "Fritz," so I have adhered to this practice.
65. Egon Fritz to Kracauer, 5 July 1931, KN, DLA. Also, see Vietta, *Die Kollektivisten* (Freiburg im Breisgau, 1930); and Vietta, "Martin Heidegger und die Situation der Jugend," *Die neue Rundschau* 42, no. 2 (1931): 501–11.
66. Egon Fritz to Kracauer, 31 November 1930, KN, DLA.
67. Egon Fritz to Kracauer, 20 October 1930, KN, DLA.
68. Vietta, *Die Kollektivisten*, 13–14. Max Rychner, in his positive assessment of this work, pointed out the influence of Heidegger; see his discussion of Vietta in conjunction with a review of *Kapitalismus und schöne Literatur* by Bernard von Brentano: "Anmerkungen: Kapitalismus und schöne Literatur" *NSR* 24, no. 2 (1931): 81–94, esp. 92–94.
69. On Kracauer's rejection of this concept, see Egon Vietta to Alfred Döblin, 3 August 1931, Döblin Nachlaß, DLA. Vietta appears to have written Döblin in order to justify his own response to Döblin's work and to express his dismay that his conversations with Kracauer had been used as an entry point to criticize *Wissen und Verändern*. Also, see Egon Fritz to Kracauer, 1 February 1931, KN, DLA.
70. Kracauer to Egon Fritz, 12 January 1931, KN, DLA.
71. Here Kracauer was responding to a conversation they had had when Vietta was still in Berlin, see Fritz to Kracauer, 31 November 1930, KN, DLA.
72. Belke, "Siegfried Kracauer als Beobachter der jungen Sowjetunion," 17–38.
73. Bloch to Kracauer, 29 April 1931, and 1 June 1932, *Briefe* 1, 353–55 and 362–65.
74. Kracauer, "Instruktionsstunde in Literatur. Zu einem Vortrag des Russen Tretjakow," *FZ*, 25 April 1931, in *Der verbotene Blick*, 232–36; and Kracauer, "Ein soziologisches Experiment? Zu Bert Brechts Versuch *Der Dreigroschenprozeß*," *FZ*, 29 February 1932, in *Der verbotene Blick*, 252–60, esp. 254–55. The *Three Penny Trial* was Brecht's account of the litigation process surrounding his claims of authorship in regards to the film version of the play.

75. Kracauer to Hans Flesch, 16 February 1932, KN, DLA.
76. Kracauer to Ernst Bloch, 4 June 1932, *Briefe* 1, 365–68, esp. 367.
77. Kracauer to Ernst Bloch, 4 June 1932, *Briefe* 1, 366–67.
78. The *Hohlräumen*, a terminology used by both Bloch and Benjamin, may be compared with what Kracauer called a "hesitant openness" (*zögerndes Geöffnetsein*) in "Those Who Wait" (*Mass Ornament*, 138), and the concept of the historical anteroom in *History*. For a discussion of this theme, see Dagmar Barnouw, "*An den Rand geschriebene Träume*: Kracauer über Zeit und Geschichte," in *Siegfried Kracauer: neue Interpretationen*, 5–14. Also, see Eiland and Jennings on the contentious overlap of these terms among Benjamin and Bloch, in *Walter Benjamin*, 479. *Selbstentäußerung* was also used by Marx to refer to the alienation of the self and the world of objects.
79. Egon Vietta to Alfred Döblin, 3 August 1931, Döblin Nachlaß, DLA.
80. Egon Fritz to Kracauer, 5 July 1931, KN, DLA. Cf. Döblin, *Wissen und Verändern*, 86.
81. Egon Fritz to Kracauer, 5 July 1931, KN, DLA.
82. Kracauer, "Minimalforderung an der Intellektuellen," in *Der verbotene Blick*, 248.
83. Kracauer to Egon Fritz, 12 July 1931, KN, DLA.
84. Kracauer, "Minimalforderung an der Intellektuellen," in *Der verbotene Blick*, 252.
85. Kracauer to Egon Fritz, 12 July 1931, KN, DLA.
86. Vietta, *Die Kollektivisten*, 11–12. In his letter to Döblin of 3 August 1931, he writes that he owed to Döblin the understanding that intellect "always has a serving role and no value intrinsic to itself."
87. Theodor Adorno, "The Actuality of Philosophy," *Telos* 31 (Spring 1977): 123. Kracauer remained hostile to Heidegger and his work after 1945. After having participated in a seminar in hermeneutics at Columbia in 1964, Kracauer wrote to Adorno that "after this experience of profound chatter round about Heidegger, the necessity and full beauty of your *Jargon of Authenticity* has become fully appreciated... I have by way of Werner Marx reckoned with the later development of Heidegger which is just as revelatory as it is abominable" (Kracauer to Adorno, 16 January 1964, *Briefwechsel, 1923–1966*, 640–41. The reference is to Werner Marx, *Heidegger und die Tradition* (Stuttgart, 1961).
88. Pecora, *Secularization and Cultural Criticism*, 1.
89. Pecora, *Secularization and Cultural Criticism*, 204–5.
90. Pecora, *Secularization and Cultural Criticism*, 2–4.
91. Pecora, *Secularization and Cultural Criticism*, 59–66.
92. Though, as Pecora points out, Blumenberg does not argue for a total break whereby the secular is established on its own foundations; modern ideas of progress are, for instance, "in part the consequence of earlier Christian thought." See Pecora, *Secularization and Cultural Criticism*, 61–62. See also, Roberts, "'Political Religion,'" 396–97.
93. Indeed, Kracauer and Blumenberg corresponded during the period that Blumenberg was working on his major study, *The Legitimacy of the Modern Age*. Their letters are in KN, DLA. In his letter of 22 December 1964, Blumenberg told Kracauer that he hoped he would find traces of their discussion in his work.
94. Kracauer, "Minimalforderung an der Intellektuellen," in *Der verbotene Blick*, 251. In this respect, Kracauer anticipates the dilemma that Pecora finds in the work of Habermas: a problem of reconciling a secular idea of modernity with its genealogy

that in some sense derives from the ethical impulses of religion. When Habermas speaks of the "semantic potentials" in religious thought, one is reminded of Kracauer's idea of religious "truth contents" to be recovered for secular modernity. Habermas writes: "As long as religious language bears within itself, inspiring, indeed unrelinquishable semantic concepts which elude (for the moment?) the expressive power of a philosophical language and still await translation into a discourse that gives reasons for its positions, philosophy, even in its postmetaphysical form, will neither be able to replace nor to repress religion." See Pecora, *Secularization and Cultural Criticism*, 49.
95. Karl Löwith, *Meaning in History* (Chicago, 1949).
96. Rudolf Pannwitz, *Die Krisis der europäischen Kultur*. (Nuremberg, 1917), 242. Benjamin cites this essay in his discussion of translation; see "The Task of the Translator," in *Illuminations: Essays and Reflections*, trans. Harry Zohn (New York, 1969), 80.
97. Kracauer, "Minimalforderung an der Intellektuellen," in *Der verbotene Blick*, 251. According to his letter of 5 July 1931, Vietta had discussed the issue raised in this passage with Heidegger, but I have not seen any indication that Heidegger responded to this in writing. According to Löwenthal, Heidegger did know of some of Kracauer's early writing—a piece on Scheler that he judged unfavorably. See Kracauer to Löwenthal, 14 January 1921, in Jansen and Schmidt, *In steter Freundschaft*, 18.
98. Gregor Streim, *Das Ende des Anthropozentrismus: Anthropologie und Geschichtskritik in der deutschen Literatur zwischen 1930–1950* (Berlin and New York, 2008), 261–317.
99. Streim, *Das Ende des Anthropozentrismus*, 263–99, esp. 266–67.
100. Kracauer to Egon Fritz, 12 January 1931, KN, DLA.
101. Max Rychner argued a related point about *The Collectivists*, seeing the work as an assertion of "metaphysical fundaments" opposed to a positivist world view. See Rychner, "Anmerkungen: Kapitalismus und schöne Literatur." *NSR* 24, no. 2 (1931): 81–94.
102. Egon Fritz to Kracauer, 8 April 1930, KN, DLA.
103. Kracauer, "Minimalforderung an die Intellektuellen," in *Verbotene Blick*, 251. Vietta did join the NSDAP in 1937, though he also appears to have had some contacts with the Hamburg White Rose group. He had worked as a civil councilor after 1932, and he continued in this position until 1944 when he did not return to Germany after a work-related trip to Italy. See Streim, *Das Ende des Anthropozentrismus*, 261–62, n. 5.
104. Burrin, "Political Religion," 322–26.
105. Raymond Aaron, "L'Avenir des religions séculières," *La France Libre* (July–August 1944), quoted in Burrin, "Political Religion," 325.
106. Burleigh, *Earthly Powers*, 2–10.
107. Kracauer, "Prophetentum," *Werke* 5.1, 460–69.
108. Kracauer, "Zwei Arten der Mitteilung," in *Der verbotene Blick*, 222.
109. Neil Gregor, "Nazism—a Political Religion? Rethinking the Voluntarist Turn," in *Nazism, War and Genocide: Essays in Honour of Jeremy Noakes*, ed. Neil Gregor (Exeter, 2005), 11–12.
110. Peter Godman, *Hitler and the Vatican: Inside the Secret Archives That Reveal the New Story of the Nazis and the Church* (New York, 2004), 149.

111. Burrin, "Political Religions," 330–31. Burrin cites as examples of this tendency the work of Voegelin, Norman Cohn, and Alain Besançon.
112. Roberts, "'Political Religion,'" 390–91.
113. Burrin, "Political Religions," 329.
114. Mark Lilla, *The Stillborn God*, 279–85.
115. This phrase is borrowed, slightly modified, from Derrida, see "Force of Law," 63.
116. Burrin, "Political Religion," 330.
117. Burrin, "Political Religion," 326.
118. Rowan Ireland, quoted in Michael P. Hornsby-Smith, "Recent Transformations in English Catholicism: Evidence of Secularization?" in *Religion and Modernization: Sociologists and Historians Debate the Secularization Thesis*, ed. Steve Bruce (Oxford, 1992), 120.
119. Luhmann, *Die Religion der Gesellschaft*, 308.
120. Pecora, *Secularization and Cultural Criticism*, 202–5.
121. Kracauer, "Kritik der Oeffentlichen Meinung," FZ, 24 November 1922, in *Werke* 5.1, 525–27.
122. Kracauer, "Group as Bearer of Ideas." *Archiv für Sozialwissenschaft und Sozialpolitik* 49, no. 3 (August 1922), in *Mass Ornament*, 143–70.
123. Luhmann, *Die Religion der Gesellschaft*, 284.
124. Said, *The World, the Text, and the Critic*, 1–30.
125. Luhmann, *Die Religion der Gesellschaft*, 311–14.
126. Luhmann, *Die Religion der Gesellschaft*, 311.
127. Franz Marc, *Briefe, Aufzeichnungen und Aphorismen* I (Berlin, 1920), 50, 54 and 126–32.
128. Luhmann, *Die Religion der Gesellschaft*, 311.
129. Luhmann, *Die Religion der Gesellschaft*, 313.
130. Kracauer, "Der Prozeß," FZ, 1 November 1925, reprinted in *Werke* 5.2, 306–8.
131. This is a recasting of the situation that Kracauer believed he saw in the novels of Julien Green, where fate determined the course of all characters, and most especially, those who sought to manipulate it. See his review of Green's *Léviathan*, "Betrachtungen zu Greens: *Léviathan*," FZ, 1 December 1929, in *Der Verbotene Blick*, 214–19.
132. Kracauer, "Ginster," in *Werke* 7, 81 and 97.
133. Kracauer, "Ginster," in *Werke* 7, 148.
134. Roth quoted in Belke and Renz, *Siegfried Kracauer*, 52.
135. Kant quoted in Kracauer, *Der Detektiv-Roman*, 40.
136. Hoeges, *Kontroverse am Abgrund*, 56–57; Istvan Deak, *Weimar Germany's Left-Wing Intellectuals: A Political History of the* Weltbühne *and Its Circle*. Berkeley, 1968; and Jürgen Kuczynski, *Über die Unpraktischheit des deutschen Intellektuellen*. London, 1944.
137. See Kracauer to Reifenberg, 12 February 1933, 18 February 1933, and 25 February 1933, KN, DLA.
138. Herwarth Kreher to Kracauer, 29 September 1931 KN, DLA. The letter from Kreher, a self-professed admirer of Kracauer and his work, is nonetheless riddled with anti-Semitic statements; his demand that Kracauer and the FZ respond to the "Jewish Question" must have struck Kracauer as offensively presumptuous, but also disturbing as Kreher also describes himself in terms that identify him as precisely the audience (young and white collar) he was trying to reach.

139. Coleridge cited in Zadie Smith, "Speaking in Tongues," *New York Review of Books* 56, no. 3 (26 February 2009): 42.
140. Bloch to Kracauer, 1 June 1932, in *Briefe* 1, 363–64.
141. Kracauer, "Was soll Herr Hocke tun?" in *Werke* 5.3, 487.
142. Pierre Viénot, *Ungewisses Deutschland: Zur Krise seiner bürgerlichen Kultur* (Frankfurt am Main, 1931), 87–88. Viénot (1887–1944), a diplomat who served in Morocco and later a member of the French resistance, was acquainted with Kracauer. They probably met when Viénot was living in Germany during the late 1920s. *Ungewisse Deutschland* first appeared in French and then was translated and published by the Frankurter Societäts-Druckerei, which suggests more extensive contacts with the *FZ*. During his exile in Paris, Kracauer appears to have received some assistance from Viénot, and it was to him that he applied when he tried to bring his mother and aunt to Paris from Frankfurt.
143. Viénot, *Ungewisses Deutschland*, 89–90.
144. See the discussion of this work in Tom Kindt and Hans-Harald Müller, "Zweimal Cervantes: Die *Don-Quijote*-Lektüren von Ernst Jünger und Ernst Weiß. Ein Beitrag zur literarischen Anthropologie der zwanziger Jahre," *Jahrbuch zur Literatur der Weimarer Republik* 1(1995): 234–35. A second version of *Das Abenteuerliche Herz* was published in 1938. See the introduction by Eliah Bures and Elliot Neaman, in Jünger, *The Adventurous Heart: Figures and Capriccios*, trans. Thomas Friese (Candor, 2012), xiii–lii.
145. Kracauer to Fränze Herzfeld, 14 November 1933, KN, DLA.
146. See Inka Mülder-Bach, "Introduction," to Kracauer, *The Salaried Masses*, 6–14.
147. Kracauer to Bloch, 5 January 1928, in *Briefe* 1, 289–90; and Jay, "The Extraterritorial Life of Siegfried Kracauer," in *Permanent Exiles*, 164–65.
148. Kracauer, *The Salaried Masses*, 88–95 and 102–6.
149. Egon Fritz to Kracauer, 8 April 1930, KN, DLA.
150. Egon Fritz to Kracauer, 31 November 1930, KN, DLA.
151. See the discussion of this issue in the review article by Peter Fritzsche, "Did Weimar Fail?" *Journal of Modern History* 68, no. 3 (September 1996): 640. See also Thomas Childers, *The Nazi Voter: The Social Foundations of Fascism in Germany, 1919–1933* (Chapel Hill and London, 1983), 91–93 and 169–174.

AFTERWORD

From Don Quixote to Sancho Panza

> There the soul of Don Quixote, light as thistledown, snatched up in the illusory vortex, goes whirling like a dry leaf; and in its pursuit everything ingenuous and sorrowing still left in the world will go forevermore.
> —José Ortega y Gasset, *Meditations on Quixote*, 133

> If today our nation lacks the force of Don-Quixoticism in its conduct of life, it will lack the power to resurrect itself.
> —Paul E. Kipper, "Don Quixotes," *FZ*, 19 January 1921, 2nd Morgenblatt

Detectives, spies, and confidence men were the figures that Kracauer saw as representatives of the crisis of modernity. They were ciphers of hidden truths that had been lost through secularization, and they were potential dynamite that could explode the facades of everyday reality. To these figures one should also add two more from literary tradition: Don Quixote and Sancho Panza. These characters share with the others the capacity to exist in an uncertain zone, where concrete reality is viewed as a code, a "conjectural paradigm" that demands interpretation.[1] The detective reads the random chaos of the world according to the interlocking categories of *ratio*; he draws out the confidence man who hides behind the ordered appearances created by social conventions and the customary patterns of thought. The detective reads an encrypted world, while Kracauer the critic reads the detective for his potential to negatively illuminate the conditions of modernity. Quixote is related to these figures as he too is an interpreter; according to one of Kracauer's contemporaries, he is "the reader *par excellence* . . . the original model of the literary man" in terms of both his pitfalls and promises.[2] It is with the ambiguous pair of Quixote and Panza that I want to conclude, as it sheds light on the problems that confronted Kracauer and his intellectual milieu.

By inserting figures from the baroque era here, I do not mean to diminish our sense of Kracauer as a figure who engaged with modernity; but rather to deepen this engagement by emphasizing the contradictory tendencies that distinguished Weimar modernity—the unsettling juxtaposition of old and new that was remarked upon by Döblin. Hence, Quixote, as was the case with Kierkegaard, is much closer to modernity than might at first seem, and indeed, some of Kracauer's contemporaries appreciated this fact.

The more conventional interpretation of Quixote and Panza views the former as the arch-idealist who transfigures the world according to his overwrought imagination. He has read too many romances, and he now projects what he has read onto the world. As Dolf Sternberger wrote in 1929 (in an article that he may have discussed with Kracauer) Quixote represented a form of adventurous existence whereby the "I" devoured all reality, absorbing the world into its own inwardness.[3] This formulation is very near to Kracauer's view of the detective as a model of the transcendental subject who subordinates all traces of the real to autonomous *ratio*. In contrast, Sancho Panza is then understood as the voice that rises up in protest from the hard ground of reality with which Quixote constantly collides.

However, this reading of the Quixote story was rendered in a more complex fashion in the literature of the 1920s. On this point, one can look back again to Kierkegaard who also deployed the Cervantes characters in a polyvocal fashion. As was the case with the spy, the figure of Quixote takes on very different meanings at different points in his writing. In *Either/Or* Quixote and Panza are included among a catalog of paired figures (King/Fool, Faust/Wagner, for instance) whereby the "grand dialectic of life" is represented, with one figure representing the "totality" while the other "compensates for the disproportionate greatness of the [former] in actual life."[4] Here, the relationship between Panza and Quixote becomes more significant than the symbolic meanings derived from them separately; the two become different aspects of a whole, or at least two entities that strive to become a whole. Elsewhere in his work, Quixote is emblematic of the "passion of inwardness" that "grasps a particular fixed finite idea."[5] He is a "prototype of subjective lunacy", Kierkegaard states, but his inwardness endows his madness with more validity than the lunacy that leads the modern "assistant professor" towards absolute skepticism. However, not only skepticism is questioned by means of Quixote but also theology; for Kierkegaard suggests an analogy between the end of chivalry and the demise of "literalist theology." To Kierkegaard Quixote represents both of these fading values, and in him they both come to an end.[6] With the figure of Quixote as a touchstone, one thus arrives at a position that is not without some affinity for the position of waiting described by Kracauer in 1922, with positive theology on one side and modern skepticism on the other.

The problem of interpretation is also important for Kierkegaard though, to be sure, his radical Christianity separates him from Kracauer. At times, Kierkegaard seems to welcome an almost quixotic confusion of reading and misreading; the "eternal and the merely momentary are so folded together that each place and each time retains the memory of the possibility of the other" even as "essential differences" are drawn out by this juxtaposition.[7] Thus, when Kierkegaard proposes reading the Bible as a travel guide in order to discover that the modern café where you smoke your cigar was once a hideout for robbers and murderers, he suggests that it is the modern age that is deluded by denying that no connection exists between the imagined past and the concrete present. Thus, in one sense, the windmills actually may have been giant monsters, just as the modern café is still related to the den of thieves.

To the extent that Quixote's radical subjectivity places him at odds with his world, the younger Kracauer appears to have identified with this "knight of the tragic countenance"; yet at some point during the 1920s his identification altered. He begins as Quixote but ends as Panza (though this is by no means a straightforward transformation).[8] In his story "Grace," the protagonist Ludwig Loos is identified with Quixote. A close friend accuses him of possessing a faulty relationship with reality; he is one whose imagination and intellect blocks his access to life, and thus he becomes a victim of his own "Don-Quixote nature."[9] His disconnectedness from the world is only overcome by the successive shock of his failed intent to commit suicide and a sexual encounter. Thus, the story ends with a gesture of crude sentimentalism. Indeed, Kracauer himself was not entirely liberated from this quixotic romanticism. In a letter to Susman written seven years later in February 1920, he described his life as that of a Don Quixote—a solitary life, devoted to philosophy ("the most severe of all the goddesses") just as the knight-errant was devoted to Dulcinea. There is a further resonance between these two references to the Quixote figure. In "Grace" Ludwig has an ambiguous but platonic relationship with a woman of religious convictions trapped in an unhappy marriage, and to whom he confides his ambitions and sorrows. While Susman does not match this character exactly, there are some resemblances. She too had an uneasy marriage, and her religious views were the cause of some friction between her and Kracauer.[10] His letters to her suggest that he was eager to impress her with his intellectual labors on behalf of the "severe goddess" of philosophical rigor. Indeed, he twice referred to his "quixotic" labors in the intellectual arena.[11] Since the story was written before these letters, it is not a matter of a portrait of his relationship with Susman, but rather, in a much more surprising gesture, his aesthetic constructions have become a model for his conduct in reality.

This aestheticizing impulse is one of the aspects of the Quixote myth that Kracauer abandoned in the shift towards Sancho Panza. Kracauer would regard with suspicion the idea that art could subsume the fullness of human experience. As a theme it emerged in the superficial aesthetic unities permitted by *ratio* in *The Detective Novel*, again in his programmatic manifesto, "The Artist of this Age," and, most directly, in his Holzapfel polemic. Similarly, artists could not become prophets. Culture could reveal the world in its negativity; it could gesture towards a vanished truth, but it could not take over the role that religion had once occupied. This meant that culture had to be accepted in its present fragmentary state; moreover, it should not be condemned for its alleged superficiality and incoherence, but rather must be interpreted for what this fragmentation reveals about the society that created it. In this way the vanished "truth contents" of religion, disfigured and scattered throughout the multiplicity of cultural forms, might yet be glimpsed. This privileging of religion over culture is, thus, not a position that is meant to short-change culture, but rather to restrict it to certain bounds; religion becomes a negative foil to culture. Nonetheless, it is remarkable that Kracauer was still voicing this position in 1924, two years after he had distanced himself from the pioneers of religious revival. The reference to grace in his review of Holzapfel is all the more striking when one compares it with his earlier usage in his novella of the same name. "Do you not believe in something like an inner grace that at some moment steps into the life of every individual?" asks Frau Ilse, the protagonist's ambiguously platonic friend[12]. This theological subtext persisted in Kracauer's work, and, I would argue, determined his position in his dispute with Vietta. This was not the result of a concealed religious sentiments; but rather a theological impulse to secularize what was valuable from religion, to find its secular components where they lay fragmented in modernity. In a sense, it is a theology of the flâneur who finds no shelter in the churches and synagogues, but also rejects the promises of material progress and secularized versions of the messianic. In this sense, as Pecora has argued, Kracauer can only be described as a purely "secular critic" with some reservations.[13]

This means that secular criticism was intertwined with theological undercurrents and that the relationship between culture and religion remained unresolved. The philosopher Ortega y Gasset wrote in his 1914 study of Quixote:

> Faced with the problematic character of life, culture . . . represents a treasury of principles. We can argue about the principles best suited to solve that problem, but whatever they may be, they must be principles; and a principle, to be a principle, must begin by not being a problem. This is the difficulty with which religion is faced and which has always kept it at variance with other forms of human culture, especially with reason. The religious spirit links the mystery of life with still darker and higher mysteries, whereas life appears to us to be potentially solvable or, at least not unsolvable *a limine*.[14]

Kracauer was probably not aware of this work, though certainly by the end of the 1920s the Spanish philosopher was familiar to him.[15] Nonetheless, Ortega y Gasset's references to a connection with the higher mysteries (*spheres* in Kracauer's preferred terminology) suggests that the nexus of religion and culture remained a thorn in the side of critical discourse more generally, and indeed, it is reminiscent of Brod's division between "noble" and "ignoble" misfortune. Culture can be deployed against the latter, but not the former. From Ortega y Gasset's perspective the entrance of religion in cultural criticism would be a complicating factor, a confusion of unsolvable mysteries with the quotidian problems of society; in Kracauer's terms it would run the risk of allowing cultural forms to be masked by an aura of timeless mystery and, therefore, to become naturalized. Thus, Kracauer directed his critical efforts against "natural forces" and "myth," where the aura of religion threatens to become ideology. Yet, the theological dilemma persisted as a negative condition of his criticism, as if he could not dispense with theological concepts as a necessary spur to his writing.

This is most evident in his critique of the rational autonomous subject that was elaborated in *The Detective Novel*. The detective is the representative of *ratio*, an unreflective or "clouded reason" that subordinates reality but never actually grasps it. To Kracauer the real was conceptualized in material and theological terms, as a sphere that resists the quantifying impulses and categories of instrumental reason. As a result the door is opened for a different kind of reason, what he referred to as a "genial cleverness . . . that in no way was identical with capitalist *ratio*."[16] For Kracauer, the representative of this "genial cleverness" was Sherlock Holmes, whom he described as a "knight" or a "Don Quixote in reverse" (*umgekehrten Don Quichote*). However, the quixotic figure was incomplete in itself, Kracauer argued, which was why Conan Doyle invented the complimentary figure of Dr. Watson. The close connections between the genial form of reason and the claims of reality were expressed in this partnership with Watson, whom Kracauer described as the most "striking" demonstration of Conan Doyle's "powers of intuition." Watson, he stated, "circled around Holmes as the earth circles around the sun"; the duo were "twin stars."[17] Here, he still valorizes Quixote, but in a more complex variation; now he incorporates the earthbound dimension of Watson/Panza even as he retains its orientation to the Quixotic or utopian element. This orientation toward the quixotic is why, as Dagmar Barnouw has argued, Kracauer was adamantly opposed to Adorno's understanding of Panza as an uncritical allegiance to empiricism.[18]

It is only after 1945 that Kracauer conceives of the Quixote/Panza relationship in terms that emphasize the decisive significance of Panza. To Adorno he wrote near the end of 1963 that "there is, as you know, a good bit of Sancho Panza in me."[19] Similarly, he contrasted himself to the quixotic impulses of his friend Bloch. "Your tempestuousness," he wrote to Bloch in 1965, "takes the breath away from the Sancho Panza in me."[20] Bloch countered by pointing out that Cervantes never allowed Panza to appear without Quixote, that Panza was no "proxy" (*Statthalter*) for Quixote, and, moreover, that he doubted that Panza on his own could have written a novel such as *Ginster*. Kracauer conceded the point, but also noted that the "utopian impulse" was not reserved to Quixote, but resided in Panza as well.[21] Indeed, he referred to the vision of Panza that appeared in a short tale by Kafka published posthumously in 1935.[22] In the Kafka parable, Quixote is a "devil" created by Panza who then has adventures in the world and who Panza follows out of a sense of obligation. This attitude towards the Quixote figure allowed Kracauer to distance himself from the problem of Quixote's fraught relationship with reality; instead the crux of the problem is an internal conflict in the individual in which Panza represents the contact with the real that, for instance, Kracauer's protagonist in "Grace" was unable to support.[23] Quixote was then conceived of as a representative of the utopian ideal, the negative ground that spurred the critical approach to the material world. Thus, he draws out of Panza the "genial cleverness" that was expressed in his proverbial wisdom and pragmatism; the two figures become part of an inner dialectic. In this respect, Quixote has a function that is reminiscent of Kracauer's view of photography, whereby the photographic image exposed ideas of order as something temporary and fundamentally "provisional."[24] As one of his fellow German émigrés stated, the madness of Quixote "illuminates everything that crosses his path and leaves it in a state of gay confusion." In the fallout of this chaos, Panza "lives himself into" Quixote.[25] Therefore, the shift from Quixote to Panza should not be understood as a simple abandonment of the utopian, but rather it was a means of redefining utopian desires.

The relationship of Quixote and Panza, with its shifting emphases, was readily amenable to different interpretations. As Carl Schmitt wrote in one of his earliest essays, numerous writers had tried to resist the conventional readings of Quixote in order to connect his legendary persona to a specific philosophical or political agenda.[26] As one study of the reception of Cervantes in Weimar Germany has argued, the figure of Quixote was informed by a wide array of meanings in the cultural politics of Weimar.[27] Ernst Jünger, for instance, read Cervantes with what he called a genuine "Spanish earnestness" that found little humor in the novel.[28] He revered Quixote for his desire to coerce hidden meaning from a disenchanted world. In the fight against the windmills, Jünger saw a "real and, at the same time, magical experience" in which Quixote revealed our absolute subordination to chance (*Zufall*). In the moment that the supreme rule of fortune is uncovered, Jünger imagines himself as a "knight upon the cusp of the divine error of life and the divine truth in which this error meaningfully expires."[29] In this framework the quixotic impulse was not simply madness, and he lamented that Cervantes chose to end his novel with Quixote's final submission to the church—a "deplorable concession to morality of lower natures."[30] Instead, the quixotic impulse to find deeper meaning hidden behind the real was nothing less than the "transformation" of the "will to power" into a "will to interpretation." For Jünger then, Quixote is a heroic model for the modern subject.[31] The relationship to Panza has little place in this reading, and, hence, there is no resistance to the hero's wildest imaginings.

Jünger's use of Quixote to validate a heroic model of the interpreting individual should cause some alarm, and Jünger's contemporaries were alert to the problems that could arise from his conception. Jünger allows the simple assertion of the will to compensate for error; moreover, he incorporates the will in a fashion that renders it difficult to imagine any means of distinguishing between the relative merits or flaws of different interpretations. In this situation, Jünger readily emphasizes feeling and instinct over intellect, reason and science.[32] We are in a Schmittian universe where what matters most is the principle of decision or will in itself, for governance is based on the sovereign decision. By including Panza in his model of the quixotic, Kracauer sought to defuse precisely this danger; Panza represented a check on the quixotic imagination. Whether this check was successful, however, is another matter. As the Kafka parable suggests, Panza also preserves a utopian ingredient, a potentially unfettered drive to elicit hidden meanings from prosaic reality. Kafka was not alone in this attempt to complicate the relationship of Quixote and Panza; contemporaries such as Miguel de Unamuno, Ernst Weiß, and, later, Erich Auerbach all saw in the figure of Panza a torch bearer of the quixotic legacy, a figure who was deeply entwined in the quixotic adventure. In 1926, an excerpt of Unamuno's *The Life of Don Quixote and Sancho* appeared in the feuilleton of the *FZ*. The excerpt was drawn from the final chapter concerning the knight's death.[33] Death, however, is a misnomer as Unamuno declares that Sancho is actually the "inheritor" of the quixotic spirit, and that Sancho will venture out into the world again and continue the legacy of his master: "Preserve, O my God, Sancho in his dreams and faith." Unamuno even mentions the possible resurrection of Quixote. To be sure, Kracauer never went this far in his references to Panza. Indeed, in the aftermath of World War II, Kracauer questioned the consuming rage for interpretation that he believed distinguished Weimar culture. In a surprisingly deprecating and unpublished essay, he even went as far as to attribute this trait to Jewish intellectuals; but a post-1945 reckoning of this sort probably should be understood, in part, as a response to the trauma of the war.[34]

After 1945 hindsight led others to explore their misgivings concerning the meaning of the Quixote figure. In 1947, Wilhelm Hausenstein, a translator and art historian, and a close friend to both Reifenberg and Picard, published a short dialogue to celebrate the 400th anniversary of the birth of Cervantes. The celebration was not unclouded, however, and Hausenstein's text mingled admiration with suspicion. In the course of the work, the positive estimates of Quixote are interrogated by two friends named Cardenio and Lucinde. True, argues Cardenio, there was none "bolder" than Quixote in terms of connecting thought and action; nonetheless, he does so in ways that violently force together the imaginative and the practical, and he compromises both as a result. Quixote suffers in his dealings with the world. Moreover, he suffers in a way that offends "human dignity" and reminds us that "out of the humanity of the Renaissance there emerged an unsettling inhumanity."[35] Prodding further in this direction, Cardenio then asks, has not Cervantes shown that "amid human relations, the truth, more or less always and in general remains placed amid the obfuscating and overshadowing danger of error"?[36] In other words, does Quixote not risk a fall into the mistaken and the inhumane? Given the year the dialogue appeared, this statement crosses into murky territory, a full discussion of which cannot be undertaken here. The potential to conflate truth and error, however, does not lead Hausenstein to pursue an apologetics grounded in the limits of reason, but rather towards its opposite—a warning that "one must become a *reasonable* Don Quixote."[37] Here, I would argue, he had in mind a reflective reason close to what Kracauer meant when he spoke of "genial cleverness."

How one should arrive at this position in a flood of interpretations and opinions was difficult to see, and Kracauer's efforts, throughout his career, were addressed to this problem of grounding one's interpretations in a world of relative judgments and infinite perspectives. This multiplicity made interpretation a risky and potentially dangerous endeavor. As Thomas Mann wrote, while reading Cervantes on his first voyage to the United States in 1934:

> History is the common reality for which humanity is born, for which one must be capable, and in which Don Quixote's maladjusted gallantry fails. That is endearing and laughable. However, what if it was a matter of an anti-idealistic, a dark and pessimistic Don Quixote who believed in violence, a Don Quixote of brutality, who nonetheless remained a Don Quixote? The humor and melancholy of Cervantes has not brought us so far.[38]

These questions concerning the nature of the quixotic legacy, questions raised by Mann, Kracauer, and Hausenstein, do not lend themselves to easy answers. To be sure, the more malignant Don Quixotes of these years were recognizable, and Kracauer was quite willing to abandon the means of "indirect communication" where it was a clear question of political barbarism and violence. Thus, he chastised the *FZ* for taking a much too tolerant line against the rise of National Socialism.[39] However, he did not address his work towards those who readily embraced Nazism, but rather to those who he saw as wavering in a confused state, beset by competing ideologies and by religious sentiments and skepticism. One ought to recognize the darker side of Quixote when it wears the uniform of the SA or SS, but Kracauer was concerned with more than this. He also feared what he saw as a collapse of the minute and often unspoken values and codes of behavior that constituted the fabric of everyday life; here the task of interpretation was more difficult but just as important. It was in this domain that the changes threatening German society frightened him just as much as the conduct of politics. In a letter to Adorno in 1930, he discussed what he thought was part of a deeper rupture in German society:

> A devastation rules over this land, and I know for sure that it is not just a matter of capitalism. That this country can become so bestial has in no way only an economic reason. How should I formulate this? When in France, where there is also much to criticize, I always notice what has been destroyed at home: basic decency, the whole of good nature, and with it all the trust that men and women have in one another. Since for us, no revolution will enliven an exhausted folk—as perhaps in Russia—I do not believe in the healing powers of the revolutionary urge. I recognize only a general mess (*Schlamassel*) and it would be best to me if we could manage to muddle forward in this fashion.[40]

Here, Kracauer describes a pervasive cynicism and indifference that Hausenstein would later identify with the age of Cervantes. Quixote too arose out of a period very close to our "modern indifferentism," a period given over to the "frivolity of artistic and theological improvisations."[41] The problem of Quixote was a modern problem, and one could revere him on account of his challenge to indifference and the status quo, but there was a danger present whenever Quixote appeared without the necessary corrective of Panza.

In one of the famous episodes of Cervantes's novel, the knight interrupts his squire as he is telling a story that recounts the shepherding of many goats across a river.[42] Quixote objects to Panza's insistence that the crossing of every goat must find its place in the narrative. Quixote remonstrates with Panza that this is no way to tell a story, that if they all went across he should just say so and not recount the details concerning the crossing of each and every goat. Quixote here insists on the need to shape experience; he gives precedence to the claims of aesthetic unity over and above that of truthful chronicle. The claims of a generalizing and rational narrative triumph over an unseemly chaos of particulars.[43] Panza, of course, states that he knows of no other way to tell the story and, on account of his lord's interruption, he is no longer able to finish. Kracauer's criticism attempts to mediate this dispute. He argues, with Panza, that the concrete details of experience do matter, that each goat does have its legitimate claim, and that these claims represent an existential imperative that should be set against the claims of *ratio* or any totalizing system of philosophy, art, or politics. In this regard, the triumphant narrative of secularization and the counternarrative of religious revival both served the fragmented modern subject poorly. An act of mediation between them was needed, the cultivation of a "secular hermeneutics" that would afford the individual a foothold in a bewildering modern landscape. Kracauer's call to "use your intellect" was, in this context, a demanding one that found limited resonance. The desire to do justice to reality, to represent it in all of its complexity, was drowned out by the totalizing ideologies that poisoned political life in the first part of the century. The story of Sancho Panza was abruptly broken off, though as Panza stated, there were a good many interesting things still to tell.

Notes

1. Carlo Ginzburg, "Clues: Roots of an Evidential Paradigm," in *Clues, Myths, and the Historical Method*, trans. John and Anne C. Tedeschi (Baltimore, 1989), 96–125. See also Olivier Agard, "Les elements d'autobiographie intellectuelle dans *History*," in *Siegfried Kracauer: penseur de l'histoire*, ed. Philippe Despoix and Peter Schöttler (Paris, 2006), 149–50.
2. Wilhelm Hausenstein, *Zwiegespräch über den Don Quijote* (Munich, 1948), 12–13.
3. Dolf Sternberger, "Charlie Chaplin, der Idiot, Don Quijote: Versuch über die komische Existenz," *Die Kreatur* (1929–1930): 392–99; and Kracauer to Sternberger, 18 August 1928, Sternberger Nachlass, DLA.
4. Søren Kierkegaard, *Either/Or: A Fragment of Life*, trans. Alastair Hannay (London, 1992), 95.
5. Søren Kierkegaard, *Concluding Unscientific Postscript to* Philosophical Fragments I. *Kierkegaard's Writings* 12.1, trans. Howard V. Hong and Edna H. Hong (Princeton, 1992), 195–96.
6. Kierkegaard, *Concluding Unscientific Postscript*, 35.
7. See the discussion of *The Moment of Vision* in Pattison, *Kierkegaard, Religion, and the Nineteenth-Century Crisis of Culture*, 22–23.
8. See the comments on the significance of Quixote in Oschmann, *Auszug aus der Innerlichkeit*, 28–29.
9. Kracauer, "Die Gnade," in *Werke* 7, 550.
10. Susman separated from her husband, the painter Eduard Bendemann, in 1928.
11. Kracauer to Susman, 10 February 1920 and 2 May 1920, SN, DLA.
12. Kracauer, *Werke* 7, 558.
13. Pecora, *Secularization and Cultural Criticism*, 2–6 and 67–100.
14. José Ortega y Gasset, *Meditations on Quixote* (New York, 1963), 99.
15. Kracauer was close to the Spain correspondent of the *FZ*, Fritz Wahl, who knew Ortega y Gasset. After Kracauer's flight to France, Wahl tried unsuccessfully to find work for Kracauer writing for the *Revista de Occidente*. See Wahl to Kracauer, 4 January 1934, quoted in Belke and Renz, *Siegfried Kracauer*, 77–78. While *Meditations on Don Quixote* was not translated into any other language before World War II, Ernst Robert Curtius referred to the work in a more general discussion of Ortega y Gasset in 1924; see "Spanische Perspektiven (Ortega y Gasset)" *Die neue Rundschau* 35, no. 2 (1924): 1229–47.
16. Kracauer, "Conan Doyle," *FZ*, 9 July 1930, Abendblatt; reprinted in *Werke* 5.3, 274–75.

17. Kracauer, "Conan Doyle," in *Werke* 5.3, 275.
18. Barnouw, *Critical Realism*, 151.
19. Kracauer to Adorno, 23 December 1963, in *Briefwechsel, 1923–1966*, 633. In this case, his identification also serves the purpose of placing him at odds with both Hegel and Heidegger, and expressing his sympathy for Kant and his "aversions to ontological remnants." He declared himself to be in complete sympathy with the Adorno's polemic against Heidegger in his *Jargon of Authenticity*.
20. Kracauer, letter to Bloch (1965) in Bloch, *Briefe* 1, 401.
21. Bloch to Kracauer, 11 September 1965, *Briefe* 1, 404; and Kracauer to Bloch, 15 September 1965, 405. He also stated that his Erasmus interpretation in *History* corresponded to Panza's utopian motives, concluding his remarks on Erasmus with the reflection that "the middle way was the direct road to Utopia," see Kracauer, *History*, 9–15.
22. Franz Kafka, *Parables and Paradoxes* (New York, 1961), 178–79.
23. Oschmann, *Auszug aus der Innerlichkeit*, 28–30.
24. Kracauer, "Photography," in *Mass Ornament*, 62.
25. Erich Auerbach, *Mimesis: The Representation of Reality in Western Literature* (New York, 1957), 309–10.
26. Carl Schmitt, "Don Quijote und sein Publikum," *Die Rheinlande* 22 (1912): 348–50. Schmitt expresses some disdain for many of these "foolish" or "learned interpretations."
27. Kindt and Müller, "Zweimal Cervantes," 230.
28. Jünger, *The Adventurous Heart*, quoted in Kindt and Müller, "Zweimal Cervantes," 231–232.
29. Jünger, *Briefen eines Nationalisten*, quoted in Kindt and Müller, "Zweimal Cervantes," 233–34.
30. Jünger, *Briefen*, quoted in Kindt and Müller, "Zweimal Cervantes," 233.
31. Kindt and Müller, "Zweimal Cervantes," 240.
32. Kindt and Müller, "Zweimal Cervantes," 249.
33. Miguel de Unamuno, "Don Quixotes Tod," *FZ*, 19 May 1926, 1st Morgenblatt.
34. Kracauer, Untitled (72.3591), KN, DLA. Miriam Hansen suggests that this essay was probably written before Kracauer had full knowledge of the Holocaust. See Hansen, "Decentric Perspectives," 52 n.11.
35. Hausenstein, *Zwiegespräch*, 22–23.
36. Hausenstein, *Zwiegespräch*, 45–46.
37. Hausenstein, *Zwiegespräch*, 48.
38. Thomas Mann, *Meerfahrt mit Don Quijote* (Frankfurt am Main, 2002). See the diary entry dated 20 May 1934, 26–28.
39. Kracauer to Reifenberg, 12 February 1933, KN, DLA.
40. Kracauer, letter to Adorno dated 24 August 1930, in *Briefwechsel, 1923–1966*, 246–47.
41. Hausenstein, *Zwiegespräch*, 44.
42. Cervantes, *The Adventures of Don Quixote*, trans. J. M. Cohen (Hammondsworth, 1987), 153–55.
43. Anthony J. Cascardi, "Don Quixote and the Invention of the Novel," in *The Cambridge Companion to Cervantes*, ed. Anthony Cascardi (Cambridge, 2002), 73–74.

Select Bibliography

Archives

Bayerische Staatsbibliothek, Munich
  Otto Crusius Papers—Crusiusiana I

Bundesarchiv, Berlin-Lichterfelde
  Das Neue Tagebuch

Deutsches Literaturarchiv, Marbach am Neckar (DLA)
  Gottfried Benn Papers
  Alfred Döblin Papers
  Wilhelm Hausenstein Papers
  Siegfried Kracauer Papers
  Max Picard Papers
  Benno Reifenberg Papers
  Max Rychner Papers
  Dolf Sternberger Papers
  Margaret Susman Papers

Deutsches Exilarchiv 1933–1945, Deutsches Nationalbibliothek, Frankfurt am Main
  Werner Thormann Papers

Johannes Senckenberg Bibliothek, Frankfurt am Main
  Leo Löwenthal Archive

International Institute for Social History, Amsterdam
  Gottfried Salomon-Delatour Papers

Leo Baeck Institute, Berlin and New York
  Franz Rosenzweig Collection (New York)
  Efraim Frisch Collection (Berlin)
  Kurt Hirschfeld (Berlin)

Württembergische Landesbibliothek, Stuttgart
  Hermann Herrigel Papers

Newspapers and Periodicals

Frankfurter Zeitung (FZ)
Die Literarische Welt
Die Neue Rundschau (NR)
Neue Schweizer Rundschau (NSR)
Die Tat

Works by Kracauer and Contemporaries

Adorno, Theodor W. "Kierkegaard noch einmal." *Neue deutsche Hefte* 10, no. 95 (1963): 5–25.
———. *The Jargon of Authenticity*, translated by Knut Tarnowski and Frederic Will. Evanston, IL: Northwestern University Press, 1973.
———. "Henkel, Krug und frühe Erfahrung." *Noten zur Literatur IV*. Frankfurt am Main: Suhrkamp, 1974.
———. "The Actuality of Philosophy." *Telos* 31 (Spring 1977): 120–33.
———. "Spengler after the Decline." *Prisms*, translated by Samuel and Sherry Weber. Cambridge, MA: MIT Press, 1981.
———. "Fällige Revision: Zu Schweppenhäusers Buch über Kierkegaard und Hegel." *Gesammelte Schriften: Vermischte Schriften* 20.1, edited by Rolf Tiedemann, 257–261. Frankfurt am Main: Suhrkamp, 1986.
———. "Nach Kracauers Tod." *Gesammelte Schriften. Vermischte Schriften* 20.1, edited by Rolf Tiedemann, 194–96. Frankfurt am Main: Suhrkamp, 1986.
———. *Kierkegaard: Construction of the Aesthetic*, edited and translated by Robert Hullot-Kentor. Minneapolis: University of Minnesota Press, 1989.
———. "The Curious Realist: On Siegfried Kracauer." *New German Critique* 54 (Autumn 1991): 159–77.
———. "The Idea of Natural-History." In Robert Hullot-Kentor, *Things beyond Resemblance: Collected Essays on Theodor W. Adorno*, edited and translated by Robert Hullot-Kentor, 252–69. New York: Columbia University Press, 2006.
Apollinaire, Guillaume. *Alcools: Poems by Guillaume Apollinaire*, translated by Donald Revell. Hanover and London: Wesleyan University Press, 1995.
Arendt, Hannah. "Søren Kierkegaard." *FZ*, 29 January 1932. In *Essays in Understanding, 1930–1954*, translated by Robert and Rita Kimber, 44–49. New York: Harcourt, Brace and Company, 1994.
Aster, Ernst von. "Die Krise der bürgerlichen Ideologie." *Die neue Rundschau*, 42, no. 2 (1931): 1–13.
Astrow, Wladimir. "Holzapfels *Panideal*." *Die Tat* 16 (1924/1925): 506–20.
———. "Holzapfels *Panideal*: eine Erwiderung." *FZ*, 19 March 1924, Morgenblatt.
Auden, W. H. "The Guilty Vicarage: Notes on the Detective Story, by an Addict." *Harper's Magazine* 196 (May 1948): 406–12.

Auerbach, Erich. *Mimesis: The Representation of Reality in Western Literature.* New York: Doubleday, 1957.
Benjamin, Walter. *Illuminations: Essays and Reflections,* translated by Harry Zohn. New York: Schocken, 1969.
———. *Reflections: Essays, Aphorisms, Autobiographical Writings,* translated by Edmund Jephcott. New York: Schocken, 1986.
———. *Selected Writings. Volume Two, 1927–1934,* translated by Rodney Livingstone and others, edited by Michael W. Jennings, Howard Eiland, and Gary Smith. Cambridge, MA: Harvard University Press, 1999.
———. *The Writer of Modern Life: Essays on Charles Baudelaire,* translated by Howard Eiland, Edmund Jephcott, Rodney Livingstone, and Harry Zohn. Cambridge, MA: Harvard University Press, 2006
———. *Kairos: Schriften zur Philosophie,* edited by Ralph Konersmann. Frankfurt am Main: Suhrkamp, 2007.
Benn, Gottfried. *Doppelleben: Zwei Selbstdarstellungen,* 2nd ed. Stuttgart: Klett-Cotta, 2005.
Bloch, Ernst. "Aktualität und Utopie: Zu Lukács *Geschichte und Klassenbewußtsein.*" In *Philosophische Aufsätze zur objektiven Phantasie. Gesamtausgabe* 10. Frankfurt am Main: Suhrkamp, 1969.
———. *The Utopian Function of Art and Literature,* translated by Jack Zipes and Frank Mecklenberg. Cambridge, MA: MIT Press, 1988.
———. *Heritage of our Times,* translated by Neville and Stephen Plaice. Cambridge: Polity, 1991.
———. *The Spirit of Utopia,* translated by Anthony Nassar. Stanford, CA: Stanford University Press, 2000.
Breton, André. *Break of Day,* translated by Mark Polizzotti and Mary Anne Caws. Lincoln: University of Nebraska Press, 1999.
Briefs, Goetz. *Untergang des Abendlandes. Christentum und Sozialismus: Eine Auseinandersetzung mit Oswald Spengler.* Freiburg im Breisgau: Herder, 1920.
Brod, Max. *Heidentum, Christentum, Judentum: Ein Bekenntnisbuch.* 2 vols. Leipzig: Kurt Wolff, 1921.
———. *Paganism, Christianity, Judaism: A Confession of Faith,* translated by William Wolf. Tuscaloosa: University of Alabama Press, 1970.
Bry, Carl Christian. *Verkappte Religionen: Kritik des kollektiven Wahns.* Gotha: Verlag Friedrich Andreas Perthes, 1924.
Buber, Martin. *Ich und Du.* Leipzig: Insel, 1923.
Buber, Martin, and Franz Rosenzweig. *Scripture and Translation,* translated by Lawrence Rosenwald with Everett Fox. Bloomington: Indiana University Press, 1994.
Chesterton, G. K. "A Defense of Detective Stories." In *The Defendant.* London and New York: Dodd, 1904.
Curtius, Ernst Robert. "Spanische Perspektiven (Ortega y Gasset)." *Die neue Rundschau,* 35, no. 2 (1924): 1229–47.
Döblin, Alfred. "Nochmal: Wissen und Verändern." *Die neue Rundschau,* 42, no. 2 (1931): 181–201.

Döblin, Alfred. "Vorwort zu einer erneuten Aussprache." *Die neue Rundschau*, 42, no. 2 (1931): 100–103.

———. *Wissen und Verändern! Offene Briefe an einen jungen Menschen*. Berlin: Samuel Fischer, 1931.

———. *Schriften zur Politik und Gesellschaft*, edited by Walter Muschg. Olten and Freiburg im Breisgau: Walter, 1972.

———. "Vom alten zum neuen Naturalismus." *Schriften zu Ästhetik, Poetik und Literatur*, edited by Erich Kleinschmidt, 263–69. Olten: Walter, 1989.

Doyle, Arthur Conan. *The Adventures of Sherlock Holmes and the Memoirs of Sherlock Holmes*. London: Penguin, 2001.

Editorial. "Nun sag,' wie halt Du's mit der- Politik?" *FZ*, 25 December 1928, Morgenblatt.

Epstein, Tilly. "Ein Leben im Philanthropin." In *Frankfurter jüdische Erinnerungen: ein Lesebuch zur Sozialgeschichte, 1864–1951*, edited by the Kommission zur Erforschung der Geschichte der Frankfurter Juden, 201–8. Sigmaringen: Thorbecke, 1997.

Fiesel, Eva. *Die Sprachphilosophie der deutschen Romantik*. Tübingen: Mohr, 1927.

Flake, Otto, Erich Mosse, and Siegfried Kracauer. "Stimmen zu 'Schule der Weisheit': Schlußwort." *FZ*, 20 October 1921, Morgenblatt.

Gadamer, Hans-Georg. *Philosophische Lehrjahre: eine Rückschau*. Frankfurt am Main: Klostermann, 1977.

———. "Die deutsche Philosophie zwischen den beiden Weltkriegen." *Neue deutsche Hefte* 195, no. 4.3 (1987): 451–67.

Gött, Ludwig. "Der geistige Mensch und sein sozialer Beruf." *Die neue Rundschau*, 42, no. 2 (1931): 76–82.

Guardini, Romano. *Liturgische Bildung: Versuche*. Berg Rothenfels am Main: Deutsches Quickbornhaus, 1923.

Haas, Willy. *Gestalten: Essays zur Literatur und Gesellschaft*. Zurich: Propyläen, 1962.

———. ed. *Zeitgemäßes aus der Literarischen Welt von 1925–1932*. Stuttgart: Cotta, 1963.

Haecker, Theodor. "Nachwort." *Der Brenner* 4, no. 20 (15 July 1914): 886–908.

Hausenstein, Wilhelm. *Zwiegespräch über den Don Quijote*. Munich: Kösel, 1948.

Hegemann, Werner. "Kathedralen, Bodenwacher und das Kollektiv. Aufsatz über Kollektivkunstwerke und die Neugestaltung des Leipziger und Potsdamer Platzes in Berlin." *Die Weltbühne*, 27, no. 1 (1931): 692–96.

———. "Der historische Schicksals- und Detektivroman. *Die neue Rundschau*, 43, no. 2 (1932): 260–271.

Herrigel, Hermann. "Zur Kritik des deutschen Idealismus—Vorrede eines ungedruckten Buches." *Die Tat*, 14, no. 2 (May 1922): 114–21.

———. *Das neue Denken*. Berlin: Schneider, 1928.

———. *Zwischen Frage und Antwort. Gedanken zur Kulturkrise*. Berlin: Lambert Schneider, 1930.

———. "Denken dieser Zeit: Fakultäten und Nationen treffen sich in Davos." *FZ*, 23 April 1931, Abendblatt.

Herwegen, Ildefons. *Lumen Christi: Gesammelte Aufsätze*. Munich: Theatiner Verlag, 1924.

Heuser, Kurt. "Glauben und Verändern." *Die neue Rundschau*, 42, no. 2 (1931): 86–91.

Hirsch, Leo. "Der platonische Film." *Neue Schweizer Rundschau*, 23, no. 1 (January 1930): 63–72.

Hocke, Gustav René. *Im Schatten des Leviathan: Lebenserinnerungen 1908–1978*. Munich: Deutscher Kunstverlag, 2004.

Holzapfel, Rudolf Maria. *Panideal: Psychologie der sozialen Gefühle*. 2nd ed. Jena: Eugen Diederichs, 1923.

Huelsenbeck, Richard. *Memoirs of a Dada Drummer*, translated by Joachim Neugroschel. Berkeley: University of California Press, 1991.

Jaspers, Karl. *Vernunft und Existenz: Aula-Voordrachten der Rijksuniversiteit te Groningen 1*. Groningen: J. B. Wolters, 1935.

Jünger, Ernst. *The Adventurous Heart: Figures and Capriccios*, translated by Thomas Friese. Candor: Telos, 2012.

Kafka, Franz. *Parables and Paradoxes*. New York: Schocken, 1961.

Kessler, Harry. *Berlin in Lights: The Diaries of Count Harry Kessler*, edited and translated by Charles Kessler. New York: Grove, 1999.

Keyserling, Hermann. *The World in the Making: Die neuentstehende Welt*. London: Jonathan Cape, 1927.

Kierkegaard, Søren. "Kritik der Gegenwart I and II," translated by Theodor Haecker. In *Der Brenner* 4, no. 19 (1 July 1914) and 4, no. 20 (15 July 1914): 815–49 and 869–86.

———. "Die Gesichtspunkt für meine Wirksamkeit als Schriftsteller." In *Gesammelte Werke* 10, translated by Christoph Schrempf and Albert Dorner. Jena: Eugen Diederichs, 1922.

———. *The Present Age*, translated by Alexander Dru. New York: Harper and Row, 1962.

———. *Fear and Trembling*, translated by Alastair Hannay. London: Penguin, 1985.

———. *Philosophical Fragments/ Johannes Climacus. Kierkegaard's Writings* 7, translated by Howard V. Hong and Edna H. Hong. Princeton, NJ: Princeton University, Press, 1985.

———. *Either/Or: A Fragment of Life*, translated by Alastair Hannay. London: Penguin, 1992.

———. *Concluding Unscientific Postscript to* Philosophical Fragments I. *Kierkegaard's Writings* 12.1, translated by Howard V. Hong and Edna H. Hong. Princeton, NJ: Princeton University Press, 1992.

Kipper, Paul E. "Don Quixotes." *FZ*, 19 January 1921, 2nd Morgenblatt.

Klabund. "Zu Holzapfels Panideal." *FZ*, 20 February 1924, Abendblatt.

Klemperer, Viktor. *Curriculum Vitae: Erinnerungen eines Philologen II, 1881–1918*, Berlin: Rütten & Loening, 1989.

———. *Leben sammeln, nicht fragen wozu und woran: Tagebücher, 1918–1924*, vol. 2. Berlin: Aufbau, 1996.

Kluckhohn, Paul. *Persönlichkeit und Gemeinschaft. Studien zur Staatsauffassung der Deutschen Romantik. Deutsche Vierteljahrsschrift für Literaturwissenschaft und Geistesgeschichte 5.* Halle and Saale: Max Niemeyer, 1925.

Kracauer, Siegfried. *From Caligari to Hitler: A Psychological History of the German Film.* Princeton, NJ: Princeton University Press, 1947.

———. *Schriften.* 8 vols. Frankfurt am Main: Suhrkamp, 1971–1990.

———. *Der Detektiv-Roman: ein philosophischer Traktat.* Frankfurt am Main: Suhrkamp, 1979.

———. *Der verbotene Blick: Beobachtungen, Analysen, Kritiken,* edited by Johanna Rosenberg. Leipzig: Reclam, 1992.

———. *History: The Last Things before the Last.* Princeton, NJ: Markus Weiner, 1994.

———. "Murder Trials and Society." *Die neue Rundschau* 42 (March 1931). In *The Weimar Republic Sourcebook,* edited by Anton Kaes, Martin Jay, and Edward Dimendberg, 740–41. Berkeley: University of California Press, 1994.

———. *The Mass Ornament: Weimar Essays.* Cambridge, MA: Harvard University Press, 1995.

———. *Berliner Nebeneinander: Ausgewählte Feuilletons, 1930–1933,* edited by Andreas Volk. Zurich: Epoca, 1996.

———. *Theory of Film: The Redemption of Physical Reality.* Princeton, NJ: Princeton University Press, 1997.

———. *The Salaried Masses: Duty and Distraction in Weimar Germany,* translated by Quintin Hoare. London: Verso, 1998.

———. *Jacques Offenbach and the Paris of His Time,* translated by Gwenda David and Eric Mosbacher. New York: Zone Books, 2002.

———. *Werke.* 9 vols, edited by Inka Mülder-Bach and Ingrid Belke. Frankfurt am Main: Suhrkamp, 2004–2012.

Kuczynski, Jürgen. *Über die Unpraktischheit des deutschen Intellektuellen.* London: Free German League of Culture, 1944.

Lerbs, Karl, ed. *Der Griff aus dem Dunkel: Detektivgeschichten zeitgenossisches Erzählers.* Leipzig: J. Singer, 1924.

Lessing, Theodor. "Nach dem Urteil." *Prager Tagblatt,* 6 February 1931.

Lion, Ferdinand. "Bemerkungen zu Spenglers 'Untergang des Abendlandes.'" *Der neue Merkur* 4, no. 4 (April to September 1920): 208–22.

Löwenthal, Leo. *Mitmachen wollte ich nie: Ein autobiographisches Gespräch mit Helmut Dubiel.* Frankfurt am Main: Suhrkamp, 1980.

Lukács, Georg. *Die Seele und die Formen. Essays.* Berlin: E. Fleischel, 1911.

———. *History and Class Consciousness,* translated by Rodney Livingstone. London: Merlin, 1971.

———. *Theory of the Novel: A Historic-Philosophical Essay on the Forms of Great Epic Literature,* translated by Anna Bostock. Cambridge, MA: MIT Press, 1971.

———. *Selected Correspondence 1902–1920. Dialogues with Weber, Simmel, Buber, Mannheim and Others,* edited by Judith Marcus and Zoltán Tar. Budapest: Corvina Kiadó, 1986.

———. *Soul and Form*, translated by Anna Bostock, edited by John T. Sanders and Katie Terezakis. New York: Columbia University Press, 2010.
Mach, Ernst. "Vorwort." In Rudolf Maria Holzapfel, *Panideal: Psychologie der sozialen Gefühle*, vii-viii. Leipzig: Barth, 1901
Mann, Thomas. *Three Essays*, translated by Helen Lowe-Porter. New York: Knopf, 1929.
———. *Reflections of an Unpolitical Man*, translated by Walter Morris. New York: F. Ungar, 1983.
———. "Verjüngende Bücher: Kafka—Schwob—Schmeljow—Graf." *FZ*, 17 April 1927. Reprinted in *Franz Kafka: Kritik und Rezeption, 1924–1938*, edited by Jürgen Born, 168–69. Frankfurt am Main: Suhrkamp, 1983.
———. *Meerfahrt mit Don Quijote*. Frankfurt am Main: Fischer, 2002.
Marc, Franz. *Briefe, Aufzeichnungen und Aphorismen*. 2 vols. Berlin: Paul Cassirer, 1920.
Mehnert, Klaus. "Das Kollektiv auf dem Vormarsch." *Die neue Rundschau* 42, no. 2 (1931): 82–85.
Messac, Régis. *Le "detective novel" et l'influence de pensée scientifique*. Paris: H. Champion, 1929.
Michel, Ernst, ed. *Kirche und Wirklichkeit: ein katholisches Zeitbuch*. Jena: Eugen Diederichs, 1923.
Michel, Wilhelm. *Der abendländische Zeus. Aufsätze über Rudolf Steiner/ Oswald Spengler/ Hölderlin u.a.* Leipzig and Hannover: P. Stegemann, 1923.
Mirgeler, Albert. "Jugendbewegung vor dem Ende: Eine Abrechnung mit Romano Guardini und dem Quickborn." In *Kirche und Wirklichkeit: Ein katholisches Zeitbuch*, edited by Ernst Michel, 180–185. Jena: Eugen Diederichs, 1923.
Musil, Robert. *Precision and Soul: Essays and Addresses*, edited and translated by Burton Pike and David S. Luft. Chicago: University of Chicago Press, 1990.
———. *Man without Qualities*, translated by Sophie Wilkins. 2 vols. New York: Knopf, 1995.
Neue Rundschau. "Wissen und Verändern. Vorbemerkung." *Die neue Rundschau* 42, no. 2 (1931): 71.
Noth, Ernst Erich. *Erinnerungen eines Deutschen*. Hamburg and Düsseldorf: Claasen, 1971.
Ortega y Gasset, José. *Meditations on Quixote*, translated by Evelyn Rugg and Diego Marin. New York: W. W. Norton, 1963.
Pannwitz, Rudolf. *Die Krisis der europäischen Kultur*. Nuremburg: Hans Carl, 1917.
Picard, Max. *Das Menschengesicht*. Munich: Delphin, 1929.
———. *Die Grenzen der Physiognomik*. Erlenbach-Zürich and Leipzig: Rentsch, 1937.
Pleßner, Helmuth. "Die Untergangsvision und Europa." *Der neue Merkur* 4, no. 5 (April–September 1920): 265–79.
Polgar, Alfred. "The Small Form." In *The Vienna Coffeehouse Wits, 1890–1938*, edited and translated by Harold B. Segel, 279–81. West Lafayette, IN: Purdue University Press, 1995.
Rosenzweig, Franz. *Franz Rosenzweig: Der Mensch und sein Werk: Gesammelte Schriften, Briefe und Tagebücher*, edited by Rachel Rosenzweig and Edith Rosenzweig-Scheinmann. 2 vols. The Hague: Martinus Nijhoff, 1979.

Rosenzweig, Franz. *The Star of Redemption*, translated by William Hallo. Notre Dame, IN: Notre Dame Press, 1985.

———. *Philosophical and Theological Writings*, translated and edited by Paul W. Franks and Michael L. Morgan. Indianapolis: Hackett, 2000.

Roth, Joseph. *Die Flucht ohne Ende: ein Bericht*. Reprinted in *Joseph Roth: Romane I*. Köln: Kiepenheuer & Witsch, 1975.

———. *Right and Left*, translated by Michael Hofmann. New York and Woodstock: Overlook, 1992.

Rychner, Max. "Was ist Modern?" *NSR* 23, no. 9 (September 1930): 641–44.

———. "Anmerkungen: Kapitalismus und schöne Literatur." *NSR* 24, no. 2 (1931): 81–94.

———. "Anmerkungen: Döblin warnt: weg von den Gebildeten." *NSR* 24, no. 5 (1931): 321–25.

———. "Eine Antwort Döblins." *NSR* 24, no. 9 (1931): 641.

———. *Zur europäischen Literatur zwischen zwei Weltkriegen*. 2nd ed. Zurich: Manesse, 1951.

Scheler, Max. *Die Ursachen des Deutschenhasses: Eine nationalpädagogisch Erörterung*. Leipzig: Kurt Wolff, 1917.

———. "Zur religiösen Erneuerung." *Hochland* 17, no. 1 (1918–1919): 5–21.

———. "Phänomenologie und Erkenntnis." In *Schriften aus dem Nachlass I: Zum Ethik und Erkenntnislehre*, edited by Maria Scheler. Bern: Francke, 1957.

Schmitt, Carl. "Don Quijote und das Publikum." *Die Rheinlande* 22 (1912): 348–50.

———. *Political Theology: Four Chapters on the Concept of Sovereignty*, translated by George Schwab. Chicago: University of Chicago Press, 2005.

Simmel, Georg. *Essays on Religion*, edited and translated by Horst Jürgen Helle with Ludwig Nieder. New Haven, CT: Yale University Press, 1997.

———. "Der Begriff und die Tragödie der Kultur." In *Aufsätze und Abhandlungen, Gesamtausgabe 12.1*, edited by Rüdiger Kramme and Angela Rammstedt, 194–223. Frankfurt am Main: Suhrkamp, 2001.

———. *Miszellen, Glossen, Stellungnahmen, Umfrageantworten, Leserbriefe, Diskussionsbeiträge, 1889–1918—Anonyme und pseudonym Veröffentlichungen, 1888–1920, Gesamtausgabe 17*, edited by Klaus Christian Köhnke. Frankfurt am Main: Suhrkamp, 2004.

Spengler, Oswald. *Der Untergang des Abendlandes. Umrisse einer Morphologie der Weltgeschichte. Gestalt und Wirklichkeit*. Vol. 1. Munich: Beck, 1920.

———. *The Decline of the West*. Abridged edition; translated by C. F. Atkinson. New York: Vintage, 2006.

Spier, Selmar. *Vor 1914: Erinnerungen an Frankfurt geschrieben in Israel*. Frankfurt: Kramer, 1961.

Sternberger, Dolf. "Charlie Chaplin, Der Idiot, Don Quijote: Versuch über die komische Existenz." *Die Kreatur* 3 (1929–1930): 372–402.

Susman, Margarete. "Die Seele und die Formen." *FZ*, 5 September 1912.

———. "Der Exodus aus der Philosophie." *FZ*, 17 June 1921 (Morgenblatt).

———. "Die Theorie des Romans." *FZ*, 16 August 1921 (Morgenblatt).

———. "Der Stern der Erlösung." *Der Jude*, 6 (1921–1922): 259–64.

———. *"Das Nah- und Fernsein des Fremden."* Essays und Briefe, edited by Ingeborg Nordmann. Frankfurt am Main: Jüdischer Verlag, 1992.

Thormann, Werner. "Die Aufgabe des katholischen Dichters in der Zeit." In *Kirche und Wirklichkeit: Ein katholisches Zeitbuch*, edited by Ernst Michel, 136–148. Jena: Eugen Diederichs, 1923.

Tucholsky, Kurt. "Die Herren Belohner." In *Gesamtausgabe: Texte und Briefe 14: Texte 1931*, edited by Antje Bonitz, Dirk Grathoff, Michael Hepp, et al., 107–9. Reinbek bei Hamburg: Rowohlt, 1996.

Unamuno, Miguel de. "Don Quixotes Tod." *Frankfurter Zeitung*, 19 May 1926.

———. *The Tragic Sense of Life in Men and Nations*, translated by Anthony Kerrigan. Princeton, NJ: Princeton University Press, 1972.

Valéry, Paul. "The Spiritual Crisis." *The Athenaeum* (11 April 1919): 182–84.

———. "The Intellectual Crisis." *The Athenaeum* (2 May 1919): 279–80.

Vietta, Egon. *Die Kollektivisten*. Freiburg im Breisgau: Urban Verlag, 1930.

———. "Martin Heidegger und die Situation der Jugend." *Die neue Rundschau* 42, no. 2 (1931): 501–11.

———. *Theologie ohne Gott: Versuch über die menschliche Existenz in der modernen französischen Philosophie*. Zürich: Artemis Verlag, 1946.

———. *Die Seinsfrage bei Martin Heidegger*. Stuttgart: Schwab, 1950.

Viénot, Pierre. *Ungewisse Deutschland: zur Krise seiner bürgerlichen Kultur*. Frankfurt am Main: Societäts-Verlag, 1931.

Weber, Max. *The Protestant Ethic and the "Spirit" of Capitalism and Other Writings*, edited and translated by Peter Baehr and Gordon C. Wells. London: Penguin, 2002.

Weiger, Joseph. "Neue Menschen und katholisches Erbe: ein Versuch über Max Scheler." *Die Tat* 14, no. 1 (April 1922): 55–60.

Weiss, Ernst. "Cervantes zu ehren." *Die Kunst des Erzählens: Essays, Aufsätze, Schriften zur Literatur*. Gesammelte Werke 16. Frankfurt am Main: Suhrkamp, 1982.

Werfel, Franz. "Die Christliche Sendung: ein offener Brief an Kurt Hiller." *Die neue Rundschau* 28 (January 1917): 92–105.

Zbinden, Hans, ed. *Ein Künder neuer Lebenswege: Einzelbilder zur Seelenforschung Rudolf Maria Holzapfels*. Jena: Eugen Diederichs, 1923.

———. *In Strom der Zeit: Gedanken und Betrachtungen*. Berlin and Munich: Francke, 1964.

Ziegler, Leopold. *Der ewige Buddho: Ein Tempelschriftwerk in vier Unterweisungen*. Darmstadt: Otto Reichl, 1922.

Zuckerkandl, Viktor. "Alte und neue Bildung." *Die neue Rundschau*, 42, no. 2 (1931): 94–99.

Correspondences

Benjamin, Walter. *Briefe an Siegfried Kracauer. Marbacher Magazine 27*, edited by Theodor W. Adorno Archive. Stuttgart: Deutsche Schillergesellschaft, 1988.

———. *The Correspondence of Walter Benjamin*, edited by Theodore W. Adorno and Gershom Scholem, translated by Manfred R. Jacobson and Evelyn M. Jacobson. Chicago: University of Chicago Press, 1994.

Bloch, Karola, ed. *Ernst Bloch: Briefe, 1903–1975*, 2 volumes. Frankfurt am Main: Suhrkamp, 1985.

Breidecker, Volker, ed. *Siegfried Kracauer—Erwin Panofsky. Briefwechsel*. Berlin: Akademie Verlag, 1996.

Buber, Martin. *Briefwechsel aus sieben Jahrzehnten II, 1918–1938*, edited by Grete Schaeder. Heidelberg: L. Schneider, 1973.

Gödde, Christoph, and Henry Lonitz, eds. *Theodore W. Adorno/Max Horkheimer. Briefwechsel, 1938–1944*, vol. 4.2. Frankfurt am Main: Suhrkamp, 2004.

Hausenstein, Wilhelm. *Ausgewählte Briefe, 1904–1957*, edited by Hellmut H. Rennert. Oldenburg: Igel, 1999.

Jansen, Peter-Erwin, and Christian Schmidt, eds. *In steter Freundschaft: Leo Löwenthal–Siegfried Kracauer, Briefwechsel, 1921–1966*. Lüneburg: Zu Klampen, 2003.

Kesten, Hermann, ed. *Joseph Roth: Briefe, 1911–1939*. Köln and Berlin: Kiepenheuer & Witsch, 1970.

Lonitz, Henry, ed. *Theodore W. Adorno/Alban Berg: Briefwechsel, 1925–1935*. Frankfurt am Main: Suhrkamp, 1997.

———. *Theodore Adorno and Walter Benjamin: The Complete Correspondence, 1928–1940*. Cambridge, MA: Harvard University Press, 1999.

Meier-Graefe, Julius. *Kunst ist nicht für Kunstgeschichte da: Briefe und Dokumente*, edited by Catharine Krahmer. Göttingen: Wallstein, 2002.

Rammstedt, Otthein, and Angela Rammstedt, eds. *Georg Simmel: Gesamtausgabe 23. Briefe, 1912–1918: Jugendbriefe*. Frankfurt am Main: Suhrkamp, 2008.

Schopf, Wolfgang, ed. *Theodor W. Adorno/Siegfried Kracauer: Briefwechsel, 1923–1966*. Frankfurt am Main: Suhrkamp, 2008.

Zenck, Claudia Maurer, ed. *Die hoffnungslose Radikalismus der Mitte. Der Briefwechsel Ernst Krenek—Friedrich T. Gubler, 1928–1939*. Wien and Köln: Böhlau, 1989.

Works on Kracauer, German Culture, and the Weimar Republic

Agard, Olivier. *Kracauer: Le chiffonier mélancholique*. Paris: CNRS, 2010.

Albert, Marcel. *Die Benediktinerabtei: Maria Laach und der Nationalsozialismus. Kommission für Zeitgeschichte*. Paderborn: Schöningh, 2004.

Arnsberg, Paul. *Bilder aus dem jüdischen Leben im alten Frankfurt*. Frankfurt am Main: Kramer, 1970.

Asad, Talal. *Formations of the Secular: Christianity, Islam, Modernity*. Stanford, CA: Stanford University Press, 2003.

Aschheim, Stephen E. *The Nietzsche Legacy in Germany, 1880–1990*. Berkeley: University of California Press, 1992.

———. *In Times of Crisis: Essays on European Culture, Germans and Jews*. Madison: University of Wisconsin Press, 2001.

Audoin-Rouzeau, Stéphane, and Annette Becker. *14–18: Understanding the Great War*. New York: Hill and Wang, 2002.

Band, Henri. *Mittelschichten und Massenkultur*. Berlin: Lukas, 1999.

Barnouw, Dagmar. *Weimar Intellectuals and the Threat of Modernity*. Bloomington: Indiana University Press, 1988.

———. "*An den Rand geschriebene Träume*: Kracauer über Zeit und Geschichte." In *Siegfried Kracauer: Neue Interpretationen*, edited by Michael Kessler and Thomas Y. Levin, 1–15. Tübingen: Stauffenberg, 1990.

———. *Critical Realism: History, Photography, and the Work of Siegfried Kracauer*. Baltimore: Johns Hopkins University Press, 1994.

———. "Vielschichtige Oberflächen: Kracauer und die Modernität von Weimar." In *Denken durch die Dingen: Siegfried Kracauer im Kontext*, edited by Frank Grunert and Dorothee Kimmich, 13–28. Munich: Wilhelm Fink, 2009.

Bärsch, Claus-Ekkehard. *Max Brod im Kampf um das Judentum: zum Leben und Werk eines Deutsch-Jüdischen Dichters aus Prag*. Vienna: Passagen Verlag, 1992.

Belke, Ingrid. "Siegfried Kracauer als Beobachter der jungen Sowjetunion." In *Siegfried Kracauer: Neue Interpretationen*, Edited by Michael Kessler and Thomas Levin, 17–38. Tübingen: Stauffenberg, 1990.

———. "Von Simmel zu Lenin: zu Siegfried Kracauers Schrift, "Sind Menschenliebe, Gerechtigkeit und Duldsamkeit an eine bestimmte Staatsform geknüpft und welches Staatsform gibt die beste Gewähr für ihre Durchführung?" *Simmel Studies* 13 (2003): 15–35.

Belke, Ingrid, and Irina Renz, eds. *Siegfried Kracauer: 1889–1966*. Marbacher Magazine 47. Marbach am Neckar: Deutsche Schillergesellschaft, 1988.

Benjamin, Andrew. "Denaturing Time." A paper given at the colloquium *Provisional Insight: Siegfried Kracauer in the 21st Century*, Monash University, 2008. Accessed 7 June 2010 at: http://www.arts.monash.edu/film-tv/colloquia/provisional-insight/2008/podcast/#benjamin.

Benson, Timothy, ed. *Expressionist Utopias: Paradise, Metropolis, Architectural Fantasy*. Berkeley: University of California Press, 2002.

Beßlich, Barbara. *Faszination des Verfalls. Thomas Mann und Oswald Spengler*. Akademie Verlag; Berlin, 2002.

———. "Kulturtheoretische Irritationen zwischen Literatur und Wissenschaft. Die Spengler-Debatte in der Weimarer Republik als Streit um eine Textsorte." *Jahrbuch zur Kultur und Literatur der Weimarer Republik* 10 (2005/2006): 45–72.

Bialas, Wolfgang, and Georg G Iggers, eds. *Intellektuelle in der Weimarer Republik*. Schriften zur politischen Kultur der Weimarer Republik. Vol 1. Frankfurt am Main: Peter Lang, 1996.

———. "Krisendiagnose und Katastrophenerfahrung: Philosophie und Geschichte im Deutschland der Zwischenkriegszeit." In *Geschichtsdiskurs* 4:

Krisenbewußtsein, Katastrophenerfahrungen und Innovationen, 1880–1945, edited by Wolfgang Küttler, Jörn Rüsen, and Ernst Schulin, 189–216. Frankfurt am Main: Fischer, 1997.

Blackbourn, David. "The Catholic Church in Europe since the French Revolution." *Comparative Studies in Society and History* 33 (1991): 778–90.

Blankenberg, Heinz. *Politischer Katholizismus in Frankfurt am Main, 1918–1933*. Mainz: Matthias Grünewald Verlag, 1981.

Bollenbeck, Georg. "Kulturkritik: ein unterschätzter Reflexionsmodus der Moderne." In *Philosophie und Zeitgeist im Nationalsozialismus*, edited by Marion Heinz and Goran Gretić, 87–99. Würzburg: Königshausen & Neumann, 2006.

Daniel Borg, *The Old-Prussian Churches and the Weimar Republic: A Study in Political Adjustment, 1917–1927*. Hanover: University Press of New England, 1984.

Bonnell, Victoria, and Lynn Hunt, eds. *Beyond the Cultural Turn: New Directions in the Study of Society and Culture*. Berkeley: University of California Press, 1999.

Braiterman, Zachary. *The Shape of Revelation: Aesthetics and Modern Jewish Thought*. Stanford, CA: Stanford University Press, 2007.

Brenner, Michael. *The Renaissance of Jewish Culture in Weimar Germany*. New Haven, CT: Yale University Press, 1996.

Brodersen, Momme. *Siegfried Kracauer*. Reinbek bei Hamburg: Rowohlt, 2001.

Bronner, Stephen Eric. *Modernism at the Barricades: Aesthetics, Politics, Utopia*. New York: Columbia University Press, 2012.

Brown, Callum. "The Secularization Decade: What the 1960s Have Done to the Study of Religious History." In *The Decline of Christendom in Western Europe, 1750–2000*, edited by Hugh McLeod and Werner Ustorf, 29–46. Cambridge: Cambridge University Press, 2000.

Bruce, Steve, ed. *Religion and Modernization: Sociologists and Historians Debate the Secularization Thesis*. Oxford: Oxford University Press, 1992.

Buck-Morss, Susan. *The Origin of Negative Dialectics: Theodor W. Adorno, Walter Benjamin, and the Frankfurt Institute*. New York: Free Press, 1977.

Bullivant, Keith, ed. *Culture and Society in the Weimar Republic*. Manchester: Manchester University Press, 1977.

Burleigh, Michael. *Earthly Powers: The Clash of Religion and Politics in Europe from the French Revolution to the Great War*. New York: Harper Collins, 2005.

Burrin, Philippe. "Political Religion. The Relevance of a Concept." *History and Memory* 9, no. 1/2 (Fall 1997): 21–349.

Burrow, John. *The Crisis of Reason: European Thought, 1848–1914*. New Haven, CT: Yale University Press, 2000.

Calhoun, Craig, Eduardo Mendieta, and Jonathan VanAntwerpen, eds. *Habermas and Religion*. Cambridge: Polity, 2013.

Cancik, Hubert, ed. *Religions- und Geistesgeschichte der Weimarer Republik*. Düsseldorf: Patmos, 1982.

Cascardi, Anthony J. "Don Quixote and the Invention of the Novel." In *The Cambridge Companion to Cervantes*, edited by Anthony Cascardi, 58–79. Cambridge: Cambridge University Press, 2002.

Chadwick, Owen. *The Secularization of the European Mind in the Nineteenth Century*. Cambridge: Cambridge University Press, 1975.

———. *History of the Popes, 1830–1914*. Oxford: Oxford University Press, 1998.

Childers, Thomas. *The Nazi Voter: The Social Foundations of Fascism in Germany, 1919–1933*. Chapel Hill and London: University of North Carolina Press, 1983.

Congdon, Lee. *Exile and Social Thought: Hungarian Exiles in Germany and Austria, 1919–1933*. Princeton, NJ: Princeton University Press, 1991.

Coole, Diana. *Negativity and Politics: Dionysus and Dialectics from Kant to Poststructuralism*. London and New York: Routledge, 2000.

Deak, Istvan. *Weimar Germany's Left-Wing Intellectuals: A Political History of the* Weltbühne *and Its Circle*. Berkeley: University of California Press, 1968.

Derrida, Jacques. "Force of Law: The 'Mystical Foundation of Authority.'" In *Deconstruction and the Possibility of Justice*, translated by Mary Quaintance, edited by Drucilla Cornell, Michael Rosenfeld, and David Gray Carlson, 3–67. New York: Routledge, 1992.

Despoix, Philippe, and Peter Schöttler, eds. *Siegfried Kracauer: penseur de l'histoire*. Paris: Éditions de la Maison des sciences de l'homme, 2006.

Deuber-Mankowsky, Astrid. "Walter Benjamin's *Theological-Political Fragment* as a Response to Ernst Bloch's *Spirit of Utopia*." *Yearbook of the Leo Baeck Institute* 47 (2002): 1–19.

Dobbelaere, Karel. *Secularization: An Analysis at Three Levels*. Brussels: Peter Lang, 2002.

Doering-Manteuffel, Anselm, and Kurt Nowak, eds. *Religionspolitik in Deutschland. Von Der Frühen Neuzeit bis zur Gegenwart. Martin Greschat zum 65. Geburtstag*. Stuttgart: Kohlhammer, 1999.

Dorn, Anton Magnus. *Leiden als Gottesproblem: Eine Untersuchung zum Werk von Max Brod*. Freiburg im Breisgau: Herder, 1981.

Douglass, Paul F. *God among the Germans*. Philadelphia: University of Pennsylvania Press, 1935.

Durkheim, Émile. *The Elementary Forms of Religious Life*, translated by Carol Cosman. Oxford: Oxford University Press, 2001.

Easton, Laird McLeod. *The Red Count: The Life and Times of Harry Kessler*. Berkeley: University of California Press, 2002.

Eiland, Howard, and Michael W. Jennings. *Walter Benjamin: A Critical Life*. Cambridge, MA: Harvard University Press, 2014.

Eksteins, Modris. "The *Frankfurter Zeitung*: Mirror of Weimar Democracy." *Journal of Contemporary History* 6, no. 4 (1971): 3–28.

———. *The Limits of Reason: The German Democratic Press and the Collapse of Weimar Democracy*. Oxford: Oxford University Press, 1975.

———. *Rites of Spring: The Great War and the Birth of the Modern Age*. Toronto: Lester & Orpen Dennys, 1989.

———. "Rag-Picker: Siegfried Kracauer and the Mass Ornament." *International Journal of Politics, Culture and Society* 10, no. 4 (1997): 609–13.

———. "Drowned in Eau de Vie." *London Review of Books* 30, no. 4 (21 February 2008): 23–24.

Eksteins, Modris. *Solar Dance: Van Gogh, Forgery and the Eclipse of Certainty.* Cambridge, MA: Harvard University Press, 2012.
Farrenkopf, John. *Prophet of Decline: Spengler on World History and Politics.* Baton Rouge: Louisiana State University Press, 2001.
Field, Geoffrey G. "Religion in the German Volksschule, 1890–1928." *Yearbook of the Leo Baeck Institute* 25 (1980): 41–72.
Föllmer, Moritz, and Rüdiger Graf, eds. *Die "Krise" der Weimarer Republik: zur Kritik eines Deutungsmusters.* Frankfurt and New York: Campus Verlag, 2005.
Friedman, Maurice. *Martin Buber's Life and Work: The Middle Years 1923–1945.* New York: Dutton, 1983.
Frisby, David. *Fragments of Modernity: Theories of Modernity in the Work of Simmel, Kracauer, and Benjamin.* Cambridge, MA: MIT Press, 1986.
———. "Between the Spheres: Siegfried Kracauer and the Detective Novel." *Theory, Culture and Society* 9, no. 2 (1992): 1–22.
Fritzsche, Peter. *Reading Berlin 1900.* Cambridge, MA: Harvard University Press, 1996.
———. "Did Weimar Fail?" *Journal of Modern History* 68 (September 1996): 629–55.
———. *Germans into Nazis.* Cambridge, MA: Harvard University Press, 1998.
Gauchet, Marcel. *The Disenchantment of the World: A Political History of Religion*, translated by Oscar Burge. Princeton, NJ: Princeton University Press, 1997.
Gay, Peter. *Freud, Jews and Other Germans: Masters and Victims in Modernist Culture.* New York: Oxford University Press, 1978.
———. *Weimar Culture: The Outsider as Insider.* New York: W. W. Norton, 2001.
Geuss, Raymond. *Morality, Culture, and History: Essays on German Philosophy.* Cambridge: Cambridge University Press, 1999.
———. "The Actual and Another Modernity: Order and Imagination in *Don Quixote.*" In *Politics and the Imagination*, 61–80. Princeton, NJ: Princeton University Press, 2010.
Gillessen, Günther. *Auf verlorenem Posten: Die Frankfurter Zeitung im Dritten Reich.* Frankfurt am Main: Siedler, 1986.
Ginzburg, Carlo. "Clues: Morelli, Freud and Sherlock Holmes." In *The Sign of Three: Dupin, Holmes, Peirce*, edited by Umberto Eco and Thomas A. Sebok, 81–118. Bloomington: Indiana University Press, 1983.
———. "Clues: Roots of an Evidential Paradigm." In *Clues, Myths, and the Historical Method*, translated by John and Anne C. Tedeschi, 87–113. Baltimore: Johns Hopkins University Press, 1989.
Glatzer, Nahum. "The Frankfort Lehrhaus." *Yearbook of the Leo Baeck Institute* I (1956): 105–22.
Gleber, Anke. *The Art of Taking a Walk: Flanerie, Literature and Film in Weimar.* Princeton, NJ: Princeton University Press, 1999.
Gluck, Mary. *Georg Lukács and His Generation, 1900–1918.* Cambridge, MA: Harvard University, Press, 1985.
Godman, Peter. *Hitler and the Vatican: Inside the Secret Archives that Reveal the New Story of the Nazis and the Church.* New York: Free Press, 2004.

Gordon, Peter Eli. *Rosenzweig and Heidegger: Between Judaism and German Philosophy*. Berkeley: University of California Press, 2003.
Graf, Friedrich Wilhelm. "Rettung der Persönlichkeit: Protestantische Theologie als Kulturwissenschaft des Christentums." In *Kultur und Kulturwissenschaft um 1900: Krise der Moderne und Glaube an die Wissenschaft*, edited by Rüdiger vom Bruch, Friedrich Wilhelm Graf, and Gangolf Hübinger, 103–31. Stuttgart: Steiner, 1989.
———. "God's Anti-Liberal Avant-Garde: New Theologies in the Weimar Republic." *German Historical Institute London: Bulletin* 32, no. 2 (November 2010): 3–24.
———. *Der heilige Zeitgeist: Studien zur Ideengeschichte der protestantischen Theologie der Weimarer Republik*. Tübingen: Mohr Siebeck, 2011.
Graf, Rüdiger. *Die Zukunft der Weimarer Republik: Krisen und Zukunftsaneignungen in Deutschland, 1918–1933*. Munich: Oldenbourg, 2008.
———. "Either/Or: The Narrative of 'Crisis' in Weimar Germany and Historiography." *Central European History* 43 (2010): 592–615.
Gray, John. "Faith in Reason: Secular Fantasies of a Godless Age." *Harper's Magazine* (January 2008): 85–88.
Green, Martin. *Mountain of Truth: The Counterculture Begins, Ascona 1900–1920*. Hanover: University Press of New England, 1986.
Gregor, Neil. "Nazism—a Political Religion?" In *Nazism, War and Genocide: Essays in Honor of Jeremy Noakes*, edited by Neil Gregor, 1–21. Exeter: University of Exeter Press, 2005.
Grimm, Reinhold, and Jost Hermand, eds. *High and Low Cultures: German Attempts at Mediation*. Madison: University of Wisconsin Press, 1994.
Gross, David L. "*Kultur* and Its Discontents: The Origins of a 'Critique of Everyday Life in Germany, 1880–1925.'" In *Essays on Culture and Society in Modern Germany*, edited by Gary Stark and B. K. Luckner, 70–97. College Station: Texas A&M University Press, 1982.
Gross, Raphael. *Carl Schmitt and the Jews: The "Jewish Question," the Holocaust, and German Legal Theory*. Madison: University of Wisconsin Press, 2007.
Grunert, Frank, and Dorothee Kimmich, eds. *Denken durch die Dinge: Siegfried Kracauer im Kontext*. Munich: Wilhelm Fink, 2009.
Günter, Manuela. *Anatomie des Anti-Subjekts. Zur Subversion autobiographischen Schreibens bei Siegfried Kracauer, Walter Benjamin und Carl Einstein*. Würzburg: Königshausen & Neumann, 1996.
Habermas, Jürgen. *Der philosophische Diskurs der Moderne: Zwölf Vorlesungen*. Frankfurt am Main: Suhrkamp, 1986.
———. "Pre-political Foundations of the Democratic Constitutional State?" In Jürgen Habermas and Joseph Ratzinger, *Dialectics of Secularization: On Reason and Religion*, translated by Brian McNeil. San Francisco: Ignatius Press, 2008.
Haenlein, Leo. *Der Denk-Gestus des Aktiven Wartens im Sinn-Vakuum der Moderne*. Frankfurt am Main: Lang, 1984.
Hake, Sabine. *The Cinema's Third Machine: Writing on Film in Germany, 1907–1933*. Lincoln: University of Nebraska Press, 1993.

Handelman, Matthew. "The Forgotten Conversation: Five Letters from Franz Rosenzweig to Siegfried Kracauer, 1921–1923. *Scientia Poetica* 15, no. 1 (2011): 234–51.
Hansen, Miriam. "Decentric Perspectives: Kracauer's Early Writings on Film and Mass Culture." *New German Critique* 54 (Autumn 1991): 47–76.
———. *Cinema and Experience: Siegfried Kracauer, Walter Benjamin and Theodor W. Adorno*. Berkeley: University of California Press, 2012.
Heuberger, Rachel. *Hinaus aus dem Ghetto: Juden in Frankfurt am Main, 1800–1950*. Frankfurt am Main: Fischer, 1988.
Hoeges, Dirk. *Kontroverse am Abgrund: Ernst Robert Curtius und Karl Mannheim: Intellektuelle und 'freischwebende Intelligenz' in der Weimarer Republik*. Frankfurt am Main: Fischer, 1994.
Hogen, Hildegaard. *Die Modernisierung des Ich: Individualitätskonzepte bei Siegfried Kracauer, Robert Musil und Elias Canetti*. Würzburg: Königshausen & Neumann, 2000.
Hughes, H. Stuart. *Oswald Spengler: A Critical Estimate*. New York: Scribners, 1952.
———. *Consciousness and Society: The Reconstruction of European Social Thought, 1890–1930*. New York: Vintage, 1970.
Huguet, Louis. *Bibliographie Alfred Döblin*. Berlin and Weimar: Aufbau Verlag, 1972.
Hunsinger, George. "A Marxist View of Kierkegaard: Georg Lukács on the Intellectual Origins of Fascism." *Union Seminary Quarterly Review* 30 (1974/1975): 29–40.
Hunter, Ian. "Secularization: The Birth of a Modern Combat Concept." *Modern Intellectual History* 12, no. 1 (2015): 1–32.
Iggers, Georg. Review of *History: The Last Things before the Last*, by Siegfried Kracauer. *American Historical Review* 75, no. 3 (February 1970): 816–17.
Iserloh, Erwin. "Innerkirchliche Bewegungen und ihre Spiritualität." In *Handbuch der Kirchengeschichte: Die Weltkirche im 20. Jahrhundert*. Vol. 7. Edited by Hubert Jedin and Konrad Repgen, 301–337. Freiburg: Herder, 1979.
Jacobs, Jack. "A Most Remarkable Jewish Sect"? *Archiv für Sozialgeschichte* 37 (1997): 73–92.
———. *The Frankfurt School, Jewish Lives and Antisemitism*. Cambridge: Cambridge University Press, 2012.
Janik, Allen. "Haecker, Kierkegaard and the Early *Brenner*: A Contribution to the History of the Reception of *Two Ages*." In *International Kierkegaard Commentary: Two Ages*, edited by Robert L. Perkins, 189–222. Macon, GA: Mercer University Press, 1984.
Jay, Martin. *Marxism and Totality: The Adventures of a Concept from Lukács to Habermas*. Berkeley: University of California Press, 1984.
———. *Permanent Exiles: Essays on the Intellectual Migration from Germany to America*. New York: Columbia University Press, 1985.
———. *The Dialectical Imagination: A History of the Frankfurt School and the Institute of Social Research, 1923–1950*. Berkeley: University of California Press, 1996.
———. "Afterword: Kracauer, The Magical Nominalist." In Siegfried Kracauer, *Siegfried Kracauer's American Writings: Essays on Film and Popular Culture*, edited

by Johannes von Moltke and Kristy Rawson, 227–36. Berkeley: University of California Press, 2012.
Jedin, Hubert, and Konrad Repgen, eds. *Handbuch der Kirchengeschichte: Die Weltkirche im 20. Jahrhundert.* Vol. 7. Freiburg: Herder, 1979.
Jones, Gareth Stedman. "Introduction." In Karl Marx and Friedrich Engels, *The Communist Manifesto*, translated by Christopher Moore, 3–187. London: Penguin, 2002.
Jung, Martin H. *Der Protestantismus in Deutschland von 1870 bis 1945. Kirchengeschichte in Einzeldarstellungen* Vol 3, no. 5. Leipzig: Evangelische Verlagsanstalt, 2002.
Kaes, Anton, Martin Jay, and Edward Dimendberg, eds. *The Weimar Republic Sourcebook.* Berkeley: University of California Press, 1994.
Katz, Jacob. "The German Jewish Utopia of Social Emancipation." *Studies of the Leo Baeck Institute*, edited by Max Kreutzberger. New York: Leo Baeck Institute, 1967.
Kelly, George Armstrong. *Idealism, Politics and History: Sources of Hegelian Thought.* Cambridge: Cambridge University Press, 1964.
Kennedy, Emmet. *Secularism and Its Opponents from Augustine to Solzhenitsyn.* New York: Palgrave Macmillan, 2006.
Kessler, Michael, and Thomas Y. Levin, eds. *Siegfried Kracauer: Neue Interpretationen.* Tübingen: Stauffenberg, 1990.
Kindt, Tom, and Hans-Harald Müller. "Zweimal Cervantes: Die *Don Quijote*-Lektüren von Ernst Jünger und Ernst Weiß, ein Beitrag zur literarischen Anthropologie der zwanziger Jahre." *Jahrbuch zur Literatur der Weimarer Republik* 1 (1995): 230–54.
Kniesche, Thomas W., and Stephen Brockmann, eds. *Dancing on the Volcano: Essays on the Culture of the Weimar Republic.* Columbia, SC: Camden House, 1994.
Koch, Gertrud. *Siegfried Kracauer: An Introduction.* Princeton, NJ: Princeton University Press, 2000.
Köpke, Wulf. "Alfred Döblins Überparteilichkeit: Zur Publizistik in den letzten Jahren der Weimarer Republik." In *Weimars Ende: Prognosen und Diagnosen in der deutschen Literatur und politischen Publizistik, 1930–1933*, edited by Thomas Koebner, 318–29. Frankfurt am Main: Suhrkamp, 1982.
Koepke, Wulf. "Döblin's Political Writings during the Weimar Republic." In *A Companion to the Works of Alfred Döblin*, edited by Roland Dollinger, Wulf Koepke, and Heidi Thomann Tewarson, 83–193. Rochester, NY: Camden House, 2004.
Kohlenbach, Margarete, and Raymond Geuss, eds. *The Early Frankfurt School and Religion.* New York: Palgrave Macmillan, 2005.
Koselleck, Reinhart. *The Practice of Conceptual History: Timing History, Spacing Concepts*, translated by Todd Samuel Presner et al. Stanford, CA: Stanford University Press, 2002.
Langewiesche, Dieter. "German Liberalism in the Second Empire, 1871–1914." In *In Search of a Liberal Germany: Studies in the History of German Liberalism from 1789 to the Present*, edited by Konrad Jarausch and Larry Eugene Jones, 217–35. New York: Berg, 1990.

Lazier, Benjamin. *God Interrupted: Heresy and the European Imagination between the World Wars*. Princeton, NJ: Princeton University Press, 2012.

Le Rider, Jacques. *Modernity and Crises of Identity: Culture and Society in Fin-de-siècle Vienna*, translated by Rosemary Morris. New York: Continuum, 1993.

Lehmann, Hartmut, ed. *Säkularisierung, Dechristianisierung, Rechristianisierung im neuzeitlichen Europa: Bilanz und Perspektiven der Forschung*. Göttingen: Vandenhoeck & Ruprecht, 1997.

Lethen, Helmut. *Neue Sachlichkeit 1924–1932. Studien zur Literatur des "Weißen Sozialismus."* Stuttgart: Metzler, 1970.

———. "Sichtbarkeit: Kracauers Liebeslehre." In *Siegfried Kracauer: neue Interpretationen*, edited by Michael Kessler and Thomas Y. Levin, 195–227. Tübingen: Stauffenberg, 1990.

———. *Cool Conduct: The Culture of Distance in Weimar Germany*. Berkeley: University of California Press, 2002.

Levin, Thomas. "Siegfried Kracauer in English: A Bibliography." *New German Critique* 40 (1987): 140–89.

———. "Walter Benjamin and the Theory of Art History." *October* 47 (Winter 1988): 77–83.

———. *Siegfried Kracauer: eine Bibliographie seiner Schriften*. Marbach: Deutsche Schillergesellschaft, 1989.

———. "The English-Language Reception of Kracauer's Work." *New German Critique* 54 (Autumn 1991): 183–89.

Levinas, Emmanuel. *Proper Names*, translated by Michael B. Smith. Stanford, CA: Stanford University Press, 1996.

Lidtke, Vernon. "Social Class and Secularisation in Imperial Germany: The Working Classes." *Yearbook of the Leo Baeck Institute* 25 (1980): 21–41.

Liebersohn, Harry. *Fate and Utopia in German Sociology, 1870–1923*. Cambridge, MA: MIT Press, 1988.

Liebeschütz, Hans. "Max Weber's Historical Interpretation of Judaism." *Yearbook of the Leo Baeck Institute* 9 (1964): 41–68.

Lilla, Mark. *The Stillborn God: Religion, Politics, and the Modern West*. New York: Random House, 2007.

Löwenthal, Leo. "As I Remember Friedel." *New German Critique* 54 (Autumn 1991): 5–17.

Löwith, Karl. *Meaning in History*. Chicago: University of Chicago Press, 1949.

———. *From Hegel to Nietzsche: the revolution in nineteenth-century thought*, translated by David E. Green. New York, 1991.

Lowitsch, Bruno. *Der Kreis um die Rhein-Mainische Volkszeitung*. Wiesbaden and Frankfurt am Main: Knecht, 1980.

Löwy, Michael. *Redemption and Utopia: Jewish Libertarian Thought in Central Europe, a Study in Elective Affinity*. London: Athlone Press, 1992.

Lübbe, Hermann. *Politische Philosophie in Deutschland. Studien zu ihrer Geschichte*. Basel and Stuttgart: Schwabe, 1963.

———. *Säkularisierung. Geschichte eines ideenpolitischen Begriffs.* 3rd ed. Freiburg and Munich: Karl Alber, 2003.
Luhmann, Niklas. *Die Religion der Gesellschaft.* Frankfurt am Main: Suhrkamp, 2000.
Malik, Habib C. *Receiving Søren Kierkegaard: The Early Impact and Transmission of His Thought.* Washington, DC: Catholic University of America Press, 1997.
McCole, John. "George Simmel and the Philosophy of Religion." *New German Critique* 94 (Winter 2005): 8–35.
McLeod, Hugh. *Secularisation in Western Europe, 1848–1914.* Basingstoke: St. Martin's Press, 2000.
Meier, Heinrich. *Leo Strauss and the Theologico-Political Problem,* translated by Marcus Brainard. Cambridge: Cambridge University Press, 2006.
Mendes-Flohr, Paul. *Divided Passions: Jewish Intellectuals and the Experience of Modernity.* Detroit: Wayne State University Press, 1991.
———. *German Jews: A Dual Identity.* New Haven, CT: Yale University Press, 1999.
Meyer, Jochen. *Berlin Provinz: Literarische Kontroversen um 1930. Marbach Magazin* 33. Marbach: Deutsche Schillergesellschaft, 1985.
———. *Alfred Döblin. 1878–1978.* Munich: Kösel, 1978.
Meyer, Martin, ed. *Intellketuellendämmerung? Beiträge zur neuesten Zeit des Geistes.* Munich: Carl Hanser, 1992.
Meyer, Michael A. "The Emergence of Jewish Historiography: Motives and Motifs." *History and Theory* 27 (1988): 160–75.
Mommsen, Hans J. *The Rise and Fall of Weimar Democracy.* Chapel Hill and London: University of North Carolina Press, 1996.
Mommsen, Wolfgang J. "Culture and Politics in the German Empire." In *Imperial Germany, 1867–1918: Politics, Culture and Society,* 119–40. London: St. Martin's Press, 1995.
Mooney, Edward F. "Exemplars, Inwardness and Belief: Kierkegaard on Indirect Communication." In *International Kierkegaard Commentary 12: Concluding Unscientific Postscript to Philosophical Fragments,* edited by Robert Perkins, 129–48. Macon, GA: Mercer University Press, 1997.
Moretti, Franco. *Signs Taken for Wonders: On the Sociology of Literary Forms.* London: Verso, 2005.
Morgan, Michael L. *Interim Judaism: Jewish Thought in a Century of Crisis.* Bloomington: Indiana University Press, 2001.
Moyn, Samuel. *Origins of the Other: Emmanuel Levinas between Revelation and Ethics.* Ithaca: Cornell University Press, 2005.
Mülder, Inka. *Siegfried Kracauer—Grenzgänger zwischen Theorie und Literatur: Seine frühen Schriften, 1913–1933.* Stuttgart: Metzler, 1985.
Mülder-Bach, Inka. "Der Umschlag der Negativität: zur Verschränkung von Phänomenologie, Geschichtsphilosophie und Filmästhetik in Siegfried Kracauers Metaphorik der 'Oberfläche.'" *Deutsche Vierteljahrsschrift für Literaturwissenschaft und Geistesgeschichte* 61, no. 2 (1987): 359–73.

———. "History as Autobiography: The Last Things before the Last." *New German Critique* 54 (Autumn 1991): 139–57.
Müller-Doohm, Stefan. *Adorno: A Biography*. Cambridge: Polity Press, 2005.
Müller-Salget, Klaus. "Döblin and Judaism." In *A Companion to the Works of Alfred Döblin*, edited by Roland Dollinger, Wulf Koepke, and Heidi Thomann Tewarson, 233–46. Rochester, NY: Camden House, 2004.
Negt, Oskar. "Ernst Bloch, the German Philosopher of the October Revolution." *New German Critique* 4 (Winter 1975): 3–16.
Nipperdey, Thomas. *Religion im Umbruch. Deutschland, 1870–1918*. Munich: C. H. Beck, 1988.
Nowak. Kurt. *Geschichte des Christentums in Deutschland: Religion, Politik und Gesellschaft vom Ende der Aufklärung bis zur Mitte des 20. Jahrhunderts*. Munich: C. H. Beck, 1995.
Oschmann, Dirk. *Auszug aus der Innerlichkeit. Das literarische Werk Siegfried Kracauers*. Jenauer germanistische Forschungen 6. Heidelberg: Carl Winter Verlag, 1999.
Pachter, Henry. *Weimar Etudes*. New York: Columbia University Press, 1982.
Pan, David. *Primitive Renaissance: Rethinking German Expressionism*. Lincoln: University of Nebraska Press, 2001.
Papapetros, Spyros. *On the Animation of the Inorganic: Art, Architecture, and the Extension of Life*. Chicago: University of Chicago Press, 2012.
Pattison, George. *Kierkegaard, Religion and the Nineteenth-Century Crisis of Culture*. Cambridge: Cambridge University Press, 2002.
Pecora, Vincent P. *Secularization and Cultural Criticism. Religion, Nation and Modernity*. Chicago: University of Chicago Press, 2006.
Petro, Patrice. "Kracauer's Epistemological Shift." *New German Critique* 54 (Autumn 1991): 127–38.
Peukert, Detlev. *The Weimar Republic: The Crisis of Classical Modernity*. New York: Hill and Wang, 1992.
Poewe, Karla. *New Religions and the Nazis*. New York and London: Routledge, 2006.
Poole, Roger. "The Unknown Kierkegaard: Twentieth-Century Receptions." In *The Cambridge Companion to Kierkegaard*, edited by Alistair Hannay and Gordon D. Marion, 49–75. Cambridge: Cambridge University Press, 1998.
Puknat, Siegfried B. "Max Picard and Ernst Wiechert." *Monatshefte* 42, no. 8 (December 1950): 371–84.
Rabinbach, Anson. *In the Shadow of Catastrophe: German Intellectuals between Apocalypse and Enlightenment*. Berkeley: University of California Press, 1997.
Reeh, Henrik. *Ornaments of the Metropolis: Siegfried Kracauer and Modern Urban Culture*. Cambridge, MA: MIT Press, 2004.
Rentschler, Eric. *The Ministry of Illusion: Nazi Cinema and Its Afterlife*. Cambridge, MA: Harvard University Press, 1996.
Repp, Kevin. *Reformers, Critics and the Paths of German Modernity: Anti-politics and the Search for Alternatives, 1890–1914*. Cambridge, MA: Harvard University Press, 2000.

Richter, Gerhard. *Thought-Images: Frankfurt School Writers' Reflections from Damaged Life*. Stanford, CA: Stanford University Press, 2007.
Roberts, David D. "'Political Religion' and the Totalitarian Departures of Inter-war Europe: On the Uses and Disadvantages of an Analytical Category." *Contemporary European History* 18, no. 4 (2009): 381–414.
Rochlitz, Rainer. *The Disenchantment of Art: The Philosophy of Walter Benjamin*. New York: Guilford, 1996.
Rodowick, David. "The Last Things before the Last: Kracauer and History." *NGC* 41 (Spring–Summer 1987): 109–39.
Rosenstock, Martin. "Ernst Jünger's *Dangerous Encounter*—the Detective Closes the Case on the Adventurer." *Monatshefte* 100, no. 3 (Fall 2008): 283–99.
Rosenwald, Lawrence. "On the Reception of the Buber-Rosenzweig Bible." *Prooftexts* 14, no. 3 (1994): 141–65.
Ruh, Ulrich. "Bleibende Ambivalenz: Säkularisierung/ Säkularisation als geistesgeschichte Interpretationskategorie." In *Ästhetik, Religion, Säkularisierung I: Von der Renaissance Zur Romantik*, edited by Silvio Vietta and Herbert Uerlings, 25–36. Munich: Wilhelm Fink, 2008.
Ruster, Thomas. *Die verlorene Nützlichkeit der Religion: Katholizismus und Moderne in der Weimarer Republik*. Paderborn: Schöningh, 1994.
Said, Edward. *The World, the Text and the Critic*. Cambridge, MA: Harvard University Press, 1983.
Schatz, Klaus. *Zwischen Säkularisation und zweitem Vatikanum: Der Weg des deutschen Katholizismus im 19. und 20. Jahrhundert*. Frankfurt am Main: Josef Knecht, 1986.
Schivelbusch, Wolfgang. *Intellektuellendämmerung: Zur Lage der Frankfurter Intelligenz in den Zwanziger Jahren*. Frankfurt am Main: Suhrkamp, 1982.
Schlösser, Manfred. *Für Margarete Susman. Auf gespaltenem Pfad*. Darmstadt: Erato Presse, 1964.
Schlüpmann, Heide. *Ein Detektiv des Kinos: Studien zu Siegfried Kracauers Filmtheorie*. Basel and Frankfurt am Main: Stroemfeld, 1998.
Scholem, Gershom. "The Tradition of the Thirty Six Hidden Just Men." In *The Messianic Idea in Judaism and Other Essays in Jewish Spirituality*. New York: Schocken, 1971.
Schorske, Carl. *Fin-de-siècle Vienna: Politics and Culture*. New York: Random House, 1981.
Schröter, Michael. "Weltzerfall und Rekonstruktion: Zur Physiognomik Siegfried Kracauers." *Text und Kritik* 68 (1980): 18–40.
Schulz, Ursula, ed. *Hermann Herrigel, der Denker und die deutsche Erwachsenbildung. Bremer Beiträge zur freien Volksbildung*. Bremen: Volkshochschule, 1969.
Schütz, Alfred. "Don Quixote and the Problem of Reality." In *Collected Papers II: Studies in Social Theory*, 135–58. The Hague: Martinus Nijhoff, 1976.
Sorkin, David Jan, and Frances Malino, eds. *Profiles in Diversity: Jews in a Changing Europe: 1750–1870*. Detroit: Wayne State University Press, 1988.
Spector, Scott. *Prague Territories: National Conflict and Cultural Innovation in Franz Kafka's Fin de Siècle*. Berkeley: University of California Press, 2000.

Spiegelberg, Herbert. *The Phenomenological Movement: A Historical Introduction.* 2nd ed, 2 volumes. The Hague: Martinus Nijhoff, 1982.
Stalder, Helmut. *Siegfried Kracauer: das journalistische Werk in der 'Frankfurter Zeitung' 1921–1933.* Würzburg: Königshausen & Neumann, 2003.
Staude, John Rafael. *Max Scheler, 1874–1928.* New York: Free Press, 1967.
Staudenmaier, Peter. "Rudolf Steiner and the Jewish Question." *Yearbook of the Leo Baeck Institute* (2005): 127–47.
Stark, Michael, ed. *Deutsche Intellektuelle, 1910–1933: Aufrufe, Pamphlete, Betrachtungen.* Heidelberg: L. Schneider, 1984.
Stern, Fritz. *The Politics of Cultural Despair: A Study of the Rise and Fall of the Germanic Ideology.* Berkeley: University of California Press, 1974.
Stewart, Jon. ed. *Kierkegaard's Influence on Literature, Criticism and Art: Tome 1: The Germanophone World.* Farnham: Ashgate, 2013.
Streim, Gregor. *Das Ende des Anthropozentrismus: Anthropologie und Geschichtskritik in der Deutschen Literatur zwischen 1930–1950.* Berlin and New York: Walter de Gruyter, 2008.
Struve, Walter. *Elites Against Democracy: Leadership Ideals in Bourgeois Political Thought in Germany, 1890–1933.* Princeton, NJ: Princeton University Press, 1973.
Thierfelder, Jorg. "Religionspolitik in der Weimarer Republik." In, *Religionspolitik in Deutschland. Von der frühen Neuzeit bis zur Gegenwart*, edited by Kurt Nowak and Anselm Doering-Manteuffel, 195–213. Stuttgart: Kohlhammer, 1999.
Tilgner, Wolfgang. *Volksnomostheologie und Schöpfungsglaube: Ein Beitrag zur Geschichte des Kirchenkampfes. Arbeiten zur Geschichte des Kirchenkampfes.* Göttingen: Vandenhoeck and Ruprecht, 1966.
Traverso, Enzo. *Siegfried Kracauer: itinéraire d'un intellectuel nomade.* Paris: Éditions la Découverte, 1994.
———. "Sous le signe de l'extraterritorialité: Kracauer et la modernité juive." In *La pensée dispersée: Figures de l'exil judéo-allemand*, 183–2008. Paris: Lignes Scheer, 2004.
Treitel, Corinna. *A Science for the Soul: Occultism and the Genesis of the German Modern.* Baltimore: Johns Hopkins University Press, 2004.
Voegelin, Eric. "Ersatz Religion." In *Science, Politics and Gnosticism: Two Essays*, 55–78. Chicago: Regnery, 1997.
Volk, Andreas, ed. *Siegfried Kracauer. Zum Werk des Romanciers, Feuilletonisten, Architekten, Filmwissenschaftlers und Soziologen. Soziographie 7, 1/2* (1994). Zurich: Seismo, 1996.
Ward, Janet. *Weimar Surfaces: Urban Visual Culture in 1920s Germany.* Berkeley: University of California Press, 2001.
Weber, Thomas. "La réalité emphatique. Le roman policier. Un traité philosophique. Une première interprétation de la culture de masse." In *Culture de masse et modernité: Siegfried Kracauer, sociologue, critique, écrivain*, edited by Philippe Despoix and Nia Perivolaropoulou, 23–39. Paris: Éditions de la Maison des sciences de l'homme, 2001.

Weitz, Eric D. *Weimar Germany: Promise and Tragedy*. Princeton, NJ: Princeton University Press, 2007.
Weltsch, Robert. *Max Brod and His Age: The Leo Baeck Memorial Lectures* 13. New York: Leo Baeck Institute, 1970.
Willett, John. *Art and Politics in the Weimar Period: The New Sobriety, 1917–1933*. New York: Da Capo, 1978.
Williamson, George S. *The Longing for Myth in Germany: Religion and Aesthetic Culture from Romanticism to Nietzsche*. Chicago: University of Chicago Press, 2004.
Winter, Jay. *Sites of Memory, Sites of Mourning: The Great War in European Cultural History*. Cambridge: Cambridge University Press, 1995.
Witte, Bernd. *Walter Benjamin, der Intellektuelle als Kritiker: Untersuchungen zu seinem Frühwerk*. Stuttgart: Metzler, 1976.
Witte, Karsten. "'Light Sorrow': Siegfried Kracauer as Literary Critic." *New German Critique* 54 (Autumn 1991): 77–94.
Wolin, Richard. *The Seduction of Unreason: The Intellectual Romance with Fascism from Nietzsche to Postmodernism*. Princeton, NJ: Princeton University Press, 2004.
Wuthenow, Ralph-Rainer. "Literaturkritik, Tradition und Politik: zum deutschen Essay in der Zeit der Weimarer Republik." In *Die deutsche Literatur in der Weimarer Republik*, edited by Wolfgang Rothe, 434–57. Stuttgart: Reclam, 1974.
Ziemann, Benjamin. "Säkularisierung, Konfessionalisierung, Organisationsbildung: Dimensionen der Sozialgeschichte der Religion im langen 19. Jahrhundert," *Archiv für Sozialgeschichte* 47 (2007): 485–508
Žižek, Slavoj. *The Puppet and the Dwarf: The Perverse Core of Christianity*. Cambridge, MA: MIT Press, 2003.
Zohlen, Gerwin. "Text-Straßen: zur Theorie der Stadtlektüre bei Siegfried Kracauer." *Text und Kritik* 68 (October 1980): 62–72.
Zudeick, Peter. *Der Hintern des Teufels: Ernst Bloch, Leben und Werk*. Moos: Elster, 1985.

Volume 12 of *Austrian and Habsburg Studies*

"Vienna Is Different"
Jewish Writers in Austria from the Fin de Siècle to the Present
Hillary Hope Herzog

CHOICE OUTSTANDING ACADEMIC TITLE 2012

This thoroughly researched, lucid book offers a broad, insightful discussion of a complex subject. Steven Beller is Herzog's immediate scholarly predecessor, yet Herzog goes beyond the excellent work of her predecessors . . . Her choices of the writings to discuss are thoughtful and sometimes unexpected . . . Posing challenging questions while keeping the city always in view, Herzog concludes that though this rich tapestry of artists and viewpoints is irreducible, there are similarities and verities to reveal. This is the book's unique contribution. Highly recommended. **CHOICE**

This work is on the cutting edge of renewed interest in Jewish Austria. It is a comprehensive road map of a culture uprooted but replanted and blossoming anew into the twenty-first century. This is recommended reading for the scholar of Austrian literary history. **JOURNAL OF AUSTRIAN STUDIES**

In tracing a tradition of Jewish writing in Vienna from the fin de siècle to the present, Herzog's book forms an important contribution to our understanding of Austrian literature and culture of the twentieth century. By focusing her analyses on the ways in which these writers conceptualized their identities as Jews, Herzog illuminates the complicated, yet continually changing relationships between Jewish writers and the city of Vienna. **H-JUDAIC**

[M]eticulously researched and clearly presented . . . Each chapter begins with a brief, well-informed overview of the period and the experiences of Jews in Austria during that time . . . This informative work successfully probes the engagement of an impressive range of writers with both their own self-identifications and Vienna. Sensitive and nuanced, it will serve scholars and others as the go-to guide for exploring issues of Jewishness in Austrian literature. **HABSBURG**, H-Net Reviews

Hillary Hope Herzog is Associate Professor of German Studies at the University of Kentucky.

Cover photos: Clockwise, from upper right: Arthur Schnitzler, Theodor Herzl, Hugo von Hofmannsthal, Felix Salten, and an Austrian coffeehouse

History / Jewish Studies

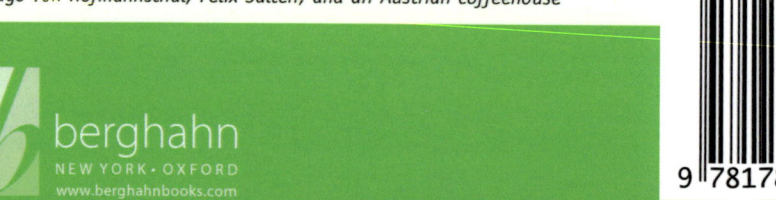

Index

Adorno, Theodor W., 6–7, 8, 10–11, 15, 19, 29n39, 38, 45, 47, 50–51, 70–71, 90, 94, 98n46, 106, 115, 116–17, 119–20, 122, 144n23, 146n79 nd 82, 159, 165, 175, 184, 202n99, 211–12, 224, 231, 240n87, 248, 252

Ahasuerus (The Wandering Jew), 142, 196

Alexander, Franz, 134

Angerstein (Angerstein Trial), 129–30, 134, 212

Antamoro, Giulio, 158

Anthroposophy, 75, 161. See also Steiner, Rudolf.

Anti-Semitism, 38, 41, 43, 81, 175, 213, 215 233, 242n138

Apollinaire, Guillaume, 15–16, 46

Arendt, Hannah, 6, 14, 107, 115, 116, 118

Arnold, Eberhard, 164, 200n56

Asad, Talal, 21, 225

Astrow, Wladimir, 188–90

Auden, W. H., 114

Auerbach, Erich, 250

Augustine, 18, 191

Avenarius, Richard, 187

B

Baader, Franz von, 189, 206n184

Baeck, Leo, 184

Bäumer, Gertrud, 205n170

Barth, Karl, 4, 18, 21, 25, 166, 168–69, 193

Beckmann, Max, 4

Beckett, Samuel, 18

Benjamin, Walter, 16, 18, 25n2, 38, 72–3, 75, 77, 93, 95, 100n90, 115, 127–28, 147n95, 148n110, 149n137, 151n207, 154, 156, 179, 190, 211, 231, 240n78

Bergson, Henri, 39, 44, 48

Bloch, Ernst, 8, 13, 16, 18, 49, 72–80, 82, 85, 95, 100n90, 105n194, 108, 128, 166, 181, 198n23, 211, 221–22, 227, 234, 248–49

Blumenberg, Hans, 23. 225, 240n92–93

Bourdieu, Pierre, 74

Briefs, Goetz, 181, 229

Brod, Max, 46, 73, 80–85, 92, 101n107, 115, 116–17, 232, 248

Bry, Carl Christian, 13, 17

Buber, Martin, 1, 18, 19, 21, 25, 38, 42, 47, 81–83, 115, 117, 155, 170, 172, 191–92, 193, 195, 200n57, 202n101, 230

Buddhism, 161, 165, 183

Bultmann, Rudolf, 21

Burckhardt, George, 3

Burckhardt, Jacob, 143n6

C

Cassirer, Ernst, 37, 170, 173

Catholicism, 1–2, 16, 25, 46, 68, 71, 116–17, 140, 161, 164, 166–67, 173–81, 197, 199n43, 204n131, 214, 228–29

Chaplin, Charlie, 129, 238n54

Chesterton, G. K., 25, 106, 111–12

Christianity, 54–55, 81, 83, 90–92, 166–83. See also Catholicism and Protestantism.

Claudel, Paul, 46

Cocteau, Jean, 160, 173

Communism (Communist Party of Germany), 3, 36, 86, 216, 218, 229, 235

Confucianism, 165

culture
    cultural criticism, 32n82, 50–51, 56–57, 86–87, 90–91, 95–96, 110, 208–209, 215–16
    tragic conception of, 45, 47–48, 51, 53, 57–58, 87, 136
    modern culture and religion, 2–5, 11–12, 15–16, 19–20, 44, 46, 48, 56–58, 67, 72–73, 87–88, 93–94, 160, 167, 178–79, 186–191, 195, 227–29, 231–32, 247–48

Curtius, Ernst Robert, 215, 217, 253n15

D

Degenerate Art Exhibit (1937), 236
Derrida, Jacques, 127, 149n137
detective fiction, 110–13, 120–22 and Chapter Three *passim*
Diederichs, Eugen, 117, 142n1, 175, 187
Dilthey, Wilhelm, 44, 115, 167
Dobbelaere, Karl, 17, 21
Döblin, Alfred, 7, 9, 74, 106, 213–19, 221, 223–27, 234–35, 239n57, 239n69, 240n86, 245
Dostoevsky, Fyodor, 13, 40, 87, 134
Doyle, Arthur Conan (Sherlock Holmes), 110–11, 112, 119, 131, 132, 139, 248

E

Ebner, Ferdinand, 116–17
Ehrenberg, Hans, 166
Ehrenberg, Rudolf, 88
Eichendorff, Joseph von, 181
Eliot, T. S., 46, 61n64
Engels, Friedrich, 143n6
Enlightenment, 21, 115, 126, 167–68, 227
Epstein, Tilly, 41
Erasmus, 36, 254n21
Expressionism, 53–54, 236
Extraterritorialism, 9, 36, 106–7, 149n137, 191, 193–94, 195–96

F

Feuilletons, 153–157
Flaischlen, Cäsar, 136
Flake, Otto, 184–86
flânerie (flâneur), 2, 17, 165, 170, 171, 173, 182, 185, 186, 191, 196–97, 214, 247
Fleg, Edmond, 196, 207n220
Flesch, Hans, 222
Flesch, Max, 39, 45
Förster-Nietzsche, Elisabeth, 40
France, Anatole, 125
Frankfurt School (*Institut für Sozialforschung*), 10, 19, 43, 198n29, 224
Frankfurter Zeitung, 1, 4, 8–9, 10, 11, 114, 153–54, 158–59, 187, 192, 202n99, 233, 251

Free Jewish School (*Freie jüdische Lehrhaus*), 4, 38, 192
Freud, Sigmund, 46, 95, 117

G

Gaboriau, Émile, 111
Gadamer, Hans-Georg, 103n148, 115, 117
George, Stefan, 37, 216
German Christian Movement (*Deutsche Christen*), 169, 171, 173, 197, 202n99
Gide, André, 154
Gies, Ludwig, 236
Ginzburg, Carlo, 139, 141
Goethe, Johann Wolfgang von, 1, 54, 55, 92, 151n197, 191, 216, 222
Gogarten, Friedrich, 25, 33n96, 168, 169, 170–71, 201n82, 202n99
Gogh, Vincent van, 181
Goldstein, Moritz, 38
grace (*Gnade*), 45, 82–83, 84–85, 128, 159, 188–90, 196, 246–47
Grisebach, Eberhard, 171
Grünberg, Carl, 93
Grune, Karl, 195
Guardini, Romano, 21, 98n46, 176–80
Gubler, Friedrich T., 114, 144n21
Guttmann, Bernhard, 9

H

Haas, Willy, 121–22, 147n94–95, 231
Habermas, Jürgen, 25, 35n130, 225, 240–41n94
Haecker, Theodor, 7, 73, 117
Hainebach, Otto, 39
Hartmann, Nicolai, 70, 136
Hausenstein, Wilhelm, 140, 173, 202n101, 250–51, 252
Hausherr, Otto, 187
Hebbel, Christian Friedrich, 39
Hegel, G. W. F., 76, 77, 86, 107–8, 116, 137
Heidegger, Martin, 7, 25, 170, 219–20, 221, 223, 224, 226, 239n68, 240n87, 241n97, 254n19
Hentschel, Felix, 40
Herrigel, Hermann, 25, 47, 120, 147n86, 169–73, 197, 202n99–101, 229

Herwegen, Ildefons, 177–78, 203n127
Hesse, Hermann, 140
Hirsch, Emmanuel, 7
Hirsch, Leo, 208, 210
Hocke, Gustav René, 213–15, 217–18, 219, 234
Holzapfel, Rudolf Maria, 187–91, 227, 230, 247
Horkheimer, Max, 7, 19, 175
Huelsenbeck, Richard, 117–18
Hughes, Langston, 154
Husserl, Edmund, 9, 61n76, 98n40

I
indirect communication, 108–9, 113–14, 121–22, 156–57, 182–83, 221, 224, 228, 233, 251
Islam, 165

J
Jaspers, Karl, 116, 117, 168–69
Jones, Gareth Stedman, 19
Judaism, 1, 4, 8, 17, 18, 20, 37–39, 40–43, 46–47, 55, 73–74, 76, 80–81, 84, 92, 127, 161, 164, 166–67, 191–97, 213–14, 250. *See also* Zionism.
Jung, Carl, 184
Jünger, Ernst, 106, 235, 249–50

K
Kafka, Franz, 46, 114, 115, 117, 149n139, 151n185, 163, 165, 211, 219, 220, 232, 249–50
Kant, Immanuel, 40, 76, 107, 108–9, 110, 111–12, 116, 119, 122, 123, 125, 127, 136, 183, 232
Kassner, Rudolf, 140, 152n212
Kayser, Rudolf, 9, 239n56
Kessler, Harry, 10
Keyserling, Hermann von, 49, 72, 88, 162, 170, 184–86, 189
Kierkegaard, Søren, 6–7, 25, 47, 73, 80, 85–86, 91, 104n175, 106–19, 124, 127, 135, 137–39, 154, 214, 220, 245–46
    reception of in Germany, 115–18
    on indirect communication, 113–14
Kircher, Rudolf, 10, 202n99
Klages, Ludwig, 140, 141

Klemperer, Viktor, 10, 65–66, 68, 69, 154
Korsch, Karl, 102n136
Kracauer, Adolf, 40–41, 46
Kracauer, Elisabeth (née Elisabeth Ehrenreich), 2, 10
Kracauer, Hedwig, 8, 11, 39, 176
Kracauer, Isidor, 8, 40–41
Kracauer, Rosette, 11, 39, 176
Kracauer, Siegfried, *passim*
    biographical sketch, 8–11
    and World War One, 2–3, 10, 35n121, 39–40, 57, 65–69, 72
    on political engagement 3–4, 12, 16, 23–24, 44, 55, 56, 65, 73–74, 126, 129, 167, 172–173, 174, 185, 212–13, 217–18, 221, 228, 233–35, 251–52
    friendship and collaboration with Adorno, 6–7, 10, 106, 119–20, 122, 146n79
    influence of George Simmel, 8, 45–53, 56–58, 126, 136
    influence of Max Scheler, 8, 67–72
    influence of Marx, Marxism, 11, 19, 20, 23–24, 54–55, 78–79, 85–86, 93, 218–19
    influence of Kierkegaard, 6–7, 107–10, 113–14, 118–19, 124, 135, 137–38
    on Nietzsche, 39, 40, 47, 51, 54–55
    on Ernst Bloch, 18, 74–82, 221–22, 227–28, 248–49
    on Max Brod, 80–83
    on Christ, 54–55, 69, 138
    on Oswald Spengler, 88–92
    on Georg Lukács, 78–79, 85–88
    on detective fiction, 110–12, 121–22, 123–25, 130–39
    attitudes to religious revival, 2–5, 15–18, 20, 91–94, 109–10, 118, 136, 159–66, 228
    on Catholicism, 54, 71, 164, 166–67, 173–81, 197, 228–29
    on Protestantism, 164, 166–69
    relationship to Herrigel, 120, 169–70, 172
    relationship to Rosenzweig, 1, 43, 136, 155, 162, 164–65, 166, 191–96

relationship to Susman, 8, 16, 40, 49, 162–64
friendship with Löwenthal, 10, 40, 42–43, 75, 80, 119, 157–58
and Judaism 18, 38–43, 191–97
controversy with Alfred Döblin, 217–19
dispute with Egon Vietta, 219–27, 230
on National Socialism, 187, 218, 233, 251–52
Kracauer Nachlaß, 39–40

L
Landauer, Gustav, 8, 74–75, 148n129
Langbehn, Julius, 197
Lange, Friedrich Albert, 41
Lao Tzu, 164
Laplace, Pierre-Simon, 44, 124, 131
Lebensreform (Life Reform movements), 13, 161–62
Leblanc, Maurice (Arsène Lupin), 111, 132, 138
Levinas, Emmanuel, 21, 140
Liebert, Arthur, 13
Liturgy Movement, 177–79. *See also* Catholicism; Guardini, Romano.
Löwenthal, Leo, 10, 40, 42–43, 46, 55, 75, 77–78, 80, 92–93, 95, 119, 120, 140, 157–58, 162, 171, 182, 191
Löwith, Karl, 107–8, 225–26
Lourdes, 1–2, 15
Ludwig, Emil, 55
Lüttge, Willy, 90
Luhmann, Niklas, 21, 22, 24, 230, 231
Lukács, Georg, 8, 13, 78–79, 85–88, 95, 102n136, 115, 157, 160, 170
Luther, Martin, 166–67, 169, 182, 216

M
Mach, Ernst, 187
Malraux, André, 9
Man, Hendrik de, 9, 37, 98n46, 238n39
Mann, Golo, 154
Mann, Heinrich, 121, 157
Mann, Thomas, 2–3, 26n5, 44–45, 57–58, 79, 87, 88, 108, 117, 140, 191, 251

Mannheim, Karl, 9, 37, 120, 147n86, 231
Marc, Franz, 231
Marcel, Gabriel, 9, 29n36
Maritain, Jacques, 160–61
Marrou, Henri-Irénée, 190
Marx, Karl (Marxism), 11, 19, 20, 24, 36, 46, 76, 77, 85–86, 93–94, 95, 213–14, 216, 218–19, 220, 222
Meier-Graefe, Julius, 10
Meinecke, Friedrich, 46–47
Messac, Régis, 111
Meyerhof-Hildeck, Leonie, 154
Michel, Ernst, 71, 98n46, 170, 175–76, 178, 180, 184, 229
Monism, 54, 83
Monod, Jean-Claude, 23
Müller, Johannes, 184
Musil, Robert, 15, 18, 49, 74, 84, 231

N
National Socialism, 25, 169, 171, 173, 187, 200n56, 202n99, 213, 217, 218, 220, 227, 228–29, 233, 235, 251–52
Natorp, Paul, 170, 173
negative theology, 18, 86–87, 110, 137–38, 160, 163, 189, 193, 232
Neumann, Lieschen, 129, 212
Nielsen, Asta, 9
Nietzsche, Friedrich, 39, 40, 41, 44, 47, 51, 54–55, 83, 109, 115, 116, 183, 216
Nipperdey, Thomas, 17, 182
Nobel, Nehemia Anton, 4–5, 55, 163, 164
Nordau, Max, 115

O
Ortega y Gasset, José, 220, 244, 247–48, 253n15
Otto, Rudolf, 21

P
Pannwitz, Rudolf, 226
Panza, Sancho, 7, 80, 244–53
Paquet, Alfons, 13, 77, 170
Paulhan, Jean, 9–10
Pestalozzi, Johann Heinrich, 41
Pfeiffer-Raimund, Kristina, 13
Phenomenology, 9, 70–72, 120, 176, 230

Philo, 192
Physiognomy, 139–42, 218
Picard, Max, 93, 140–41, 216–17, 228, 250
Polgar, Alfred, 154
political religion, 21, 23–24, 33n106, 212–13, 227–30
Protestantism, 20–21, 164, 166–69, 171, 186, 193, 199n43, 229

Q
Quickborn Youth Movement, 176, 179, 180
Quixote, 7, 80, 244–53

R
Ranke, Leopold von, 167
ratio (instrumental reason), critique of, 12, 54, 123–24, 132–34, 136, 138–39, 209, 232–233, 248
redemption (*Erlösung*), 12, 75–76, 81–83, 94, 116–17, 157, 159, 189, 211–12, 232
Reformation, 36, 166–67, 169
Reifenberg, Benno, 8, 9, 10, 23, 140, 153, 156, 250
religious revival, 2–5, 13–18, 47, 67, 70–72, 89, 91–92, 118, 120, 153, 160–66, 170, 192, 225, 230, 252
Renoir, Jean, 9
Rhein-Mainische Volkszeitung (RMV), 71, 175, 180
Riefenstahl, Leni, 52
Riesman, David, 142
Rittelmeyer, Friedrich, 184
Roesmann, Matwej, 196
Rolland, Romain, 187
Rosenstock-Heussy, Eugen, 47, 164, 165, 171
Rosenzweig, Franz, 1, 18, 21, 42–43, 46–47, 49, 50, 73, 80, 88, 116, 136, 155, 157, 162, 164–65, 166, 170, 171, 191–96, 203n122
Roth, Joseph, 10, 23, 87, 96, 106, 140, 153–54, 184, 196, 232
Rychner, Max, 57, 208, 216–17

S
Said, Edward, 42, 231

Schäfer, Wilhelm, 200n68
Scheler, Max, 4–5, 8, 21, 37, 39–40, 67–72, 83, 97n18, 158, 162, 165, 175–76, 184, 220, 230
Schelling, F. W. J., 107, 143n6, 143n11
Schickele, René, 184
Schmitt, Carl, 21, 25, 124, 127–29, 130, 179, 220, 249
Schnitzler, Arthur, 159, 187
Scholem, Gershom, 42
Schomerus, Hans, 171
Schopenhauer, Arthur, 108, 136, 157, 212
Schrempf, Christoph, 142n1
Secularization, 2, 5, 12, 14–16, 20–25, 43, 53, 72, 79–80, 93–94, 110, 118, 159–60, 166–67, 181, 190–91, 197, 221–34, 244, 247, 252
Seipel, Ignaz, 175, 181
Sekles, Bernhard, 37
Seligmann, Caesar, 41
Sénéchal, Christian, 187
Sewell, William H., 20
Sieburg, Friedrich, 10
Silone, Ignazio, 9
Simmel, Georg, 8, 19, 39–40, 45–46, 47–53, 56–58, 67, 75, 87, 89, 91, 126, 136, 190
Simon, Ernst, 162, 199n49, 230
Simon, Heinrich, 8, 10, 203n115, 233
Socialism (German Social Democratic Party), 3–4, 19, 24, 41, 54–55, 79, 83, 108, 214, 216, 217–19, 221, 223
Sombart, Werner, 67
Sorel, Georges, 95, 127
Spengler, Oswald, 49, 50, 58, 73, 88–92, 94
Spier, Selmar, 37–38
Stapel, Wilhelm, 171
Staub, Hugo, 134
Steiner, Rudolf, 75, 184
Sternberger, Dolf, 237n15, 245
Stolpe, 129, 134. *See also* Neumann, Lieschen.
Strauss, Leo, 25, 136
Susman, Margarete, 3, 8, 16, 18, 26n9, 32n92, 40, 49–50, 70, 74, 75, 77, 86, 155, 157, 162–64, 165, 170, 246

T
Tagore, Rabindranath, 184
Tauler, Johannes, 214
Taut, Bruno, 52
Thormann, Werner, 1–2, 120, 170, 175–76, 178, 181, 187
Tillich, Paul, 19, 21, 37, 175
Tönnies, Ferdinand, 52, 230
Treitschke, Heinrich von, 83
Tretjakow, Sergei, 221–22
Troeltsch, Ernst, 195
Troß, Erich, 187, 203n125
Tucholsky, Kurt, 184

U
Unamuno, Miguel de, 250

V
vagabond religion, 17, 92, 159, 181–82, 183–84
Valéry, Paul, 210, 211
Vaupel, Karl, 156
Viénot, Pierre, 234–35, 243n142
Vietta, Egon (Egon Fritz), 219–27, 230, 234–35, 247
violence, 15, 16, 95–96, 124–25, 127–28, 212, 234

Voegelin, Eric, 227, 230

W
Wandervogel (youth movement), 174
war books, 72–73
Weber, Max, 15, 20, 25, 51, 56, 84, 162–63, 232
Weiger, Josef, 71, 176
Weiß, Ernst, 250
Werfel, Franz, 81
white collar workers, 9, 85, 235
Wigman, Mary, 9
Wirth, Joseph, 175
World War One, 2–3, 13, 14, 38, 58, 72–73, 75, 81, 85–86, 115–16
Wundt, Wilhelm, 65

Z
Zaddikim (The Thirty Six, *Lamedvovniks*), 55, 141–42
Zbinden, Hans, 187
Zenker, Thomas, 183
Ziegler, Leopold, 49, 183
zionism, 1–2, 15, 38, 81, 196, 213. *See also* Judaism.
Zuckerkandl, Viktor, 215
Zweig, Stefan, 155

www.ingramcontent.com/pod-product-compliance
Lightning Source LLC
Chambersburg PA
CBHW072146100526
44589CB00015B/2118